ELABORATING MULTILITERA
MULTIMODAL TEXTS

Elaborating Multiliteracies through Multimodal Texts: Changing Classroom Practices and Developing Teacher Pedagogies is the complementary volume to *Foundations of Multiliteracies: Reading, Writing and Talking in the 21st Century*, which provides a comprehensive introduction to multiliteracies, classroom talk, planning, pedagogy and practice. This second volume embeds an action learning model, encouraging readers to explore classroom practice around multiliteracies, collect data about their pedagogy and enact change. It provides in-depth examination of the five semiotic systems, including a suggested school-wide sequence, explores reading and writing processes with multimodal texts and explains how to develop dialogic practices through talk around multimodal texts. The links between inquiry and action learning are explored in order to demonstrate how these approaches can change classroom practices and talk around multimodal texts.

Several features have been designed to help translate knowledge of multiliteracies into effective classroom practice:

- **Graphic Outlines** orient the reader to the concepts in the chapter.
- **Reflection Strategies** enable the reader to gauge their understanding of key concepts.
- **Theory into Practice** tasks enable the trialling of specific theoretical concepts in the classroom.
- **Auditing Instruments** inform assessment of student performance and evaluation of teacher pedagogy.
- **QR codes** address the multimodal and digital nature of new literacies and link the reader to multimodal texts.
- **Action Learning Tasks** enable readers to investigate specific aspects of their multiliterate pedagogy, and plan and implement change, based on their findings.

Dr Geoff Bull is Co-director of ABC: Anstey and Bull Consultants in Education and formerly Associate Professor at the University of Southern Queensland, Toowoomba. He was national president of the Australian Literacy Educators' Association.

Dr Michèle Anstey is Co-director of ABC: Anstey and Bull Consultants in Education and formerly Associate Professor at the University of Southern Queensland, Toowoomba. She was also a teacher in Victoria, NSW, and Queensland and editor of *Australian Journal of Language and Literacy*.

Together, Geoff Bull and Michèle Anstey, provide professional development, conduct tendered research, commissioned writing, speak at conferences, prepare professional development packages for trainers and advise on curriculum.

ELABORATING MULTILITERACIES THROUGH MULTIMODAL TEXTS

Changing Classroom Practices and Developing Teacher Pedagogies

Geoff Bull and Michèle Anstey

LONDON AND NEW YORK

First published 2019
by Routledge
2 Park Square, Milton Park, Abingdon, Oxon OX14 4RN

and by Routledge
711 Third Avenue, New York, NY 10017

Routledge is an imprint of the Taylor & Francis Group, an informa business

British Library Cataloguing-in-Publication Data
A catalogue record for this book is available from the British Library

Library of Congress Cataloging in Publication Data
A catalog record for this book has been requested

ISBN: 978-1-138-55504-4 (hbk)
ISBN: 978-1-138-55502-0 (pbk)
ISBN: 978-1-315-14928-8 (ebk)

Typeset in Interstate
by Apex CoVantage, LLC

CONTENTS

FIGURES, TABLES AND QR CODES

QR codes

ACKNOWLEDGEMENTS

As with all our work, the focus of this book has been informed by our discussions and engagement around multiliteracies and multimodality with teachers and teacher leaders throughout Australia in recent years. We thank them for their willingness to share their thoughts and ideas with us. In doing so they have revealed their passion for teaching and learning and their deep commitment to the education of their students. We would particularly like to thank Jan Mansfield for allowing us to share transcripts from her classroom.

Thank you also to the many people associated with Routledge who have supported and advised during the process. In particular, we wish to thank Lucinda Knight and Matt Bickerton for their guidance and assistance. We would also like to thank Jennifer Fester, Marie Louise Roberts and Emma Sudderick for their editorial advice and to Jac Nelson for her work on the index.

INTRODUCTION

Why two complementary volumes?

This book is the second of two complementary volumes. Our professional development work and research with teachers and students across all education systems since we wrote *Teaching and Learning Multiliteracies: Changing Times, Changing Literacies* (2006) and *Evolving Pedagogies: Reading and Writing in a Multimodal World* (2010) stimulated the idea of writing two complementary volumes. We discovered that it is not sufficient to know and understand the concepts and research that inform understandings about **multiliteracies** and **multimodal texts**. To fully understand these concepts in their teaching context it was necessary for teachers to investigate and apply this knowledge in classrooms, to examine and change their **pedagogy**. We found that engaging in a continuous cycle of Action Learning enabled teachers to elaborate and apply their understandings in ways that were appropriate to the social, cultural context of the community in which they were teaching. Engagement in Action Learning Cycles resulted in not just new understandings about literacy but radical shifts in pedagogy.

Therefore, each of the complementary volumes was designed with very specific objectives in mind. *Foundations of Multiliteracies: Reading, Writing and Talking in the 21st Century* provides a comprehensive introduction to multiliteracies and the ideas and concepts that inform it, together with information about the changes to classroom talk, planning, pedagogy and practice that are necessary as a result of adopting a multiliterate pedagogy. This complementary volume, *Elaborating Multiliteracies through Multimodal Texts: Changing Classroom Practices and Developing Teacher Pedagogies*, builds upon the previous volume by embedding an action learning model throughout the book, encouraging readers to explore classroom practice around multiliteracies, collect data about their pedagogy and practice and enact change. Its aim is to build a more refined and in-depth understanding of literacies, multiliteracies and multimodal texts and concurrently develop a multiliterate pedagogy.

Design of this book

Throughout the book we refer to writing and reading as a process of **designing** and **redesigning** text in order to convey or make meaning, that is, to fulfil a particular communicative purpose. In *Elaborating Multiliteracies through Multimodal Texts: Changing Classroom Practices and Developing Teacher Pedagogies*, our aim is to assist teachers in designing and redesigning their pedagogy. Therefore, we have designed this book around six intertwined themes which are investigated through six chapters:

- The value of **action research** and learning in developing teachers' pedagogies,
- **Inquiry** as an essential component for developing multiliteracies and multimodality,

- The origins and development of the concepts of multiliteracies and multimodality and the five **semiotic systems** (linguistic, visual, audio, spatial and gestural) that underpin texts,
- The use of **dialogic talk** as the vehicle for enhancing the teaching and learning multiliteracies and multimodality,
- Reconsidering reading and **consuming** text in a multiliterate multimodal world,
- Reconsidering writing and **producing** text in a multiliterate multimodal world.

As always, our overarching goal is to blend theory and practice and provide readers with the opportunity to reflect upon and develop their own understandings, as well as apply this knowledge to the educational setting in which they are based. Therefore, we have also designed particular features to help the reader in these endeavours and in the development and implementation of their Action Learning Cycle as they read:

- Graphic Outlines for each chapter are designed to orient the reader to the concepts contained in the chapter and the relationships among them.
- Reflection Strategies provide activities and tasks that enable the reader to gauge their understanding of key concepts.
- Theory into Practice tasks provide ideas and activities that enable the trialling of specific theoretical concepts in the classroom.
- Auditing Instruments provide specific tasks related to assessment of student performance and evaluation of teacher pedagogy.
- QR Codes are used to address the multimodal and digital nature of new literacies. They immediately link the reader to multimodal texts and further references that illustrate and enhance the concepts being developed.
- A Glossary at the end of the book enables the reader to access definitions of key concepts.
- Action Learning Tasks are designed to assist the reader to develop an individual Action Learning Cycle as they progress through the six chapters.

1 The action learning cycle: Designing multimodal pedagogies

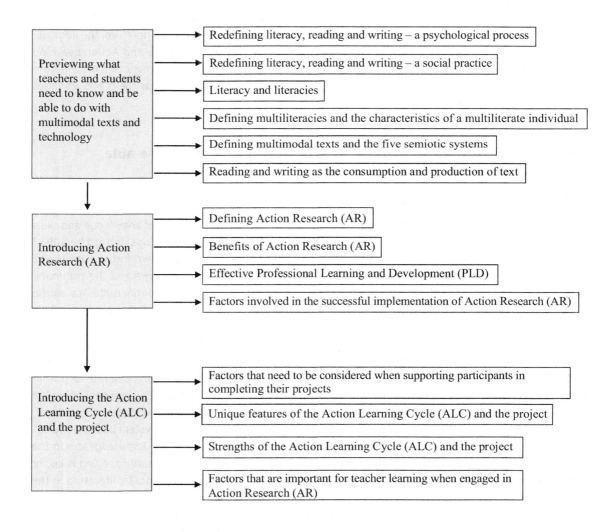

Previewing what teachers and students need to know and be able to do with multimodal texts and technology

- Redefining literacy, reading and writing – a psychological process
- Redefining literacy, reading and writing – a social practice
- Literacy and literacies
- Defining multiliteracies and the characteristics of a multiliterate individual
- Defining multimodal texts and the five semiotic systems
- Reading and writing as the consumption and production of text

Introducing Action Research (AR)

- Defining Action Research (AR)
- Benefits of Action Research (AR)
- Effective Professional Learning and Development (PLD)
- Factors involved in the successful implementation of Action Research (AR)

Introducing the Action Learning Cycle (ALC) and the project

- Factors that need to be considered when supporting participants in completing their projects
- Unique features of the Action Learning Cycle (ALC) and the project
- Strengths of the Action Learning Cycle (ALC) and the project
- Factors that are important for teacher learning when engaged in Action Research (AR)

This chapter will investigate what students need to know and be able to do with multimodal texts by tracing the change in the concept of literacy to consideration of literacies and multiliteracies. It will define the characteristics of a literate and multiliterate person through exploring semiotic systems and the changing nature of texts and will propose that reading and writing might be more usefully seen as **consumption** and **production**. The chapter will introduce the Action Learning Cycle as a way of examining and changing teaching practices around new texts, multiliteracies and multimodality. It will introduce new tools that have been designed by Anstey and Bull to support understanding the relationships among professional knowledge, planning and teacher practice. Finally, the chapter will explain how the Action Learning Cycle and how it can be used to support the **design** and **redesign** of teachers' **pedagogy**. As stated in the introduction to this book, the purpose of *Elaborating Multiliteracies* is to increase the readers' knowledge about multiliteracies and enable the implementation of a multiliterate pedagogy. Therefore, the information about the Action Learning Cycle in this chapter provides specific knowledge and Action Learning Tasks for the reader to begin an action learning project focussing on the development of a multiliterate pedagogy in their classroom. The project can be further refined and implemented as the reader engages with subsequent chapters and the Action Learning Tasks within them.

Reviewing what teachers and students need to know and be able to do with multimodal texts and technology

Redefining literacy, reading and writing - a psychological process

In the period following the end of World War Two, literacy was seen as a collection of knowledge and skills that enabled individuals to participate effectively in the society of the time. This was defined by a 1962 UNESCO document (cited by Oxenham, 1980, p. 87) as attaining a level of reading, writing and arithmetic that made it possible to adequately function and to 'use those skills toward his own and the community's development'. Earlier UNESCO (cited by Harris & Hodges, 1995, p. 140) had defined literacy as the ability of a person '... who can with understanding both read and write a short, simple statement on his everyday life'. This view of literacy as a finite and unique set of skills pertaining to a particular society was reinforced by the idea that literacy was a form of communication that was language dominated. It followed that language was predicated on the understanding that the basics of grammar, spelling, punctuation and comprehension were essential requirements for both reading and writing and provided what Luke (1995) referred to as a basic toolkit. Cope and Kalantzis (2000, p. 5) suggested when describing the literacy of this era as 'What we might term "mere literacy" remains centred on language only, and usually on a singular national form of language at that, being conceived as a stable system based on rules'. Later Kalantzis et al. (2016, p. 4) commented that students of this era '... became knowledgeable in the sense that they recognised received rules and **conventions**. They learned complicated spelling rules, or the grammar of adverbial clauses, or the lines of great poets'. At this time in Australia, literature in the form of poetry, prose and plays was dominated by the British tradition, possibly because the population was almost entirely of British heritage. This led some cynics to suggest that Australian students spent their time in English lessons studying the writing of 'dead English males'. Street (1993, p. 2) suggested that these traditional approaches were 'highly biased' because they focussed mainly on genres from the Western literary canon that were mainly concerned with '... the literate activities and output of the intellectual elite'. During this time, it was not possible to study Australian literature at university level because it was not seen as part of the canon that was worthy of attention or to have sufficient prestige. Literacy was therefore defined by what educationists of the time thought was appropriate for the civic, economic and work contexts that students would be entering, or as the Organisation for Economic Co-operation and Development (OECD; cited by Lo Bianco & Freebody 2001, p. 21) stated, students '... who are able to use their skills to function fully in the workplace, the community, and the home'. It was also socially and culturally determined by the values held by the community of the time, as the goal of education generally was to pass on and maintain the heritage and literacy skills needed to maintain it. The literacy of this period has been variously described as old basics by Luke (1995) and Luke and Freebody (1997), as traditional by Anstey and Bull (2004, 2006) and heritage based by Kalantzis et al. (2016). Further information about these ideas can be found in Chapter One of the complementary volume *Foundations of Multiliteracies: Reading, Writing and Talking in the 21st Century*.

This view of literacy and literature as old basics was challenged firstly by the mass migrations following the war that not only affected the population of Australia, but also populations in the U.S. and the U.K. At the same time, the development of affordable air travel made it more likely that individuals would meet people from different backgrounds, societies and cultures. These two developments increased the diversity of populations around the world and made available a range of views about what literacy was and how it might be enacted. The view that literacy could be regarded as a set of knowledge and skills, essentially a psychological process, was no longer sufficient. The greater diversity of populations together with increasing mobility meant that literacy had to be regarded not only as a psychological process, but also as a social process with concomitant **social practices**. It was during this time that a significant amount of research was carried out in the U.K. and the U.S. about the social and cultural factors that affected the development of language and literacy in particular groups. It marked a change in the way literacy was perceived, as researchers were now focussing on the practices associated with literacy and about how language was used in social settings.

REFLECTION STRATEGY 1.1

- The purpose of this Reflection Strategy is to determine what views about literacy are held by the individuals in your educational setting.
- Ask the people who you work with in your school/setting to reflect on their views about the nature of literacy. Have them commit these views in writing and then collect them. (Make sure that you inform participants beforehand that their views are to be collected and analysed. It may be that the group will prefer their views to be anonymous.)
- The views should be analysed and placed into one of four categories:
    o   Those individuals who define literacy as a psychological process – a belief that literacy is a unitary set of skills and knowledge,
    o   Those individuals who define literacy as a *social practice* – a belief that literacy is a communicative process relating to interaction among different sociocultural groups,
    o   Those individuals who define literacy as a balance between psychological processes and social processes,
    o   Those individuals who do not have a clear definition of literacy.
- Use these four categories in a discussion about how these disparate ideas may influence students learning about literacy. At this point it may be useful to have a further discussion about the benefits of a school-wide developmental approach and sequence to literacy instruction.

Redefining literacy, reading and writing – a social process

One of the first researchers in the U.K. to investigate the social origins of literacy and language develop-ment was Bernstein who, in his earlier work (Bernstein, 1960, 1961, 1962, 1964, 1971), proposed that there was a link between the literate practices involving talk in the home and social class membership and sociocultural practices in families. He suggested that there was a relationship between particular family types found in working class and middle class families and what he termed codes. He advanced a theory that **restricted codes** developed in working class families and **elaborate codes** in middle class families. Bernstein suggested (1964, pp. 118–139 and 1971, pp. 170–189) that elaborate code users drew their **utter-ances** from a broad range and variety of alternatives and therefore their language use was less predict-able, more explicit and therefore more complex (elaborate). The literacy that developed in such families was more flexible and creative. Conversely, restricted code was more predictable and implicit and less complex. It followed that the restricted code was therefore less flexible and less creative. Bernstein fur-ther suggested that working class families could be identified as **position-oriented families** because they were more regulated and less open to change in family social structures, whereas middle class families, or **person-oriented families**, had more fluid roles and family structures and were therefore less regulated. A more detailed discussion of the codes and family types can be found in Anstey and Bull (2004, 2006, 2018) and Edwards-Groves, Anstey and Bull (2014). See also a detailed explanation in Chapter Two of the complementary volume *Foundations of Multiliteracies: Reading, Writing and Talking in the 21st Century*.
Bernstein's theory became widely accepted and led to the belief that students from working class families could be seen as 'culturally disadvantaged' or 'culturally deprived'. Some schools adopted the position that failure at school was determined by family background and therefore families were held responsible for lack of student success rather than the school. This shift in accountability became widely accepted in educational circles and resulted in some teachers adopting the position that students from working class homes were somehow deficient in literacy. This led to the formation of the term **Deficiency Hypothesis** as a way of relating student performance to family background and child-rearing practices. The defi-ciency hypothesis was not proposed by Bernstein but its effect was to 'blame the victim' and shift respon-sibility away from teachers and the schools. This may explain why this misinterpretation of Bernstein's ideas gained such wide acceptance even though they were controversial and were the subject of many challenges in the U.S., the U.K. and Australia.

It is interesting to note that despite the challenges and the controversies surrounding the work of Bernstein, his ideas continue to be widely accepted and researchers still find evidence for teacher beliefs and acceptance of the central ideas underlying the theory. In their study of literacy practices in low socioeconomic communities, Freebody and Ludwig (1998) found that schools continued to hold to the belief that poor student performance was related to working class membership some three decades after Bernstein proposed his initial theory. This is in spite of the fact that Bernstein (1973, 1975, 1990) reviewed and revised his theory in his later research.
There was some support for Bernstein's proposals in the early stages of the development of his theory in Australia (Poole, 1972), the U.K. (Lawton, 1968) and the U.S. (Williams & Naremore, 1969). However, there were also some questions raised about the efficacy of his theory. Labov (1966, 1969a, 1969b), while disagreeing with the proposition that poor performance could be explained by social class membership, did not abandon the theory altogether but rather suggested important modifications. He agreed with Bernstein's view that sociocultural factors affected, and partly determined, literacy performance. In his study of African American students, he proposed that difference in student performance could be better explained through the concepts of standard English (SE) and non-standard English (NSE) rather than restricted and elaborate codes. Labov suggested that African American students learnt a non-standard

variant of English at home that was not valued by the school. This position became known as the **Difference Hypothesis** and reversed Bernstein's theory that the home was accountable for poor student performance by suggesting that the school was accountable because of its refusal to acknowledge that NSE was an acceptable dialect of English, albeit with its own rules of grammar and syntax and its own logic. Labov proposed that it was a question of linguistic relativity and should not be judged as a deficit.

The Deficiency Hypothesis would view these dialectic differences as a problem created by the home whereas the Difference Hypothesis would interpret them as a problem generated by the school or teacher. Therefore, the Difference Hypothesis was a more culturally appropriate theory because it valued the literacy that students brought from home to school.

Just as Bernstein's theory was modified by Labov, so Labov's position was modified by Cazden. Cazden (1967, 1970, 1972, 2015) agreed with Labov's rejection of Bernstein and the Deficiency Hypothesis but felt that linguistic relativity and the Difference Hypothesis did not adequately account for difference. She suggested that both working class and middle class students had access to restricted and elaborate codes or standard and non-standard forms of English. Cazden, drawing on the work of Habermas (1970) and Hymes (1972), suggested that it was a matter of **communicative competence**, that is, while middle class students knew which code was appropriate to use in which context, working class students did not. It was therefore not so much about knowing a particular code or dialect, but rather a question of use. She suggested that middle class children were able to distinguish between conventional or more formal situations (school and workplace) and casual or less formal situations (family and playground) and therefore able to judge when SE or NSE was more appropriate to use.

The work of these three researchers, in investigating the relation of home and school literate practices, provided an important impetus to broadening the concept of literacy to include consideration of literacy as a social process. This approach to literacy has been taken up more recently through the research of Heath (1983), Hull and Schultz (2002), Dyson (2003) and D'warte (2014) who have investigated the various literate practices to be found in the home and other out-of-school sites. Heath added an additional factor when studying the effect of culture and context by focussing on social behaviour, thus further broadening the concept of literacy. This approach was later followed by Gee (1990, 1992, 2004) and Kress and van Leeuwen (2001) in their studies of *discourse* and *Discourse*.

REFLECTION STRATEGY 1.2

- The purpose of this Reflection Strategy is to investigate the views held in your educational setting/school about the factors that affect students learning about literacy in the home and how this might impinge upon performance in school.
- Have a discussion with all participants similar to the one in the previous Reflection Strategy. Make sure that the discussion includes debates about the Deficiency and Difference Hypotheses, Communicative Competence and Discourses/discourses. It may require more than one session to cover all these ideas.
- The outcome of these discussions is to challenge views that are culturally inappropriate and to design an agreed-upon approach to literacy learning throughout the school. This may be included in school policy documents.

Literacy and literacies

The research by Heath (1983, 1986), as did much of the research that followed, challenged the idea of literacy encompassing one basic toolkit by concluding that literacy was a set of social practices that varied according to culture and context. She concluded (1983, p. 10) in her study of two communities in the American South that 'The various approaches of these communities to acquiring, using and valuing language are the products of their history and current situations'. Literacy began to be seen as an active, flexible, dynamic and interactive repertoire of practices that could occur in the home, at school, in the playground, in religious settings and in different social or cultural groups. As Lankshear and Lawler (1987, p. 43) stated, 'In other words, what literacy is is entirely a matter of how reading and writing are conceived and practised within particular social settings'. Literacy was no longer regarded as a unitary skill but rather a repertoire of practices that led to the formation of a multiplicity of literacies. This idea was supported by earlier work by many researchers in the area such as Halliday (1973) in Australia, Smith (1973) in the U.S. and Street (1984) in the U.K. Interestingly, Heath, Smith and Halliday all approached the developments in literacies, rather than literacy, by proposing functions or purposes of literacy, while Street focussed on the social practices around literacies.

In summary, the literacy toolkit proposed in the 1950s and 1960s, though still necessary, was no longer seen as sufficient. Literacy was no longer to be regarded as only a psychological process. Literacy was now defined as a social practice that required the acquisition and use of a variety of literacies and the associated behaviours, to be used in a range of social and cultural settings. In other words, literacies and literate practices are shaped by society and society shapes literacies.

Defining multiliteracies and the characteristics of a multiliterate individual

The advent of literacies, or the new literacies as Street (1993, 1997) described them, set the scene for a rethink of literacy. The growing diversity of societies around the world and the development of new technologies reinforced the need for a variety of literacies. Change became the new constant, necessitating a further reconsideration of the nature of literacies. In 1996 the New London Group, comprised of educators from around the world, published a seminal paper describing what they termed **multiliteracies**. Their first concern was to reconsider literacy as primarily encompassing only notions about language and the linguistic. As Cope and Kalantzis (2000, p. 6) suggested, they were concerned that individuals were also required to '... interact effectively using multiple languages, multiple Englishes, and communication patterns that more frequently cross cultural, community, and national boundaries'. They stated that multiliteracies should support learners to specify differences in language, and promote meaning making, in a range of contexts and cultures at the regional, state and national levels.

The *multi* in multiliteracies refers to the range of literacies and literate practices used in all facets of life and how these practices are similar and different. Various writers such as the New London Group (1996), Cope and Kalantzis (2000), Carrington and Robinson (2009) and Mills (2011) all suggest that the range of literacies and literate practices are a result of the growing diversity of populations at the local and global levels. They also suggest that the increasing pace of technological change creates a variety of new texts that have been created through the new and emerging live and digital technologies (Zammit & Downes, 2002) as well as those texts produced by the more traditional paper technology. As a result of these changes, Kalantzis et al. (2016, p. 7) state that students '... will be able to navigate change and diversity, learn as they go and communicate effectively in a wide range of settings. They will be flexible thinkers, capable of seeing things from multiple perspectives'. Therefore, the *multi* in multiliteracies not only refers to multiple literacies and literate practices, but also to a growing variety of new texts and new technologies. As Mills (2011, p. 124) concluded, 'Previous conceptions of literacy as monolingual, mono-cultural and monomodal – one language, culture and mode – have been transformed for the new times as multiliteracies'. Multiliterate individuals must therefore be strategic, able to recognise what is required in a particular context, examine what is already known, and then, if necessary, modify that knowledge to develop a strategy that suits the situation. They need to be problem solvers, strategic and critical thinkers (Anstey & Bull, 2006, p. 23).

Anstey and Bull (2006), Anstey (2009) and Bull and Anstey (2010a) have proposed a set of character-istics of a multiliterate person. They suggest that in order to be multiliterate, a person must:

- Be flexible and able to deal with change – be analytical and reflective problem solvers, be strategic, creative and critical thinkers who can engage with new texts in a variety of contexts and audiences.
- Have a repertoire of literate knowledge and practices – understand that new texts that have differing purposes, audiences and contexts will require a range of different behaviours that draw on a reper-toire of knowledge and experiences.
- Understand how social and cultural diversity effects literate practices – know that experiences and culture influence and produce a variety of different knowledges, approaches, orientations, attitudes and values that will influence the interpretation and occurrence of literate practices.
- Understand, and be able to use, traditional and new communication technologies – understand the semiotic systems and recognise that the increasing variety of new texts are delivered by paper, live and digital technologies, and realise that purpose, audience and context determine which semiotic system and which technology is appropriate.
- Be critically literate – understand that in every literate practice it is necessary to determine who is participating and for what reason, who is in a position of power, who has been marginalised, what is the purpose and origin of the texts being used and how these texts are supporting participation in society and everyday life.

AUDITING INSTRUMENT 1.1

- **The purpose of this Auditing Instrument is to investigate the classroom practices that are present across the school community.**
- **Conduct lesson observation exercises in each classroom in the school to investigate teachers' practices to discover whether teachers are addressing literacy as a single unitary concept or if there is evidence of multiple literacies being introduced.**
- **Develop a checklist based on the five characteristics of a multiliterate person to explore which characteristics are present in students' literacy learning.**

These five characteristics can form the basis for teachers to create opportunities for students to investigate, learn about and engage with literacies, literate practices and multiliteracies. While the central concepts involved in the exploration of multiliteracies have largely remained constant, recent research has addressed its application to particular issues relating to schooling and the workplace. These issues include how to support teachers to address the diversity and inequalities manifest in classrooms, how to introduce and teach about the multiplicity of texts that have been delivered by new and evolving technologies, how multiliteracies can be applied to different disciplines other than English, and specific approaches to the planning and teaching multiliteracies (Unsworth, 2001, Anstey & Bull, 2006, 2018; Baker, 2010, Bull and Anstey, 2010b, Cole & Pullen, 2010, Mills, 2011).

Defining multimodal texts and the five semiotic systems

The concept of multiliteracies has necessitated that students and teachers engage with texts arising out of paper, live and digital technologies. The diversity of contemporary populations and the increasing rates of technological change have produced a variety of literacies and texts that were not available in earlier times. The advent of digital technologies has produced an array of new texts that were not possible in the late 20th century. Live technologies which were once limited to face-to-face interactions can now, through the development of the internet and through apps such as Skype, permit real-time interactions between individuals in different contexts. It is important to note that these technological developments often result in the production of contested sites. As Hawisher and Selfe (2000, p.15) stated with reference to the internet,

> … this system of networked computers is far from world-wide; it does not provide a culturally neutral conduit for the transmission of information; it is not a culturally neutral or innocent communication landscape open to the literacy practices of all global citizens.

Even texts produced through the traditional paper technologies have been transformed through developments in technology. The concept of text as limited to the written word is now outmoded. Paper texts presented through such technological developments as the desktop computer and the internet can be read or written in much more flexible ways, creating new ways of meaning making that individuals need to access. Texts produced through live technologies require individuals to engage with elements from music, art and drama, while texts produced through digital technologies require interpretation of such elements as colour, movement, sound effects or images such as those presented in film or video.

AUDITING INSTRUMENT 1.2

- The purpose of this Auditing Instrument is to investigate which technologies are evident in teachers' planning and practice.
- Construct a simple checklist containing the three technologies (paper, live and digital) and conduct classroom observations of teachers' practices to see which technologies feature in everyday lessons.
- Use the same checklist to analyse teachers' planning for evidence of the three technologies.
- Look at the selection of texts that are present in lessons and planning to judge what balance has been struck across the range of texts.
- Use the data from the checklists to implement a uniform approach across the school.

The proliferation of new technologies has produced a range of new texts which in turn has created the need for a variety of new meaning making systems. As has been already stated in this chapter, when the characteristics of a multiliterate person were defined, in order to be conscious of the increasing variety of new texts that are delivered by paper, live and digital technologies, both students and teachers need to understand the semiotic systems. A **semiotic system** is a system of signs and **symbols** that have agreed-upon meanings within a particular group and is particularly suited to the interpretation of these new texts (Anstey & Bull, 2004, 2006, 2018 and Bull & Anstey, 2010a). Semiotic systems, being based on group interpretations of meaning making involving social processes, are therefore subject to variation between, and across, different cultures. Therefore, semiotic systems are:

- Comprising a set of signs and symbols that are called codes that are employed according to agreed-upon conventions,
- By definition culture specific and may not be shared by every student in a classroom or by every teacher in a school,
- Inextricably involved in the learning process and engaged in through the metalanguage of the semiotic system,
- Where meaning is negotiated and regulated, but is also imprecise, requiring individuals to have a tolerance for difference,
- Meaningful only when they are used and shared,
- Essentially a social process that develops roles and relationships among individuals because they are used for different purposes and in different contexts,
- Empowering or marginalising as they can either provide access to, or exclude, individuals from life experiences.

Each one of these semiotic systems has a grammar of elements, or codes and conventions, that are particular to that semiotic system. As Kress and van Leeuwen (2006, p.1) suggested,

> Just as grammars of language describe how words combine in clauses, sentences and texts, so our visual 'grammar' will describe the way in which depicted elements – people, places and things – combine in visual 'statements' of greater or lesser complexity and extension.

They proposed that the grammar of the visual would contain such elements as colour, the meaning of which would be culture specific.

Beyond the linguistic and visual grammars that have been discussed so far, there are other semiotic systems that are required to deal with the ever-increasing diversity of texts. These have recently been explored by Anstey and Bull (2004, 2006, 2018) and Bull and Anstey (2010a, 2010b, 2013), who proposed five semiotic systems. These are briefly outlined below (for a more in-depth discussion of semiotic systems see Chapter Three and also Chapter Three in *Foundations of Multiliteracies: Reading, Writing and Talking in the 21st Century*).

- Linguistic (written language, incorporating choice of nouns, verbs, adjectives and conjunctions);
- Visual (still and moving images, incorporating choice of colour, **vectors** and **point of view**);
- Audio (music, sound effects, incorporating **volume, pitch** and rhythm);

- Gestural (**facial expression** and **body language**, incorporating eyebrow position, movement of head, arms, hands and legs);
- Spatial (layout and organisation of objects and space, incorporating **proximity**, direction and **position**).

AUDITING INSTRUMENT 1.3

- This Auditing Instrument is intended to determine the balance of the five semiotic systems in classrooms across the school.
- Devise a checklist containing the five semiotic systems (linguistic, visual, audio, spatial, gestural) and use during observations in each class to determine how often each semiotic system is regularly incorporated into daily lessons.
- Use the same checklist to determine how often each semiotic system is regularly incorporated in daily lesson plans.
- Use the data from both checklists to implement a uniform approach across the school.

The *codes* and *conventions* of the visual, audio, gestural and spatial semiotic systems are more dynamic and flexible sets of rules for engaging in meaning making as distinct from the linguistic semiotic system that was often associated with a set of rigid and unchanging rules that were related to 'correct usage'. Kress and Leeuwen (2006, p. 266) had suggested that a visual grammar should be interpreted as '... a flexible set of resources that people use in ever new and ever different acts of visual sign-making'. The audio, gestural and spatial, through further research in the area, came to be interpreted in a similar fashion. The concept of the codes and conventions of the five semiotic systems allowed the plethora of texts that arose from the development of the new literacies, multiliteracies and the new technologies to be further analysed. It is important to note that the application of the semiotic systems and their codes and conventions should be treated carefully since the determination of all these texts is a complex process that relies on careful and thoughtful introduction. As early as 1996 the New London Group (quoted in Cope & Kalantzis, 2000, p. 31) had cautioned that '... knowledge is inextricably tied to the ability to recognise and act on patterns of data and experience, a process that is acquired only through experience, since the requisite patterns are often heavily tied and adjusted to context'.

Analysis of these texts revealed that they were not only delivered through different technologies (paper, live or digital) but also through different combinations of the codes of the semiotic systems. The codes of each semiotic system provide a terminology that enable the reader/viewer to identify and describe how attention is captured, how emphasis is created and therefore how meaning is shaped. A ballet performance delivered through live technology relies on codes such as music, involving the audio semiotic system, gestures and proximity of the dancers to convey meaning. Similarly, the home page of a website delivered by digital technology conveys meaning through codes such as sound effects, music and still or moving images. Texts delivered by paper technology are nearly always accompanied by images employing codes such as colour, **line** or **shape** on the cover, between chapters or on the dust jacket or, in the case of a picture book, throughout the whole book. All these texts rely on multiple semiotic systems to convey meaning and are therefore termed **multimodal texts** (Anstey & Bull, 2006, 2018, Bull & Anstey,

2010a, Bull & Anstey, 2010b, Kress, 2003, 2010, Jewitt et al., 2016) that can be delivered through paper, live or digital technologies. As Kress and van Leeuwen (2006, p.177) suggested, '... any text whose meanings are realised through more than one semiotic code is multimodal', and '... we see the multimodal resources which are available in a culture used to make meanings in any and every sign, at every level, and in any mode' (Kress and van Leeuwen, 2001, p. 4). Similarly, Jewitt and Kress (2008, p.1) proposed that '... meanings are made, distributed, received, interpreted and remade in interpretation through many representational and communicative modes – not just language'. It is therefore critical that teachers and learners understand what is involved in the application of both multiliteracies and multimodality in order to understand how texts are created and how meaning is conveyed.

Reading and writing as the consumption and production of text

In applying knowledge about multiliteracies and multimodality, a multiliterate person needs to become familiar with a whole range of new texts and increase understandings about the composition of texts and how to engage with them. Engagement with the new texts requires more than the terms reading and writing imply. These terms have traditionally been used when referring to the linguistic semiotic system. While it seems appropriate to describe a text generated through the linguistic semiotic system as written, or suitable to be read, it is not pertinent to suggest that a text generated using the visual, audio, spatial or gestural semiotic systems should be written or read. *Production* is a more suitable term to use when referring to the 'writing' process involved in all the semiotic systems. Similarly, *consumption* is more applicable to all semiotic systems rather than reading. There are a number of understandings that an individual requires in order to engage in the production and consumption of texts, and the practices around texts, across the five semiotic systems. (This has been discussed in some detail in Chapter Two of *Foundations of Multiliteracies: Reading, Writing and Talking in the 21st Century.*)

These understandings are represented below:

- All texts are consciously constructed and have particular social, cultural, political or economic purposes.
  - o All producers of text have some conscious purpose in mind when constructing a text.
- Texts will continue to change as society and technology changes.
  - o Texts are being constructed in more flexible and dynamic ways as producers attempt to deal with rapid societal and technological changes.
- All texts are multimodal.
  - o All multimodal elements of a text need to be attended to as both producers and consumers have realised that important meanings are not only contained in the written word.
- Texts can be interactive, linear or non-linear.
  - o Consumers of text, particularly digital and live texts, can become actively involved in the construction of the text. Paper texts, because they are read page by page, are linear, whereas digital texts are consumed idiosyncratically and are therefore non-linear.
- Texts may be intertextual.
  - o Texts, whether they be paper, live or digital, may draw or make reference to other texts to make meaning.
- Texts are tending to become more screen-like as design and designing become more central to the production of texts.

- o   The layout and organisation of paper texts is increasingly taking on some of the characteristics of screen-like texts.
- Texts can be created by the consumer using the links in digital texts to produce **hypertexts**.
- o   The consumer creates his or her own hypertext by navigating through the digital texts in an idiosyncratic manner.
- The social and cultural background of individuals influences the production of, and engagement with, text.
- o   Individuals may bring their own notions about how texts are produced dependent upon their social and cultural background and experiences. Therefore, individuals may respond quite differently to texts in school and in other contexts.
- A text may have several possible meanings.
- o   There may be many possible meanings in a text depending on the social, cultural, economic or political background of the reader/viewer and the context in which it is read. An individual's response to a text should be considered rather than the adoption of a single, authorised interpretation.
- The consumer interacts with the text to actively construct the meaning of the text.
- o   The author or producer of a text constructs it in a particular way in order to convey certain meanings. However, the consumer of a text reconstructs the text in his or her individual way in order to gain meaning. The consumer is an active participant in meaning making rather than a passive receiver. It is important that students realise that they have an important (active) role in the construction of meaning in any given text.
- The complexity of multimodal texts means that consumers have to consciously differentiate the focus of their attention across the semiotic systems.
- o   When a consumer interacts with a text, they may focus on a particular semiotic system as part of their analysis. However, all the semiotic systems may play a part of the meaning making process while engaging with a text. It is important not to focus on the one semiotic system, or the same semiotic system, when interpreting a text. The consumer needs to be conscious of this process and be capable of realising when to engage with the text in a particular way.
- No text is neutral.
- o   Every producer of a text expects that the consumer will learn something from engaging with the text. Therefore, every text has a particular purpose that is designed to change the consumer in some way. The consumer should always be asking themselves, among other things, 'What is this text trying to get me to do or believe?' Any text has a message or belief to convey and is, as a result, not neutral.

Because of the development of multiliteracies and multimodal texts generated by rapid changes in technology and the growing diversity of populations, students and teachers have access to an expanding, and ever-changing, variety of texts at school and other sociocultural contexts. This proliferation of texts can potentially engage students and teachers in new and interesting ways that go beyond simple access. The twelve understandings enumerated above require teachers and students to engage in discussions about multiliterate practices, to uncover the purposes of texts, to decide which texts to attend to, and to decide which are the most powerful and of most use to them.

THEORY INTO PRACTICE 1.1

- The purpose of this Theory into Practice is to support discussions about the purposes of the variety of texts now available.
- To guide such discussions, the following questions may be helpful in determining the purpose of a particular text. These questions can be used in teacher discussions with the students or alternatively by the students themselves as they engage with texts.
  - o What was your purpose for using the text?
  - o Where or when have you come across this topic or subject before? What did you do?
  - o What do you already know that might help?
  - o What else do you need to know or find out that might help you?
  - o Have you used a text like this before? How did you use it?
  - o What prior experiences can help you here?
  - o Which semiotic systems were used in the construction of this text?
  - o Have you engaged with these semiotic systems in texts like this before? How does this help you?
  - o What is the purpose in using each semiotic system in the construction of the text?
  - o Have you used this technology or software before, or something similar? How does that prior experience help you?
- Discuss with the staff of the school which of the twelve understandings about texts should be a feature of literacy teaching and learning within the school and how they might be taught.

The questions in the preceding Theory into Practice have been adapted from the work of Kress (2003), Walsh (2007) and Bearne (2009) and were originally proposed by Bull and Anstey (2010a). The questions focus attention on what it is that teachers and students need to know and be able to do. It is now important to consider how to move beyond knowing what it is that teachers and students need to know and explore how such knowledge can be incorporated into everyday classroom practice.

Introducing Action Research (AR)

The complexities of the concepts of multiliteracies and multimodality necessitate the provision of support in order to change teachers' pedagogy and practice. Professional learning and development (PLD) that is practical and classroom based has been effective in encouraging teachers and schools to adopt these concepts to build capacity for sustainable improvement in student performance. In recent years, the introduction of action research as a way of addressing the issue of changing teachers' pedagogy and practice has received increasing attention. Wells (2001) suggested that the concept of teachers as researchers was a powerful way of modelling successful learning to students. Ingvarson et al. (2003) and Ingvarson (2005) suggested that PLD was an important way of changing teacher practice, and Ingvarson (2005, p. 66) reported on '… the importance of making practice, and evidence about practice, the site for professional learning'. This type of approach to research that involved teachers gathering data in their own classrooms is commonly referred to as action research, although it is sometimes termed cooperative inquiry, action inquiry, practitioner or teacher research, practice-based research, case study research or participatory research.

Defining Action Research (AR)

As a methodology, *Action Research* originated in the 1940s and Lewin (1946) is credited with popularis-ing the approach. As Adelman (1993, p. 7) suggested, 'Kurt Lewin is often referred to as the originator of action research'. Since then there have been many, and varied, definitions proposed by researchers in the area such as:

- AR can be seen as a critical and systematic inquiry into teacher practices based on gathering data about the processes of teaching and learning that occur in classrooms and schools. Normally it is carried out by teachers but can sometimes be supplemented by outside experts (Mills, 2003; Nolen & Putten, 2007).
- AR generally takes the form originally proposed by Stenhouse (1981, 1983, 1985), who influenced later theorists such as Noffke in the U.S., Alexander in the U.K., and Kemmis in Australia. Among the first to apply it to educational settings was Corey (1953, p. 70) who concluded that '... the con-sequences of our own teaching is more likely to change and improve our practices than is reading about what someone else has discovered of his teaching'. Action Research follows a number of com-monly accepted sequential steps:
  - o   Identifying a research problem or question,
  - o   Developing a plan of action and collecting data/evidence,
  - o   Analysing and evaluating of data and establishing findings,
  - o   Reflecting on findings and modifying practice and/or pedagogy,
  - o   Sharing findings,
  - o   Identifying a further research question and beginning a new cycle of research.

  As Denscombe (2010, p. 6) stated, the purpose of action research is to solve a particular issue and to propose guidelines for best practice. It is therefore based on problem solution and active learning on the part of the teacher and/or school. It requires engagement in an **inquiry** process that involves what Reason and Bradbury (2007) term 1st, 2nd or 3rd person research, that is research conducted by an individual teacher, a team of teachers, or a whole school or network of schools (see also Ferrance, 2000, p. 6).
- AR research, according to Dick (2000, pp. 1-2) tends to be:
  - o   Cyclic - a recurrent process,
  - o   Participative - participants play an active role in the research process,
  - o   Qualitative - focusses more on qualitative than quantitative data,
  - o   Reflective - involves critical reflection in each cycle of the research process,
  - o   Responsive - responds to the changing needs of the research context,
  - o   Emergent - the research process develops gradually and, because of its cyclical nature, informs later cycles of action research,
  - o   Often based on some version of the Carr and Kemmis (1986) and Kemmis and McTaggert (1988) cycle of plan - act - observe - reflect.

In summary, Action Research can be understood as a research methodology that is based on systematic and critical inquiry about teaching and learning carried out by teachers in their classrooms/schools. It arose from the need to relate theory to practice by investigating the nature of theory while addressing teacher concerns about everyday pedagogy and practice.

REFLECTION STRATEGY 1.3

- The purpose of this Reflection Strategy is to explore how important action research is in your school.
- Discuss with other teachers in your school whether they have been involved in action research, and if so, whether they engaged in it by themselves, with other teachers, or with the whole school.
- Try to determine whether one type of action research was preferred over others. This will give some direction as to how you might embark on action research yourself.
- Have a meeting with the leadership team in your school to gauge what support there is for the introduction of action research and what support strategies the team might be willing to provide.
- If action research is to be encouraged, then it will be useful to determine whether PLD is needed and what outside expert help might be needed and/or available.

Benefits of Action Research (AR)

There are a number of benefits arising from engaging in AR that make it attractive to teachers and schools. As has been stated earlier in this chapter, teachers find PLD (professional learning and development) particularly helpful when it is practical and informs pedagogy and practice. The idea of supporting engagement in AR with focussed PLD is therefore particularly appealing. AR develops a relationship between acquiring knowledge about the teaching and learning around a certain issue with engaging in action at the coalface of the classroom. As Coghlan and Brannick (2010, p. 4) suggested, AR is '... research in action rather than research about action'. Its focus is about improving or modifying practice through the generation of new knowledge by involvement in research. It can also encourage teachers to form cooperative partnerships that focus on joint planning, reflection and sharing knowledge (Rose et al., 2015, p. 2). Coghlan (2007, p. 293) refers to these benefits as 'actionable knowledge'. Earlier Adelman (1993, p. 7) had stated that AR, as different from scientific or empirical approaches to research, promoted development of social relationships within, and between, groups that led to sustained communication and cooperation. Mertler and Charles (2008, p. 308) concluded that teachers often used AR because it:

- Dealt with real-life personal issues or problems rather than general ones relating to education as a whole,
- Could be started without delay and could provide immediate results,

- Provided opportunities to understand and improve educational practices,
- Promoted the building of stronger relationships among teachers,
- Provided teachers and schools with a variety of alternative ways of understanding and investigating educational issues and, in addition, new ways of examining their own practices.

The benefits of AR that have been discussed so far point to the fact that it addresses the relationship of theory and practice and makes it possible for teachers to have a practice-based theory of teaching and learning. This relationship allows teachers to make good use of theory in their day-to-day teaching rather than judging theory as somehow impractical. In the research reported by Bull and Anstey (2010b), the participants in the study accorded theory an important part of their action research projects and rejected the proposition that good practice did not need to relate to good theory.

ACTION LEARNING TASK 1.1

- The intention of this Action Learning Task is to determine how you might begin action research in your classroom.
- In your discussions with other teachers find out what issues are of concern or interest to other teachers.
- The purpose of discussing issues with other teachers is that this may give you alternative ideas about the topic of your research or, alternatively, assist you in deciding whether to join other teachers in a joint project.
- It will be very useful if, at this point, you raise the possibility of forming a community of learners. This does not imply that everyone will be researching the same issue but rather that the community can provide mutual support and advice.

Effective Professional Learning and Development (PLD)

Edwards-Groves, Anstey and Bull (2014, p.140) developed a set of characteristics for effective PLD drawn from the work of Alexander (2001, 2004, 2005a, 2008b) and Wells (1999, 2001) in the U.K., Noffke (2008) and Hendricks (2002) in the U.S., and Kemmis and McTaggert (1988, 2005) and Ingvarson (2005) in Australia. These characteristics supported teachers in transforming their practice, particularly in situations where teachers were involved in AR. Edwards-Groves, Anstey and Bull suggested that effective PLD should:

- Address teacher concerns related to their classrooms and not be drawn from research in other educational contexts,
- Be school based,
- Emphasise modelling and demonstration of teacher practices,
- Involve a community of learners that is based upon joint planning and sharing and emphasises reflection,

- Incorporate spaced learning over a significant period of time,
- Provide for follow-up sessions between each set of PLD days,
- Focus on the change process as well as practices, pedagogy and talk,
- Address the relationship of theory to planning, practice and pedagogy,
- Mandate the collection of evidence from a variety of sources to indicate that change in planning, practice and pedagogy has occurred,
- Provide opportunities for participants to develop a sense of ownership of the process of action research,
- Involve external experts from outside the context of the school,
- Include provision for extended periods of time when participants can discuss issues pertaining to planning, practice, pedagogy or talk.

These twelve characteristics are similar to the work of many researchers and writers who have explored both AR and PLD and the positive relationship between them. This work has enabled teachers and other researchers to develop successful programs and approaches to action research following the benefits enumerated by this research. Rose et al. (2015) explored the benefits of AR and suggested that it should be:

- Based on the structuring of social relationships and practices,
- Flexible and require judgements to be made about appropriate practices,
- Include monitoring of results that depended upon analysis, interpretation and synthesis of results that enabled conclusions to be drawn.

Dick (2000) suggested that benefits of AR accrue when it is seen as a cyclical process that needs to be based on a number of iterations of the cycle that enable multiple sources of data to be analysed. There are a number of other factors that have been identified that lead to the successful implementation of Action Research.

Factors involved in the successful implementation of Action Research (AR)

Developing a *community of learners* has been identified as having an important influence on AR. Meiers (2010, p. 1), quoting the work of Bolam et al. (2005), reported that a community of learners had the capacity to promote and sustain the learning of both teachers and learners. Meiers (2010, p. 1) further referenced the work of Stoll et al. (2006), which concluded a community of learners produced positive results when displaying the following characteristics:

- Shared values and vision,
- Collective responsibility for students' learning,
- Collaboration focussed on learning,
- Group as well as individual learning, reflective professional enquiry,
- Openness, networks and partnerships,
- Inclusive membership,
- Mutual trust, respect and support.

Reason (1994) developed the concept of cooperative, or collaborative, inquiry within a community of learners to emphasise active participation and group decision-making and encapsulated this approach as 'research with' rather than 'research on'. Lefstein and Snell (2014, p. 4) also recommended teachers sharing their practice with colleagues in order to learn from each other and suggested 'This approach is better than best practice because it helps to develop and support thoughtful, flexible and insightful practitioners'.

The provision of *long-term Professional Learning and Development* (PLD) in action learning settings has been a focus of recent attention. This is not so much a question of providing longer sessions, but rather spreading PLD over a longer period of time by introducing spaced learning. According to Edwards-Groves and Ronnerman (2012), teachers are more likely to participate in collegial discussions if they are a part of a community of learners that is part of long-term PLD. Similar findings were suggested by Kemmis et al. (2012), Ronnerman and Olin (2012) and Edwards-Groves, Anstey and Bull (2014), who concluded that teachers were more likely to engage in successful AR because of the greater opportunities created through spaced learning.

Based on the work of Schon (1983) who proposed reflection-in-action (when teachers engaged in *reflection* about their practices while they were actually engaged in those practices), the process of reflection, particularly *collaborative reflection*, has become an important part of both AR and PLD. Kemmis and Grootenboer (2008) and Kemmis and Heikkinen (2012) found that reflection, as with a number of other factors, played a part in successful PLD in their work in Australia and Sweden. However, reflection was accorded a more prominent role in the work of Edwards-Groves (2003, 2008), who suggested that teachers in what she termed reflective learning communities – that is engaging in collaborative reflection – asked significant numbers of questions involving reflection that modified classroom practices. She concluded (2003) that collaborative focussed reflection resulted in a number of benefits that were later adapted by Edwards-Groves, Anstey and Bull (2014, p.145) and encouraged teachers to:

- Join a community of learners and engage in collaborative reflection,
- Investigate, and modify, their classroom practices,
- Tape their lessons in order to analyse their pedagogy,
- Engage in critical analysis and self-monitoring of their PLD,
- Acknowledge that reflection should result in action,
- Realise that teacher talk shapes classroom practices,
- Reshape their practices through explicit instruction.

Edwards-Groves, Anstey and Bull (2014, p.146) concluded that this type of reflection-based PLD is best supported through AR conducted over the long term. This position was supported by Lefstein and Snell (2014, p.34) through what they termed their reflection workshops that encouraged participating teachers to engage in collaborative reflection.

Successful PLD is achieved by a focus on *pedagogy*. As Lefstein and Snell (2014, p. 3) suggested in their approach, which they described as 'better than best practice', they outlined '... an approach to pedagogy and professional development that is sensitive to and appreciative of the tensions and dilemmas inherent to teaching and learning in classrooms'. They describe a pedagogy that is sensitive to 'critical moments, problems and/or opportunities', interprets various situations that arise in the classroom and about making judgements about the possibilities that are likely to unfold (Lefstein & Snell, 2014, pp.8–9).

As they conclude (2014, p. 9), 'Professional teaching practice involves sensitivity, interpretation, judge-ment and a flexible repertoire of methods'. It is therefore critical that teachers' actions in developing their pedagogy and the way they talk about pedagogy should be at the core of their everyday practices. Bull and Anstey (2010b) recommended that such a pedagogy can be successfully developed through PLD that is situated in a program of action learning and is based on validation of learning through promoting change in pedagogy and practice. Ingvarson et al. (2003) reviewed eighty professional learning programs involving three thousand teachers and concluded that PLD was a vital part of changing teachers' prac-tices. Ingvarson (2005) later reported that it was important to make practice the site for professional learning and development.

In his report Ingvarson (2005, p. 66) concluded that not only was it important to make practice an important part of professional learning, but also it was critical to gather *evidence* about practice. Both Ferrance (2000) and Bull and Anstey (2010b) recommended that gathering evidence about change in pedagogy and practice should be an essential part of AR and PLD. They further stated that any con-clusions arising from the gathering of evidence should be based on the triangulation of three sources of data that might include such things as transcripts of lessons, interviews, lesson observations, ques-tionnaires, case studies, surveys or samples of student work. The focus on the gathering of evidence to support change in pedagogy or practice is crucial in determining whether change has been effective in a program of AR or PLD rather than relying on teachers or students reporting enjoyment in engaging in a particular activity.

Collaborative dialogue occurs when teachers discuss issues or problems that they have in common. This often occurs when teachers engage in collaborative reflection but may, as Ferrance (2000) reported, when teachers or principals work together to mutually assist one another. Both Ferrance and Rose et al. (2015) report on the benefits of collaborative action through dialogue and its value in increased participation of participants. Bull and Anstey (2010b) suggested that collaborative dialogue resulted in teachers developing shared knowledge of a particular issue which led to increased success in programs of AR and PLD. Bull and Anstey (1995, 1996, 1997) also reported that teachers reading about the research on educational issues increased the amount of collaborative and professional dialogue. Dialogue, whether it is referring to talk or pedagogy, is accorded a central place in the discussion about teacher practices by Lefstein and Snell (2014). As Hattie (2012, p. 39) stated, '… learning is collaborative and requires dialogue'.

When teachers are attempting to modify their pedagogy and practices, they need support in *dealing with change*. Ferrance (2000, p. 8) concluded AR is increasingly becoming an instrument for addressing school reform or school renewal. In each of these cases, there is a requirement for teachers to change their behaviour, whether it be through talk, pedagogy or practice or perhaps some combination of all three. Meiers (2010) referring to the research of Stoll et al. (2006) identified response to change as being one of the factors that impacted on '… schools' overall capacity for change and development, including individuals, orientation to change, group dynamics, school context influences'. Bull and Anstey (2010b), drawing on the work of Comber and Hill (2000), Comber (2005), Comber and Kamler (2005) and Kamler and Comber (2008) in Australia, suggested that teachers who were engaged in an action learning model of PLD were supported to implement change successfully.

Much of the research that looks at the nature of change and how teachers deal with it is based on the work of Fullan (2001, 2002, 2004, 2005, 2007, 2008), who traced how teachers lead in a culture of change. His later work identified factors such as resilience and sustainability that promoted and supported long-term change in pedagogy and practice. A recurring theme in much of the work around change is that change is a complex process where some teachers and schools have difficulty in dealing with it and some do not. Hendricks (2002) suggested that success in dealing with change was influenced by who was driving the change. She concluded that when AR was guided by researchers or by teachers it met with limited or no success, whereas if AR was implemented through a collaboration of both groups it was more likely to succeed. Change in pedagogy and/or practice was achieved when all stakeholders had ownership of the process and had a degree of control over its direction. Change was also more likely to be successful, according to Ingvarson (2005, p. 69), when participating teachers had some knowledge of, and confidence in, the theory on which it was based. Earlier Wells (2001) had proposed that the relationship between theory and practice was important in that good practice needed to be grounded on good theory and that good theory grew out of good practice – one needed to inform the other. Another note of caution was sounded by Alexander (2004a, 2005a) in his work on changes in practice and in talk when he stated that some teachers were achieving real change in their classrooms whereas others were struggling. He concluded that those teachers who took time to set up the conditions and routines for classroom interaction before attempting to change pedagogy, practice or talk were more likely to successfully implement change.

Finally, both Bull and Anstey (2010b) and Edwards-Groves and Ronnerman (2012) reported that change was more likely to occur when there were high expectations about the amount of change in participants' teaching and learning. They concluded that the result of being challenged encouraged teachers to make greater degrees of change in their practice.

There appears to be a relationship between the *culture of the school* and the likelihood of achieving measurable change. The fact that some schools have clear and shared understandings about their goals and well-defined ideas about the nature of good teaching and learning suggests that they are more likely to successfully implement change. Conversely, those schools that struggle to achieve consensus on issues are not likely to be prepared to undergo change and more likely to remain content with conditions as they are. There have been attempts to classify schools according to how open they are to the introduction of new ideas and approaches. Gossen and Anderson (1995) proposed three types of schools according to the characteristics that they exhibited. The following characteristics are a summary adapted from Gossen and Anderson (1995, pp. 117–146):

- The conventional school – having a traditional atmosphere and belief system where school is seen as a place to work; teachers work in isolation from each other and tend to teach without regard to others; teachers tend to be competitive.
- The congenial school – where social relationships are friendship based and are regarded as important as work; belonging to a group is important; there is an aversion to conflict; when a difficult issue is raised, it often results in silence or a lack of discussion so that the issue is put off for another day or ignored.
- The collegial school – vigorous discussion is encouraged where there is no fear of disagreement; staff openly examine beliefs and practices; there is a willingness to modify or shift paradigms; ideas and differences of opinions are shared; all staff are encouraged to air their opinions while others listen.

Another set of characteristics are those proposed by Stoll and Fink (1996) and adapted in the typology of cultures below:

- Moving – encourages student performance; responds to change through cooperation of staff; clear identification of goals and standards.
- Cruising – appears to be effective; often an affluent school; students learn in spite of the quality of teaching; standards inhibit change because they are not clearly defined; staff does not deal effectively with change.
- Strolling – seems to be marking time so is neither effective or ineffective; change dealt with inadequately; needs of students not addressed; goals are not clearly defined and often conflicting so progress is inhibited.
- Struggling – staff are aware of ineffectiveness and have the will but lack the skills to succeed; expend considerable energy to improve but progress is unproductive; often identified as failing.
- Sinking – loss of faith in progress which inhibits improvement; ineffective with staff unable to change; tends to blame others, such as parents, for lack of student performance; often in a deprived or disadvantaged area where dramatic action and significant support is required.

It is important to treat these two typologies of school cultures with a certain amount of caution. It is not intended by either group of researchers that any school should fulfil all the characteristics of a particular type of school. Nor is it their intention that just because a school appears to be 'sinking' or 'conventional' that there would not be pockets or groups of teachers who could be judged as 'moving' or 'collegial'. It was concluded by Gossen and Anderson (1995) and by Stoll and Fink (1996) that the categories of schools tended to be accurate only in terms of general tendencies across most characteristics. Different teachers in a particular school might judge their school in diverse ways or individuals from outside the school might hold different views from those from within the school. There may also be occasions when a school moves from one category to another because of staff changes or change in goals. A shift in category might also be caused when different issues are addressed. Despite these notes of caution, the two typologies can be used to explore why some schools are more open to change than others by alerting teachers to some characteristics that can be investigated. Many of the teachers in the research reported by Bull and Anstey (2010b) found the characteristics most useful in exploring the conditions for change in their schools and the reasons why it might be impeded or encouraged. The teachers were also able to analyse their school in terms of both cultures and characteristics and found this categorisation useful in planning PLD and AR at their site.

REFLECTION STRATEGY 1.4

- The purpose of this Reflection Strategy is to decide which factors will be considered in how you conduct your action research.
- It will be useful to discuss with the community of learners in your school which factors will be considered. If you do not have such a community in your school, it will be important to have discussions with other teachers. It may be useful to review the eight factors discussed

in the preceding section titled 'Factors Involved in the Successful Implementation of Action Research (AR)'. As an example, it will be crucial to decide in what period of time the research will be conducted. Long-term research, as with any PLD you decide is important, will be more likely to be successful if it is conducted over a period of at least one year.

- It is important to go through a period of careful planning before you begin your research. If you rush into a project because you are excited about it, it is likely that you will run into trouble and have a negative experience.

Introducing the Action Learning Cycle (ALC) and the project

Having discussed the factors that contribute to successful professional learning and development and the role of action research in professional learning, the remainder of this chapter provides information about the Action Learning Cycle developed by Anstey and Bull. It also provides tools and Action Learning Tasks that enable the reader to commence their own Action Learning Project as an individual, or as part of a group or school engaging in an Action Learning Cycle.

Using the research literature concerning the factors that affect AR, the various definitions and benefits of AR and what contributes to effective AR that have been previously discussed in this chapter, Anstey and Bull devised what they termed the Action Learning Cycle (ALC). They drew firstly on their earlier research (Anstey, 1998, 2003; Anstey and Bull, 2005; Bull and Anstey, 1993, 1994, 2000) in the areas of multiliteracies, multimodality and PLD. Secondly, they referred to their more recent research (Bull and Anstey, 2004, 2005b, 2007) that explored the relationship of PLD and AR. Their ALC was similar to AR but differed in a number of important ways that will be discussed later in this chapter. Two early decisions were made about the conduct of the ALC. The first was that participants would engage in the ALC only on a voluntary basis. Secondly, the participants would decide whether their research would be conducted over a period of one, two or three years. The overall structure of the ALC was determined by selecting a number of characteristics drawn from the research about action learning that assisted in framing the project.

It was at this point that Anstey and Bull decided to use the term 'action learning' rather than 'action research' since they felt that learning was a more appropriate expression because it emphasised that participants were learning through the application of research. It was also decided to add the term 'cycle' to draw attention to the fact that classroom-based research was not a one-shot approach but rather should be seen as a continuous cycle that, as it addressed one issue of interest to the researcher, raised other areas of possible future research. Participants were therefore engaged in a succession of investigations, each building on the previous one to form a cycle of action research. Once the nature of the ALC was determined, it was then possible to ascertain which characteristics of action learning were essential to the implementation of the cycle.

The following characteristics were adopted:

Adoption of the term project. It was decided for ease of reference that participants would describe what they were doing as a project that involved an ALC.

Duration of the project. The duration of the project was seen as critical to the processes involved in the ALC. This was based on the belief that significant and lasting change in pedagogy and teacher practices can only be attained over time. As previously stated, it was up to the teachers and the school to decide whether the project would run over one, two or three years.

Site-based professional learning and development. One of the recommended conditions of appropriate PLD is that it results in teachers having a shared knowledge of a particular area or discipline. In the case of the ALC, because of the structure of the project it was mandated that participants have a thorough background in multiliteracies, multimodality, the change process and the nature of pedagogy. The project was therefore designed around an intensive period of PLD that was conducted over two days at the beginning of the project, which was followed by three more days at intervals throughout the year (with additional days if the project ran over two or three years, or if the group desired). The sessions of PLD were developed around the needs identified by the teachers concerned so that they were particular to the site but also included some sessions that were common to all projects.

Multiliteracies Matrix and Reflection Tool. This tool, reported by Anstey and Bull (2010b) and Bull and Anstey (2000, 2004, 2005b, 2007), was specifically devised by Anstey and Bull to support the ALC in a number of ways. For the purpose of future discussion, it will be referred to as the Matrix and will be examined in more detail later in this chapter (see Table 1.1). The Matrix was initially designed to define the concepts of multiliteracies and multimodality by requiring participants to engage with the 26 items outlined in it that addressed knowledge, understandings and practices about the two concepts. Some of the 26 items had sub-categories that provided participants with the opportunity to rate themselves on 40 elements. These elements were divided into three broad categories that addressed the areas of text (16 elements), context (10 elements) and pedagogy (14 elements).

The Matrix was also used as a reflection tool by requiring participants to evaluate their classroom pedagogy and practice by rating themselves for their current knowledge about, and practice implementing, each of the 26 items. They were then asked to justify why they rated themselves at a particular level. In this way, the Matrix was intended to increase teachers' awareness of their knowledge about multiliteracies, multimodality and pedagogy and encourage them to engage in reflection.

Once all 40 elements were addressed and justified, participants were asked to select two or three elements that would form the basis of their research in the classroom. One element had to be selected from the pedagogy section in order to ensure that teacher pedagogy was investigated, and the remaining element/elements could be chosen from any of the three broad categories. Allowing participants to select items from the Matrix was designed to assist in deciding the focus of their research, thereby overcoming the perennial problem of determining which issue in the classroom to investigate. Limiting the choice of elements to two or three was predicated on the tendency of teachers to attempt to solve too many issues in their classroom-based research that produced a project that became unmanageable, leading to negative outcomes for teachers.

Participants were expected to fill out the Matrix a number of times throughout their project as a way of collecting data about their change in knowledge and approach. It was therefore seen as important that each time teachers filled out the Matrix, a new copy would be filled in so that developing changes could be analysed to increase the validity of the data being collected. Teachers were also supported to form learning pairs, or small groups, to engage in professional dialogue as they deliberated about the Matrix. Table 1.1 below represents all of the categories and elements of the Matrix.

Table 1.1 Multiliteracies Matrix and Reflection Tool

Instructions for using the Multiliteracies Matrix and Reflection Tool.

The purpose of this tool is to identify the characteristics of a multiliterate classroom in terms of three Domains: Text, Context and Pedagogy. In the first two columns, the Domains and a description of characteristics associated with each Domain is provided. In the Text and Context Domains, each characteristic is accompanied by an italicised example. The example indicates what a *student* might have engaged in and learned if that characteristic was *fully embedded* in the classroom. The example is intended as an aid to you in interpreting how the characteristic might be implemented in a classroom and what the actual learning might look like, that is how a student might talk about their learning. In the Pedagogy Domain, each characteristic is accompanied by an italicised example of how you might describe the enactment of that feature in your classroom if it was *fully embedded*. Again, the example is there to help you translate the characteristic into classroom practice.

Use these characteristics and examples to reflect upon, evaluate and rate your knowledge, planning and practice in relation to these descriptors, on a scale rated from 1 to 5. The scale is presented below.

Scale for Rating Personal Knowledge Planning and Practice.

1. This is a **new concept** to me and I have **no understanding** of it.
2. I have **some understanding** of this concept but have **not attempted to apply** it in my classroom planning and practice.
3. I **understand** this concept and have **begun** exploring ways I can implement this as part of my classroom planning and practice.
4. I **fully understand** this concept and it is an **important part** of my classroom planning and practice.
5. This concept is **fully embedded** in my understanding and **consistently implemented** in my classroom planning and practice.

Two additional columns are provided as part of the reflection tool. In the first column, Justification and Comments, you can provide specific information and clarification about why you rated yourself as you did. You are encouraged to differentiate between *beliefs* and *practice* when rating yourself, to ensure your ratings reflect your *current* knowledge and classroom practice.

The final column is designed for use after the rating and comments columns have been completed. Its purpose is to encourage you to reflect about what area you wish to prioritise in terms of your personal learning and action in your classroom and what form that action might take.

Multiliteracies Matrix and Reflection Tool: Name _____ Year level/Subject _____ School _____

Domain	In a multimodal literacy classroom:	1	2	3	4	5	Justification and Comment Ensure you differentiate between *belief* and *practice*	Possible Strategy or Action
TEXT	1. Students **use, interpret, & produce** texts using:							
	• paper,							
	• live, and							
	• digital technologies.							
	For this purpose and in this context, it would be better to conduct a conversation face to face rather than send an email because…							

TEXT						
2. Students know, understand and use **individual and combined semiotic systems:**						
• linguistic (vocabulary, grammar)						
• visual (still & moving images, page & screen layouts)						
• audio (music, sound effects, silence)						
• gestural (facial expression & body language)						
• spatial (environmental & architectural spaces & layouts)						
*As I watched this video I could see that the character was being developed not only by the way the plot dictated his actions, but through the costuming, soft **lighting** and close-up camera shots. This was achieved by…*						
3. Students engage in explorations that develop knowledge and understandings about *how and why* **meanings are actively constructed.**						
My friend and I went to the movies and afterwards we discovered we had quite different views about the way the plot was re-solved. We discussed what had shaped our views and discovered that we had very different life experiences and this had shaped our interpretation and understanding of the plot. These were…						
4. Students engage in explorations which develop knowledge and understandings about **how and why a text may have several possible meanings.**						
Although I was amused by this ad, if I was a recent immigrant to this country I believe that I would find it offensive because….						
5. Students engage in explorations which develop knowledge and understandings about **how and why** texts may be:						
• multimodal						
• interactive						
• intertextual						
• linear and non-linear						
We looked at a website today. Its audience is mostly…and it had lots of video and music. You could enter competitions online and download stuff. It had hotlinks to other sites. I think the website worked well for its audience because…						

Table 1.1 (Continued)

Domain	In a multimodal literacy classroom:	1	2	3	4	5	Justification and Comment Ensure you differentiate between *belief* and *practice*	Possible Strategy or Action
	6. Students explore and develop understandings about the concept that all texts have a purpose and therefore 'no text is neutral', that is, they explore **how and why texts are produced and distributed.** *We explored smartphone ads and found that smartphones are marketed as a form of entertainment. This was evident because... Smartphone manufacturers do this because...*							
	7. Students investigate **how and why texts have and will continue to change.** *We were looking at SMS messages today and comparing them with notes we handwrite and email messages. We found that the way we write notes has changed and think this is because...*							
	8. Students explore & develop understandings about how **social practices shape texts and behaviours with texts.** *Today we looked at places where we do not always use correct spelling and grammar (such as SMS messages and shopping lists) and then we talked about why this was acceptable in these contexts but not in others. We concluded that....*							
CONTEXT	9. Students explore & develop understandings about how literacy can be:							
	• cultural (behaviours, stories, dialects)							
	• economic (advertising, marketing)							
	• ideological (beliefs, values, attitudes)							
	• political (bias, propaganda)							
	• psychological (thinking)							
	• social (dress, behaviour, vocabulary)							
	Today we looked at the fairy stories we grew up with and found out that although in some cultures we have three wishes and three bears, in other cultures they have a motif of four, like four wishes.							

	10. Students **explore their unique literacy identity** and how it affects their literate practices. *When I started to do this task, I thought about what previous school and other life experiences might help me or hinder me and then I worked out a strategy for completing the task based on these reflections.*				
	11. Students learn about literate practices and literacy **in all key learning areas.** *We looked at report writing in science today and compared it with writing a report about an historical event. We found the following similarities and differences… and concluded…*				
	12. Students explore how audience and context influences **how and why texts are produced.** *We looked at all the Harry Potter books and products and identified who might buy them and why. Then we talked to someone from an advertising firm about how these products might have been developed and marketed*				
PEDAGOGY	13. The class literacy learning and teaching program is informed by reference to the **Four Resource Model.** There is not only a **balance** between the four practices but the program clearly articulates what each practice looks like in **different disciplines** and year levels. *When I am planning, I ensure that students are engaged in all four practices across all disciplines. I am also careful to select appropriate materials and teaching strategies for the practice I am focussing upon.*				
	14. The desired **learning outcome informs** the selection of **teaching strategies.** *When I plan lessons, I start by working out what I want the students to know and be able to do at the end. Then I select activities, materials and strategies that best achieve that, rather than starting with the materials and activities.*				

(Continued)

Table 1.1 (Continued)

Domain	In a multimodal literacy classroom:	1	2	3	4	5	Justification and Comment Ensure you differentiate between *belief* and *practice*	Possible Strategy or Action
PEDAGOGY	15. Students engage in **strategy development** rather than activities (problem solving, strategic approaches, knowledge as problematic). *When we engage in a task we focus on the strategy to be used, when it should be applied, and why it is being used and not just what is to be done to complete the task. In this way, the students get the idea that things change, and sometimes you have to modify what you know in order to address the task at hand.*							
	16. Teachers and students have a **metalanguage** for exploring and talking about texts and their semiotic systems. *When we discuss texts the students and I use the correct terminology, so for example we talk about **parallel cutting** and close-ups when we consume or produce moving images.*							
	17. Teachers use **explicit pedagogy** that focusses on the **what, how, when and why** of literacy learning and literate practices. *Whenever we start a task and even during the task, we constantly refer to why we are doing it, what we are learning and how and when this learning might be used in other contexts and with other texts.*							
	18. **Explicit teacher talk** focusses on the **what, how, when and why of literacy** rather than classroom organisation and discipline and is a feature of all literacy teaching and learning. *I have been audiotaping my lessons and analysing them in order to change my talk around texts. I try to have substantive conversations rather than simple question and answer sequences where students have to 'guess what's in my head'.*							

PEDAGOGY					
19. Classroom talk is **dialogic**, there are **extended, explicit and purposeful exchanges between teacher and student and student and student.** *I am concentrating on shifting my classroom talk from monologic to dialogic to allow students the space to ask questions and initiate learner talk.*					
20. Teacher talk is **not dominated by IREs** that restrict exchanges with students to initiation, response and evaluation, creating the perception that learning is only about getting right answers. *I am allowing more time for learner talk by vacating the floor, encouraging more student reflection, by employing wait time and extending exchanges.*					
21. Students are engaged in the **consumption, production and transformation** of knowledge about literacy. *I am really aware that I must provide different learning opportunities for my students. Sometimes it's necessary to engage in focussed learning episodes, but sometimes they actually need to work out the learning for themselves. Other times they need practice in applying that knowledge in new ways and in different contexts.*					
22. The literacy teaching and learning is balanced. Students **learn literacy, use literacy to learn** and **learn about how literacy operates and functions** in society. *It's not just enough for my students to be able to identify the features of a genre, they need to know how to use it to learn and how it is used in society to shape social practices and behaviours.*					
23. All learning encourages the development of **metacognitive skills.** Students monitor their learning in four ways: *knowing that, knowing how and knowing when and why a particular strategy needs to be employed.* *I encourage the students to develop a plan for every task and then monitor its use. Afterwards I get them to reflect on their learning and the success of their strategy.*					

(Continued)

Table 1.1 (Continued)

Domain	In a multimodal literacy classroom:	1	2	3	4	5	Justification and Comment Ensure you differentiate between *belief* and *practice*	Possible Strategy or Action
PEDAGOGY	24. Students investigate how literate practices operate in the social, cultural, political, ideological and economic world in order to develop understandings about the **relationship between literacy and power.** *When we investigate a genre or any piece of text we discuss the purpose of the text, who constructed it and how it constructs the world. We identify the power of the text for different groups in different contexts. I want the students to understand that no text is neutral, that being literate is about gaining control over your life.*							
	25. Literacy teaching and learning is planned in response to students' social and cultural diversity in order to ensure **connectedness** between home, school and community. *Initially I used the school's community audit data to inform my selection of materials and teaching strategies, and then I conducted some further investigations with my class to fill in gaps in that data. This helped me make the learning more relevant and empowering for my students.*							
	26. Approaches to the teaching and learning of literacy are part of a **shared vision about literacy** to which the whole school has committed. *I know that the literacy teaching I do is part of a clearly articulated whole school approach and that my students will encounter similar approaches in other classes and disciplines.*							

ACTION LEARNING TASK 1.2

- The purpose of this Action Learning Task is to introduce the ALC and support you in beginning a project designed to change your literacy pedagogy, to introduce you to the characteristics of a multiliterate classroom and to a methodology suitable for action research.
- Spend some time reading through the 26 items in the first column on the Matrix to make yourself familiar with them.
- Start the process of rating yourself in the second column against the 26 items, remembering that there are 40 individual elements within the items. As you rate yourself on each item, there are some important points to consider.
    - o There are detailed suggestions on the first page of the Matrix that will assist you in rating yourself from 1 to 5.
    - o The 40 elements are *not* belief statements. If they were, then you would likely say that you believe all elements are important to you and rate yourself as a 5 for each element. When you rate yourself on each element, what you are doing is making a judgement about how well each element is established in your classroom.
    - o In order to help you with making this judgement, there are statements in italics for each item that reflect what students in your class would say about their understanding of each item. The italicised statements are meant to reflect the understandings of an average student in your class who has mastered this knowledge and understanding. There will necessarily be some students who have not reached this level of understanding and others who have exceeded it.
    - o It is important that you address all 40 elements so that you get an accurate assessment of your practice and pedagogy.
    - o There may be a tendency for you to rate yourself as a 3 for each element. This could be interpreted as 'fence sitting' or as avoiding making a decision about the items. This is not to say that the 3 rating should be avoided, but rather if you have a preponderance of 3 ratings, then you might be focussed more on 'getting the Matrix done' rather than making judgements about your teaching.
    - o In order to assist you to make accurate judgements in the third column, you need to justify each rating that you make against the 40 characteristics. Remember that you are making judgements about your practice and not about whether you believe some characteristic is important.
    - o The fourth column is there only if you wish to add any reminder to yourself about ideas that you might have about addressing a particular practice. It is important to add those comments as you go, as leaving them till you have finished all items on the Matrix may lead you to forget some good ideas.
    - o As a guide, most participants take 2 to 3 hours to fill in the Matrix. Most participants also return to the Matrix a number of times during their project to adjust some of their ratings. It might be useful to complete the Matrix in pencil to aid in this process of revision, or alternatively if completed as a Word document, save each revision as a separate file so you can trace the development of your ideas and reflections. It is important to approach

filling in the Matrix as a work in progress and not a document that is set in concrete from the beginning of your project.

o   Once you have completed the Matrix, it is time to select some items that will form the basis of your project. It is advisable that you limit your choices to two but no more than three elements in order to make your project manageable. It is important that you select at least one element or item from the pedagogy section of the Matrix, as it is a project designed to change your pedagogy. As an example, a number of participants selected the visual semiotic system from Item 2 and then selected Item 15, 16 or 18 depending on whether they were investigating strategy development, metalanguage or explicit teacher talk. You will have noticed that the element visual semiotic system was selected by the participants and not Item 2. Selection of Item 2 would have resulted in five foci, one for each semiotic system, creating a project that was unmanageable for the scope of the project as it is envisaged.

o   You need to give careful consideration to which items you are going to select from the Matrix. While the ratings on the Matrix lend themselves to revision, once you have selected the items from the Matrix and begin to frame your project, it is very time-consuming to change your focus by selecting alternative items. Nevertheless, it is possible and sometimes necessary.

Action plan

Anstey and Bull designed the action plan as a proforma that teachers completed in order to devise a sequenced and carefully balanced research-in-action project. With over 1,500 possible combinations of elements, the Matrix enabled teachers to self-select their research focus. The Action Plan Proforma was designed to allow teachers to conduct their research at a level that matched their capabilities and at a pace that suited their experience and expertise with the research process. From its inception, the proforma was designed to focus attention on changing teacher practice and pedagogy rather than on improving student performance. In this way, the Action Plan Proforma and the Matrix were teacher focussed rather than student focussed. In order to quantify change in pedagogy and practice, teachers were expected to focus their attention on collecting a variety of data so that any conclusions that they drew were evidence based.

The proforma had two broad categories of action and validation. These were further divided into the sub-categories of aim, method, data collection, analysis and reporting. These sub-categories were specified so that participants would become familiar with the format of a research project so that they would be able to repeat the process in further cycles of the ALC. The format was seen as way of preparing teachers for more formal research projects as part of further postgraduate study or as a way of supporting them in any future application for recognition of prior learning (RPL) as part of a university course. The Action Plan Proforma also required teachers to specify any visits to other schools that they undertook and any conversations that occurred with fellow teachers as well as providing evidence of change in practice, pedagogy and planning and evidence of professional reading. This came to be termed 'the 4P's of evidence of change' because it was based on the idea that any change in teacher belief or behaviour brought about by one of these factors had to influence the other three. For example, any theoretical change brought about through professional reading would change teacher practice and therefore modify pedagogy and planning.

It was pointed out to participants that both the Matrix and the Action Learning Proforma were not to be understood as absolute or immutable but rather open to change or modification as part of the normal process of engagement in research. The Action Plan Proforma is presented in Table 1.2.

Factors that need to be considered when supporting participants in completing their projects

Role of the leadership team

A feature of the ALC was the expectation that the leadership team in the participating schools including principals, deputy principals, curriculum specialists and any other teachers in leadership positions would be involved in the action learning and research process. It was a case of leading by example – do as I do, not do as I say. This became a crucial factor in influencing completion rates and satisfaction with the outcomes of the projects by the participating teachers.

Follow-up support

Follow-up support was provided to participants by access to Anstey and Bull via telephone and email and also by the appointment of trained on-site specialist advisors. This was necessary because of the vast distances involved in the Australian context. The on-site specialists were responsible for addressing day-to-day problems as they arose and also conducting sessions devised to address set tasks that were designed to be accomplished between the visits that were focussed on PLD sessions.

Analysis of pedagogy

As part of the collection of data in their action plan, participants were required to audiotape at least one lesson and prepare a transcript. It was decided that an audiotape of a lesson was more appropriate than a videotape because it focussed attention on the role of teacher talk. Analysis of a videotape requires investigating the gestural, visual and spatial semiotic systems, a complex process involving the many codes of each system. As most participants were novice researchers, it was important to make data collection and analysis focussed and manageable in order to promote positive outcomes. The gestural semiotic system alone contains 47 separate codes and would involve an onerous process of analysis. It was felt that to make some selection of the codes from the three semiotic systems to reduce the size of the task would potentially lead to some important data being ignored. (For further details about the codes and conventions of the five semiotic systems, see Chapter Five.)

The audiotapes were analysed to identify the different types of teacher talk and the different phases present in each lesson. Teachers were then able to identify which types of teacher talk were absent in their lessons and which types of talk were over-represented and whether they were appropriate to the desired learning outcomes for the lesson. Similarly, phase structure could also be analysed to identify lesson structures and which phases were absent or over-represented. In terms of teacher talk, participants often found the categories of classroom organisation and literacy management over-represented and process and utility talk under-represented. In other words, teacher talk was more concerned with

Table 1.2 Action Plan Proforma

ACTION		VALIDATION	
Aim or Goal	**Method (focus on action)**	**Method (focus on validation) #**	**Data Collection, Analysis and Reporting #**
What are the items identified for change? *What is your desired outcome?*	*How will you go about achieving this?* *What will you do?*	*What would you expect to see as evidence of change or improvement?* *Where would you look for this evidence?* *How would you recognise it?* *What would it look like?*	*How would you collect this evidence?* *How would you collate it?* *How will you analyse it and report it?*
Items	**Professional Reading, Visits, Conversations**		
	Pedagogy and Practice		
Desired Outcomes	**Planning**		
	Resources		

Examples of data collection methods: Reflection journals about professional reading; reflection logs by teacher and students on teacher practice; student interviews; student work samples; observations of your work by critical friend; discussion with critical friend; field notes about conversations/discussions with colleagues; samples of your planning (before, during, after); samples of lesson transcripts (before, during, after).

controlling behaviour and less concerned with explaining strategies, thinking processes and how and why the lessons might be useful. As far as lesson structure was concerned, the review phase was not regularly used, and when it was present it usually occurred at the end of the lesson. Further, only a small number of phases were used while others were rarely employed. Interestingly, when the focus, review, guided identification, guided practice and guided transfer phases were used in lessons, they were accompanied by significant amounts of process and utility teacher talk. Participants were often surprised, and dismayed, at the imbalances they found in the analyses of their talk and lesson structures but were always successful in addressing these imbalances, over time, in further transcripts. More information about these ideas can be found in Chapter Four of the complementary volume *Foundations of Multiliteracies: Reading, Writing and Talking in the 21st Century* and in Anstey (2003). The types of teacher talk and phases of lessons are presented in Tables 1.3 and 1.4.

Knowledge about change management

The ALC was specifically designed to engage participants in classroom-based action research with one of the central goals to change pedagogy and practice. There is therefore an expectation that significant change will take place at the classroom and school levels. It was felt that if participants had a knowledge of the change process, then they would be more likely to be able to deal with the highs and lows of the process. Teachers would then appreciate that there would be times when they would experience positive feelings about the changes that were occurring in their classrooms and sometimes they would experience negative reactions. They also needed to realise that there would be some plateaus where little change would occur. For these reasons participants were introduced to the research of Michael Fullan (2001, 2002, 2004, 2005, 2007, 2008) on how to deal with the culture of change. From Fullan's work, Bull and Anstey (2010b, p.145) identified the concepts of capability, sustainability and thriveability as critical to the support of teachers engaging in the ALC by establishing the means by which teachers could measure the success of their project. Capability was developed by providing teachers with increased knowledge about literacy, pedagogy and the change process. Sustainability was addressed firstly by encouraging teachers to change current practices and pedagogies rather than approaching their projects as an 'add-on' to their already crowded teaching programmes. Secondly, suggestions were made to school leadership teams regarding providing support to teachers to maintain and increase capability and also to create extra time and space for teachers to undertake their research. Thriveability, the potential to continually grow and create new knowledge, was maintained by presenting the ALC as a cyclical process where the process of action learning would be continuous, as each project would lead further questions to be explored that had arisen in the original study.

Production of a written report

As part of the ALC, participants submitted an evidence-based report of approximately 1,000 words on their action research. Appendices were used to provide summaries of data that might include such items as examples of planning, transcripts and student work. It was intended to record the process of change in classroom practices and pedagogy that traced development of capability, as well as suggestions for further study that promoted sustainability and thriveability. The report was structured into sections that reflected the format and categories outlined in the Action Plan Proforma. The format of the report was adopted so that it could be used as a submission to a university for part of an independent study in a postgraduate degree programme.

Table 1.3 Functions of teacher talk (Developed by Anstey, 1993b, 1998, 2003 and adapted from Anstey and Bull, 2018)

Category/Type of Talk	Description Questions or statements that focus on:	Example	Focus and Function of talk
Classroom Management	• Physical, social and organisational management • School rituals	• Turn around, Mandy • Pens down • Get out your...	**Organisation**
Literacy Management	• Management of literacy tasks and lesson • Functional aspects of literacy not teaching about literacy	• Read the first page • Write... • Look at the cover	
Reconstruction Restatement	• Construct, reconstruct paraphrase or rephrase oral written or pictorial text • Repeat students' answers • Confirm a correct answer – but no more • Require literal thinking • Provide implicit modelling	• Mary ran away (paraphrasing text) • John said Mary is frightened (repeating student answer) • Yes, right, well done • I would write... • I think there are two ideas	**Doing Literacy**
Elaboration Projection	• Require inferential thinking • Require drawing on own experience or knowledge from previous lessons	• Why might he do that? • What can you tell me about ...	
Informative	• Provide information or definitions about literacy • Do not provide explanations about how to use the information to complete the task	• Every sentence has a verb • Usually the first sentence in the paragraph provides the main idea	
Process	• Focus on cognitive aspects of task, decision-making processes • Explicitly model cognitive activity and thinking processes	• What is a better strategy than guessing? • How would you work that out? • I am writing... because ...	**Learning How When, and Why about Literacy**
Utility	• Explain how the strategies or process might be useful in other situations • Explain why it is useful to be able to do this	• It is useful to do... because... • You skim to work out whether there is useful information present • Why do we use paragraphs?	

Validation day

At the conclusion of their project, participants made an oral presentation on a feature of their research that they felt would be of interest to others. This was sometimes presented to the rest of the group as a way of sharing expertise with their colleagues, but more often delivered at an area or network conference held specifically for the purpose of informing a wider audience of interested teachers. This process was designed to validate the participants' study by describing the progress they had made and sharing the evidence they had gathered. Participants often spontaneously referred to this as a celebration day, which encapsulated how they felt about the process and their outcomes.

Table 1.4 Phases of lessons

Phase	Definition	Example statements or description of activity
Attention	How the lesson begins. Not necessarily an introduction. For example getting students' attention and organising for beginning of lesson.	*Boys and girls, who's ready? My that is good to see.*
Focus	The part of the lesson as indicated by the teacher's tone, language etc., where the focus of the lesson is identified. Some information may be imparted.	*Now today we are going to talk about the structure of stories.*
Guided Implementation	Where teacher and student construct, practise, or implement the knowledge which is the focus of the lesson but the activity is led by the teacher. Specific aspects of Guided Implementation:	
	(a) **Identifying** Identifying examples of new knowledge. May include writing on whiteboard or in books/laptops/iPads.	*Identifying* *Teacher leads students in identification of main idea in paragraph.*
	(b) **Practising** Using new skills or knowledge learned to practise in a similar task.	*Practising* *Teacher leads students finding main idea in a new paragraph and making notes about the main idea.*
	(c) **Transferring** Using new skills or knowledge learned in a different combination or to carry out a different task.	*Transferring* *Teacher leads students in using notes taken about main idea to construct a paragraph.*
Report	Sharing presentation of work/task by student	*Students share answers or discuss completed work to class as requested by teacher.*
Display	Teacher displays/presents/reads aloud/models task he or she has completed.	*Teacher might show work and say, 'When I was looking for information on this topic the first thing I did was…'*
Unguided Implementation	Same as Guided Implementation but student must perform on own. Same sub-categories as for Guided Implementation. Independent student-driven or student-led work.	*As for Guided Implementation examples, except student led or done by student independently.*
Review	Teacher reviews definitions/information/skills presented in previous phases at a general level. It is not a complete reworking or re-teaching of examples but a review of what has been done and learned.	*Teacher might use following phrases in such a phase:* *'Now what we have learned so far…'* *'First we found out that…'*
Presentation of Text	Teacher reads text to students, or students read text. Random exchanges between teacher and students may occur during this phase.	*Reading of story to class as part of a shared book activity.*
Coda	Teaching aspect of lesson has concluded but teacher or students may continue exchanges in some way related to topic or content of lesson.	*Having finished the actual literacy lesson using a text about Eskimos, continuing to talk about Eskimos.*
Transition Out	Signals end of lesson and tidying up or reorganisation of class for subsequent lessons.	*Usually signalled by activity and teacher instructions such as 'Put your work away' or 'Forward out'.*

ACTION LEARNING TASK 1.3

- The purpose of this Action Learning Task is to assist you to frame your project by completing the Action Plan Proforma.
- As has been previously outlined in this chapter, the Action Plan Proforma has a dual focus on action and validation, so it is important that you are clear about the goals of your project and what methods you are going to use to validate it.
- In the first column of the Proforma, you need to specify which items you have selected from the Matrix and also what are your desired outcomes of the project, that is what you expect to achieve in your action research.
- In the second column, you are asked to specify what methods you will employ to achieve your outcomes. You will need to consider the 4P's of professional reading, pedagogy, practice and planning and give some initial thought to suitable resources. You will need to decide what areas of reading you are going to do, whether you are going to visit other classrooms and if there are any experts with whom you plan to have conversations. You will also need to decide what changes in pedagogy and practice you are going to introduce and how these changes will affect your planning. In the third and fourth columns, you will need to specify what evidence you are going to collect, how you are going to collect this evidence, and how you are going to analyse the evidence and report it to others.
- The Proforma also has a horizontal dimension. For example, when you indicate which professional reading you are going to do, you need to signify what evidence you are going to collect about how you have changed as a result of your reading, how you are going to collate it, how it will be analysed and how you will report it. You will also need to do the same things for pedagogy, practice and planning. When you review your Proforma, you will need to read it horizontally and vertically to ensure that you have a clear idea of what you intend to do and how you are going to do it.
- There are a number of suggestions on the Proforma about methods for collecting data including proposals to collect evidence before the project begins, while it is in progress and once it has been completed. The idea of collecting data before, during and after treatment provides a good indication of how change has been achieved.
- Keep a record or a journal that records ideas about further research that occur to you as you engage in your action research.
- It may appear that completion of the Action Plan Proforma could be quite onerous. However, the more clearly and concisely the project is defined, the more likely it is going to achieve measurable change. It is interesting to note that participants consistently report a growing sense of excitement about their projects as they complete the Proforma.

Unique features of the ALC and the project

The eleven characteristics of the ALC outlined serve to describe the structure of the approach that was developed by Anstey and Bull. While it can be seen that this approach is similar to others that sought to link PLD with action research, there are features that are unique to the ALC that contributed to its success. These can be summarised as follows:

- The development of the Matrix as a tool for promoting reflection provided an important stimulus and structure to assist teachers in engaging in reflection rather than just expecting them 'to reflect'.
- The Matrix provided a detailed definition of multiliteracies, multimodality and pedagogy.
- The Action Plan Proforma made available a detailed structure for engaging in an action learning project that addressed professional reading, practice, pedagogy and planning.
- The ALC addressed the change process as part of PLD.
- The ALC provided detailed information about the **functions of teacher talk** and the **phase structure of lessons**.
- The requirement of participants submitting a written report together with an oral presentation describing the processes undertaken in their study.

Strengths of the ALC and the project

One of the most striking features of the ALC is that, despite the considerable amount of work required by the project, participants remained overwhelmingly positive about their experiences. This has been reflected in the written comments in their reports, the remarks in their presentations and their willingness to recommend the project to other teachers. The following, taken from Bull and Anstey (2010b, p. 155), is an extract from a written report submitted by one of the teachers that is indicative of the responses found in most of the reports and presentations.

> This project has been highly significant to my teaching practice. It has been an exhilarating experience for me as a professional . . . The paradigm shift I have made . . . has provided enormously enhanced learning for my students. I have made positive growth as a teacher and learner.

Another positive indicator was the resilience of the participants. Despite the extra effort required to complete the project, the drop-out rate was negligible. Aside from a small number of withdrawals caused by personal or family illness and the transfers of teachers from one school to another, there were remarkably few participants who did not complete their projects. This is despite the fact that there were a considerable number of projects conducted in preschool, primary and secondary schools in the state, Catholic and independent systems in different social and cultural contexts across Australia.

It is interesting to explore why the projects were as successful as they were. Participants were asked to respond anonymously to a number of questionnaires requesting their opinions on the success, or otherwise, of the projects they had undertaken. This was in addition to analyses of their reports and presentations. The following statements are representative of the comments made by participants across all of the projects conducted. What is of particular importance about these participants' comments is the extent to which they reflect the unique features of the ALC and the project as identified by Anstey and Bull.

- This action research has inspired me to change what I am doing wrong rather than blaming the students for their behaviour. If I improve my teaching pedagogy and learn new strategies to engage students, anything is possible.
- The process of the Matrix was interesting as it made me aware of what I was doing and what I can do better.

- The project has given me a chance to reflect on my teaching practice.
- Putting some achievable (yet challenging) goals in front of me that I see value in is highly motivating.
- I have realised that I have struggled to teach literacy effectively in the past.
- We have a group of very committed, interested teachers to work with. It has been very worthwhile to learn from each other.
- The Matrix has been an amazing reflective tool. Some areas where I originally believed I was strong in have now become the major focus for improvement.
- This has been a really valuable experience so early on in my career. I can see and hear progress within myself.
- The whole process has made me reflect on my own teaching practice, not only in literacy but across the curriculum.
- The project has inspired me to look at my teaching pedagogy and reflect on what I can improve. It has become very apparent that sometimes we need to be pushed in order to make these changes.
- I've really critically assessed where I am as a teacher and feel this action research has been the catalyst for change.
- Ultimately to know that I have improved my pedagogy which will in turn improve learning outcomes for my students.
- The ALC highlighted the value of transcript analysis on changing pedagogy and practice.
- The project foregrounded the role of teacher talk in supporting interaction in the classroom and promoting different learnings.

All of the participants' comments above highlighted a broad range of positive features of both the ALC as a process and the project as an approach to PLD. While comments were overwhelmingly positive, there were some negative responses in a minority of cases. Two themes were identified that typified teachers' comments, and these were related to space and time. Comments about space referred to the covering of what was seen as required content of the curriculum that was being followed by the school. Comments about time involved the provision of time for teachers to meet, consult and engage in professional dialogue in their school context with fellow researchers as a means of advancing their projects. While these are perennial issues for teachers, it is interesting to note that the significance of the issues was related to the participation of the leadership team in the project. In schools where members of the leadership team were themselves involved in the ALC and were engaged in a project, it was more likely that arrangements would be made to address the issues of time and space. In these schools, measures such as cancelling staff meetings and replacing them with a school intranet system provided more time for participants to meet. Sometimes participants were taken out of supervision of students during lunch breaks or sporting practice to further increase professional sharing. As a way of creating space, participants were sometimes placed in team teaching situations that allowed them to specialise in particular subject areas to minimise preparation time. There were a variety of different arrangements that were put in place in these schools that were not found to be common in schools where the leadership teams were not directly involved in the projects. There were distinct advantages for participants when their leaders were participating in the projects that were perhaps related to a greater appreciation of what was involved in action research.

Factors that are important for teacher learning when engaged in action research

Having analysed teachers' participation and responses to the ALC and the projects, it is now possible to draw some conclusions about which factors are important in successful teacher research and learning.

Value of professional dialogue

Throughout all of the projects time was provided where participants could discuss an issue of common concern. This dialogue often occurred in small groups particularly when teachers were undertaking similar projects. Dialogue amongst the whole group was encouraged by requiring each teacher to give a short summary of their progress, be it successful or problematic, at the start of each day of PLD. The ensuing dialogues were sometimes positive and encouraging and sometimes critical (but supportive) by proposing alternative ideas or approaches. At all times teachers were encouraged to explore and think through ideas rather than making evaluative comments. The underlying assumption behind participating in these dialogues was that they would promote understanding, and learning about, a variety of issues arising from teachers' research. Participants consistently rated opportunities for professional dialogue very highly in their reports and presentations and in their day-to-day conversations throughout the projects. It is important to realise that the dialogues were carefully structured and not just an opportunity for a 'talk fest' when extroverts could monopolise the discussion. Interestingly, teachers frequently reported that there were few opportunities for such dialogues in their schools.

Involvement of the leadership team

As has already been reported, participation in the ALC and the projects by the leadership team resulted in the introduction of differing arrangements that supported teachers in implementing their projects. However, there were other benefits that arose from leadership team participation. One such benefit was the provision of what Fullan (2001, p.8–9) referred to as external and internal commitment. External commitment is achieved when the leadership team puts in place strategies or protocols, such as the provision of time and space, that support teachers to successfully engage in their projects. Internal commitment, which often results from the provision of external commitment, is intrinsically rewarding because it is driven by the personal desire to get something done. It was a consistent finding across all the projects that the thriveability of the projects was directly related to the provision of external commitments.

Another finding was the relationship between leadership team participation in the projects and participants withdrawing from the projects. As reported earlier, withdrawal rates from the projects were low. However, teachers were more likely to withdraw from their projects when leadership participation was low or non-existent.

Whole school participation

There were a number of projects in the state, independent and Catholic school systems where the whole school was involved in the project. When networks of schools were involved in the projects, typically two or three teachers from each school would be involved. Sometimes only one teacher from a particular school would be involved because of the size of the school. While all participants achieved varying degrees of success, there appeared to be an increasing benefit according to the size of the community of learners taking part in the projects. When the whole school was involved, there was a higher occurrence of professional dialogue and external and internal commitment. Teachers who were the single representative from their school reported fewer opportunities to engage in professional dialogue at school and were more likely to withdraw from the project than other participants.

Focus on teachers

An important part of the project was the emphasis on teachers which was central to achieving pedagogical change and the major focus of the Action Plan Proforma. What arose from this focus was the reporting by the teachers right across all of the projects that while all had been involved in the assessment of student performance, almost none of them had been involved with investigating change in pedagogy or practice. They reported that attendance at PLD sessions was usually designed to support delivering content in new ways and was nearly always of the 'quick fix' variety over one or two days at best with no follow-up. While it would be expected that PLD would address change in teacher practice, the teachers themselves stated that such PLD rarely resulted in change. A small minority of participants reported some form of taping of lessons which sometimes resulted in the construction of transcripts. The outcome of these trends was that a considerable proportion of participants tended to focus on student change rather than teacher change when designing their project, particularly when dealing with the Action Plan Proforma. Accordingly, participants had to be continually reminded about the focus on teacher change in the early phases of the projects. As a result, the focus on teachers came to be seen as an important contributing factor in teacher learning when engaged in action research.

Whether these reported teacher comments were only due to the nature of the design of the projects is not possible to determine. However, in the period of eleven years that the projects operated, upwards of one thousand teachers took part, from all systems and year levels, so it is reasonable to assume that this group of teachers were representative of the majority of teachers.

The importance of data collection

The collection of data as evidence that teacher change in pedagogy had taken place, or was effective, was not identified by many teachers as part of their everyday practice. Gathering evidence therefore emerged as an essential factor as part of the projects as evidenced in the design of the Action Plan Proforma. It therefore became necessary to have conversations with participants about the relative merits of qualitative data, as compared to quantitative data, since this was the type of data they were collecting. Discussions revolving around transcript analysis, functions of teacher talk and phases of lessons enabled participants to total up categories of data and quantify the qualitative data they had collected so that their interpretations were more robust. The concept of triangulation of data was also discussed so that participants did not rely on one source of data to draw conclusions and have some confidence in the validity of their conclusions.

Value of lesson transcripts

Few participants reported that they had previously prepared a transcript of a recorded lesson. There was some initial resistance from participants to the preparation of lesson transcripts because of the time and effort involved in their preparation. At the time, there were few reliable programs or services that could be accessed to prepare transcripts, so participants were required to prepare them by themselves. The categories, presented in this chapter in Tables 1.3 and 1.4, were used to analyse teacher talk and lesson phases. Once the transcripts were prepared, they provided detailed in-depth analysis of lessons that the participants found particularly useful in studying their lessons. Many teachers in their oral and written reports and in their presentations remarked that the transcript preparation was one of the most useful features in the analysis of data. They reported that it clarified a gap between what they *thought* they were doing and saying and what they *actually were* doing and saying. Once the initial transcript had been prepared, it enabled teachers to identify which phase, or phases, they wished to concentrate on. This made the preparation of further transcripts much simpler because a small section, or phase, of the lesson could be focussed on. It also meant that teachers could chart the change in their pedagogy over time by comparing one transcript with another.

Duration of PLD

The project came to be judged as very successful in changing teacher behaviour over time. Feedback from schools, leadership teams and various sections within education departments in the three systems (state, independent, Catholic), as well as evidence from the participants themselves, judged the projects to be successful where short-term PLD was seen as less effective. It was not just the amount of time spent on PLD that was seen as crucial, but also the fact that change in pedagogy and the concepts surrounding multiliteracies and multimodality were seen as complex processes that needed to be implemented carefully over considerable periods of time, whether it be one, two or three years.

Value of professional reading

One of the requirements of both the ALC and the project was that participants would engage in professional reading around the topics that they had selected from the Matrix. The participants had, previous to the introduction of the Matrix, undergone PLD in the areas of multiliteracies and multimodality, and often teachers were supplied with their own copies of a text written by Bull and Anstey (2010a) by their school or the education system they taught in. The combination of these design features was aimed at encouraging teachers to engage in professional reading. Despite the issue of finding time to engage in reading that the teachers often referred to, they nevertheless exhibited a willingness to read about professional matters and share ideas with their colleagues. Given that teachers are often constructed as reluctant to undertake professional reading, this was a positive outcome. It would appear, as far as the projects were concerned, that if teachers were given a reason to read, saw value in the reading and were provided with the appropriate literature, they were amenable to engage in professional reading.

Providing a challenge

As discussed in the previous section in this chapter on the strengths of the project, it was common for participants to make comments such as:

- Putting some achievable (yet challenging) goals in front of me that I see value in is highly motivating.
- It has become very apparent that sometimes we need to be pushed in order to make these changes.

Far from being confronted by challenges, participants seemed to welcome challenge and be excited and motivated by it. The processes involved in the project were intentionally designed by Anstey and Bull to be challenging. The very idea of changing pedagogy and practice is full of challenge, and at no time did participants say 'This is too hard and I cannot do it'. The presence of challenge seemed to be an important factor in providing the foundation for teacher learning.

Community of learners

Without a doubt, the most common response of participants to the question of what factor in the projects most supported teacher learning was participating in a community of learners. While they did not use that exact expression, the participants frequently made reference to the opportunities provided to have conversations in PLD sessions with teachers from within their school and across other schools. They set a high value on the provision of time to have discussions with each other and to learn from each other. The concept of a community of learners emerged as a factor that was a powerful way of motivating teachers to learn and to change their behaviours around pedagogy and practice. Its usefulness goes far beyond the boundaries of the ALC and the projects.

Successful action research is not limited to 'good' schools

Participants in the various projects volunteered from a variety of types of schools. There were participants from schools that were achieving at a high level of performance. As a principal of a large school engaged in the project suggested, 'These students would be very successful even if all the teachers stayed at home'. That school was not focussed on learning how to be good educators but rather how to be better, or as Lefstein and Snell (2014) would say, 'better than best'. On the other hand, there were participating teachers from schools that were very challenging in terms of isolation, disinterested students, severe behavioural problems, socially and economically depressed areas and parents who did not value education and had no ambition for their children to do any better than they had. There was no appreciable difference in the changes in pedagogy and practice achieved by teachers from the different schools in terms of the quality of change, only in terms of the quantity of change. What was remarkable was the resilience exhibited by the teachers from the challenging schools, many of whom were in their first years of teaching. What this illustrated in a powerful way was that action research and learning is not the province only of good schools or experienced teachers.

Finally, as many participants stated, 'I can never go back'. This was a measure of the success of the ALC and the projects that the participants undertook and of the framework designed by Anstey and Bull. It was very reassuring that not only were capability and sustainability developed, but also that thriveability was established.

ACTION LEARNING TASK 1.4

- The purpose of this Action Learning Task is to illustrate how you will conclude your project and address the concept of thriveability.
- Once you have completed your action learning project, analysed your data and drawn conclusions about how successful you have been in achieving your desired outcome, prepare a brief report. This report will provide an outline of your action research project, the data that you gathered and analysed, and the conclusions that you came to. The following headings may be useful in preparing your report:
  o Aim of Project
  o Method: What did I do and what evidence did I collect?
  o Method: Data Analysis and Reporting
  o Conclusions and Implications
  o Appendices
- Refer back to the journal of ideas that you kept and select one of these ideas for your next ALC. This addresses the point that the process is most valuable when it is a cycle of action research rather than a one-off project.
- Select one part of your report that would be suitable to share in a presentation and would be of interest to your teaching colleagues. Attempting to share your whole report in one presentation is not possible in terms of the time required. Your project would be more successfully shared through a number of presentations spaced out over time.

Conclusion

This chapter has traced the changing concepts about literacy by exploring the research addressing the development of literacies and multiliteracies. It also investigated what students need to know and be able to with multimodal texts. The semiotic systems were defined together with the changing nature of texts in order to examine the characteristics of a literate and multiliterate person. It was proposed that reading and writing might be more usefully defined as consumption and production.

A detailed description of the Action Learning Cycle (ALC) and the projects that were undertaken was provided as a way of implementing concepts about the new texts, multiliteracies and multimodality in the classroom. The tools developed by Anstey and Bull that were developed to support engagement in the ALC, the Matrix and the Action Plan Proforma, were examined in detail. These tools were designed to support understanding of the relationships among professional knowledge, planning, teacher practice and teacher pedagogy (the 4P's). The reader was encouraged to address changes in their pedagogy and practice through the application of the ALC in their own individual Action Learning Project as they engaged with the Action Learning Tasks in this and subsequent chapters.

2 Multiliteracies and inquiry: Implications for pedagogy, planning and practice

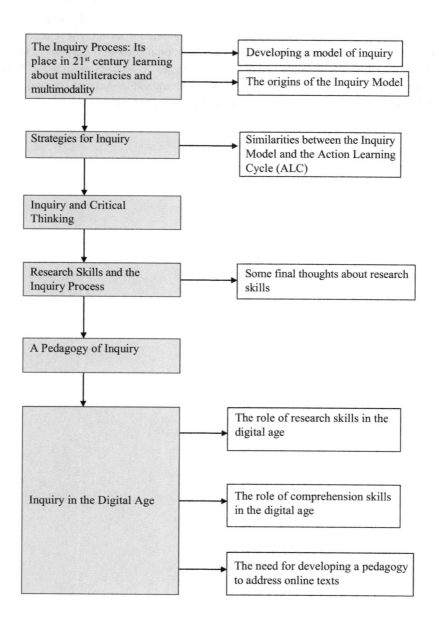

In this chapter a model of the inquiry process will be developed as a framework that goes across disciplines and informs students' approach to literacy tasks. It is introduced as a way of focussing on the need to problem solve and demonstrates that consideration of **multiliteracies** focussing on **inquiry** will assist students to develop understandings about the complexities of communicating with **multimodal texts**. A model for implementing inquiry in the classroom will also be advanced. The chapter will address how the Action Learning Cycle (ALC) relates to inquiry and how teachers are better able to communicate the process of inquiry to their students and engage more deeply with their own inquiry when engaging in Action Learning Cycles. It will explore the need to equip students with the knowledge to cope with the continuous change that will occur in texts and technology.

The chapter will discuss the processes underlying inquiry and the strategies that students will need to learn in order to successfully engage in the inquiry process. It will explore the relationship of critical literacy skills and research skills to the inquiry process. The chapter will also develop a **pedagogy** of inquiry and explore the processes of **design** and **redesign**. It will examine how inquiry using digital texts is similar to, and different from, inquiry with print-based texts.

The inquiry process: its place in 21st-century learning about multiliteracies and multimodality

As has been previously argued in Chapter One, literacies, multiliteracies and multimodal texts are continuously changing. This process of change has been exacerbated by globalisation and the explosion of knowledge. It is no longer possible to reduce knowledge to a finite number of facts that can be memorised in order to produce a citizen who can effectively function in contemporary society. In order to address this issue, many countries have embarked on a highly contested program designed to define a set of facts that would form the core of knowledge to be learnt in schools. Questions immediately arise about what facts are to be included in school curricula and which facts are to be left and who should make these decisions. In Australia, as in other countries, there has been debate about the balance of knowledge about local, national and international issues that might be appropriate for students in primary/elementary and secondary schools to learn. At one point this debate resulted in a former Australian prime minister making statements about which knowledge should be available in museums and which should be removed. This is aside from the ever-present debate about what is a fact and how factual information can be tested and determined.

As a result of these developments, much recent discussion has centred around developing curricula that involve teachers and students in learning how to learn. Such an approach to learning relies on the ability of students to acquire strategies to research and investigate in order to elicit the information that is appropriate to complete the learning tasks in which they are engaged. What has become known as the *Inquiry Process* has been adopted in many educational systems as a method for teaching students the strategies of inquiry and for teachers to become familiar with **inquiry-based teaching**. The inquiry process grew out of the discovery learning movement of the 1960s and the constructivist learning theories of writers such as Vygotsky (1962), Freire (1984), and Bruner (1961), which had their origins in the work of Dewey (1910).

REFLECTION STRATEGY 2.1

- The purpose of this Reflection Strategy is to determine what part inquiry plays in your class-room.
- Record some of your lessons over a number of weeks, or have a colleague come into your class to observe some of your lessons, to ascertain how often you engage your students in learning about the skills and processes of inquiry.
- Review your lesson planning over a number of weeks in order to judge how often you plan to engage your class in the inquiry process.

In order to assist both students and teachers to engage in the inquiry process, many models of inquiry have been developed. While all of these models have some particular differences, there are nevertheless a number of commonalities in the stages of inquiry that have been proposed.

Developing a model of inquiry

The stages of inquiry that are present in many proposed models are equivalent to those suggested by Leu et al. (2011, p. 5) and Lynch (2017, p.189). The following stages have been adapted from both Leu et al. and Lynch and include:

- Identify problem or issue to be investigated and decide what is already known,
- Locate relevant information and generate further questions,
- Organise and evaluate the information and undertake research to develop answers to questions,
- Create new knowledge and share results with others.

This model, like many other earlier ones, has formed the basis for alternative models that have provided more detail about the process of inquiry. Anstey and Bull (2012) and Bull and Anstey (2013) proposed generic processes to be engaged in during inquiry similar to those suggested earlier in the discipline of history by Vass (2004) and Levesque (2008):

- Formulating a focus and/or creating an overview,
- Locating and collecting information,
- Defining and hypothesising,
- Interpreting, evaluating and **synthesising** information,
- Recording and sharing solution and conclusions,
- Seeking reactions and translating information.

AUDITING INSTRUMENT 2.1

- The purpose of this Auditing Instrument is to have you review your understanding about the Inquiry Process.
- Does the Inquiry Process form an important part in the teaching and learning practices in your classroom?
- How many of the different stages of the Inquiry Process feature in your everyday teaching practices?
- How confident are you that you understand the Inquiry Process?
- How competent are your students in engaging in the Inquiry Process?

Adapting these six processes Anstey and Bull (2012) and Bull and Anstey (2013) developed a seven-stage model of inquiry which is represented in Figure 2.1.

As indicated in Figure 2.1, inquiry is a recursive process where individuals move backwards and forwards from one stage to the next. As a case in point, an individual having developed an initial question might go on to locate relevant information and then analyse this information. In the light of gaining new perspectives from this information, the individual might reformulate the initial question and then continue with the inquiry. While there is no set sequence of engagement with the stages, it is nevertheless most likely that the inquiry will begin at the engagement stage and conclude at the review stage where a new inquiry may begin. The inquiry model, in its most useful form, is not only recursive but also cyclical. Bull and Anstey (2013) further explicated the seven stages by describing the learning experiences that teachers might engage students in at each stage of the inquiry model.

- Engagement stage – create excitement, motivation, curiosity and a sense of wonder about a particular question of topic, encourage students to listen and participate in the discussion;
- Exploration stage – support students to collaborate with others to plan inquiry, to develop a research focus, identify and prioritise inquiry questions, develop a plan for conducting the inquiry and identify what is already known about the topic and where are the gaps in students' knowledge;
- Investigation stage – recommend to students the use of skimming and scanning skills to locate relevant information and promote reference to table of contents, indexes, chapter headings, accessing and bookmarking websites; have students identify useful sources of information such as websites, artefacts, site visits, films and photographs; encourage students to ask themselves questions such as 'What do I want to know?' and 'I wonder why this is so?'; assist students to narrow the focus of their investigation;
- Evaluation stage – promote critical analysis and synthesis of information by the students through the detection of bias and propaganda and interpreting different points of view; encourage students

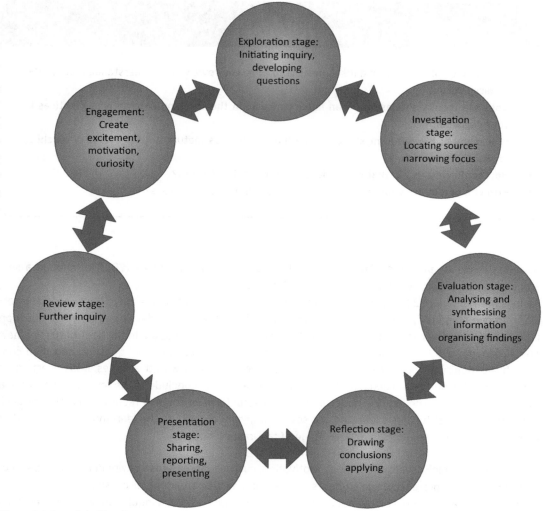

Figure 2.1 A model of inquiry

to organise information both on paper and digitally through note-making, research folders and out-lining, checking reliability of sources and using graphic organisers to arrange information; prompt students to ask themselves questions such as 'Does this information answer my original question?' and 'How will I record my findings?';

- Reflection stage – assist students to draw conclusions and generate new interpretations or perspectives, support students to make generalisations and judgements about information they have gathered, prompt students to review their predictions and draw inferences from their conclusions, discuss with students how they might demonstrate what they have learnt;
- Presentation stage – encourage students to identify ways results and conclusions might be shared with colleagues; demonstrate to students how to create an overview of the structure of the presentation; suggest to students that they should consider which **semiotic systems** they will use to present results and how they are going to display data depending upon which technology is to be used (paper, live,

digital); discuss with students who will be the audience of their presentation and how they will share their findings to meet the needs of their audience; students will need to decide whether they will use PowerPoint or other methods such as web pages, blogs, wikis, displays or plays;

- Review stage – take students back to their original question or investigation to check whether it has been answered, review the processes used during the inquiry to judge how well they worked, have students go back through their inquiry to identify questions that have arisen during their inquiry and whether there are issues or topics that need modification for future investigations; students need to ask themselves questions such as 'How well did my inquiry go?' and 'Where do I go next?'

ACTION LEARNING TASK 2.1

- **The purpose of this Action Learning Task is to review your project that you began at the end of Chapter One as part of your participation in the Action Learning Cycle (ARC).**
- **Do you need to modify the aim of your project?**
- **Will you need to change, or add to, the evidence that you are gathering?**
- **Does your method of data analysis need to be reviewed?**
- **Can you retain the style of reporting that you have selected? If not, in what ways will it need to be modified?**

As has been argued, access to the stages of the inquiry model and the processes involved in those stages puts students and teachers in an advantageous position when responding to changes in contemporary developments in pedagogy. However, there are further advantages to engaging in the processes of inquiry. As Leu et al. (2011, p. 5) have argued, 'Workplace settings are increasingly characterized by the effective use of information to solve important problems within a global economy'. They further suggested that such uses have become more critical because digital technologies have created even greater access to increasingly large amounts of information. They concluded (2011, p. 5) that individuals, groups and networks of individuals and even societies that can access such uses effectively '... will succeed in the challenging times that await us'.

The origins of the inquiry model

The model of inquiry developed by Anstey and Bull (2012) and Bull and Anstey (2013) that has been previously discussed in this chapter had its origins in earlier research by Bull (1989). Bull interviewed acknowledged leaders in various disciplines regarding the model of inquiry and thinking processes central to their discipline. From this he developed a generic model of the processes associated with each discipline from which similarities across disciplines were identified, enabling the development of a model of inquiry first reported in 1989 and then adapted in Anstey and Bull (2004) and Bull and Anstey (2013). While similarities were identified, it is important to realise that each discipline had discipline-specific terminology, or a **metalanguage**, that supported discussion in the subject area and enabled inquiry to be undertaken. In Table 2.1 the processes of inquiry across disciplines are presented and in Table 2.2 the processes common to all disciplines are represented.

Table 2.1 Processes of inquiry in each discipline

Model of Inquiry Suggested	Thinking Processes Engaged In					
Inquiry Process in Literacy (e.g. reading)	What do I know and what do I want to know?	Locate the information in the sources	Brainstorm and create possible solutions	Revise possible solutions through interpreting and evaluating	Draw conclusions and share ideas	Seek a response, criticism or appreciation Translate ideas to a new situation
Inquiry Process in Social Science (geography and history)	What do I want to know? Develop questions Create an overview	Use various sources to gather information and be aware of the context of the time	Ask probing questions and arrive at alternative explanations Hypothesise tentative answers	Analyse, interpret and synthesise information to verify hypothesis	Record conclusions and share solutions from the data gathered	Seek a response to test validity
Problem Solving Process (mathematics)	Define the question	Data collection and observation	Define alternative solutions Create hypothesis	Choose appropriate solution	Demonstrate solution	Seek response and affirmation
Scientific Process (chemistry, physics, biology)	Use imagination to define problem	Design a test to gather information	Interpret data and define alternative solutions Predict hypothesis	Proof through experimentation	Write report	Further inquiry Pose new questions to lead to new investigations
Artistic Process (music, art, drama)	Decide on project What can I do?	Immersion and engagement in task Select techniques	Preliminary sketch, model or rehearsal	Complete final work by reshaping model, sketch or rehearsal	Exhibit Performance	Seek a response, criticism or appreciation

Table 2.2 Common processes across the disciplines

Generic Thinking Processes Engaged In During Inquiry	Formulating a focus and/ or creating an overview	Locating and collecting information	Defining and hypothesising	Interpreting, evaluating and synthesising information	Recording and sharing solutions and conclusions	Seeking reactions and translating information

REFLECTION STRATEGY 2.2

- The purpose of this Reflection Strategy is to review how you are implementing the Inquiry Process in your classroom.
- Did you introduce the Inquiry Process in your literacy/multiliteracies lessons?
- If so, in retrospect, why did you introduce the process in these types of lessons?
- What other subject/discipline area could you have chosen to implement the Inquiry process in? How would this have changed your approach?
- Are you implementing the Inquiry Process across other subject/discipline areas?

There have been attempts by others working in the area to study the inquiry process in a number of subject areas. The Ontario Library Association (1999) proposed a series of processes associated with each subject under a generic model that contained four stages equivalent to defining a question, locating information, evaluating information and presenting information. The following terminology has been adapted from the Ontario Library Association.

- Social science (geography and history) independent study – focus, locate information, develop a question, extract information, organise information, communicate/share information,
- English writing – choose topic, brainstorm and group data, organise information and write an initial outline, revise, edit and draw conclusions, final report, communicate/share,
- Mathematical problem solving – understand problem, construct a plan and carry it out, review the work carried out, communicate/share the results,
- Scientific method – identify the problem, predict outcomes, make a plan and collect information, decision-making, communicating/sharing, evaluating, applying.

While there are some differences in terminology for processes and stages, there are significant similarities between the Ontario model and the one proposed by Bull and Anstey. There is, in fact, a significant degree of agreement among all the models of inquiry sufficient to have confidence in the model proposed by Bull and Anstey. The generally agreed-upon characteristics of inquiry are that it is an active process where:

- Students lead the investigations,
- There is a degree of student collaboration,

- Investigations involve a 'hands-on' approach,
- Teachers adopt the role of facilitator,
- There is a degree of interactivity among the students and between teacher and student.

AUDITING INSTRUMENT 2.2

- The purpose of this Auditing Instrument is to review how you are implementing the Inquiry Process in your classroom.
- Are you implementing the Inquiry Process in the same way in different subject/discipline areas?
- Do you use different metalanguage in different discipline/subject areas? Can you give reasons for this?
- What are the potential advantages/disadvantages in using the same terminology across different subject/discipline areas?
- Which of the five characteristics of inquiry mentioned above have you implemented in your classroom? Why is this so?

Strategies for inquiry

These characteristics of inquiry feature, to one degree or another, depending on the type of inquiry that is being undertaken. There are three types of inquiry – structured, guided, and open or independent – depending on the amount of teacher intervention in the investigative process.

Structured inquiry is the most teacher-centred approach, where the teacher provides structured procedures that students follow in their investigations. It is perhaps the most common type of inquiry and is sometimes seen as the traditional approach. It is usually used either when students are being introduced to the inquiry process, when new work is being covered, or if the teacher is implementing a change in pedagogical approach from teacher-centred to student-centred instruction. In each case students need a high level of guidance. As Bull and Anstey (2010a, p.141) pointed out, teachers need to be aware of where on the continuum from teacher-centred to student-centred pedagogy their approach is focussed. As Bain (2005, p.180) concluded when discussing the teacher-focus, student-focus dichotomy, the choice is not an either/or decision even though '... often teachers see it as something either on the margins or as a replacement for traditional teaching'. Nevertheless students should still be supported to carry out the investigation and determine the outcomes.

When students are becoming more proficient with the inquiry process, teachers can implement a guided approach. This approach usually involves teachers in devising the initial problem or question and students determining the process and the outcomes. As suggested by Kuhlthau et al. (2007), an important aspect of guided inquiry is that it be based on real-life contexts that incorporate authentic activities and allow students some exercise of choice in determining the initial question. The initial question should also draw on students' prior knowledge. The teacher may still intervene if the students need further guidance, but essentially the students are responsible for carrying out the inquiry process. However, there need to be opportunities for sustained dialogue between students and teachers.

The open or independent approach to inquiry requires little, or no, teacher intervention where the student is responsible for determining the initial question, carrying out the investigation and establishing the outcomes. In this type of inquiry, the students often work in groups to collaborate in the inquiry process so that they seek guidance from each other rather than from the teacher. As with guided inquiry, there need to be opportunities for sustained dialogue between students and teachers. It is important in this type of inquiry that the teacher closely monitors the class in order to identify those students who may be finding the process more challenging than their classmates and therefore exhibiting some signs of frustration. As Levesque (2006, p.5) pointed out, part of the problem with students' experiences with inquiry is lack of guidance and the belief that research in the disciplines can automatically '... be transplanted to a body of novices'. Both Lynch (2017) and Coiro (2011) point out that students find comprehension of materials a challenging task when they are required to develop their own inquiries.

THEORY INTO PRACTICE 2.1

- The purpose of this Theory into Practice is to review the type of inquiry that you are implementing in your classroom.
- Which of the three types of inquiry (structured, guided, open/independent) form your approach to inquiry?
- Review your teaching and planning to determine how you are introducing the different types of inquiry.
- What strategies are you employing in each of the different types of inquiry?
- Which of the strategies that you are using are your students finding most helpful?
- What, if any, changes do you need to make? Why?

When teachers decide which type of inquiry they are going to implement in their classroom, it is important that they are aware of the issues that impact on their students' learning. As has been discussed, there are advantages in students undertaking inquiry in terms of self-motivated and self-directed learning. The shift from a reliance on teacher-centred pedagogy to achieving a balance between teacher-focussed and student-focussed pedagogy has advantages in terms of catering for different learning styles and incorporating higher levels of student choice. However, as Lynch (2017, p.190) reported, there are risks involved when students waste time or become lost in their inquiries. She continued that students may then neglect the performance required by the teacher, have trouble with comprehending material beyond their reading level or be simply overwhelmed by the amount of information available. Teachers need to be aware of firstly which type of inquiry is suitable for the capabilities of their students and secondly which approach to inquiry is required to complete particular tasks that they have designed. One of the factors not related to student involvement that can contribute to the successful implementation of the inquiry approach in the classroom is whether the teacher is involved in the inquiry process at a personal level.

Similarities between the inquiry model and the Action Learning Cycle (ALC)

Those teachers who are taking part, or have taken part, in an Action Learning Cycle (ALC) or some other form of inquiry will be better placed to appreciate the advantages and challenges associated with implementing the inquiry process in their classrooms. The processes involved in the ALC have been carefully explicated in Chapter One. In Table 1.1, the processes involved in choosing a topic for action research and learning in the class or school were addressed in detail in the Matrix, and the processes for conducting the ALC were specified in Table 1.2, which outlined the Action Plan Proforma. Taken together, these two tables suggested the following guidelines for conducting an inquiry through the ALC:

- Choosing a topic – what am I interested in?
- Specifying a goal or aim – what is my desired outcome?
- What method will I use – how will I go about achieving my goal?
- What evidence or information will I gather – how will I decide what is relevant?
- How will I analyse the information – in what ways will I collate it?
- How will I prepare my report – what is the best way to share/report to my audience?

It can be seen that the processes involved in the ALC are similar to those in the Inquiry Model represented in Figure 2.1 earlier in this chapter. When Anstey and Bull (2012) first developed this model of inquiry they drew heavily on the ALC that, in its earliest form, was generated in 2003 and reported in 2004 (Bull & Anstey, 2004). The important point here is that when teachers are engaged in action research, they are drawing on the same inquiry processes that their students are involved in while engaged in learning about, and through, inquiry. The potential for teachers and students to learn about inquiry from one another is thereby established. This learning relationship between teacher learning and student achievement has been the subject of contemporary research into inquiry. Glasswell et al. (2016, p.22) refer to this approach as co-inquiry, where their aim was to investigate whether '... a co-inquiry model of instructional reform, could bring about intended teacher and student learning effects'. They cite research in Australia by Singh et al. (2014) and Lai and McNaughton (2013) in New Zealand as supporting this approach to inquiry. As Glasswell et al. suggested, the purpose of this type of co-inquiry was a collaboration of various stakeholders designed to address the effectiveness of student learning. In this way, teachers could 'learn about their own teaching' and investigate their effect on student learning.

This relationship between teaching and learning has the potential to shape pedagogy particularly with reference to how content is taught and learnt. Wiggins and McTighe (2005), Levesque (2008) and Bull and Anstey (2013) have addressed the question of how content might be covered in contexts where the inquiry process is being implemented. Wiggins and McTighe (2005, p. 340) defined coverage as 'A teaching approach that superficially teaches and tests content knowledge irrespective of student understanding or engagement'. Student learning is therefore equated with covering the content and the memorisation of facts, usually in a specific time frame. As such, this approach is the antithesis of the inquiry process. Wiggins and McTighe suggested that inquiry could be seen as a teaching approach that was based on understanding and in-depth learning. The terms 'covering' and 'uncovering', as Wiggins and McTighe defined them, describe the essential difference between a classroom that is focussed on the inquiry process and one that is not. In the uncovering approach, '... the student can verify, induce or justify the content through inquiry' (Wiggins & McTighe 2005, p.352). As Levesque (2008, p.35) suggested when discussing uncoverage, '... students inquire, interrogate, and go into depth, so as to find defensible answers to meaningful questions'. He further suggested (2008, p. 172) when discussing how students might learn history that '... by uncovering (as opposed to covering) the past, educators put students in a position to learn far more on their own than they ever could learn from history textbooks, educators, or any authority'. As Bull and Anstey (2013) proposed, the choice is between the passive consumption of knowledge and the active and critical engagement with a range of different sources of information – surface knowledge or deep understanding. Given the definition of a multiliterate person, a multiliterate pedagogy should be encouraging and developing active consumption and critical engagement to ensure students develop the deep understandings necessary to translate and transform the understandings to new contexts.

REFLECTION STRATEGY 2.3

- The purpose of this Reflection Strategy is to review the pedagogical approach that you are using in your class.
- Are you using a student-centred or teacher-centred pedagogy in your classroom? Give the reasons for this.
- Is your pedagogy based on covering content or students developing understandings through inquiry?
- If you are using both pedagogies, how are you attempting to achieve a balance between the two?

Inquiry and critical thinking

In order to employ active and critical engagement with a range of different sources of information, students need to apply critical thinking skills. According to the Ontario School Library Association (1999), one of the purposes of inquiry is to encourage high levels of critical thinking so that the processes of inquiry are appropriate, leading to conclusions and problem solutions that are based on supporting evidence. The word critical is derived from two Greek roots: *kriticos*, meaning making a judgement, and *kriterion*, meaning a standard or criterion. The concept of critical thinking therefore suggests making a discerned judgement based on specified criteria. Critical thinking is that mode of thinking whereby an individual improves the quality of their thinking and problem solving abilities by analysing, assessing and reconstructing his or her thoughts. It is essentially a self-directed and self-monitored activity that checks for accuracy, relevance of reasoning, and significance and depth of information. As Ritchhart et al. (2006, p. 16) suggested,

perhaps the most obvious message is that learning involves actively doing something with the topic at hand, rather than just absorbing information. This view, often called 'active learning' contrasts with a traditional view of learning in which knowledge is passively received – something you *get* rather than *do*.

Critical thinking skills require active engagement by students in dealing with information contained in a variety of texts. The idea of addressing these skills was popularised in the early 1950s when Bloom et al. (1956) devised their taxonomy of educational objectives which were later revised a number of times by different authors but lately by Anderson and Krathwohl (2001). In the original taxonomy, Bloom et al. suggested six levels beginning with knowledge and going on to include comprehension, application, analysis, synthesis and evaluation. When they were implemented in schools, they were commonly used to define the goals of lessons, the objectives, or as a way of devising a series of questions at increasing levels of difficulty. While this proved useful for classroom teachers, it was teacher focussed and did not address the question of what students should know and be able to do. As an alternative, Anstey and Bull (2006, p.23) suggested critical thinking should result in students '... having the ability to analyse texts, identify their origins and authenticity, and understand how they have been constructed in order to perceive their gaps, silences, and biases', that is critical thinking skills should be student focussed. Anstey and Bull (2006, p. 23) further suggested that students and teachers '... must be aware that the texts we access or are exposed to have been consciously constructed to share particular information in particular ways, shaping our attitudes, values, and behaviours'. Anstey and Bull (2006) maintained that texts should include traditional linguistic dominant paper texts, together with texts that include the visual, audio, gestural and spatial semiotic systems delivered by various technologies. Walker (2006, p.34) similarly suggested that students needed experience in using critical thinking skills in order to interpret films, and that 'Critical thinking and problem-solving skills are not inherent in students and must be taught'.

AUDITING INSTRUMENT 2.3

- The purpose of this Auditing Instrument is to establish what form critical thinking skills take in your teaching of inquiry in your classroom.
- Review your lesson plans and the teaching practices you use in your classroom to discover how often you address critical thinking skills.
- How often do you engage students in critical thinking skills that require dealing with information contained in a variety of texts?
- Do you engage your students in critical thinking skills by asking them a series of questions of increasing levels of difficulty, or engage them in strategies that require active learning?
- How often do you explicitly model or teach critical thinking skills?
- When addressing critical thinking skills, how often do you limit your selection of texts to the linguistic semiotic system?
- What is the balance of texts that you draw on from all available semiotic systems (linguistic, visual, audio, spatial and gestural) and technologies (paper, live and digital) when teaching critical thinking skills?

Beyond the question of pedagogical focus and the broadening of concepts surrounding the nature of texts, there is the issue of how students might best learn to be critical thinkers. Bain (2005) established a group reading procedure when he asked students to use critical thinking skills in their analysis of historical material. He used structured, guided and independent inquiry based on the work of Palincsar and

Brown (1984). Bain (2005, p. 203) reported that 'I established reading procedures that enabled a group of students to read and question sources together in ways they did not on their own'. Other researchers, such as Harpaz and Lefstein (2000), have reported on the value of a community of learners in assisting students to engage in critical thinking. Other strategies have been developed to support the development of critical thinking by students. Ritchhart et al. reported, as part of the Visible Thinking Team at Project Zero at the Harvard Graduate School of Education, on the development of what they termed routines for making thinking more visible. They suggested (2006, p. 4) that 'Thinking routines focus on the establishment of structures that weave thinking into the fabric of the classroom and help to make the thinking of everyone in the classroom more visible and apparent'. They recommended strategies such as **Think-Pair-Share, KWL** and **PMI** (2006, pp. 6-10). These strategies, along with many others, are discussed in detail by Kruse (2009, 2010, 2012) and Ditchburn and Hattensen (2012).

Anstey and Bull (2004, 2006) and Bull and Anstey (2010a) developed a number of sets of questions designed to promote critical thinking in students and critical awareness in teachers' pedagogy in order to make the processes of inquiry more available. The following have been adapted from the original questions proposed by Anstey and Bull:

- Who produced this text?
- What is the purpose of this text?
- Who is this text produced for?
- Of what relevance is this text to my reading purpose?
- Why is this topic being written about?
- From whose perspective is this text constructed?
- Are there other possible constructions from different points of view?
- Whose interests are being served by this text?
- Who is included in or excluded from this text? Why?
- What assumptions about the potential audiences of this text have been made?
- Are there particular attitudes, values and ideologies that are foregrounded in this text?
- Who is silenced or marginalised by this text?
- Who is empowered by this text?
- Are there any stereotypes represented or challenged in this text?
- What kinds of person(s) with what interests and values produced this text?
- What are the origins (social, cultural, historical) of this text?
- After examining this text, what action can be taken?
- In what way does this text transform the reader?

The preceding questions do not represent a definite list but rather some of the queries that can be addressed before, during or after the inquiry process. It is not intended that all of these questions would, or should, be asked in a single lesson. It is more than likely that a teacher might focus on a single question, particularly if the class has not engaged in the type of critical thinking that is necessary to answer a specific question. In their current form, most of the questions are directed towards the teacher and would need to be reworded in order to make them appropriate for students. Individual schools would need to develop a school-wide approach to critical thinking skills in order to determine which questions would be suitable for investigation at which year level. It is also important for teachers and schools to realise that while critical thinking skills are a crucial part of the inquiry process, they are by no means the only skills that are involved.

THEORY INTO PRACTICE 2.2

- The purpose of this Theory into Practice is to review your questioning and strategy use.
- Review the eighteen question types above, proposed by Anstey and Bull, to determine whether the range of questions that you are asking is broad enough in your approach to the teaching of critical thinking skills. Are your questions ranging over a number of levels such as inferential or critical, or are you mainly focussing on literal comprehension?
- Check the range of strategies you are teaching the students in your class to use when they engage in inquiry. Do you use a variety of strategies, or do you tend to rely on just two or three favourites?

(Further information on critical thinking skills can be found in Chapters Five and Six.)

Research skills and the inquiry process

A significant part of the inquiry process is the gathering of information that will be needed to form the basis of the inquiry. Gathering relevant information requires a set of specific skills to be learnt. These skills are sometimes referred to as study skills, information skills, information literacy or research skills. In this chapter, they will be referred to as research skills since the term research is most closely aligned to the process that is involved in inquiry. Interestingly, there is little research about research skills. Some research focusses on the relationship of comprehension and research, such as Coiro (2003, 2011) and Coiro & Dobler (2007), while others investigate students researching on the internet (Lynch, 2017). There are many writers who argue for the importance of research skills such as Scott and O'Sullivan (2005), Ritchhart et al. (2008) and Julien and Barker (2009). There is a degree of agreement about what are the relevant research skills. As Taylor (2003, p.2) suggested, undertaking research involved '... developing research skills such as gathering and using evidence, analysing sources and identifying the origin of sources and their ownership'. This view of research skills is supported by many writers in the area such as the Ontario School Library Association (1999), Leu et al. (2011) and Lynch (2017). The general consensus is that research skills involve locating (including skimming and scanning), organising, evaluating and reporting.

However, both Bain (2005) and Lynch (2017) were careful to point out that research should also involve students in considering factors outside the text, such as the audience for which the text was designed, when and by whom it was constructed, the circumstances and context that the text arose from, and the intended purpose of the text. Interestingly, for some time primary, secondary and tertiary students have employed what has often been referred to as a CRAAP procedure as a way of addressing some of these issues. The procedure suggests that the following questions should be at the forefront of their minds when information is being explored:

Currency – Is it recent information and up to date?
Relevance – How does the information relate to the research topic?
Authority – What are the qualifications and reliability of the source?
Accuracy – Can the information be confirmed or verified from another source?
Purpose – From what point of view is it written?

It is important that students not be tempted to trivialise this strategy because of its acronym, but rather appreciate the usefulness of the CRAAP procedure. Any strategy that supports students to apply the research skills successfully should be treated seriously. As Leu et al. (2011, p. 5) pointed out, those societies that carefully engage in the research process '... will succeed in the challenging times that await us'. It is crucial that students and teachers do not see the research and inquiry processes as linear beginning with locating skills, moving through organising and evaluating, and ending with reporting. They are better considered as cyclical processes, that is recursive. As a case in point, students engaged in research might locate some information about a particular topic, organise the information and then begin to evaluate the information only to realise that they need to go back and retrieve further information about the topic before they report on it. Accordingly, teachers might be better able to represent research to students as a cycle rather than a list of skills.

AUDITING INSTRUMENT 2.4

- The purpose of this Auditing Instrument is to investigate the importance that you attribute to research skills.
- Do you have a well-thought-out program for teaching research skills in your classroom that involves the skills associated with locating (including skimming and scanning), organising, evaluating and reporting?
- What is the balance that you have achieved among the four groups of skills? (For example do you spend the majority of your research skill instruction on locating skills?)
- What form does the school-wide approach to research skills take in your school?
- How aware are you of what skills your students learnt last year and what skills they are likely to learn next year?

One area of the research process that seems to be most challenging for students are those skills related to organising, particularly taking notes and making an outline. Morris and Stewart-Dore (1984) developed a series of strategies that was expressly designed to support students' abilities to extract and organise information. They drew on the earlier work of writers such as Herber (1978), Meyer and Freedle (1979) and Bartlett (1978) to construct a series of graphic displays based on **top-level structures**. As Morris and Stewart-Dore (1984, p. 118) suggested, 'These top-level structures are found both at the macro-level, that is, underlying the whole section, article or chapter, and also at the micro-level, that is, within smaller units such as paragraphs and sentences'. These structures, or organisational sections of text, were based on common patterns of text structure such as comparison–contrast or cause-effect and were further developed by Turner (1992).

Morris and Stewart-Dore incorporated these strategies into their ERICA (Effective Reading in the Content Areas) program for working with both teachers and students. This program was later modified by them into the LTLTR (Learning To Learn From Reading) program. Anstey and Bull (2012) and Bull and Anstey (2013) represented the top-level structures illustrating their relationship with various text types or genres. They also indicated the common graphic representations associated with them. Table 2.3 has been adapted from these earlier representations.

Because each of the top-level structures in Table 2.3 has been related to a graphic display, students find them particularly useful in taking notes rather than copying down whole sections of texts from paragraphs or chapters. They also find them useful in organising their notes into an outline that represents their own thoughts. The graphic displays also focus students on visual as well as linguistic ways of organising and representing information in text. Teachers find Table 2.3 useful because it relates each top-level structure and graphic display to a particular text type.

Some final thoughts about research skills

The top-level structures outlined in Table 2.3 are especially useful because they can be applied across all discipline areas, semiotic systems and technologies. These structures are easier to apply in disciplines such as science or mathematics which are largely fact based. In history, particularly with the use of primary or original sources, this is not the case. Primary sources, which rely on eyewitness accounts, artefacts, memoirs or autobiographies, are fundamental to the study of history and are often delivered by multimodal texts and a variety of technologies. However, as Marwick (1997) suggested, primary sources are frequently fragmentary, often ambiguous and usually difficult to analyse or interpret. Teachers need to be aware of the different factors that are involved with each discipline and adjust their expectations of students' performance accordingly. The use of the CRAAP procedure is ideal for addressing some of these issues related to historical research and is also applicable to research in other disciplines. Therefore it can be incorporated into teacher practice when it is most needed.

While research is normally associated with non-fiction text types, fiction can also be used as a source of factual information. Fiction is sometimes discounted as a source of factual information based on a false dichotomy that non-fiction is 'true' and fiction is 'not true'. This distinction does not always hold up in either case. The content of non-fiction texts may be 'not true' because they are out of date or based on a false premise or belief held by the author. In the case of a fictional text, there may be factual details about the social, cultural or historical conditions of the time in which the characters live, or the plot or theme of the text may address important issues of the time. There are also those texts that might best be described as historical fiction which, while still containing a strong fictive element, have been especially constructed to include historical facts. Finally, there is a category of text, *faction*, where there is a significant amount of factual information presented (hence the term faction) in the context of a narrative. Researchers such as Vass (2004), Hoodless (2004) and Johansen and Sendergaard (2010) all reported that it was essential for students to discriminate between fiction, faction and non-fiction.

REFLECTION STRATEGY 2.4

- The purpose of this Reflection Strategy is to establish how wide-ranging is your approach to teaching research skills.
- What part do top-level structures play in your research skill program?
- How do you make distinctions between fiction and non-fiction for your students?
- In what way do you incorporate fiction and non-fiction texts in your research skill program?
- How will you address the differences among fiction, faction and non-fiction for your students?

Table 2.3 Organising information using top-level structures

Top-Level Structures (TLS) and Explanation	Examples of Linguistic Indicators	Examples of Graphic Displays for Top-Level Structures	Examples of Types of Text and Organisation in Which Particular TLS and Graphic Displays Might Be Used
Simple List – contains a main idea and supporting ideas	for example and then next		**Report:** Opening general statement, sequenced facts. **Explanation:** Opening general statement, followed by a series of statements and a conclusion.
Time Order – sequence of ideas over time, distance or order	at this point finally after before	Time line Flow chart Map	**Recount:** Orientation, series of events in chronological order, concluding personal comment. **Procedure:** Opening general statement, materials or skills required in order of use, sequential list of steps.
Problem and Solution – an answer or solution must be found to a problem	consequently whereas alternatively therefore	Retrieval Chart	**Discussion:** Opening statement presenting issue/problem, arguments for different solutions, recommendation.
Cause and Effect – one set of events leads to another	because due to reason thus	Retrieval Chart	**Explanation:** Opening general statement, followed by a series of statements and a conclusion.

(Continued)

Table 2.3 (Continued)

Top-Level Structures (TLS) and Explanation	Examples of Linguistic Indicators	Examples of Graphic Displays for Top-Level Structures	Examples of Types of Text and Organisation in Which Particular TLS and Graphic Displays Might Be Used
Compare and Contrast - how events can be the same or different	likewise similarly in contrast instead	Retrieval Chart |		
---	---	---
				Discussion: Opening statement presenting issue, arguments for different and against, recommendation.
Argument - for and against	nevertheless on the other hand however on the contrary		**Discussion:** Opening statement presenting issue, arguments for different and against, recommendation. **Exposition:** Opening statement of position, stages of argument, summing up/conclusion.

Top-level structures, the use of primary sources, engagement with fiction, faction and non-fiction and the strategies and processes relating to inquiry all inform the *pedagogy* that is necessary to develop multiliterate individuals. This raises the question as to whether there are particular pedagogies that are more appropriate to accomplish a focus on the inquiry process. (Further information on research skills can be found in Chapters Five and Six.)

A pedagogy of inquiry

A detailed discussion of the concept of pedagogy was presented in Chapter Four of the complementary volume, *Foundations of Multiliteracies: Reading, Writing and Talking in the 21st Century*. This discussion addressed explicit and implicit pedagogies, visible and invisible pedagogies, and defining multiliterate and dialogic pedagogies. In Chapter Two of the complementary volume, a pedagogical approach based around the Four Resource Model proposed by Freebody and Luke was also discussed. Therefore, none of these concepts will be addressed in the current chapter.

Earlier in the current chapter there was a discussion about teachers being involved in an Action Learning Cycle (ALC) which required them to be engaged in an inquiry process. As part of addressing this process, Wells (2001) had suggested that teachers who became inquirers or researchers in their own classrooms were more likely to model successful learning to their students. Such an approach recasts teachers as inquirers themselves, engaged in the same goals as their students. This change in the teaching/learning paradigm has the potential to change students from a concentration on a 'listen to learn' focus and to move teachers away from a focus on 'talking to teach'. Such a paradigm shift requires teachers to make significant changes to their pedagogy.

Compounding the need for such a shift in paradigm is the ever-increasing change in the nature of literacy brought about by the pace of new developments in technology. Literacy has always been subject to change, but in the past the pace of change was considerably slower. As Leu et al. (2011, p. 5) suggested, 'To be literate tomorrow will be defined by even newer technologies that have yet to appear and even newer social practices that we will create to meet unanticipated needs'. Such is the pace of change in literacy that Leu (2000) and Leu et al. (2011, p. 6) have suggested that literacy should now be regarded as deictic because '... the meaning of literacy rapidly and continuously changes', necessitating a rethinking about the traditional notions of literacy. Changes in ideas about literacy necessitate changes in literacy pedagogy. Contemporary definitions of literacy pedagogy characterise teachers as facilitators, learning based on inquiry, collaboration of students in student-led investigations and involvement of students in critical thinking and problem solving. As Paris and Paris (2001, p. 94) suggested, 'Students are cognitively engaged in classrooms that have open-ended tasks, projects, and problems that are based on driving questions. These are student-centred and inquiry-driven contexts... that promote intrinsic motivation, autonomy, and self-determination'. Paris and Paris (2001, pp. 97–98) recommended a pedagogy that was based on self-regulated learning (SRL) that had a number of major features including self-appraisal and management that led to a greater understanding and engagement with learning, thinking and problem solving and resulted in learning that was adaptive, strategic and goal oriented. They also suggested that SRL could be taught directly through explicit instruction and indirectly through modelling that could be enhanced by the establishment of a reflective community. The role of indirect teaching and modelling in the teaching of thinking and problem solving was also recommended by Ritchhart et al. (2008) and Ritchhart and Perkins (2008).

Given the preceding discussion, it is now possible to devise a pedagogy of inquiry that has the following characteristics:

- Teachers as facilitators,
- Inquiry-based learning and teaching incorporating student-led investigations,
- Collaboration of students in learning contexts,
- Student centred,
- Self-regulated learning,
- Includes critical thinking and problem solving skills,
- Adaptive and goal oriented,
- Incorporates explicit teaching and indirect teaching through modelling.

These characteristics also inform a multiliterate pedagogy.

AUDITING INSTRUMENT 2.5

- The purpose of this Auditing Instrument is to investigate which of the preceding eight characteristics feature in your approach to the Inquiry Process.
- What is the balance in your pedagogy between direct teaching and your role as a facilitator of student learning?
- What part do student-led investigations and self-regulated learning play in your approach to the Inquiry Process?
- How important in your pedagogy of inquiry learning are a student-centred focus and collaborative learning?
- How do you account for an adaptive and active approach to inquiry in your pedagogy?
- What is the balance between explicit instruction and modelling in your pedagogy?

The Gradual Release Model first proposed by Pearson and Gallagher (1983) and later adapted by Anstey and Bull (2011b) and Bull and Anstey (2013) is a pedagogical model that satisfies the eight characteristics mentioned above. The attraction of the original model proposed by Pearson and Gallagher (1983, pp. 34–35) was that it was '. . . conceptualised as requiring differing proportions of teacher and student responsibility'. This adjustment of student and teacher responsibility according to the type of learning and teaching that was being attempted avoided the dichotomy of teacher-centred versus student-centred pedagogy that has been the subject of so much discussion in recent times. In recommending modelling and explicit instruction as part of a structured pedagogy, guided practice where teachers and students share responsibility for learning, and independent practice and learning where students are solely responsible for learning, Pearson and Gallagher varied pedagogy according to the type of engagement in learning or teaching. The eventual goal was that '. . . every student gets to the point where she is able to accept total responsibility for the task' (Pearson & Gallagher, 1983, p. 35). Pearson and Gallagher

(1983, p. 36) also emphasised that students would be continually self-monitoring their learning and that teachers would provide feedback at every stage, even at the independent practice stage when they reported that 'Feedback at stages is critical (even when the teacher is not the "teacher" he must provide feedback about how well the group is accomplishing its goals along the way)'. They were also careful to point out that the explicit instruction that they were recommending was different from direct instruction because the model did not assume that complex strategies could be broken down into sequentially ordered subskills and did not suggest that there was a single best way of applying a strategy.

The model presented in Figure 2.2 represents an amalgamation of, and adaption of, the original devised by Pearson and Gallagher (1983) and those suggested by Anstey and Bull (2011b) and Bull and Anstey (2013).

There are some important considerations to be taken into account when applying this model. Essentially, the model in Figure 2.2 has been developed to provide a pedagogy for the inquiry process that can be applied in a multiliterate classroom. However, the model should not be seen as only applying in literacy contexts. As the model suggests, the goal of the gradual release of responsibility approach is that students will be able to independently apply the skills and processes of the inquiry process with a variety of texts and in contexts across the curriculum. It should also be noted that while the gradual release of responsibility implies a continuous progression from explicit teacher instruction to independent student practice, it is not intended that this should be seen as an invariant sequence. Not every teacher will follow the same sequence, nor will every teacher interpret each type of practice in the same way. Therefore, the model should not be interpreted as linear and the practices should not be depicted as static or fixed. The model represents a flexible and adaptive approach to the inquiry process. It is based on the understanding that students need clear models of thinking processes and strategies, together with definitions and knowledge when in the early stages of inquiry. This early stage should be followed by appropriate guidance and scaffolding as their understanding and knowledge increases and they gradually take control of their learning. Ultimately, students will develop a level of sophistication in their learning that will enable them to independently apply their learning to other settings and contexts. Teachers support this process by providing appropriate pedagogical guidance by adapting their practices and planning.

ACTION LEARNING TASK 2.2

- The purpose of this Action Learning Task 2.2 is to refocus your attention on your action research project that you began at the end of Chapter One as part of your participation in the Action Learning Cycle (ARC).
- How have the foci on the Inquiry Process, critical thinking skills and research skills in this chapter changed your understanding of pedagogy?
- Will you need to make changes to the aim or goal of your project?
- Will you need to make adjustments to your methods of gathering or analysing data?
- How will your report change in the light of the possible changes in pedagogy that you have made?

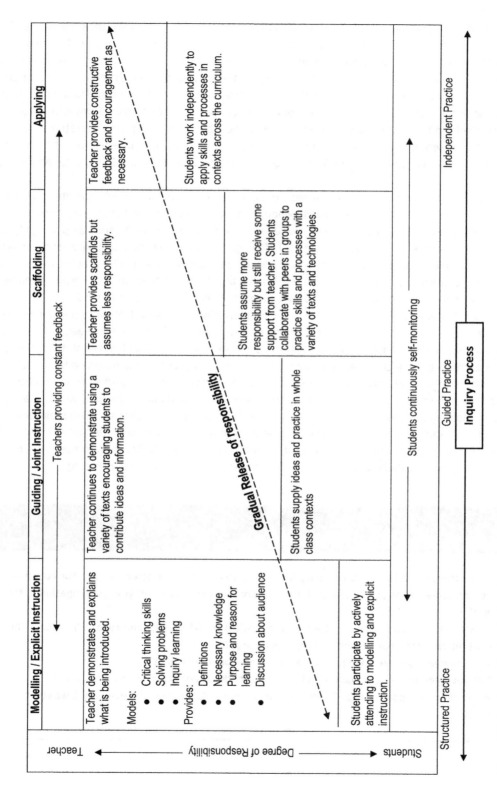

	Modelling / Explicit Instruction	Guiding / Joint Instruction	Scaffolding	Applying
	Teacher demonstrates and explains what is being introduced. Models: • Critical thinking skills • Solving problems • Inquiry learning Provides: • Definitions • Necessary knowledge • Purpose and reason for learning • Discussion about audience	Teacher continues to demonstrate using a variety of texts encouraging students to contribute ideas and information.	Teacher provides scaffolds but assumes less responsibility.	Teacher provides constructive feedback and encouragement as necessary.
		Teachers providing constant feedback		
		Gradual Release of responsibility		
	Students participate by actively attending to modelling and explicit instruction.	Students supply ideas and practice in whole class contexts	Students assume more responsibility but still receive some support from teacher. Students collaborate with peers in groups to practice skills and processes with a variety of texts and technologies.	Students work independently to apply skills and processes in contexts across the curriculum.
		Students continuously self-monitoring		

Teacher ◄—— Degree of Responsibility ——► Students

Structured Practice — Guided Practice — Independent Practice

Inquiry Process

Figure 2.2 A pedagogy for inquiry learning

Inquiry in the digital age

As was argued in Chapter One, the new literacies provide essential components for learning in the global and diverse societies that have developed in recent years. What has emerged from these developments has been a focus on multiliteracies and multimodality. As Lynch (2017, p. 186) suggested, this has led to '... the interweaving of the performance of new digital literacies with traditional print-based skills and strategies, and the mutually-supportive relationship between these traditional and new literacies'. Students now spend a considerable proportion of their time on the internet when applying the skills and strategies of the inquiry approach. These skills and strategies are referred to using a number of terms, such as traditional, print based or digital. For the purposes of discussion in this and further chapters, the terms offline and online will be used when referring to traditional/print-based skills and digital skills.

The role of research skills in inquiry in the digital age

The growth of internet use when engaging in the inquiry process has brought about significant changes in how students access information. As Levesque (2006) has pointed out, the internet has provided both students and teachers with a vastly increased amount of information available from an increasing variety of sources. Levesque (2006, p. 3) suggested that '... sources are easier to search and locate and, by extension, more rapidly and effectively manipulated'. As Lynch (2017, p. 193) pointed out when discussing the use of videos, students had access to 'information-rich online environments' where a lot can be learned in a short period of time, as compared to extracting information for an inquiry from a print text.

This increasing access to online information brings with it a number of issues. As Coiro (2005, p. 30) reported, adolescent readers '... vary tremendously in their ability to locate, understand, and use information online'. Coiro concluded that less skilled readers interact more passively with online text than do their more skilled counterparts, which impacted on the goal to produce students who were 'informed skeptics' when reading online. Somewhat similar results were obtained by Heil (2005, p. 26), who reported that students were attracted to internet use because of the ease of use and speed of finding information quickly and were less concerned about viewing the information critically. She also reported on a study by Scott and O'Sullivan (2005) that suggested that students had developed an 'infatuation with information' and regarded any information as good information provided that it was easy to obtain. Heil (2005, p. 28) concluded that '... if a site had information that students wanted, they chose to ignore clear signals that the site was inappropriate for research'. Both Heil (2005) and Levesque (2006) reported that quality control of information on the internet was a recurring issue. Allied to this issue, Eagleton et al. (2003), Buckingham (2005), Leu et al. (2011) and Lynch (2017) stated that students were either not skilled at internet use or that the self-reported expertise of students was higher than the actual expertise.

In contrast to these findings, Levesque (2006, p. 3), in exploring online historical information, stated that because the information was not structured as it was in textbooks that '... students are more directly and actively involved' in inquiry. Similarly, Walsh (2007), reporting on the work of Kress, stated that while offline information was linear and sequential, online information was non-linear and non-sequential. Walsh (2007, p. 41) further reported that online information relied on links that operated across the information and that when students negotiated these links, this was '... more likely to augment than harm the reading process'. According to Walsh this process facilitated more active and reflective reading. While these findings might appear to contradict one another, it may be that students find the comprehension processes involved in reading information less challenging than locating and extracting information. As Walsh (2007, p. 46) concluded, 'Many students found it difficult to understand how to refine a search' and would commonly accept the first information they found, but conversely 'Inferring was evident when students decided on relevance of information'. Jenkins (2009) reported that research skills assumed great importance once students began to deal with texts that had not previously screened by librarians, that is as they engaged in independent inquiry. As Leu et al. (2011, p. 7) suggested, 'The reading ability required to search for and locate information on the Internet may very well serve as a gatekeeper skill, because you will be unable to solve the problem if you cannot locate information'.

REFLECTION STRATEGY 2.5

- The purpose of this Reflection Strategy is to focus attention on how you have addressed inquiry in the digital age.
- To what extent have you addressed digital texts in your approach to inquiry?
- What do you see as the advantages in addressing digital texts?
- What are some of the challenges that you have encountered in incorporating digital texts in your approach to inquiry?

The role of comprehension skills in inquiry in the digital age

Interestingly, there has been a great deal of research carried out on the role of comprehension in following the inquiry process in online contexts. Coiro (2003, p. 463) suggested that online inquiry tasks required new comprehension skills and '... fundamentally different sets of new literacies'. She suggested that online inquiry projects demanded high levels of thinking and collaborative problem solving that were quite different from the largely literal questions associated with offline comprehension at the individual student level. She also suggested that online inquiry expected that students would adopt a range of new roles as they followed different reading pathways through online texts, that a more critical stance towards texts was needed and that students should develop the abilities to 'draw connections between resources of diverse and multiple perspectives' (Coiro, 2003, p. 461). As Coiro (2011) later stated, traditional ideas about reading comprehension may no longer be sufficient to deal with online reading that demands flexible reading comprehension skills to respond to rapidly changing research contexts and new online texts. Research has provided evidence that online reading comprehension involves skills and strategies that are unique to online texts (Afflerbach & Cho, 2008) – or at least more complex than that required for offline texts (Coiro & Dobler, 2007).

While there does seem to be a general consensus of opinion that there is some relationship between reading offline and online texts, as suggested by the research of Coiro and Dobler (2007), there are increasing claims that online texts do have their own idiosyncrasies (Coscarelli & Coiro, 2014). As Bull and Anstey (2013, p. 57) pointed out, students who are reading or viewing texts delivered via digital technologies, that is online texts, '... will require different literacy processes and skills'. This point of view was shared by Lynch (2017, p.187), who reported that '... internet reading tasks are more intense than reading traditional print-based informational texts, involving the combination of a greater number of comprehension strategies and in more rapid succession' and require new skills and strategies. Lynch also suggested, drawing on the work of Bearne (2009), Serafini (2011) and Liu (2013), that online reading involves accessing texts that include visual images, audio and gestural elements. This view has been central to the work of Anstey and Bull (2010a, 2018) and Bull and Anstey (2010b, 2013), who refer to these elements as semiotic systems. The presence of multiple semiotic systems in online texts brings with it the need for new skills and processes and involves new levels of complexities. While offline texts do incorporate the visual semiotic system through still images, online texts commonly involve a greater reliance on still images as well as the use of moving images that include audio, gestural and spatial semiotic systems. (For further details about the semiotic systems, see Chapter Three.) The greater complexity of online texts, together with the attractiveness of the texts created through the semiotic systems, increases the likelihood that students will go off-task and follow an area of interest or appeal rather than continue to investigate their original inquiry. This is compounded by the fact, as Lynch (2017, p.190) suggested, that students might be '... overwhelmed by the amount of information available on the internet, much of which is beyond their independent reading level'.

REFLECTION STRATEGY 2.6

- The purpose of this Reflection Strategy is to explore your understanding of offline and online texts.
- What do you understand about the issues surrounding students' use of offline texts?
- What do you understand about the issues surrounding students' use of online texts?
- How have you adjusted your teaching of comprehension to account for the complexity of online texts?
- What issues arise from the use of online texts that do not arise with offline texts?

(Further information on comprehension skills can be found in Chapters Five and Six.)

The need for developing a pedagogy to address online texts

The greater complexity of online texts, together with the difference between offline and online texts, suggests that a pedagogy for teaching about the use and interpretation of online texts needs to be developed. Walsh (2007) called for research to address how students learnt from online texts and to use this evidence to develop a new pedagogy. In her research Walsh (2007, p.48) found that explicit explanations about the visual semiotic system led to a '... marked increase in the incidence of *metalanguage* use during conversation with the teacher', whereas the use of metalanguage in the students' own discussions occurred far less frequently. The use of metalanguage, or a language to talk about the visual semiotic system, is not the issue here but rather that a pedagogy that includes explicit instruction and encourages frequent teacher–student talk is more likely to succeed with online texts.

Walsh went on to suggest, using Freebody and Luke's Four Resource Model, that online reading practices might include such strategies as scanning, comparing different websites, interpreting meanings, critically evaluating and detecting bias and **point of view**. (For further information about using the Four

Resource Model as a pedagogy see Chapter Five in this volume and Chapter Two in the complementary volume *Foundations of Multiliteracies: Reading, Writing and Talking in the 21st Century*).

In their research Leu et al. (2011, p. 7) suggested that reading online texts should involve a process of problem-based inquiry and the incorporation of research skills. Leu et al. (2011, p. 8) concluded that '... online reading is a self-directed, text-construction process' where readers '... read through the links that they follow as they gather information to solve a problem'. They suggested that while this process may be possible with offline text, it always occurs with online texts. They further suggested that since no two readers read the same online text to solve the same problem, such reading is an individual process that involves selecting unique segments of information. The process of using links to read through the text relies on the use of **hypertexts**.

However, when the focus changes from gathering information to comprehension, Leu et al. (2011, p. 8) concluded that '... online reading comprehension is not simply an individual process but rather a collaborative and social practice'. Both Leu and Kiili et al. (2008) found that individual readers concentrated on gathering facts whereas collaborative readers were able to gain deeper understandings and construct different perspectives. Coscarelli and Coiro (2014) also found that collaborative readers were more likely to gain deeper understandings when accessing online texts. Coscarelli and Coiro (2014, p. 768) further suggested that

> ... readers need to realise that visiting multiple sources for information is not only unavoidable, but also desired. This process prompts the need to evaluate the relevance and reliability of these different sources and languages, as well as select and/or integrate the information from different sources.

As suggested earlier in this chapter, Coiro (2003) had concluded that online inquiry demanded high levels of thinking, collaborative problem solving, a range of new roles following different reading pathways through online texts and a more critical stance towards texts.

Taking all this research into consideration, it is now possible to develop an outline of what a pedagogy of inquiry for online texts might involve by looking at the following characteristics. Note these characteristics also inform a multiliterate pedagogy:

- Explicit instruction with regard to semiotic systems (Walsh, 2007);
- Use of metalanguage, particularly with student-teacher conversations (Walsh, 2007);
- Using the Four Resource Model as a pedagogical approach (Walsh, 2007);
- Incorporation of problem-based inquiry (Leu et al., 2011);
- Inclusion of an approach to research skills (Leu et al., 2011);
- A focus on the use of hypertexts as a way of accessing information (Leu et al., 2011);
- Teaching comprehension skills as a collaborative and social process (Leu et al., 2011);
- Encouraging collaboration among readers to achieve deeper understandings and different perspectives (Kiili et al., 2008, Leu et al., 2011 and Coscarelli & Coiro, 2014);
- Using multiple sources of information to address reliability and relevance (Coscarelli and Coiro, 2014);
- Incorporate higher levels of thinking and a critical stance towards texts (Coiro, 2003).

AUDITING INSTRUMENT 2.6

- The purpose of this Auditing Instrument is to explore your understanding of what a pedagogy of inquiry for online texts might involve.
- To what extent does your pedagogy of inquiry for online texts address the explicit teaching of the five semiotic systems and a variety of technologies?
- What part do student-teacher conversations play in your pedagogy?
- How familiar are you with the metalanguage of the semiotic systems?
- In what ways does collaborative learning feature in your pedagogy?

It is important to understand that the ten characteristics specified above could also be applied to offline texts. However, what should be realised is that all the researchers involved have identified these characteristics as applying particularly to online text and reading online. Because of the greater complexity of online texts and the recent conceptualisations of multiliteracies and multimodality, more careful consideration should be given by teachers and schools to the provision of conditions that allow these characteristics to develop. Each of these characteristics needs to be addressed as part of a school-wide program in order to develop a logical sequence of development and to make teachers at each year level aware of the part they are expected to play in the individual classroom context.

ACTION LEARNING TASK 2.3

- The purpose of this Action Learning Task is to refocus your attention on your action research project that you began at the end of Chapter One as part of your participation in the Action Learning Cycle (ARC).
- To what extent has the focus on online texts changed your understanding of pedagogy?
- Will you need to make changes to the aim or goal of your project?
- Will you need to make adjustments to your methods of gathering or analysing data?
- How will your report change in the light of the possible changes in pedagogy that you have made?

Conclusion

In this chapter a model of the inquiry process was developed as a framework that applied across disciplines or subject areas to inform students and teachers about how to approach literacy tasks. It focussed on the need to address multiliteracies and the process of inquiry and how this assisted students to develop understandings about the complexities of communicating with multimodal texts. A model for implementing inquiry in the classroom was also developed. The chapter also addressed what part the inquiry process played in the Action Learning Cycle (ALC) and how teachers were better able to communicate the process of inquiry to their students if involved in inquiry themselves. It explored the need to equip students with the knowledge to cope with the continuous change that have occurred in texts and technology.

The chapter outlined the processes underlying inquiry and the strategies that students needed to acquire in order to successfully engage in the inquiry process. It explored the relationship of critical thinking skills and research skills to the inquiry process and also explored how comprehension impacted differently on offline and online texts. The chapter also identified the similarities and differences when accessing and reading offline and online texts and examined how inquiry using digital texts was similar to, and different from, inquiry with print-based texts. The chapter developed a set of characteristics for a pedagogy of inquiry based on the research into reading and comprehending of offline and online texts. The pedagogy of inquiry informs a multiliterate pedagogy.

3 The codes and conventions of the semiotic systems: Developing a metalanguage for literacy inquiry

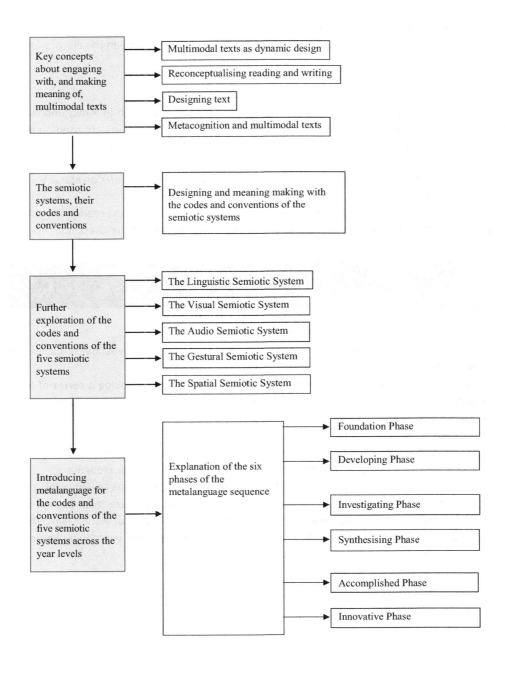

The purpose of this chapter is to build upon information about the codes and conventions of the semiotic systems that was introduced in the complementary volume, *Foundations of Multiliteracies: Reading, Writing and Talking in the 21st Century*. In the complementary volume it was established that in order to investigate multimodal texts, and the reading and writing processes associated with them, teachers and students require a metalanguage to talk about the resources that are drawn upon to construct multimodal texts. Because the codes and conventions of the five semiotic systems (linguistic, visual, gestural, spatial and audio) are one of the major resources drawn upon, a metalanguage for them is particularly important. In this chapter, there will be further definition and exploration of the codes and conventions, together with a suggested sequence for their introduction to students. As part of the exploration readers will be reminded that semiotic systems are social and culture specific resources and therefore subject to change. In addition, the social and cultural origins of the semiotic systems mean the literacy identities of the consumers and producers of the text influence meaning making.

The point will be made that the semiotic systems do not operate in isolation in a multimodal text. It is the combination of the *semiotic systems*, and how their **codes** and **conventions** are used, together with other resources that contribute to the meanings conveyed. Therefore, the chapter examines how **inquiry** into multimodal texts might be conducted by students and teachers. It will also focus on using the metalanguage of each of the semiotic systems present in a text, together with knowledge about text, purpose and context, to identify and discuss how meaning is made.

As in preceding chapters, there will be specific Action Learning Tasks that the reader can engage in. In this chapter these tasks will be addressed at both the beginning and end of the chapter.

ACTION LEARNING TASK 3.1

- Complete this task *before* reading the chapter.
- The purpose of this Action Learning Task is to provide a strategy for investigating current planning, pedagogy and practices when talking about text with students.
- Select a lesson where you will be introducing a new text or commencing a series of lessons around a text. The text can be paper or digital. For this activity, do not use a lesson based around a live text.
- Videotape or audiotape the entire lesson.
- At the end of this chapter, Action Learning Task 3.2 will provide guidance for investigating the lesson in terms of how you currently plan and talk about text with your students.
- It is suggested that you audiotape all of the Theory into Practice lessons taught in this chapter. You may wish to transcribe and analyse parts of these lessons and use them as part of your data collection and analysis once you refine the focus and goal of your Action Plan. They will provide good baseline data, and it is better to collect that data now even if you do not transcribe and analyse it later.

Key concepts about engaging with, and making meaning of, multimodal texts

In this section understandings about **multiliteracies, multimodal texts** as design, the five **semiotic systems, metacognition, metalanguage** and the concept of **literacy identity** will be revised in relation to how meaning in multimodal text is produced and consumed. The Glossary at the end of the book provides definitions of these terms. However, if these terms are unfamiliar, or further introductory information is required, Chapter Three in the complementary volume *Foundations of Multiliteracies: Reading, Writing and Talking in the 21st Century* provides foundational knowledge for this chapter.

Multimodal texts as dynamic design

Multimodal texts comprise two or more semiotic systems, and the meanings that are conveyed by them draw upon the codes and conventions of those semiotic systems and other resources. The semiotic systems and their codes and conventions have meanings that are generally accepted among a social or cultural group. Jewitt and Kress (2008) stated that because semiotic systems, together with their codes and conventions, are a social and cultural construct, they will continue to change and may have different meanings among social and cultural groups. A common example is associations with colour and particular social and cultural events. In some cultures red is an important colour for weddings, while in others white is associated with weddings. Similarly, meanings will change over time within a cultural group. In Victorian England among particular social groups, the colour mauve or lilac was associated with a stage of mourning, to be worn by a widow or other mourners instead of black after a period of time had elapsed since the death of a loved one. In the 21st century this is no longer a code or convention. As a consequence of technological advances and general social and cultural changes in societies across the globe, texts are dynamic, that is they will continue to evolve and change. Therefore, Kress (2010) suggested that the most appropriate and forward-looking way of describing the processes of representing and communicating ideas through multimodal text (that is meaning making) is to think of text as **design**. The idea of design being at the centre of meaning making was also shared by Cope and Kalantzis (2000) and Kalantzis et al. (2016), who suggested that design could be thought of as both a verb and a noun when referring to multimodal text. They suggested that by thinking of text and design in these ways, the concept of text, the components within in it that potentially convey meaning, and the process of making meaning are all encompassed in the term design. Reference to design as both verb and noun also emphasises the dynamic nature of text.

Jewitt and Kress (2008) and Jewitt (2006) were particularly concerned that the dynamic nature of text inform the ways in which concepts about texts, their semiotic systems, codes and conventions are taught. As this chapter focusses particularly on understanding and teaching about the codes and conventions of the semiotic systems, it is important to review why teaching about texts should be dynamic rather than static. As explained in the complementary volume to this book, if the codes and conventions are taught as 'rules' (as they were in traditional approaches to teaching the grammar of the linguistic semiotic system), then the social and cultural basis or agency of people in the design of texts becomes lost and a static or immutable concept of literacy is promulgated. This approach would discourage students from understanding and embracing change and realising their agency and role in designing texts as a consumer (reader) and producer (writer), both now and in the future. Potentially, it would prevent them from becoming multiliterate. Anstey and Bull (2006), Anstey (2009), Bull and Anstey (2010a) and Anstey and Bull (2018) have stated that in order to be multiliterate, individuals need to:

- Be *flexible*, actively responding to changing literacies, capable of adopting, developing and sustaining mastery over new strategies;
- Have a **repertoire of resources** *and practices* (knowledge, skills and strategies) that can be designed, redesigned and used appropriately with different technologies and for different purposes, audiences and contexts;
- Understand and employ *traditional and new communication technologies* with multimodal texts that are delivered via combinations of paper, live (face-to-face) and digital technologies;
- Recognise and respond to how *social and cultural diversity* effects literate practices through the application of different knowledges, approaches, orientations, attitudes and values;
- Be *critically literate*, understanding that every literate practice requires them to be reflective and analytical problem solvers who are strategic and creative thinkers able to make meaning of, evaluate and respond to a variety of multimodal texts.

As can be seen from the characteristics of a multiliterate individual described in the preceding list, being multiliterate requires an understanding of text as dynamic and an ability to embrace and respond to change in strategic ways. Therefore, any exploration of texts, the resources drawn upon to design them (e.g. the semiotic systems) and the designing and **redesigning** of texts must construct texts as dynamic and encourage active problem solving and analysis. Nevertheless, dynamic approaches to teaching about producing and consuming text must ensure that students develop competence with the resources that are currently available (e.g. a knowledge of the current ways of using the codes and conventions of the semiotic systems) together with an ability to apply critique. That is students need to be able to use their competence to review the ways these resources have been used in texts and then critically analyse whether these ways are suitable for their current purpose and context.

Figure 3.1 was presented by Anstey and Bull (2018) as a way of looking at text and design that would encourage talk around text as dynamic rather than static. It emphasises the concepts and ideas about text that need to be developed and the ways in which any exploration of text and design should be focussed in order to develop students' understanding of texts as dynamic.

Reconceptualising reading and writing

The concept of text as dynamic and informed by design necessitates a revision of understandings about the ways in which texts are read and written. Teaching and learning text as something complete and finite, never to be redesigned and disseminated in different ways, is simply not appropriate or reflective of current practices of communication. Bull and Anstey (2010a) and Anstey and Bull (2018) stated that in a multiliterate world dominated by multimodal texts delivered via multiple technologies, it is more appropriate to use the terms **consuming** and **producing** rather than reading and writing when discussing interactions with text. They suggest that describing a multimodal text as 'written' predisposes thinking to a linguistic text conveyed by paper, because of the historical associations of the word

Commentary: to be read in conjunction with viewing Figure 3.1

- The use of the term **Design** is central to the figure. It is a term that denotes *active processing, problem-solving and invention* in order to achieve a *purpose or outcome*. Therefore, it constructs the production and consumption of text as *dynamic*, that is, a forward looking, (prospective), inventive process. Design also means the consumer/producer must have *agency* and realise the need to *mediate* the text in order to achieve the desired purpose.

- **Communication/Meaning Making** indicates this figure refers to both the *production and consumption of text*. It also reinforces the *purpose of producing and consuming texts*.

- **Representation** indicates the *use of all available resources* to produce or consume the text in order to achieve a communicative or meaning making purpose, for example, consideration of semiotic systems, cultural and social influences, available technologies, lifeworld and school world knowledge and experiences.

- **The producer's or consumer's competence and critique** are processes that inform designing. The multiple double headed arrows indicate this process can be cyclic – that is, it may need to be *reviewed, combined and recombined in multiple ways and multiple times* to inform a design that will *achieve the desired purpose*.

- **Competence** refers to existing knowledge about texts, technology, semiotic systems, their codes and conventions. In a changing world, this knowledge may or may not be useful in its current state. If it is talked about and thought about *only as competence and is not challenged* then it encourages a *static* view of knowledge, that it cannot evolve, be modified or used in different ways when designing. *Competence is necessary, but not sufficient, it must be thought about and used in dynamic ways.*

- **Critique** refers to *examining previous designs, ways of designing, and use of resources*. It involves *reviewing how previous designs, ways of designing and use of resources, have succeeded in achieving particular purposes in particular contexts* and how they would succeed in achieving *the current purpose now*. It involves *looking backward, critically, in order to be able to look forward and design*.

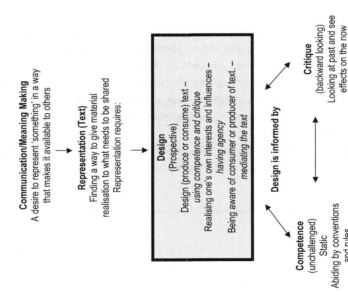

Communication/Meaning Making
A desire to represent 'something' in a way that makes it available to others

Representation (Text)
Finding a way to give material realisation to what needs to be shared Representation requires:

Design
(Prospective)
Design (produce or consume) text – *using competence and critique*
Realising one's own interests and influences – *having agency*
Being aware of consumer or producer of text. – *mediating the text*

Design is informed by

Competence
(unchallenged)
Static
Abiding by conventions and rules

Critique
(backward looking)
Looking at past and see effects on the now

Figure 3.1 Text and design: encouraging talk about texts as dynamic rather than static

From Anstey & Bull, 2018, *Foundations of Multiliteracies: Reading, Writing and Talking in the 21st Century*, Taylor and Francis, Abingdon, p. 85

REFLECTION STRATEGY 3.1

- The purpose of this Refection Strategy is to reflect upon your current approach to exploring and talking about texts with your students and whether it constructs a static or dynamic picture of text.
- Re-read Figure 3.1 before you engage with this Reflection Strategy and keep it beside you as you reflect on each of the following questions. Each of the questions focusses on an aspect of the figure.
- Do you discuss the writing or reading of text as a problem solving process, or in other words, as a process of design? How often and in what ways?
- When teaching about texts that are constructed for particular purposes (e.g. reports, instructions, stories), do you present the structure of the text and its textual features as static and unchanging, to be followed exactly in order to get the text 'right'? In other words, when teaching competence do you present the knowledge, skills and processes as static and unchanging or as dynamic and subject to change?
- How often, when discussing texts that are constructed for particular purposes (e.g. reports, instructions, stories), do you examine a variety of examples delivered by different technologies and discuss their characteristics in terms of similarities or differences and the possible reasons for the similarities and differences (e.g. different technologies, audiences, uses of semiotic systems)? In other words, do you and your students engage in critique?
- How often do you discuss the process of decision-making when reading and writing a text and actively teach strategies that might be used during the decision-making process? In other words, do you approach reading and writing texts as a process of design?
- How often do you encourage your students to think about what they bring to the text and what the writer of the text has brought to the text? Do you discuss how this influences their meaning making, reading and writing? In other words, do you encourage the students to realise their role and agency in reading and writing text and how they as readers or writers mediate the text?
- Finally, examine your planning for teaching about text (reading or writing) and consider each of these questions again in terms of the degree to which your planning for teaching addresses any of these points.

'writing'. Furthermore, multimodal texts are often produced by a group of people, each contributing particular expertise. Texts are disseminated by a range of technologies, sometimes several, simultaneously. Therefore, a better term to describe how these texts are constructed is production and the process of production is producing.

Similarly, Anstey and Bull (2018) stated that consuming should be used to describe the reading process because once again the term reading has historical associations with the written word and paper technology. Consuming a multimodal text means decisions must be made related to the purpose of reading the text and the context in which it will take place. Consideration of purpose and context informs how to engage with the text and what parts to focus upon. It is also necessary to understand how to process different technologies; for example searching online for information will require different skills and ways of processing information to using a paper text, such as a novel, for pleasure. The different technologies mean that the consumer may be attending to multiple semiotic systems together with their codes and conventions and working out what each contributes to meaning making and therefore how to attend to them. The term reading is also traditionally associated with consuming a text in isolation, while in reality multimodal texts are often consumed during interaction with others. Consuming text is an active and interactive process that involves problem solving, planning, revising strategies, sharing, listening and responding. Even when reading in isolation, active readers have a conversation with themselves as they redesign what they are consuming in ways that suit their purpose in making meaning of the text.

Two key concepts in the *consumption* and *production* of text as design are the agency of the consumer(s) or producer(s) and awareness of how the interests and influences of the consumer or producer mediate the text and the meaning making process. The interests and influences are often referred to as literacy identity. An individual's literacy identity grows from a combination of the social and cultural experiences in their lifeworld and the pedagogical activities and experiences of their school world. An individual's literacy identity evolves and changes as their experiences grow. It includes concepts to do with:

- Prior experience with texts
- Knowledge about texts
- Social and cultural knowledge and experiences
- Technological knowledge and experiences.

Being aware of your literacy identity and how that might influence your consumption or production of a text is essential to being multiliterate and actively engaging with text. Similarly, when possible and able to be accessed, consideration of the literacy identity of the producer(s) of the text and the text's origins ensures that a consumer engages critically with text and is aware of possible bias or influences that may be present. The consumer can then adjust their strategies for engagement with the text appropriately.

The concept of literacy identity informs Figure 3.1 and can help teachers guide students in developing strategies for active critical engagement with texts and design. Understanding literacy identity can also build understandings about the dynamic nature of text. The following example statements show how aspects of Figure 3.1 are informed by the concept of literacy identity. Students would draw on their literacy identity:

- Together with that of their audience when making decisions about representation;
- To determine the knowledge they have (competence) and then make decisions about what would be of assistance and how it might be used to access, create or critique what is present in a text;
- To realise their role and agency in the process of engaging with and designing text;
- In order to be critical in their meaning making by being aware of the potential influence of others' literacy identity in mediating text.

Designing text

Anstey and Bull (2018) presented a figure representing the design processes with text. It addressed both the consumption and production processes. It is re-presented here as Figure 3.2. An explanation of the main concepts and ideas underpinning it follow.

Figure 3.2 reinforces the concept of text and design as dynamic. It illuminates the processes and decision-making involved and the resources necessary to designing and redesigning. As can be seen, the process of designing may be recursive and non-sequential as indicated by the arrows on the cycle and in the centre. Designing is about meaning making. The producer of the text has a particular purpose in representing meaning to communicate a message to an audience. The consumer is attempting to make meaning of a text in order to fulfil a particular purpose. Whether consuming or producing a text there is always a purpose, and the way in which this purpose is achieved will be influenced by a range of available resources, among them audience, context and the technologies available for the design.

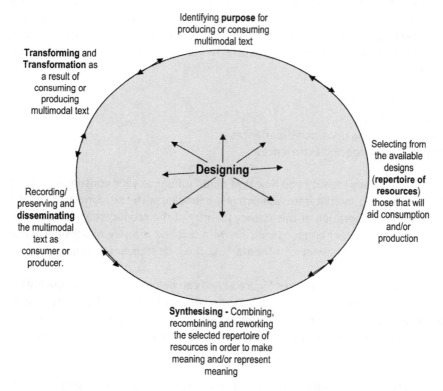

Figure 3.2 Consuming and producing multimodal text in a multiliterate world

From Anstey & Bull, 2018, *Foundations of Multiliteracies: Reading, Writing and Talking in the 21st Century*, Taylor and Francis, Abingdon, p. 91

The designing process may be interactive and involve several people, as often the purpose for, and process of, designing necessitates drawing upon multiple expertise, sharing and negotiating meaning. Kress and van Leeuwen (2001) suggested that the process of designing, and the designs themselves, can adhere to known conventions and competencies or be innovative, responding to purpose, audience, context and the available technologies.

Decisions will be made about dissemination of a text, and this may include technical preservation (as in a work of art) or recording (as in a live performance). The process and medium of dissemination means that all designs have the potential to become an archive of available designs and resources for the future (Kress & van Leeuwen, 2001).

Transformation is the result of the process of design. As designers (consumers and producers) use a repertoire of resources to *design*, they *redesign* an aspect of the world. No two redesigns will ever be the same because each designer has a unique literacy identity. The redesigns will become part of the available *repertoire of resources* to be used in the future.

The process of design involves **synthesising**, that is moving back and forth among different semiotic systems and other resources to make meaning.

The repertoire of resources that may be drawn upon to inform decisions during designing and redesigning will continue to evolve and change. They may include resources from the following areas:

- Purpose, knowledge about the purpose and how this might affect decisions about the design process, the construction, consumption and dissemination of the text.
- Audience, knowledge about the audience, for example their literacy identity.
- Contextual resources, knowledge about the context in which the text is produced or consumed.
- Social resources and cultural resources, knowledge about the social and cultural context in which the text is produced or consumed.
- Human and non-human resources, identifying what or who might be drawn upon to provide specific expertise, knowledge or a facility (e.g. software or hardware) for designing and redesigning the text.
- Textual resources, knowledge about the structure and design of text.
- Technological resources, hardware and software for producing, consuming and disseminating the text.
- Semiotic resources, the codes and conventions of the linguistic, visual, audio, gestural and spatial semiotic systems.
- Strategic resources, knowledge and understandings of skills, processes and strategies that can be drawn upon to facilitate the process of designing and redesigning.

Metacognition and multimodal texts

The preceding discussion has focussed on the processes of design and redesign during the production and consumption of multimodal text, together with the understandings, knowledge, skills and processes necessary to being a multiliterate person. It is apparent from this discussion that the consumer or producer needs to strategise, rethink, modify, combine, recombine or develop new strategies, knowledge, skills and ways of using technology, in order to achieve their purpose when consuming or producing text. In order to do this effectively they will need to develop strategies that enable self-monitoring and self-regulation during these processes.

Early in the 21st century, Paris and Paris (2001, p. 89) conducted a review of the research examining the classroom application of self-regulated learning (SRL) and defined it as follows: 'SLR... emphasises autonomy and control by the individual who monitors, directs and regulates actions toward goals of information acquisition expanding expertise and self-improvement'.

Zimmerman (2000, p. 14) described self-regulation in the following way: '(SLR) refers to self-generated thought, feelings and actions that are planned and cyclically adapted to the attainment of personal goals'.

These two definitions emphasise having and using agency in strategic ways, problem solving and lifelong learning, in order to become independent and active citizens of the future. They exemplify how self-regulated learning is relevant to becoming multiliterate and developing the ability to produce and consume multimodal texts. Self-regulated learning is sometimes referred to as metacognition, which was the focus of a large body of research in the late 20th century. The research focussed upon developing strategies that would help readers when engaging with paper texts, but the general principles and many of the strategies developed are still relevant and able to be applied to both the consumption and production of multimodal texts.

Paris et al. (1984) suggested that three kinds of metacognitive knowledge needed to be taught. They can be summarised as four ways of knowing:

- Knowing *that*: knowing a range of metacognitive strategies
- Knowing *how*: knowing how to use the strategies
- Knowing *when*: knowing the best strategy to use to achieve a specific purpose in a particular situation and at a particular time
- Knowing *why*: knowing why the strategy selected is the best one to use.

These ways of knowing can be used to prompt questions and strategies to aid self-monitoring during all aspects of design and redesign, from decisions about purpose and audience to selecting appropriate resources and synthesising them into a new design.

Anstey and Bull (2018) stated that in order to develop and apply metacognitive strategies, it was also necessary to have a metalanguage to talk about and investigate all aspects of text, not just the linguistic. Therefore, teachers and students need to develop a metalanguage for identifying, developing understandings and talking about:

- The codes and conventions of the semiotic systems
- The thinking processes involved in the consumption and production of text
- The structure of text
- Describing and navigating online text
- The technologies associated with producing and consuming text.

(Anstey & Bull, 2018, p. 98)

THEORY INTO PRACTICE 3.1

- The purpose of this Theory into Practice strategy is to use the four ways of knowing and the identification of appropriate metalanguage to plan for modelling and providing metacognitive strategies in a literacy lesson.
- You may wish to audiotape any of the lessons you teach from this Theory into Practice activity for future reference and analysis.
- Choose a lesson where you are going to teach a particular strategy for either consuming a text or producing a text – not both. For example brainstorming as a strategy that might be used when producing a text, including different ways of representing ideas, such as diagrams or word clouds.
- Before you start planning, use the four ways of knowing to unpack what you need to teach and model about this strategy and its use, together with the appropriate metalanguage.
- The following questions that have been developed around brainstorming as a strategy might aid your planning:
    - Knowing *what*: What do students need to know about brainstorming? How would you define it?
    - Knowing *how*: What do students need to know about how to brainstorm? How do you think when you brainstorm? Do you think differently to when you are doing other tasks? What questions might you ask yourself? Do you accept anything you think of? How do you decide what to keep and what to discard in the brainstorm? Do you always write or draw (represent) a brainstorm the same way? Why would you do it different ways?
    - Knowing *when*: When might you use brainstorming? At what stages of producing a text might it be helpful? Would you use it and represent it the same way at all stages? Why or why not?
    - Knowing *why*? How do you tell whether a brainstorm is a good strategy to use, how to think during the brainstorm and how to represent it? Can you present a justification for your choice?
- Having answered those questions, examine the metalanguage or terminology that is often repeated in your answers. If you have used synonyms to describe the same knowledge, skill or process, then identify the correct metalanguage (terminology) and plan to be consistent in its use, rather than confusing students by using many words to describe the same knowledge, skill or process.
- Look at your answers and consider how you might need to sequence the lesson and whether it might need to be a series of lessons taught over time.
- Think about other curriculum areas or situations in which brainstorming might be used so you can give examples relevant to students' current school world and lifeworld experiences.
- Think about how to involve students during the lesson(s) to ensure they not only see the process modelled, but trial parts of it themselves and investigate some of the different ideas and strategies you present in authentic contexts and with authentic texts.
- Teach your lesson(s) and think about whether using the four ways of knowing and focussing on correct and consistent use of metalanguage during your planning assisted your teaching, and if so, how.

The concepts of metacognition and metalanguage are discussed further in Chapters Five and Six during in-depth investigation of the consumption and production processes. However, for foundational information about metacognition and metalanguage, including examples of their application to investigating text, see Chapter Three in the complementary volume *Foundations of Multiliteracies: Reading, Writing and Talking in the 21st Century.*

The semiotic systems, their codes and conventions

As has been discussed, the semiotic systems and their codes and conventions are socially and culturally derived and will continue to change. At present, there is debate regarding whether there are more than five semiotic systems. This debate centres around the five senses – sight, taste, smell, hearing and touch – and whether these are discrete semiotic systems that have their own codes and conventions. Anstey and Bull believe that sight and hearing are already accounted for in the linguistic, visual and audio semiotic systems. However, Kalantzis et al. (2016, pp.230-233) do not include the linguistic as a single semiotic system in their modes of meaning. They refer to oral meaning and written meaning, which relate specifically to the written and spoken manifestation of the linguistic semiotic system. Anstey and Bull would argue that the linguistic semiotic system, in combination with codes related to speech in the audio system, can account for the representation of meaning in both written and oral language. Kalantzis et al. (2016) limit their definition of the audio mode of meaning to music, ambient sounds and noises. This seems an unnecessary limitation, as the inclusion of those audio codes and conventions related to speech (some of which, such as **volume**, **pitch** and **pace**, are common to music, ambient sounds and noises) accounts for spoken aspects of language without creating a separate semiotic system or mode of oral and written meaning.

There is quite widespread debate regarding taste, smell and touch. Kalantzis et al. (2016, p.379) suggested that the bodily sensations of touch, taste and smell be incorporated into the tactile mode of meaning. They suggested that tactile meanings add to the linguistic meaning of words by adding 'metaphorical powers' that indicate or initiate feelings. Regarding taste, at present there is limited technology used in paper, live or digital texts that can literally create taste as part of the text. Therefore, Anstey and Bull would argue that the semantic meaning of the words about taste – for example sweet, sour or bitter – activate memories and associated feelings around those sensations, which may add further meaning. It is the linguistic meaning that activates the memory and emotion, not the actual sensory experience of taste.

Some paper texts already incorporate 'scratch and smell' factors (for example books and advertising), and different qualities of paper have a particular smell (for example glossy paper) and may be specifically chosen during the publication process to add that sensation as part of the text. Some public spaces such as entrance foyers to hotels are also 'perfumed' using various forms of technology. Advances in technology mean that in some situations smell and touch can be incorporated into live texts, such as performances. Smoke machines and other technologies can disperse a smell into the audience at particular points in the performance. However, in all these examples of smell and taste being added to text, the question that needs to be asked is: at this point in time, are there generally agreed social and cultural codes and conventions around smell and taste that would lead to the representation of meaning, or do smell and taste simply activate individual memories and associations and provide an additional sensory experience?

The issue of touch has been debated by a number of authors and is perhaps at present the sense around which technology and use has developed so far that its identification as a semiotic system should be carefully considered. It is sometimes referred to as the Haptic Semiotic System. Bezemer and Kress (2014, 2016) provided a thorough investigation of the ways in which touch manifests as a possible meaning making system. The first point they made was that touch operated as a mode of meaning for a small but very specific group of people who are both visually and hearing impaired. This group communicates through tactile signing, where the sender of meaning communicates with the receiver by placing their hand over the receiver's hand and conveys meaning through touch and movement. In this situation, there is an agreed set of codes and conventions that conveys meaning (Bezemer & Kress, 2014, p. 77). Kalantzis et al. (2016) made a similar point regarding touch and the use of Braille for those that have a visual impairment. The question Bezemer and Kress (2014, 2016) asked is whether touch has developed as a semiotic system or mode, with codes and conventions. That is, has it moved beyond a semiotic resource that can be used among a small group with particular physiological characteristics? They firstly discussed how touch technology has activated discussion about touch as a semiotic system. For example, people use iPads, smartphones and other touch-activated technologies to find information, view images and film, use games and so forth. However, in this case touch is simply used to activate a text that has been designed and disseminated through technology. The text or design that has been accessed through touch incorporates a range of semiotic systems that provide meaning through their codes and conventions. Touch in this sense provides access; it is not a semiotic system (Bezemer & Kress, 2016, pp. 124–125).

However, there are technologies available that simulate touch including a 'tele-shake' remote handshake and the simulation of touch through a touch screen used by the 'toucher' and sensors attached to the person being 'touched'. Bezemer and Kress (2016, p. 125) discussed specific examples of these technologies and an experiment in which people in an audience listening to a story wore an armband that provided different forms of touch at particular moments in the story. This is similar to the previously discussed example of disseminating a smell at specific points in a live performance. Bezemer and Kress concluded that in these situations there is potential for using touch as a form of meaning making when constructing a text, but at present the technology and use is not widespread enough to warrant a new semiotic system.

Two further examples Bezemer and Kress (2014, 2016) used were about touch as a communication system in teaching. They conducted research with surgeons teaching medical students (Bezemer & Kress, 2014, pp. 80–83). Their research identified two ways in which touch was used in this situation. In one situation, described as 'communicating touch', a surgeon identified body parts by touching and naming them (liver, pancreas) and sometimes provided additional oral information. The medical student was not touched, nor was the medical student engaged in touch. The student simply observed what was being touched and listened to the information provided orally. Once again, touch was used to identify, but the main communication was provided by the accompanying oral (linguistic) explanation. Another example was 'exhibiting touch', where a medical student was invited to touch a lump on a patient. The surgeon then implicitly modelled the actual touching of the lump through grasping and pulling, demonstrating the depth of the touch and the angle of the hand of the surgeon when touching. No oral (linguistic) information was provided about the implicitly modelled touching by the surgeon. Instead, while touching, the surgeon simultaneously provided additional oral information about the patient obtained from other sources, such as scans and interviews with the patient.

Bezemer and Kress (2014) conclude that there is no doubt that touch can convey meaning, however they question at this point in time whether it has status as a mode. They believe that there needs to be more precise discussion and exploration of the use of touch and the ways in which it is used to convey meaning before this can happen.

> We might ask what needs, what occasions, in what ways, under what conditions, in what communities, will lead to the use of the materiality of touch, as an 'available' resource to be drawn into semiosis, and lead to the development of the mode of touch.
>
> (Bezemer & Kress, 2014, p. 85)

Given the preceding discussion regarding the development and recognition of the five senses as semiotic systems, Anstey and Bull believe it is appropriate to limit the exploration of the semiotic systems to the five previously identified: visual, linguistic, auditory, gestural and spatial.

Designing and meaning making with the codes and conventions of the semiotic systems

The five semiotic systems are some of the major resources that will be drawn upon when producing or consuming a multimodal text. The selection and use of them will be based upon the consumers' or producers' purpose; the audience for which the text was produced; the context in which it is, or will be, used; and the technology by which it will be delivered. The codes and conventions can be combined and used in particular ways to generate meaning in a multimodal text. The more students understand about the ways in which codes are brought together as signifiers of meaning in the design of a multimodal text, the more effectively they can consume or produce a text to achieve their purpose. Therefore, when introducing the codes and conventions of the semiotic systems to students it is important to provide opportunities for them to use the inquiry process to investigate how the semiotic systems, together with their codes and conventions and other resources, have been selected and combined to convey meaning in a variety of texts. In order to do this, students need to understand some basic concepts about multimodal texts and develop a metalanguage about multimodal texts in order to communicate and discuss their findings.

In order to provide a framework that might be used to guide the planning of learning episodes in which students investigate how decisions might be made about combining resources to communicate particular meanings, five concepts about multimodal texts will now be explored.

Concept One: Multimodal texts convey meaning through a combination of **meaning making elements** that draw upon several semiotic systems.

When a text draws upon two or more semiotic systems (that is the linguistic, visual, gestural, audio and spatial) in order to convey meaning, it is defined as multimodal. Examples of multimodal texts are a live ballet performance in which elements of meaning are conveyed through the use of gestural, audio and spatial semiotic systems; a picture book in which the elements of meaning are conveyed through the visual and linguistic semiotic systems; and the home page of a website in which elements of meaning are conveyed through the audio, linguistic and visual semiotic systems. All these texts are multimodal, that is they comprise a number of elements of meaning that draw upon a range of semiotic systems. Each may be delivered via different, or sometimes multiple, technologies, that is live (the ballet, and the picture book if performed as a live play), paper (the picture book) or digital (the website, the picture book as eBook, the ballet as film).

REFLECTION STRATEGY 3.2

- The purpose of this strategy and Reflection Strategies 3.4 to 3.5 is to reflect upon the five concepts about multimodal text that will be introduced by comparing two multimodal texts on the same topic, but delivered via different technology. Advertisements have been chosen as the text type because they are easily accessed and are presented via a range of technologies, even live. (For example, companies have been known to place people on public transport using a particular brand of mobile phone and then talk loudly about the phone, extolling its virtues to someone they are supposedly talking to, as an early form of an advertising campaign to get brand-name attention.) Advertising is also a text type that is designed to persuade, and therefore decisions made about selecting meaning making elements, semiotic resources and specific codes and conventions may be more easily identified. Advertising is also a good vehicle for developing critical literacy skills when considering why particular decisions about these selections might be made during the design process and how they are selected and combined to have impact on particular audiences and contexts.
- Obtain copies of two advertisements for the same item (preferably for the same product), for example shampoo, deodorant, drinks, frozen meals or junk food. One advertisement should be on paper (e.g. magazine, newspaper or advertising billboard) and one should be retrieved from television or the internet. Both should be in a format that can be explored a number of times, for example the digital electronic advertisement should be able to be viewed with and without sound, paused and played in slow motion. It may also be necessary to reproduce the paper advertisement on an A4 page in full colour to facilitate detailed investigation over time. A useful source for finding advertisements is the website www.bestadsontv.com which showcases TV, print, audio and interactive advertisements that can be viewed free of charge and downloaded for a small fee. QR Code 3.1 provides a link to the site.

QR Code 3.1 Best Ads on TV (www.bestadsontv.com)

- Analyse the two advertisements you have chosen and identify the specific meaning making elements they use and the semiotics systems present. Use the headings provided in the sample analysis of car advertisements in Table 3.1.
- Identify common and different meaning making elements and semiotic systems used across the two advertisements. Think about and try to identify possible reasons for the selection of common or different meaning making elements and semiotic systems.
- Consider how the use of a particular technology (paper or digital) has afforded the advertiser different options in terms of producing and delivering a message about this product. Think about the implications of choice of technology when consuming or producing multimodal texts.

Table 3.1 Sample analysis

Type of Text	Meaning Making Elements	Semiotic Systems
Billboard advertisement for small hatchback sedan	Image of car Young people surrounding it and gazing at it admiringly Caption identifying brand and model Phrase describing car Logo of brand	Visual Visual, gestural, spatial Linguistic Linguistic Visual
TV advertisement for small hatchback sedan	Sound effects Pop music Inaudible conversation and gasps from people Voice-over Sequence of images of car being driven by young attractive female through the restaurant and entertainment area of a city Groups of people looking at parked car and commenting Caption identifying brand and model Logo of brand	Audio Audio Audio and linguistic (however linguistic is inaudible) Audio and linguistic Visual, gestural, spatial Visual, gestural, spatial Linguistic Visual

Concept Two: Multimodal texts draw upon and cross the boundaries of the Arts (the disciplines of Art, Media Studies and the Performance Arts – Music, Drama and Dance), their knowledge, understandings and processes.

When explaining Concept One, three examples of multimodal text were described: a ballet, a picture book and the home page of a website. These three examples, and multimodal texts generally, often cross the boundaries between the disciplines of art, performance and design (Kress & van Leeuwen, 2001, p. 1). The ballet draws upon Performance Arts (Music); the picture book, if delivered by paper, draws on Art; and the website may draw on Art, Music and Media Studies, depending upon its content, purpose and audience. The role of the disciplines of the Arts and how they might be drawn upon in the production of multimodal texts is discussed further in Chapter Five of the complementary volume *Foundations of Multiliteracies: Reading, Writing and Talking in the 21st Century*. Proficient users or producers of multimodal texts need the knowledge and ability to move across and between the boundaries of other disciplines, accessing and using the knowledge and processes they afford to make and communicate meaning. Therefore, when designing learning episodes that facilitate students' inquiry into multimodal texts, planning should include explicit teaching that draws attention to, models and demonstrates drawing upon knowledge from other disciplines.

REFLECTION STRATEGY 3.3

- The purpose of this Reflection Strategy is to investigate how some multimodal texts, such as a ballet performance, draw upon the Arts, as well as several semiotic systems. Use QR Codes 3.2 and 3.3 to access two contrasting ballet performances, view them and then select one to examine further.

QR Code 3.2 Modern ballet performance (www.youtube.com/watch?v=9IOBglx2X3I)

QR Code 3.3 Traditional ballet performance (www.youtube.com/watch?v=n8CUDVpkGk4)

- Identify the semiotic systems present and any codes or conventions you already know and recognise being used. Do any of these semiotic systems share codes and conventions with other disciplines? For example, the gestural semiotic system shares gesture, **facial expression** and **appearance** (costume, make-up, hairstyle and props) with Dance and Drama.
- As both performances have been filmed, the visual semiotic system has been used (e.g. **framing** – close up, long shot and point of view: top down, bottom up). Does film draw upon any of the disciplines in the Arts? If so, what does it draw upon and how is this knowledge used in the filming of these ballet performances?
- In Dance, specific choreographic elements such as time, space, dynamics and relationships are explored and developed. Do these have anything in common with any of the semiotic systems?
- Specific technical skills are necessary in Dance – strength, control, balance, co-ordination, flexibility and endurance. How might these technical skills draw upon or cross over into other disciplines?
- How has the use of the semiotic systems, together with any prior knowledge or experience you have with the Arts or specifically, ballet, contributed to your meaning making and interpretation of what is happening (e.g. the story and characters) in the ballet?
- Consider how your exploration and analysis of the ballet, the semiotic systems and other contributing disciplines, together with your prior knowledge and experience (your literacy identity) has contributed to your meaning making and understanding of how multimodal texts work. How might you use these findings and understandings in your planning and teaching about multimodal texts?

REFLECTION STRATEGY 3.4

The purpose of this Reflection Strategy is to re-examine the two advertisements you have chosen to analyse for this series of Reflection Strategies in terms of how decisions about meaning making during their production may have drawn on the Arts.

- Identify if and how any areas of the Arts (Art, Media Studies and the Performance Arts – Music, Drama and Dance) may have been drawn upon in the production of these advertisements.
- Identify similarities and differences between the two advertisements in terms of the areas they draw upon and how they used them.
- Think about why these differences occurred and identify possible reasons.
- Identify how the similarities or differences do (or do not) contribute to the success of each advertisement.

Concept Three: The role of language in multimodal text varies; it is not always the dominant semiotic system present.

The fact that multimodal texts combine elements, semiotic systems and cross disciplines means that language (the linguistic semiotic system), which has for so long dominated meaning making, is now only one part of it (Jewitt & Kress, 2008, p. 3). In the three examples previously provided, one (the ballet) does not use language at all; the picture book may foreground the image over the words (language); and the home page website design may foreground images and symbols to capture the consumers' attention initially before engaging with the less obvious linguistic elements. Consequently, to engage productively with multimodal texts, proficient consumers or producers must not only be competent in the linguistic mode but with all modes and their semiotic systems. In addition, they need to be cognizant of how they differentiate their attention among the semiotics systems present. The consumer should identify the dominant semiotic system in a text in order to make decisions about where to focus attention when consuming the text. The consumer needs to attend to the parts which best address the purpose of their consumption at the time. Conversely, if producing a text the producer must decide which semiotic system should be dominant in order to best fulfil the purpose of the text and suit the characteristics of the audience. These decisions will also be influenced by the context in which the text is produced or consumed and the available technologies.

REFLECTION STRATEGY 3.5

- The purpose of this Reflection Strategy is to identify the dominant semiotic system in each of the two advertisements you have been analysing.
- Which meaning making elements and semiotic systems are dominant in each advertisement, and why do you think this is so?
- In the digital advertisement, does the dominant semiotic system change as the advertisement progresses? If it does, where does this occur in the advertisement (beginning, middle, end or some other point)? Why do you think the change does or does not happen?

Concept Four: In a multimodal text, meaning is distributed across all elements (parts) and each element has a role in contributing to the overall (whole) meaning of the text.

Understanding the part–whole concept of multimodal texts means understanding that meaning is distributed across all meaning making elements present in a multimodal text and that each element has a specific role or function in contributing to the overall meaning of the text. Kress and van Leeuwen (2001, p. 20) pointed out that these roles might be:

- **Complementary**: for example in a picture book, where the picture shows a child's bedroom but the words lead the consumer to look at the bedroom in a particular way.
- **Reinforcing**: for example in a ballet, when music and gesture both signify the same emotion.
- **Hierarchical**: for example at another point in the ballet, when the music fades and the action on the stage becomes the dominant signifier of meaning and the music is secondary.

It is also possible for meaning making elements to be **oppositional**, that is they have different meanings that are in opposition to or contradict one another, for example where the words imply one meaning but the image implies another, possibly opposite meaning. *Oppositional meaning making* is used less often, and therefore when it is used it is more noticeable and compelling as a device. The dissonance between the meaning making elements can be used to draw attention to something or create humour.

Proficient producers and consumers of multimodal text need to be able to identify how each **meaning making element**, semiotic system, code and convention is contributing to the overall meaning in order to engage critically with a text. Producers of multimodal texts need to be able to make informed decisions about how the role or function of each part in a multimodal text will contribute to achieving their communicative purpose.

REFLECTION STRATEGY 3.6

- The purpose of this Reflection Strategy is to use the table commenced when analysing the chosen advertisements after reading Concept One, as a basis for further review and analysis.
- Once an initial examination has been completed, identify whether any of these roles are *complementary, reinforcing, hierarchical* or *oppositional*. The example in Table 3.1 has been elaborated in Table 3.2 to demonstrate how such an analysis or reflection can refine understanding of the purpose of the text and conversely inform production of a text. In the initial analysis of the example in Table 3.1, the goal of the advertisement was clearly to showcase a car and encourage people to buy it. However, analysis of the role of each meaning making element and the specific contributions of the semiotic systems, codes and conventions revealed a more specific and refined idea of the purpose and audience of the text. It was directed very specifically at young, image-conscious females. In other words, the analysis of the roles of the meaning making elements, semiotic systems and codes and conventions (the parts) showed how some meanings were being augmented or reinforced by the way each part, semiotic system and code contributes to one (whole or overall) message. This type of analysis can also be a very useful tool for engaging in critical literacy.

Table 3.2 Elaborated sample analysis

Type of Text	Meaning Making Elements (Part)	Role of Elements	Semiotic Systems Used in Element	Contribution of Specific Codes and Conventions to Role of Element and Overall Meaning of Text (Whole)
Billboard advertisement for small hatchback sedan	Image of car	Display product	Visual	*Colour* of car is popular among young female drivers
	Young people surround car and gaze admiringly	Indicate that product is popular with the young	Visual, gestural, spatial	*Gaze* and *body position* of young is towards car, *facial expressions* indicate admiration and envy
	Caption identifies brand and model	Imprint brand memory	Linguistic	*Font, colour* and *size* have young, female appeal, *placement* across top *frames* image
	Phrase describes car	Reinforce brand memory	Linguistic	Placed at bottom with linear art completing *frame* of image and *leading* to logo
	Logo of brand		Visual	Prominent *bottom right* for memory
TV advertisement for small hatchback sedan	Sound effects	Enhances display of visual features of car	Audio	*Quality of sound* (purring throaty exhaust) attracts attention, indicates power but is not masculine
	Pop music	Engages potential purchasers of car	Audio	*Style of music* most popular with young females at present
	Inaudible conversation and gasps from people	Indicates popular appeal through sound	Audio and linguistic (however linguistic is inaudible)	Although the words are inaudible, the *pitch, pause and intonation* indicate admiration
	Voice-over	Audio identifies features of car unable to be shown visually and reinforces brand and model name	Audio and linguistic	Young female voice *pitch, pace, pause and intonation* indicating enthusiasm
		Indicates locations, contexts and segment of population to which car is suited		
	Sequence of images of car being driven by young attractive female in restaurant and entertainment area of a city	Visually reinforces popular appeal	Visual, gestural, spatial	*Camera angles* show off car's visual appeal, *wide angles* and *top-down shots* stress attractive locations and ease of steering through city
	Groups of young people looking at car	Visually reinforces brand and model memory	Visual, gestural, spatial	The camera zooms in on young female, then *follows their gaze* to features of car
	Caption identifying brand and model		Linguistic	*Font, colour* and *size* have young, female appeal, *placement* at beginning and end of advertisement sequence *frames* images and reinforces brand and model memory
	Logo of brand		Visual	*Placement* at beginning and end of advertisement sequence *frames* images and reinforces memory of brand and model

- Having completed an analysis of the role of the meaning making elements, semiotic systems and any known codes or conventions in contributing to the overall meaning of the texts, analyse the role of them in relation to one another. For example, identify the semiotic systems that are providing complementary, reinforcing, hierarchical or oppositional meanings. In the sample analysis provided in Table 3.2 it can be seen that while all semiotic systems fulfilled a reinforcing role, different combinations reinforced different meanings or messages. For example, the visual, audio, spatial and gestural semiotic systems all contributed meaning making elements that focussed on appeal to young females. The visual, audio, spatial, gestural and linguistic all contributed meaning making elements that reinforced car features. Only the visual and linguistic contributed elements that reinforced branding.
- When analyses have been completed, think about *why* particular meaning making elements and semiotic systems have been chosen by the producers of the texts to reinforce particular messages.

Concept Five: The codes and conventions of the semiotic systems in a multimodal text can be used to identify the relative importance of meaning making elements and provide coherence throughout the text.

Understanding the ways in which a multimodal text may have been constructed to provide clues as to what to attend to and how to move through the text is essential to the consumption and production of text. Previously, in a written text this might have been referred to as 'identifying a reading path', but such a description focusses more on the linguistic semiotic system. When engaging with a multimodal text where multiple meaning making elements and semiotic systems vie for the consumers' attention, it is more appropriate to think in terms of where attention should be directed and how to move through the text. There are two strategies that can be used to think about and describe this process: looking for codes and their associated conventions that indicate **salience** or importance among meaning making elements, and looking for codes and their associated conventions that provide coherence and cohesion throughout the text. Choosing how to use these strategies to focus attention and move through a text will also be directed by the purpose of engaging with or producing the text, the technology of delivery, the audience and the context in which it is to be used. As the codes and conventions of the semiotic systems are socially and culturally derived, attention to audience and context will be particularly important.

Within each semiotic system, codes and conventions can be used to draw attention to particular meaning making elements indicating *salience* or importance. For example, a bright colour in an image can immediately draw attention to a meaning making element. Similarly, codes and conventions can be employed to provide coherence throughout a text by linking elements or indicating the appropriate sequence for engaging with them. The most familiar is in the linguistic text, where conjunctions such as 'and' can indicate elements are linked and need to be thought about together, while 'but' indicates that something to follow may be an exception, qualifying information or an opposing view.

The concept of *coherence* and *cohesion* is also influenced by the text type and sometimes the technology of delivery. Cohesion or coherence may be space based, for example where relationships among meaning making elements are indicated by their layout or position in an image, diagram or a three-dimensional setting, such as a scene on the stage of a play. **Cohesion and coherence** may also be time based or chronological, for example using meaning making elements such as light to indicate the time of day to show the sequence of events in a narrative in images in a book or scenes in a film. Table 3.3 provides examples of how codes and conventions in each of the semiotic systems might provide salience or cohesion.

Understanding the five concepts about multimodal text can assist in working out how to process a multimodal text when consuming it and can also inform the decision-making processes when producing a multimodal text. Bearne (2009, pp. 163–165), Walsh (2006, p. 32) and Bull and Anstey (2010a, p. 30)

Table 3.3 Examples of the use of codes to achieve salience or coherence in a text

Semiotic System	Sample Code	Example of How Salience Might Be Achieved With This Code and Its Associated Convention	Example of How Coherence Might Be Achieved Through a Convention Associated With This Code
Linguistic	conjunction	The use of a positive conjunction like 'and' suggests an additional point is to follow, while the use of a negative conjunction like 'but' indicates alternative or qualifying information follows. This indicates to the reader the relative importance or type of information to follow.	Continued use of appropriate conjunctions facilitates the sequential development of information supporting an argument.
Visual	colour	Use a bright colour to attract attention to an object.	Repetitive use of colour to lead the eye to critical points in the image.
Audio	pause	A pause (sudden silence) in an oration indicates to the listener that something important is to follow.	Regular pauses in an oration allow **phrasing** and control of the flow of information in order to aid the listener's understanding.
Gestural	body position	If the body position of one participant is completely different to all others, then attention is drawn to that person, indicating they are significant.	Repetitive use of a particular body position at key points in a narrative reinforces aspects of character.
Spatial	proximity	If objects or people are placed in front of other objects or people, or in the foreground, this indicates importance.	Continued use of the same placement of character or object develops and reinforces understandings of the role of this object or character in the performance.

offered suggestions regarding the way in which a consumer or producer can identify or create a path through a text. Kress (2003, p.160) suggested that because of the complexity of a multimodal text there is a need to apply criteria of relevance when approaching the text, and that the criteria would be related to purpose in consuming or producing it. This would involve using metacognitive strategies such as a set of questions to think about when first approaching a text. Table 3.4 provides a sample set of questions that draw upon the work of Bearne (2009), Walsh (2006), Kress (2003), Bull and Anstey (2010a) and the five concepts about multimodal texts that have been introduced in the preceding paragraphs.

Further exploration of the codes and conventions of the five semiotic systems

In the following sections, three types of information are presented for each semiotic system. The first is a summary and definition of the main codes and conventions for each semiotic system. Following this are examples of the codes of each semiotic system, the functions or roles they might fulfil or contribute to the meaning of a multimodal text and how these roles might be realised in a text. There are also examples of commonly used conventions that indicate salience and facilitate cohesion among the elements of a text. It must be recognised that the information provided about each semiotic system, while comprehensive, is not meant to be definitive as it is socially and culturally derived and subject to change. The final part of this section provides a suggested sequence for introducing the codes and conventions of all five semiotic systems, based on the work of Anstey and Bull (2011a). Once again, this sequence should not be regarded as definitive.

Table 3.4 Metacognitive prompts for approaching the production or consumption of a multimodal text

Metacognitive Prompts	Notes/Reflections/Thoughts
1. What is my purpose or goal in producing or consuming this text? • How will this influence my approach to the text and the following questions?	
2. What do I know about the audience and context? • How will this influence my approach to the text and the following questions?	
3. What is the technology of delivery and how does this influence the text? • How it will be produced or consumed?	
4. What meaning making elements are present? • Are they complementary, reinforcing, hierarchical or oppositional?	
5. Is the text space based or time based? • How does that influence the way I approach the text and interact with it?	
6. What semiotic systems are present? • Which are dominant? • Given my purpose, which are likely to be most helpful?	
7. Are there codes and conventions that provide salience among the meaning making elements? • Given my purpose, how should I use them?	
8. Are there codes and conventions that provide cohesion and coherence among the meaning making elements? • Given my purpose, how should I use them?	
9. Given my responses to the preceding questions and examination of the text: • How should I approach the text? • What should I attend to? • What should I ignore? • What path should I follow?	

REFLECTION STRATEGY 3.7

- The purpose of this Reflection Strategy is to apply the questions in Table 3.6 to a range of text types, delivered by a range of technologies, and consider how this might inform the way you approach planning for teaching and learning about multimodal texts.
- Identify at least three multimodal texts that constitute different text types (e.g. report, explanation, narrative), have different purposes (e.g. to inform, persuade, or entertain) and are delivered via different technologies.
- Use Table 3.4 to preview the texts before engaging with them, making notes or reflective comments in the second column.
- Review your notes and consider how it informs the way you would then go about approaching the texts when you engage fully with them in order to achieve your identified purpose (e.g. to learn about a historical event or a scientific process, or to be entertained).
- Identify any differences or similarities in how you responded to the questions for each text type. Did these similarities or differences relate to the text type, the technology, the purpose of engagement with the text or any of the five understandings about text or other aspects of the text? What do the similarities and differences tell you about previewing a text in this way? How do they inform your engagement with the text?
- Having completed your analyses and refection, how might you change the way in which you talk about engaging with multimodal texts in the future?
- What do students need to know and be able to do when engaging with multimodal text?

The Linguistic Semiotic System

The Linguistic Semiotic System is the one which is most familiar and therefore it has been used to introduce the examination of the codes and conventions of the semiotic systems. It consists of the semantics and syntax of language and includes such vocabulary items as nouns, verbs, adjectives, pronouns, and compositional items such as punctuation, phrases, clauses, sentences, paragraphs, generic structure and chapters. All of these items form a grammar of the linguistic semiotic system which can be used to design (consume or produce) a linguistic text. A summary and set of definitions for the main codes and conventions of the linguistic semiotic system has not been provided in this chapter or the glossary. This is because this information is already known to readers and, unlike the other semiotic systems, can be easily accessed and confirmed in school English and literacy programs and state curriculum documents. A suggested sequence for introducing metalanguage to describe the codes and conventions for all five semiotic system across all school years is presented in Table 3.15. It includes a set of codes and conventions for the linguistic semiotic system and a sequence for their introduction, based upon, but not the same as, the scope and sequence of the Language Strand of the Australian Curriculum English (2015). Readers should use this sequence for the linguistic semiotic system in consultation with the relevant English language curriculum of their system. Table 3.5 presents examples that illustrate how salience and cohesion might be achieved with the codes and conventions of the linguistic semiotic system when consuming or producing a text.

Table 3.5 Examples for achieving salience and cohesion with the codes and conventions of the linguistic semiotic system

Codes and Conventions	Possible Functions or Roles	How Salience Might Be Achieved With This Code	How Cohesion Might Be Developed With This Code
Vocabulary Items: Parts of speech			
Noun/pronoun	Naming/identifying person, animal, place or thing in the text	By repeating the name (noun) rather than replacing with the pronoun foregrounds it, indicating importance.	Ensuring that nouns and pronouns are close to each other makes strong links throughout the text and avoids confusion.
Verb	Indicates action or process	Use a series of synonyms to emphasise the action or process being carried out.	Use the same verb for the action every time to avoid confusion about what is taking place and keep the verb close to the noun to which it is referring.
Adjective	Describes nouns	Using a string of adjectives to describe a particular noun and only one for others indicates that particular noun is more important. By putting the adjective in an unusual place (after the noun rather than before, as other adjectives have been used), it foregrounds that adjective and the information it is providing. See Table 3.3.	Use the same adjective to qualify the noun every time to create links through the text and keep the adjective close to the noun it is qualifying.
Conjunction	See Table 3.3	See Table 3.3.	See Table 3.3.
Compositional Items: Punctuation			
• Quotation marks	Indicate direct speech	By choosing to use quotation marks and direct speech rather than simply reporting what someone said, you draw attention to what was said, indicating it is important.	Separates direct speech from indirect.
• Commas	Signify pause, indicate a list	Commas can be used to highlight a particular phrase by separating it from the rest of the text, thus drawing attention to that information.	Commas can be used to separate lists of or groups of words so that they form chains or chunks of texts that are linked. This makes the sentence easier to process.

(Continued)

Table 3.5 (Continued)

Codes and Conventions	Possible Functions or Roles	How Salience Might Be Achieved With This Code	How Cohesion Might Be Developed With This Code
Compositional Items: Phrases or clauses	Qualify nouns or modify verbs by providing further information	By choosing to use a phrase rather than a single adjective or adverb to qualify nouns or modify verbs, it draws attention to that noun or verb, indicating it is more important than others. The fact that more information is being provided in this way also indicates importance. NB: As stated previously, phrases and clauses can be separated using punctuation that, in combination with the phrase or clause, can achieve salience and/or cohesion.	The addition of phrases or clauses provides more information that aids the reader's or viewer's meaning making, thus adding coherence to the text.

REFLECTION STRATEGY 3.8

- The purpose of this Reflection Strategy is to further develop understandings of these codes and conventions and practice applying them to a familiar text. An additional purpose will be to investigate how effective the codes and conventions are in contributing to the achievement of the communicative purpose of the text.
- Choose a linguistic text that is part of a multimodal text currently being used in the class-room. It can be a paper or digital text. For this introductory strategy, a live text would be too difficult to analyse as this text will be used, where possible, to investigate the other semiotic systems as well.
- Preview the text using the questions 1 to 6 in Table 3.4.
- Identify any of linguistic codes and conventions present and consider the function they are performing in the text.
- Find any examples of the codes and conventions being used to achieve salience and identify how salience is achieved.
- Find any examples of the codes and conventions being used to achieve cohesion and identify how cohesion is achieved.
- Rewrite the linguistic part of the text using the linguistic codes and conventions in different ways, and evaluate the effectiveness or lack of effectiveness that is achieved through using the codes in different ways. For example, try using no pronouns, or substituting a phrase that performs an adjectival function with one adjective, or vice versa.

THEORY INTO PRACTICE 3.2

- The purpose of this Theory into Practice activity is to use the analyses of the linguistic part of the text to inform teaching around this text.
- Examine the planning that you have completed for teaching around the linguistic part of this text.
- Given your analyses, are there any codes and conventions of the linguistic part of the text with which your students are unfamiliar and will need to be addressed prior to or as part of the planning you have completed?
- Given your analyses, are there any aspects of this planning you would change, and if so, how?
- Examine the metalanguage that you planned to use in the lesson. Do you need to revise this?
- Complete any modifications to the lesson and teach it.
- Consider the effect of your planning revisions on how you actually conducted the lesson and your talk around text.

The Visual Semiotic System

The Visual Semiotic System draws on the work of semioticians such as Kress and van Leeuwen (2001, 2006) and Trifonas (1998), together with the literature of the disciplines of art and media studies, particularly film and photography.

While phrases, words and punctuation assist meaning making in the linguistic part of a multimodal text, codes and conventions such as colour, line, **texture**, viewpoint and position are used to denote meaning in the visual part of the text. As previously stated, these meanings are not universal and may be socially or culturally specific. However the effects of globalisation and digital technology, together with the availability of banks of images via the internet, mean that there are increasingly universal interpretations as certain codes and conventions become globally consumed and therefore 'normal' to all cultures. Kress and van Leeuwen (2006, p.266) suggested the visual semiotic system should be seen as a resource for designing rather than a rigid set of rules for application in an image.

The visual semiotic system is used in both still and moving images, and there are some codes and conventions that are unique to each and some that are common to both. A summary and definitions of the main codes and conventions of the visual semiotic system is provided in Table 3.6.

A suggested sequence for introducing metalanguage to describe the codes and conventions for all five semiotic systems, across all school years, is presented in Table 3.15. In Table 3.7, examples are provided of the functions the codes and conventions of the visual semiotic system might perform in a text together with an example of how they might be used to create salience and cohesion.

Table 3.6 Codes and conventions of the visual semiotic system

Codes and Conventions	Definitions and Descriptors
Colour: • Placement	• The placement of colours on the colour wheel effects how they can be used to create meaning. Colours that are close together (e.g. blue and green) are harmonious. Those colours that are on opposite sides of the colour wheel are discordant and therefore attract attention when placed close together in a text.
• Saturation	• Saturation refers to the purity or intensity of the colour. When other colours are added, it dilutes its intensity. For example, the addition of blue to red cools or darkens it, while the addition of yellow creates a warmer or lighter red. Different saturations can create different moods and emotions.
• Tone	• Tone refers to the amount of light (white) or dark (black) in a colour. If an image is all the same tone, the eye has nowhere to land or focus. Variation in tone can attract the eye to objects of importance.
• Media/Opacity/Transparency	• The use of different media, for example watercolour, gouache or colour software, can produce transparent colours (see-through) or opaque (dense). The use of transparent or opaque colour can engender mood or indicate the quality or make-up of what is begin depicted.
Texture	Texture provides a link between tactile memory and the object depicted. It activates the viewer's memory of the feel of that object. Texture can be created using paint, or other media in works of art and in photography hard focus and close-up camera work can provide scientific information about the texture of an object.

Codes and Conventions	Definitions and Descriptors

Line:
  • **Quality**
 	
  • **Type**
 	
  • **Actual or implied**
	• The quality of a line refers to how it is depicted, and can be achieved through the media or software employed and how the line is applied. A line may be thick, thin, heavy, light or hesitant, thus invoking a particular mood or quality to what is being depicted. In scientific drawings this is a particularly important way of portraying information about the object.
	• Lines may be vertical, horizontal, diagonal, jagged, curved, right-angled or forming a doorway. Each of these has significance in Western society. For example repeated vertical lines infer loneliness or isolation; jagged and diagonal lines infer discord or anger; while horizontal or curved lines infer calm or harmony.
	• Lines can be actual, but they can also be implied through repetition of colour or objects across a page or screen, thus drawing the eye or showing relationships. This is referred to as creating a **vector or vectorality**.

Shape
 	
  • **Symbols**
	Shape refers to the actual visual outline of an object and provides a way of identifying objects. An object is identified by comparing its shape to shapes previously experienced, identified and stored in the mind.
	  • Symbols are simplified shapes used to represent items in diagrams and figures or convey information in everyday settings.

Juxtaposition	Juxtaposition has to do with the boundaries of an object and its relation to others, how objects are arranged in relation to one another. It can denote relationships or mood.

Point of view:
 	
  • **Bird's-eye or top down**
 	
  • **Eye level**
 	
  • **Worm's-eye or bottom up**
	Point of view refers to where the consumer is positioned to view the scene or image. In moving images and photographs this can be achieved through the use of camera angle. In other images or diagrams this is achieved through the angle of view at which the consumer is positioned to view the meaning making elements in the image.
	  • Bird's-eye or top down positions the consumer above the scene or image looking down on it.
	  • Eye level positions the consumer at the same level as the participants in the scene.
	  • Worm's-eye or bottom up positions the consumer below the scene or image, looking up at it.

Framing
 	
  • **Cropping**
 	
  • Close-up, medium or long shot
	Framing can be real or implied by using elements in the image. It indicates whether elements in the image are connected or disconnected by placing them together in the frame or outside it. It provides the reader with clues about how to read the image and may infer a sequence between frames.
	  • Framing can determine what is available or not available to the reader/viewer. It can be achieved by cropping an image. This means that the consumer is provided with, or deprived of, certain information and thus focusses their attention and meaning making in a particular way.
	  • In a moving image, framing is achieved through the use of long, medium or close-up shots. Long shots provide information about setting or context; medium shots allow the viewer to see characters in relationship to one another, their actions and gestures. Close-up shots focus on details and tracing small movements and help to portray character development or emotions.

Focus	Focus refers to how the objects or participants are depicted in the scene or image. It can be achieved through the camera, software or application of media. Hard (or sharp) and soft focus can be used to direct the attention of the consumer, as the eye will choose to focus on hard- or sharp-focussed objects or characters over those in soft focus. Another use of focus is to depict mood, authority, character or emotion. For example, an item or person viewed in hard focus will be more authoritative, while soft focus can be used to denote fragility.

(Continued)

Table 3.6 (Continued)

Codes and Conventions	Definitions and Descriptors
Lighting	The absence, presence or degree of light can be used to denote mood, emotion, time of day or draw attention to items or characters in a scene or image. This can be achieved through the way in which lighting is used (e.g. soft, bright, subdued, dull, spotlighting). The direction from which light comes – side, top, bottom, front or back – can highlight or modify aspects of a scene, item or character and focus the consumer's attention on particular elements of meaning.

Editing
 	
• **Parallel cutting**
 	
• **Speed**
 	
• **Inserts**
 	
• **Pacing**
 	
• **Transitions**
	Editing refers to how the director puts together (edits) the scenes that have been shot in order to achieve his or her communicative objective.
	  • Parallel cutting refers to cutting backwards and forwards from one scene or character to another to depict simultaneous events and/or create increasing tension. It can also be achieved through the use of a split screen.
	  • Action can be presented at normal or real speed, sped up or in slow motion to create particular moods or draw attention to an aspect of a scene. For example, car chases are often sped up to increase the excitement and car accidents are slowed down to focus on the destruction.
	  • When a scene is added, which appears out of place or does not advance the plot, but later its relevance is revealed.
	  • The plot or information in a film can be presented at a fast or slow pace. Fast pace focusses on action whereas slow pace focusses on character development or detail. This is not to do with the speed of what is happening in a single scene; it is about the pace at which the whole narrative of the film unfolds in over time.
	  • This is the method of moving from one scene to another. This can be achieved by fading to black or white or one scene slowly dissolving into another. It is often related to pacing, where no transitions produce fast pacing and fades and dissolves produce slow-pacing. When there are no transitions and one scene abruptly changes to another, this often suggests chaos or confusion.

Table 3.7 Examples of how the codes and conventions of the visual semiotic system might be applied to perform a function and facilitate salience and cohesion

Codes and Conventions	Possible Functions or Roles	How Salience Might Be Achieved With This Code	How Cohesion Might Be Developed With This Code
Colour	Create mood or emotion, attract attention	Use a bright colour or light tone in an otherwise dark or dull image to attract attention to an aspect of the image that is important.	In a series of images where the seasons or time of day change, the palette or set of colours used in the image will change to indicate the passage of time to the consumer. This will help the consumer to link events and time in the text and so provide coherence.

Codes and Conventions	Possible Functions or Roles	How Salience Might Be Achieved With This Code	How Cohesion Might Be Developed With This Code
Line	Create mood, or emotion indicate character, show relationships, attract attention, direct the consumer's gaze or focus	The use of fine, halting and shaky lines, applied lightly to portray one character in contrast to others could depict frailty. The repeated use of line in this way in contrast to the depiction of other characters draws attention to this particular aspect of the character.	Lines that connect elements in a diagram can indicate relationships. The relative weight of the line can indicate the strength of the relationship (e.g. heavy indicates strong, fine indicates weak). The addition of arrows to lines in a diagram can indicate direction of a relationship or cause and effect. These uses of line aid the consumer in finding coherence between the elements in a diagram.
Juxtaposition	Shows relationships, relative importance, character or emotion	The placement of a particular character in front of another in every image in a sequence establishes the importance of that character or their dominance over other characters.	The juxtaposition of items in a diagram can indicate relationships, for example items grouped together can indicate they have something in common while being placed far apart can indicates the opposite. The repetition of this juxtaposition creates coherence.
Point of View	Positions the reader to view the scene or image in a particular way. Can promote empathy or create distance with the object and characters portrayed.	The selection of a bottom-up camera angle can emphasise important aspects of a character or item. For example, it can empower a character by making them appear tall and dominating.	A bird's-eye view of a setting can provide the consumer with an overall picture of all the elements and where they are placed. This means that when these elements are presented in other scenes, the consumer has a reference point to draw upon to make sense of that element in the overall setting. The bird's-eye view becomes a link for the consumer to help place other scenes in context. It aids coherence between scenes.
Framing	Shows connection and disconnection between items, information and characters, provides or excludes information from the consumer.	By framing a part of the scene and thus separating it from the rest, it focusses the consumer on particular information, characters or action, indicating importance.	A sequence of framed images on a screen or page can indicate the passage of time, thus creating coherence for the consumer when determining the sequencing of events.
Focus	Depicts mood or authority, directs attention	The use of hard focus for some characters and soft focus for others informs the consumer as to which character is most important at this point in time.	By using hard/sharp focus on the person whose action or dialogue is important and soft focus on the rest of the scene and consistently using this pattern of focus throughout the film, coherence can be created for the consumer as they will always know where to direct their attention.
Lighting	Creates mood, provides information about setting, draws attention	A spotlight or patch of bright light can draw attention to action that is happening in a scene or image, indicating its importance to the plot or meaning of the scene/image.	If the same lighting is used on a character throughout a film, then it creates a particular character who can be recognised through the whole film. This provides coherence though character development.

REFLECTION STRATEGY 3.9

- The purpose of this Reflection Strategy is to complete analytic tasks that will further develop understandings about some of the codes and conventions presented in Table 3.6. It is not possible to provide strategies for every code and convention, however after completing these tasks it should be possible to extrapolate ways of conducting your own personal investigations for the other codes and conventions. It is suggested that where possible when conducting analyses, copies of the text should be annotated and kept for future reference (in both digital and paper form), building up your own personal repertoire of resources. This Reflection Strategy is expected to be conducted over an extended period of time.

- Colour: Use QR Code 3.4 to link to a colour theory website that commences with details of the colour wheel and characteristics of colour, and then explore the section on colour and marketing.

  o Try to find examples of the ways in which colour can be used to enhance meaning making in texts in everyday multimodal texts such as brochures, websites, advertising, magazines and newspapers (paper and digital). Find examples in paper and digital texts, and if you attend a live performance, think about how colour has been used to add meaning there as well. Annotate the examples and keep them for future reference, for example when planning lessons.

  o Once you have completed this task, reflect upon how aware you were of the ways in which colour might be used prior to this and whether the analyses you completed have made you a more critical user of multimodal texts.

QR Code 3.4 Colour theory website (www.colormatters.com/color-and-design/basic-color-theory)

- Line: Investigate how line has been used in the illustrations of picture books. Try to find examples of:

  o Actual or implied vectors that lead the eye to meaning making elements.

  o Different types of line.

  o The use of different media applied in different ways in order to contribute to the quality of the line and therefore add meaning to the element portrayed. Annotate and keep analyses.

  o QR Code 3.5 provides a link to illustrator Shaun Tan's website. Click on 'picture books' and scroll down to the cover of the book called *Memorial* (Crew & Tan, 1999). Examine the second illustration, depicting an elderly soldier. This is an excellent example of the use of line to create character. Tan has selected the medium and used the quality of the line to create the frail elderly character. Read Shaun Tan's comments to find out more about how he designed the illustrations.

QR Code 3.5 Shaun Tan's website (www.shauntan.net/)

- Find examples of the use of actual or implied vectors that lead the eye to meaning making elements, different types of line and different qualities of line in scientific drawings, or images such as photographs, diagrams and figures in other non-fiction multimodal texts. Identify how they add meaning to the element represented. QR Code 3.6 provides some images to begin analyses, but other authentic examples in context (i.e. in a full non-fiction multimodal text) should also be found, analysed, annotated and kept for future reference.

QR Code 3.6 Scientific images
(www.google.com.au/search?q=Scientific+drawing&client=firefox-b&dcr=0&tbm=isch&imgil=
CAHjf_h1uxmpEM%253A%253By5YPcivGZfyL3M%253Bhttps%25253A%25252F%25252Fwww.
slideshare.net%25252Fcristalbeam%25252Fdrawing-scientific-diagram&source=iu&pf=m&fht)

- Point of View Go back to Shaun Tan's website (QR Code 3.5) and click on Picture books. Scroll down to the cover of *Tales from Outer Suburbia*, click on it and scroll down to the image of the child looking at the buffalo. Think about where you are positioned. You are looking from behind the child and at her level, so you are seeing the buffalo through the child's eyes and are placed below it, emphasising its size. What is the effect of point of view on your meaning making?
  - o Find examples of the use of different points of view in both fiction and non-fiction texts delivered via paper and digital technology, still and moving images. Identify the effect on meaning making and why you might choose to use this point of view when including a still image or making a film as part of a multimodal text. Annotate the examples and add them to your reference collection.
- Go to the *Best Ads on TV* website (QR Code 3.1), where there are examples of still advertisements from magazine and billboards and film advertisements (moving images).
  - o Identify other examples of the codes and conventions of the visual semiotic system in some of the advertisements shown. Where possible, annotate and add to your reference collection.
  - o Add to your annotated reference collection of everyday texts (including still and moving images) by identifying and analysing other examples of the codes and conventions of the visual semiotic system.
- Applying the visual codes and conventions to film: In 2001, BMW made a series of short films of about ten minutes each and released them on the internet. They were directed by popular filmmakers from around the world, such as Ang Lee and Guy Ritchie. All feature Clive Owen as the driver, who has been hired in various scenarios. While they are not all suitable to share with all students, they are an excellent source for teaching about how the codes and

conventions of all semiotic systems are used in a narrative time-based multimodal text. From a critical literacy perspective, they are also very interesting. Clearly they are 'branded' in the sense that they advertise a BMW car and its attributes. However, they can also be interpreted as a simple narrative. After viewing them several times, it is interesting to think about what meaning making elements and codes and conventions foreground the brand and car and are 'advertising' and what elements pertain to the narrative. They are all available on YouTube. QR Code 3.7 provides a link to one of them: *The Chosen.*

o   View it several times, each time trying to address one of the different codes and conventions of the visual semiotic system introduced in Table 3.6. It may help to remove the sound after the first viewing in order to focus only on the visual codes and conventions and editing that that have been used. Remember the main purpose is to learn how to identify the codes and how they help you as the reader viewer make meaning, how they are shaping your meaning making, and how the director and producer of the film have designed the visual to convey a particular message.

o   Identify examples of long, close-up and medium shots, and then think about why those shots have been used and how they shape your meaning making at that point in the film.

o   Identify examples of soft and hard focus, and once again think about how they shape meaning making.

o   Identify different points of view and think about how they shape meaning making.

o   Examine the use of lighting, its source and the type of lighting being used. Think about how it enhances mood or character.

o   Look for examples of inserts, transitions and parallel cutting. What did each of these contribute?

QR Code 3.7 *The Chosen* (www.youtube.com/watch?v=DBav5VVzmZM)

THEORY INTO PRACTICE 3.3

• The purpose of this Theory into Practice is to identify a variety of strategies to introduce the codes and conventions of the visual semiotic system to students and also provide opportunities for them to practice applying them in both consumption and production contexts and using all technologies: live, paper and digital. When planning to teach about the codes and conventions of the visual semiotic system, remember that one of the goals of being multiliterate is to be a problem solver, able to investigate, explore and apply knowledge in different ways in different contexts. Therefore, strategies for introducing the codes and conventions should not simply provide definitions and examples, but should also include a focus on an inquiry approach (see Chapter Two) and engage students in critical examination of texts. Students should be involved in investigations that identify effective and less effective application of the codes and conventions. They should also have opportunities to conduct joint and individual investigations, collaborating and discussing findings and drawing conclusions and sharing them.

- You may wish to audiotape any of the lessons you teach from this Theory into Practice activity for future reference and analysis.
- The strategies provided in Reflection Strategy 3.9 can be adapted for use with students. Many of the links provided could be accessed using electronic whiteboards in the classroom for joint examination and discussion. This task focusses on how codes and conventions influence meaning making, investigation and application of knowledge to other texts and contexts. Similar to Reflection Strategy 3.9, students should develop an annotated personal collection of the application of the codes and conventions of the visual semiotic system in paper or digital form. A classroom reference should also be generated with examples selected for inclusion by the students themselves and also constructed by them. (Teachers Anstey and Bull have worked with report that students are far more likely to access and use a resource they have constructed than a commercially or teacher-produced one.)
- Use digital cameras to record role-plays of students or to photograph/film objects or settings from different points of view. Download them and display them next to one another on the electronic whiteboards and discuss how the point of view changes or emphasises different meanings. Discuss when and why particular points of view might be used. This task and those that follow focus on producing a text.
- Crop and display the digital images to investigate how framing and cropping changes or emphasises different meanings.
- Using a light or torch, explore the role of light from different directions and different intensities when filming or taking photographs.
- Use simple software programs for editing photos taken to change focus, adjust saturation and tone. Once again, place the series of photos next to one another and discuss the effects.
- Conduct further investigations in groups. Young students can use toys such as plastic action figures and farm sets to create scenes and photograph them. Real contexts could also be used, for example creating different images for a report or narrative students are currently producing and working out the best way to achieve their purpose. Students could start with simple investigations and then refine them and try new investigations based on what they found out. Investigations and findings could be reported in a form similar to that presented in Table 3.8 and added to their reference collection. It could be adapted for different codes and conventions.

Table 3.8 Sample format for reporting investigations

Investigating Point of View	Photographs
1. Eye Level *What we did.* We photographed the dinosaur at eye level and by itself. *What we found out.* You cannot tell how big it is. *What we did next to try and show size.* We added trees around the dinosaur and photographed the whole scene at eye level. *What we found out.* Adding trees showed the size of the dinosaur. It looked scarier because we knew how big it was.	Dinosaur on its own Dinosaur with trees
2. Eye Level and Bottom Up *What we did.* We photographed the knight figurine twice at eye level and bottom up. *What we found out.* It made him look taller and more frightening when it was from the bottom up. *What we did to make him even more frightening.* We added his weapons and photographed the knight increasing the amount of bottom up (at a more acute angle). *What we found out.* He looked taller and more frightening than before and the weapons looked big because they were in the foreground.	Knight at eye level Knight bottom up Knight with weapons and increased use of bottom up
3. Top down *What we did.* We photographed the scene of the big dinosaur chasing the others top down and with the dinosaurs running straight at the camera. *What we found out.* Top down showed the whole scene and what was happening. It showed movement.	Top down photo of dinosaurs being chased by bigger dinosaur

REFLECTION STRATEGY 3.10

- The purpose of this Reflection Strategy is to provide some tasks that will assist in developing understandings about how the codes and conventions of the visual semiotic system might be used to create salience and cohesion in meaning making.
- Revisit some of the books, advertisements and websites you have previously analysed, for example the two advertisements compared in Reflection Strategy 3.1. Try to identify examples of the visual codes and conventions being used to provide salience and/or cohesion, how this is achieved and the effect on meaning making.
- Use the text that you selected for Reflection Strategy 3.8 when focussing on the Linguistic Semiotic System. Examine the text again and this time focus on the Visual Semiotic System, for example images, diagrams, photographs or video clips.
- Find examples of the visual codes and conventions being used to achieve salience, how this is achieved and the effect on meaning making.
- Find examples of the visual codes and conventions being used to achieve cohesion, how this is achieved and the effect on meaning making.
- Consider the roles the linguistic and visual semiotic systems play individually and in combination with one another in the text and how this effects meaning making.
- Based on your analyses, make a critical evaluation of the use of the linguistic and visual semiotic systems in this text and explain your conclusions.

The Audio Semiotic System

The audio semiotic system refers to sound, how it is produced, how it is heard and interpreted. It includes non-verbal sounds such as sound effects in a movie, music or everyday sounds such as machinery. The audio semiotic system also includes voice, where speech is modified by codes such as pace, pitch and volume that augment the literal meaning of the words being uttered.

Audio codes add a dimension to moving images, video or film that is not present in still images. It is rare to encounter a video or film without a soundtrack, that is without the audio semiotic system. Multimodal texts such as films have complex soundtracks that combine dialogue, music and sound effects. The absence of any audio, that is, silence, is also part of a soundtrack. The audio codes have the potential to add realism and interest. Brice and Lambert (2009, p.53) reported that when the movie *Star Wars* was being previewed with audiences accompanied by the dialogue, but without the music and sound effects, the interest of the audience was tepid. However, when the music and sound effects were added, the audience was immediately far more engaged as the action and emotion became more real. In other words, the audio semiotic system decreased the social distance between the actors and plot and the audience. It created more affinity because it was more real.

Creating and managing the balance and relationships among dialogue, music, sound effects and silence is complex, and requires collaboration between people with a variety of expertise, for example sound editor and sound designer, sound recordist, composers, musicians and the sound rerecording mixer. A 're-recording mixer' mixes recorded dialogue, sound effects and music to create the final version of a soundtrack to accompany the film in such a way that each plays an appropriate part at the appropriate time. The layering of music, sound effects and voice is a complex process and involves critical deci-sions as to which of these three areas of audio is more important and should be foregrounded at which point in the unfolding text. An excellent discussion of the problem solving, research, decision-making and collaboration that occurs during the creation of the soundtrack of a film can be accessed through QR Code 3.8. Here a 10-minute film can be accessed that provides authentic insight into the process, as supervising sound editor and sound designer John Kassab discusses his work on the animated film of *The Lost Thing* (2010). This 10-minute film can also be accessed through Shaun Tan's website (QR Code 3.5), where it is embedded together with additional information about the production process and a trailer for *The Lost Thing*.

QR Code 3.8 Creating the soundtrack for *The Lost Thing* (http://soundworkscollection.com/videos/thelostthing)

The role of music in the audio of a film necessitates drawing on the discipline of music in order to understand how music is composed and structured for use in a soundtrack. Barton and Unsworth (2014) discussed this extensively in relation to the music in *The Lost Thing* and provided an analytical framework for examining the role of music in multimodal texts such as film. Drawing upon their work and that of Ellis and Simons (2005), some music-based codes and conventions have been embedded in the definitions of the main codes and conventions of the audio semiotic system presented in Table 3.9. It is useful to consult the relevant music curriculum and music teachers in your school for further information in order to con-struct learning experiences that help students make links between what they know about multiliteracies and what they know about music. This will enable them to draw upon more resources when they consume and produce multimodal texts.

Table 3.9 **Codes and conventions of the audio semiotic system**

Codes and Conventions	Definitions and Descriptors
Volume and audibility	Volume and audibility refer to the loudness or softness of the sound. It applies to sound effects, music and voice. The degree of loudness or softness can indicate mood or emotion. It can also create social distance between the listener and the text; for example in voice a soft whisper creates intimacy, while shouting creates distance. Different meanings and emotions can be engendered by how volume is changed over time. For example a gradual increase or decrease is less disturbing than a sudden increase or decrease.
Modulation (voice)	Modulation refers to the way in which volume and tone varies during dialogue, voice-over, narration and song lyrics.
Pitch and **tone**	Pitch refers to how high or low the sound is. Sound effects can be high-pitched, like scratching on glass, or low-pitched, like the rumble of a train. In music, the term tone refers to pitch and translates to a specific level of sound on the musical score (e.g. middle C). High-pitched voices and musical instruments can be classified as soprano and very low-pitched as bass.
Pause	Pause refers to points at which the audio message stops for a period of time, usually to draw attention to a particular part of the message or composition.
Silence	Silence is used to achieve or signal change in pace, a pause or phrasing. Creates emphasis.

Codes and Conventions	Definitions and Descriptors
Projection (voice)	Projection refers to how well the speaker or singer projects (throws) their voice out to the audience so it is easier to hear.
Articulation (voice)	Articulation refers to how clearly the speaker enunciates words.
Timbre	Timbre is the particular quality of a voice that is characteristic or unique to an individual, for example a reedy, thin quality or a dark, throaty quality. Musical instruments also have unique timbral qualities and are often selected because of them when composing music for a film, for example to reinforce particular emotions being portrayed in a scene.
Intonation and stress (voice)	Particular pitch and stress patterns may be used within an oration to emphasise particular words and can therefore change meaning.
Rhythm and rhythm patterns	In music, sound effects or oration stress patterns can be realised through rhythm, for example short, sharp rhythms might accompany fast or rough actions and a regular, flowing rhythm might accompany gentle actions.
Pace	Pace applies to music, voice and sound effects. It refers to the speed at which sound is delivered. Pace can vary throughout a text to create emotion or mood. For example fast-paced sounds tend to indicate action or excitement and slow-paced sounds a more calming effect. A sudden change in pace can draw attention to a change of atmosphere or a crucial point in a plot or the introduction of new information in a documentary. In music, pace can be referred to as tempo.
Phrasing	Phrasing refers to the way the overall audio message is broken up into smaller sections. For example, a speaker may use phrasing to break up information into smaller more easily processed pieces as it is presented in dialogue, voice-over or narration. Music and sound effects can also be phrased to aid expression and meaning.
Major key and minor key	Research indicates that the selection of a major key for music is associated with a bright, cheerful sound and engenders a positive response, while minor keys are associated with darker or sadder sounds (Ellis & Simons, 2005; Balkwill & Thompson, 1999). See music specialist and music curricula for a musical definition of major and minor.
Harmony and discord	Music that is harmonious is generally more melodic, that is there is an overall melody and it is associated with more pleasing and positive emotions. Discord describes music that is dissonant and is generally clashing and contrasting sound without melody. It is associated with less positive emotions such as anger and violence. Harmony or discord can be produced by music, sound effects or voice or a combination of them. See music specialist and music curricula for a musical definition of harmony and dissonance.
Motifs or musical phrases	A group of sounds that is composed and comes together in a short phrase may be repeated when a particular character appears or when a character exhibits particular emotions. This group of sounds or musical phrase can then referred to as a motif. Motif or musical phrases can also be produced in voice and sound effects.

A suggested sequence for introducing metalanguage to describe the codes and conventions for all five semiotic systems, across all school years, is presented in Table 3.15.

The codes and conventions of the audio semiotic system not only augment meaning but also create a relationship between the audience and the text. They can create distance, affinity, inclusion, exclusion or empathy. Using the codes carefully can draw attention to specific meaning making elements in the text and create cohesion across the text. Relationships among the semiotic systems can be built by using the codes to complement, reinforce or oppose meanings presented through the other semiotic systems. Examples of how the codes and conventions of the Audio Semiotic System can be used to create salience and cohesion are presented in Table 3.10.

Table 3.10 Examples of how the codes and conventions of the audio semiotic system might be applied to perform a function and facilitate salience and cohesion

Codes and Conventions	Possible Functions or Roles	How Salience Might Be Achieved With This Code	How Cohesion Might Be Developed With This Code
Pitch and modulation in voice	Indicate expression, question, statement or exclamation. Create mood, indicate emotion, create social distance. Direct attention to particular aspects of meaning being delivered through other semiotic systems, for example, linguistic or visual. Adds realism and interest.	Variation in pitch and modulation can draw attention to information or action.	When pitch and modulation are used consistently to indicate expression, for example, to distinguish between questions and statements and exclamations, the consumer is provided with information that assists the processing of the information presented over the whole text.
Intonation and stress in voice	Aid delivery of information and meaning making. Create mood, indicate emotion, create social distance. Adds realism and interest.	Variation in intonation or the use of stress can draw attention to information or action.	Using intonation and stress to set up a rhythm in the delivery of sound creates coherence throughout the text. The rhythm and repetition will set up a pattern of expectation for the consumer of the text, enabling them to predict and process the information conveyed by sound more easily.
Motif or phrase in music or sound effects	Create mood, indicate emotion, pique interest.	A motif or phrase can indicate a specific emotion in a particular character.	By repeating a motif whenever a particular character appears in the text, it creates continuity and reinforces this character's emotional character. The consumer can recognise and use this pattern to anticipate meaning, that is it will aid prediction about how this character will act in the scene or situation about to unfold.
Pause - in music, voice or sound effects	To provide time for the consumer to process or comprehend what has taken place before moving on, or to draw attention.	A sudden and extended pause in the audio draws attention and can indicate something major or important is about to be delivered in the text.	The repeated use of an extended pause whenever important or major information is about to be delivered, enables the consumer to make predictions about how they should attend to the next piece of text. NB: An extended pause does not necessarily mean there will be silence. For example, in a film the character may pause in their dialogue, but background music or sound effects may continue through the extended pause.

REFLECTION STRATEGY 3.11

- The purpose of this Reflection Strategy is to provide some tasks that will assist further development of your understandings about the Audio Semiotic System presented in Tables 3.9 and 3.10. Choose at least one of the texts previously analysed in Reflection Strategies 3.7 to 3.9 that included an audio track.
- Focus on the audio aspects of the text, for example sound effects, voice (delivery of dialogue or voice-over) or music. Make several passes through the text focussing on one aspect at a time (for example, sound effects). On each pass, identify any of the codes and conventions presented in Table 3.9 and determine the function they are performing in the text. Justify your conclusions about the function of the codes and conventions.
- Find examples of the audio codes and conventions being used to achieve salience and identify how salience is achieved.
- Find examples of the codes and conventions being used to achieve cohesion and identify how cohesion is achieved.
- If your previous analyses concerned the audio and/or linguistic semiotic systems in the text, analyse how the audio, visual and linguistic codes and conventions work together, for example are they complementary, reinforcing, opposing or do they indicate a hierarchy?
- Draw conclusions about the effectiveness or otherwise of the audio, linguistic and visual semiotic systems working together in text in terms of general meaning making and fulfilling the overall communicative purpose of the text.

THEORY INTO PRACTICE 3.4

- The purpose of this Theory into Practice is to identify a variety of strategies to introduce the codes and conventions of the visual semiotic system to students and also to provide opportunities for them to practice applying them in both the consumption and production of texts.
- You may wish to audiotape any of the lessons you teach from this Theory into Practice activity for future reference and analysis.
- Use these ideas to plan strategies for introducing the codes and conventions through an inquiry approach (see Chapter Two) and engage students in critical examination and production of texts. Identify effective and less effective application of the codes and conventions, provide opportunities for students to share and justify the findings from their inquiry.
- The strategies provided in Reflection Strategy 3.9 can be adapted for use with students. Many of the links provided could be accessed using electronic whiteboards that have an audio facility in the classroom for joint examination and discussion. Both classroom and personal reference materials should be generated from investigations for future use.
- Use digital cameras and mobile phones to record sound effects, different types of music, voice-overs and dialogue to accompany a specific section of text. A simple place to start this

type of activity is to use a page in a picture book or a scene students can role-play from a well-known fairy story. Oral reports for another discipline are also a useful starting point. Students could complete these tasks in groups and then share them, discussing the effectiveness of the different groups' solutions. Discussion should focus on the choice and execution of codes, how they should relate to the other semiotic systems present (e.g. the visual and linguistic) and which types of audio should be added (voice, music, sound effects) and where.

- Once a set of codes has been decided upon, try putting them together and evaluate their effectiveness. Try some alternatives and compare results.

The Gestural Semiotic System

According to Kendon (2004, p. 15) in his seminal work on gesture as a form of 'visual utterance', the gestural semiotic system refers to actions that have the features of observable, intended meaning, that is the consumer of the gesture determines that the gesture is deliberate, conscious and voluntary and is therefore intended to convey meaning. The gesture is not perceived as meaningful and significant by the consumer if it is determined to be unconscious, incidental or involuntary (e.g. a nervous tic). Because it is the consumer that determines whether a gesture is significant and therefore meaningful and relevant, purpose and context are very important to interpreting gesture. Gesture will take on different meanings in different contexts, for example gesture in acting, speech making and everyday living will be realised and interpreted differently. Similarly, gesture is socially and culturally specific and therefore meanings will not always be shared or permanent. Gesture occurs in daily lives during interaction with friends, family and workplace; it is depicted in movies and still images, as part of narrative and documentary; and it occurs as performance in speech making, seminars and performance arts such as theatre. It is important to remember that many live texts are texts of the everyday interaction in life. Therefore, when developing understandings about the gestural semiotic system it is important to focus on texts that are delivered live, not just as performance but as part of conversation, negotiation and interaction that occurs daily in a broad range of contexts.

According to Kendon (2004, p. 93) gesture occurs in and travels through space, and therefore its meaning is modified by the size and reach of the gesture (e.g. using the whole arm as opposed to just the finger), the form of the gesture (e.g. angular or circular), direction of the gesture (e.g. sideways or across) and which body parts are involved in the gesture (e.g. the eyebrows or shoulders). Jewitt and Kress (2008, pp. 158–159) discussed gesture in terms of the bodily communication that takes place through gesture, posture and facial expression. They suggested that it needs to be considered in two ways, firstly the way in which the body moves around its own axis, and secondly the way in which the body moves through space. Kalantzis et al. (2016, pp. 386–390) maintained that gestural meaning occurs though body configuration, including body spacing, orientation and posture, bodily movement and gaze. They also described gesticulation, the movement of arms and hands, as part of gestural meaning. Finally, they included aspects of appearance such as costume, hairstyle, jewellery or anything that a person does to modify their bodily appearance as part of gestural communication.

Table 3.11 draws upon the work of Kendon, Jewitt and Kress and Kalantzis et al. to provide a set of definitions of the main codes and conventions of the gestural semiotic system.

Table 3.11 The codes and conventions of the gestural semiotic system

Codes and Conventions	Definitions and Descriptors
Bodily contact	Bodily contact refers to the way in which people make contact through touch, where and how they touch, and the parts of their body that make contact may indicate emotion, relationships and the nature of those relationships.
Proximity	Proximity refers to the space (or distance) between people and can indicate a relationship and the nature of that relationship. Its meaning and interpretation are modified by cultural and social conventions. • **Personal space** is a critical aspect of proximity. It refers to the level of proximity a person can tolerate with comfort (the size of their personal space), that is how tolerant they are of how close someone is to them. The comfort of those involved and the nature of their relationship influences personal space. Personal space is also influenced by social and cultural conventions and context. For example, some social groups that live in densely populated cities will tolerate the close proximity of strangers in settings such as public transport better than those from a less densely populated rural area. The difference in their social experiences will mean that their concepts of personal space will be very different.
Body position and orientation	How the body is presented to others in the interaction, for example, whether participants face one another, are at an angle, turned to the side or away from each other. Body position can indicate power, intimacy, aggression, compliance or respect in relationships.
Appearance	Appearance refers to how the following elements: hairstyle, colouring or costume, clothing, jewellery, make-up and props such as a walking stick contribute to appearance and indicate personality, social status and culture.
Head nods	Head nods can indicate agreement or disagreement, but angle and tilt of head towards others when nodding can also effect interaction and indicate power, intimacy, aggression, compliance or respect.
Facial expression	Facial expression includes eyebrow position, shape of eye (e.g. narrowing or wide-eyed) position and shape of mouth and size of nostrils. These aspects of facial expression can all be used singly and in combination to indicate relationships and the nature of them and also emotion, mood, agreement, disagreement or disinterest. They are all are socially or culturally constrained.
Kinesics	Movement of head, arms, hands, legs and feet can indicate emotional arousal or a particular emotional state (e.g. rough or jerky movements might indicate lack of control). The nature of the gesture can indicate relationships (e.g. a very emphatic movement of the arm or hand could indicate authority or dominance).
Posture	The way in which a person stands, sits or lies can indicate interpersonal attitudes, their emotional state or the nature of their character. For example, a rigid upright posture leaning towards and over another person could indicate superiority or a person who likes to dominate. The ways in which a person uses their height, weight and build as part of their posture can indicate similar aspects of attitude, emotion and character.
Gaze and eye movement	The way in which a person's gaze is realised and where it is directed can indicate relationships or the relative importance of something. Gaze can be directed (specifically and intentionally focussed on someone or something) or non-directed (general scanning that is not focussed).

(Continued)

Table 3.11 (Continued)

Codes and Conventions	Definitions and Descriptors
	• The angle of the gaze can indicate attitude, relationships and power, for example, an eye level gaze could indicate equality between the participants, top down dominating someone or something, bottom up would indicate that someone or something has power over you. • The **length** of gaze (time spent) can indicate power, intimacy or dismissal. The nature and length of the gaze (how the eyes are used and how long the gaze lasts) can modify the intention. For example, an eye-level gaze that is prolonged with narrowed eyes could be confrontational rather than equitable. • The **stability** of gaze can also modify intent: it might be steady, fluctuating or hesitant, each of which imply different emotions, mood or relationships. For example, a hesitant gaze may indicate a relationship that is new or just beginning; a fluctuating gaze may indicate suspicion. • The gaze of a participant represented in a text can be directed at the consumer of the text. The effect of this direct gaze is to **demand** the attention of the consumer and a relationship with the participant. This will influence the meaning making of the consumer.

A suggested sequence for introducing metalanguage to describe the codes and conventions for all five semiotic systems, across all school years, is presented in Table 3.15.

Examples of how the codes and conventions of the gestural semiotic system can be used to create salience and cohesion are presented in Table 3.12.

The Gestural Semiotic System contributes much to the understanding of character and emotion. In situations where a text is to be delivered live, a public speaker will rehearse particular facial expressions and gestures to augment the oration. In day-to-day interactions in work or leisure situations, people monitor body language and facial expression in order to consider how they will respond or interact.

Often producers of text, such as animators and illustrators, will spend time developing a character by considering how that character would display themselves and their emotions in particular situations. This may include drawing multitudes of annotated sketches as part of the character development.

Anstey and Bull asked a graphic artist to develop the persona of a well-known fairy tale character, Little Red Riding Hood, for an animation. She produced many sketches to develop Little Red Riding Hood's posture, facial expressions and appearance, including the costume. Because the name of the character signifies her costume, the cloak and hood became a major part of developing the character, and the way in which the hood of the cape was depicted became an indicator of mood. Some of the graphic artist's drawings are presented in Figures 3.3, 3.4 and 3.5, together with her annotations.

In the discussion of the semiotic systems and how they combine to make meaning, there has been a particular emphasis on how the various semiotic systems relate to one another and the role they play and the types of information they convey. As stated previously, each semiotic system may provide complementary, reinforcing, hierarchical or opposing information to another. One picture book that uses the relationship between the visual, linguistic and gestural codes in a particularly clever way is *Wolves* by Emily Gravett (2005). This book was Gravett's debut publication and she won the 2006 Greenaway Award

Table 3.12 Examples of how the codes and conventions of the gestural semiotic system might be applied to perform a function and facilitate salience and cohesion

Codes and Conventions	Possible Functions or Roles	How Salience Might Be Achieved With This Code	How Cohesion Might Be Developed With This Code
Bodily contact	Can indicate relationships and the nature of those relationships.	A sudden change in the nature of bodily contact draws attention to an important aspect of plot.	The way in which the nature of bodily contact unfolds in a text indicates the development of a relationship and therefore creates cohesion throughout the narrative.
Proximity	Space between people can indicate a relationship and the nature of that relationship, for example the comfort of those involved.	As the space between people decreases the relationship between the people is seen to become closer, indicating the importance of the relationship in the development of the narrative. This can occur in live, paper or digital texts (e.g. movies, plays or picture books).	Continued use of the same space between two people in everyday life, a play or movie indicates cohesion in the nature of a developing relationship.
Orientation or body position	Body position can indicate power, intimacy, aggression, compliance or respect in relationships.	During a conversation between an employee and employer (text delivered live) the employer may suddenly change body position (e.g. stand up and bend over the seated employee) to draw attention to what is being said and assert power and authority.	During a conversation between two people (text delivered live), one of them may continuously change body positions, but all changes may indicate that they are paying attention and have empathy, for example leaning the whole body forward, leaning closer, tilting the head closer, reaching out with the arm or hand. These continuous body movements, all imparting the same message over the time of the conversation, provide the other person in the conversation with a cohesive and reassuring message.
Appearance	Can indicate personality, social status and culture.	A sudden change in appearance can draw attention to a change in circumstances, health or social status.	When a character maintains the same costume or clothing, this maintains the character throughout the play, movie or picture book (i.e. it provides cohesion).

(Continued)

Table 3.12 (Continued)

Codes and Conventions	Possible Functions or Roles	How Salience Might Be Achieved With This Code	How Cohesion Might Be Developed With This Code
Head nods	Can indicate agreement or disagreement, but angle and tilt of head towards others when nodding can also affect interaction and indicate power, intimacy, aggression, compliance or respect.	In a conversation during which information or an explanation is being provided, a sudden change in the manner of the head nod (for example, from nod to shake or change in angle) can draw attention to the fact that the recipient of the information is confused, indicating a need to pause and possibly change the flow of information or clarify the nature of confusion.	Monitoring head nods and the nature of head nods can provide feedback to the person, providing information about whether their message is coherent.
Facial expression	Aspects of facial expression (e.g. eyes and mouth) can be used singly and in combination to indicate relationships, emotion, mood, agreement, disagreement or disinterest.	A sudden change in expression indicates that something important has happened to cause the emotions of the person to change.	Participants in an interaction can use facial expression as a cohesive device to track the how the interaction is progressing, that is if it is proceeding in a logical and cohesive manner and if the other participants in the interaction are comprehending and reacting in expected or unexpected ways.
Kinesics	Movement of head, arms, hands and legs, and feet can indicate emotional arousal or a particular emotional state, or, when directed towards someone or something, the nature of a relationship.	A sudden change in the nature of a character's movement can draw attention to an important change in emotion or circumstances.	By using the same movements, an actor can construct a coherent picture of a particular character.
Gaze and eye movement	The way in which a person's gaze is realised, where and how it is directed, can indicate relationships, attitudes or the relative importance of something.	Sudden shift from undirected to directed gaze (towards something in a scene) indicates that the object is significant or important to the unfolding plot.	Repetition or maintenance of gaze indicates a continuous relationship between characters. It provides continuity in plot or relationships.

Exploring Relief

Eyebrow placement makes her look worried

phew!

cautious

Cautious

Cautious:

looking up as the things to be afraid of are often bigger a taller than you are

Figure 3.3 Developing facial expressions for Little Red Riding Hood

Figure 3.4 Developing appearance, in particular the costume of Little Red Riding Hood

Figure 3.5 Developing posture for Little Red Riding Hood

for it, a prestigious international award for illustration. A reading of *Wolves* together with the actual book is provided in QR Code 3.9.

QR Code 3.9 A reading of *Wolves* by Emily Gravett (2005)
(www.youtube.com/watch?v=NEIb88KnKYE)

REFLECTION STRATEGY 3.12

- The purpose of this Reflection Strategy is firstly to revise and apply the codes and conventions of the gestural semiotic system to a whole text, and secondly to examine how the linguistic, visual and gestural semiotic systems combine to make meaning.
- View the reading of *Wolves* (Gravett, 2005) provided through QR Code 3.9, or if you have access to the book itself, read the book.
- Having read the book once, go back and examine the way in which the gestural semiotic system has been used to portray the rabbit and the wolf. Identify particular codes and how they contribute to the meaning on individual pages and over the whole text.
- Identify examples of salience and cohesion that are achieved through the use of particular codes and conventions in the gestural semiotic system.
- Read the book several more times. Each time, focus on a different semiotic system and try to identify its role at various points – complementary, reinforcing, hierarchical or opposing. Think about how each semiotic system relates to the other and what each contributes to the meaning of each page and the overall text.
- Could the book communicate the story without one of the semiotic systems, for example without the linguistic? Why or why not?
- Could any of the semiotic systems play a different role, and would this be more or less effective?

THEORY INTO PRACTICE 3.5

- The purpose of this Theory into Practice is to use the knowledge you have gained from Reflection Strategy 3.12 to plan and teach a lesson using Wolves (Gravett. 2005) to either
  - o   Revise and apply the codes and conventions of the gestural semiotic system to a whole text
  - o   Examine how the linguistic, visual and gestural semiotic systems combine to make meaning.
- You may wish to audiotape any of the lessons you teach from this Theory into Practice activity for future reference and analysis.
- The decision about which of these lessons to teach will depend upon the experience of your students with the semiotic systems. Note that age of students is not mentioned regarding the choice of activity. Picture books are suitable for any age group, and the humour and sophistication of this particular book appeals to people of any age group, including adults.

REFLECTION STRATEGY 3.13

- The purpose of this Reflection Strategy is to further develop understanding about the codes and conventions of the Gestural Semiotic System.
- Revisit some of the books, advertisements and websites presented in Reflection Strategy 3.2 and see if you can find examples of the codes and conventions of the gestural semiotic system being used and consider how they contribute to your meaning making.
- Consider whether the gestures complement, augment or are in disagreement with the linguistic or any other semiotic system present.

THEORY INTO PRACTICE 3.6

- The purpose of this Theory into Practice is to provide strategies that enable students to practice applying the codes and conventions of the gestural semiotic system in both consumption and production contexts using all technologies (paper, digital and live).
- You may wish to audiotape any of the lessons you teach from this Theory into Practice activity for future reference and analysis.
- Use a digital camera/phone to record students developing facial expressions for different situations. Include real-life interaction (e.g. how to show interest, lack of understanding, puzzlement, disagreement when listening), as well as expressions for characters in plays and to augment formal oral presentations such as reports. Download them and display them next to one another on the electronic whiteboard and discuss the details and nuances of eyebrows, eye shape, gaze, mouth shape, head tilt and so forth.
- Discuss which would be the most effective for the different purposes of the texts and why they might be used.
- Repeat this activity with other codes, particularly body position, posture and costume.
- Having completed these activities as a whole class, provide students with a small part of a specific text type and ask students to experiment with finding appropriate gestural codes and conventions to use with the text. They can do this as live characters (themselves) or use toys to create the selected gestural codes and conventions and photograph them. Each group should annotate their photographs to explain their decisions. For example, 'We chose to use a wide-eyed expression combined with an open mouth and hands up in the air to show surprise at this point in the story because it was the major thing that was happening and we wanted to emphasise it'.

The Spatial Semiotic System

The spatial semiotic system encompasses the two-dimensional space of page and screen represented in organisation and layout and three-dimensional space, which includes architecture, actual places and settings and the way these might be represented on page and screen. Kalantzis et al. (2016, p. 373) referred to the representation of space as virtual space. Aspects of space include position, that is where things are placed and how things move from one position to another, together with directionality of that movement, for example up, down, left and right (Jewitt & Kress, 2008, p. 64). All these contribute to the concept of spatiality, that is how meaning making elements are distributed within the frame of the page, screen and actual live space (Kenner, 2008, p. 91). The consumer of a multimodal text may be a participant in the space (actual) and positioned to view the space (actual or virtual) in a particular way. The producer of the space (actual or virtual) can shape the consumer's experience of the space, interaction with it and potentially their meaning making.

The use of space to convey meaning is shaped by culture. Kress and van Leeuwen (2006, pp. 194–197) reported that in Western cultures meaning associated to spatial organisation is based around top, bottom, left and right, while in Asian cultures meaning is attributed to centre and margins. The way in which space is designed is also shaped by its use (e.g. classroom, shop, factory, website). Space can shape the way it is entered, the way in which people move around it and leave it. Kalantzis et al. (2016) referred to this as flow, that is the ways space shapes movement through it. They elaborated this concept by stating that space can be human-made, such as architecture or the layout of page and screen, but it can also occur naturally as in landscape. However, the perception and evaluation of the beauty (or otherwise) of the landscape may be shaped by actual paths created to guide the experience of it. A map may be created to guide movement through the landscape. The map might also be used to imagine the experience of moving through the space before actually doing it. Kalantzis et al. (2016, pp. 377–388) summarised spatial communication as including 'giving directions, making maps, drawing plans, creating models and diagramming flows. It also involves constructing buildings, arranging furniture in a room, creating parks, marking paths, creating transport infrastructure and building information transmission channels'.

Drawing upon the definitions of Kalantzis et al. (2016), it becomes apparent that aspects of the spatial semiotic system often overlap, draw upon and work with the visual and the gestural semiotic systems. For example, the way in which space is organised and used to represent meaning making elements (such as people in an everyday situation or characters in an image or play) can indicate the nature of relationships between those elements. If a speaker places him or herself close to the listener, this may signify an exclusive, intimate relationship. In this situation, some of the gestural codes and conventions, such as personal space and proximity, are drawn upon and others, such as facial expression, body position and posture, might clarify the nature of the relationship. In a map or diagram, lines may be used to indicate the desired flow of movement through a building in an emergency or the representation of a process such as evaporation. In this situation, the codes and conventions of the visual semiotic system might be used to clarify meaning, for example depicting the line in various qualities, types, and colours. Similarly, in a map a visual code and convention such as symbols might be used to represent the location of facilities in a park.

In Table 3.13 a summary and definitions of the main codes and conventions of the spatial semiotic system is presented.

QR Code 3.10 provides a link to Shaun Tan's website and access to images from some of his picture books. In the images from *The Rabbits* (Marsden & Tan, 2010), the 'Meeting on the Hill' illustration depicts the present occupants of the country on the left and the invaders or rabbits (the new) on the right. This follows the convention discussed in Table 3.13.

QR Code 3.10 The use of left (known) and right (new) in an illustration (www.shauntan.net/books.html)

Table 3.13 Codes and conventions of the spatial semiotic system

Codes and Conventions	Definitions and Descriptors
Position • **Left – Right** • **Top – Bottom** • **Centre – Margin** • **Foreground – Background**	In Western society, information or objects on the left and right have different values. On the left is what is known, while on the right is the new. (Kress and van Leeuwen (2006, pp.179–185). This can apply within an image or on a page or screen layout. It is demonstrated in complete texts such as newspapers: incomplete reports continued on a later page always appear on the left page (because they are already known) and only new stories appear on the right page. In Western society, information or objects placed at the top or bottom of the page have different value. Information at the top will be that which is more salient or palatable. For example, Kress and van Leeuwen (2006, p.186) found that often the information at the top of the page is the ideal, while that at the bottom was the real information. This was particularly the case in advertising, where the idealised concept of the product is at the top (an image suggesting that using a particular perfume means good things will happen), while the real (a photograph of the bottle of the perfume) will be at the bottom. In Asian culture, importance is indicated by placement at the centre of the layout, while objects or information placed at the margins are either less important or ancillary. However, these spatial relationships can be found in Western culture as well with similar meaning. Centre and margin layouts are used more frequently in non-fiction than narrative genres. For example, maps, diagrams, information pamphlets or charts may use this type of layout. The placement of objects in the foreground indicates importance, and placement in the background indicates lesser importance. Degrees of importance can be indicated by placement closer to foreground or background.
Distance • **Degree** • **Angle**	The spatial distance between objects can indicate relationships between people, places and things. Different degrees of space between people, places and things signify different degrees of formality or intimacy. The angles at which people, places and things are positioned in space as well as the distance can augment information about the relationship. A direct frontal or front-on angle can indicate stronger engagement between the people, places or things, while an oblique angle can mean someone or something is detached or sidelined (Jewitt 2006, p.44). By creating distance between the consumer and the people, places and things in the text, a closer or more distant relationship can be created between the consumer and what is being depicted. This can affect the consumer's meaning making and empathy towards the people, places or things depicted in the text.

(Continued)

Table 3.13 (Continued)

Codes and Conventions	Definitions and Descriptors
Framing	Frames, real or implied, separate or bring together people, places or things in a text. Similarly, they can separate or bring together items in a composite text (for example, bringing together or separating linguistic and visual text, or two parts of a visual or a linguistic text). This influences how the consumer will attend to a text, how they will direct their meaning making path through the text and how they might combine or relate parts of the text. This is particularly pertinent when considering the layout of texts and how semiotic systems might be combined on a screen or page to influence the consumer's meaning making. The absence of framing stresses group identity, whereas its presence signifies individuality (Kress & van Leeuwen, 2006, p. 203).

QR Code 3.11 provides a link to a figure representing the water cycle. The figure is framed by a large, thick continuous line which forms an oval. The oval has arrows on it indicating it is a continuous and recurring cycle, and the words 'water cycle' are embedded within it at the top. The oval frames all other elements of the figure. Within it, stylised representations of sky, cloud, mountains with snow, rivers and underground water systems are depicted. There are smaller arrows and labels on these items. The goal of a frame is to bring together or separate items. In this figure the oval frames all the elements of the diagram in a way that indicates all are involved in a continuous cycle and should be read and interpreted that way. A frame also influences how the consumer might attend to the text and direct their viewing path. The size of the oval, the fact that it encompasses all meaning making elements and the heading placed centre top draw the consumer's initial attention, emphasise the cyclical nature of the process and then direct the gaze inward to other elements, lines and labels. Because the frame emphasises the cyclical nature, the consumer is oriented to choose a viewing path of the remaining elements in the figure in terms of a cycle rather than taking a viewing path from left to right and top to bottom as might be used in a linguistic text.

QR Code 3.11 Framing in a diagram showing a process (https://pmm.nasa.gov/education/sites/default/files/ article_images/Water-Cycle-Art2A.png)

A suggested sequence for introducing metalanguage to describe the codes and conventions for all five semiotic systems, across all school years, is presented in Table 3.15. Examples of how the codes and conventions of the spatial semiotic system might be applied to perform a function and facilitate salience and cohesion are presented in Table 3.14.

Table 3.14 Examples of how the codes and conventions of the spatial semiotic system might be applied to perform a function and facilitate salience and cohesion

Codes and Conventions	Possible Functions or Roles	How Salience Might Be Achieved With This Code	How Cohesion Might Be Developed With This Code
Left – Right	Indicate known (left) and new (right)	If organising a report with new information that is important for people to read and note, the producer would choose a layout in which that information would be placed on the right. This might mean that in a report of several pages all new information or summaries would be placed on the right-hand page, or if it were a one-page paper summary frames may be used and images and words that summarise the new, important information would be placed in a frame on the right.	In newspaper layout, new stories are always found on the right or facing page while continuations of news items from other pages or updates of older news items are found on the left. This convention of layout creates cohesion among the newspaper articles and assists the editor in shaping the news of the day, indicating what is deemed important and new. It also aids the reader in locating the information they want or selecting those parts of the newspaper they want to read.
Top – Bottom	Indicate ideal (top) and (bottom)	In advertising, appeal is important in order to market a product and make it desirable. Therefore, idealised images of the use of that product are placed at the top of the page to get attention and draw the potential customer in. The more practical aspects of the product (size, colour, price, appearance) will be depicted in the bottom half of the page.	As consumers, we can use knowledge of how advertisers use layout to direct our reading path in advertisements and focus on the information wanted (for example, details of the product). This knowledge about the cohesion of an advertisement also enables the application of critical literacy skills – for example knowing the image at the top of the page is idealised and meant to persuade a decision can be made about whether to accept it as is or seek further clarifying information.

(Continued)

Table 3.14 (Continued)

Codes and Conventions	Possible Functions or Roles	How Salience Might Be Achieved With This Code	How Cohesion Might Be Developed With This Code
Centre – Margin	Centre indicates importance; margins are less important or ancillary	In a diagram, the producer will choose to place the most important aspect of a concept at the centre and arrange related points around it (at the margins), placing those that are more important closer to the centre point and those that are less important further away.	When organising the layout of information, a producer will need to consider how to help the consumer move among the information and gauge its importance, that is, how to use design to create cohesion. Therefore the most pertinent information, images or diagrams are placed at the centre of the page or screen with arrows pointing towards it. This placement at the centre together with the use of arrows as reinforcing cohesive devices aids the reader in finding a reading path.
Foreground – Background	Foreground indicates most important; background the least. In between indicates degree of importance, depending on proximity to foreground or background.	In the visual images of a picture book, the importance of a character may be indicated by placing him or her in the foreground of the image.	Cohesive character development is achieved by according the character the same position (foreground or background) in all images throughout the narrative.
Distance	Distance and angle between people, places and things suggests different kinds of relationships and degrees of engagement.	By placing people or objects at particular angles and distances from one another, the producer can draw attention to relationships between them.	In a live performance or film, the way in which characters are positioned in relationship to one another produces differing degrees of engagement between characters and creates coherence throughout the production.
Framing	Separates or brings together people, places and things or parts of text, indicating relationships and a suggested viewing path.	When designing the layout of a screen or page, the designer can draw attention to particular information or images by framing them with a heavy border of bright colour or placing them on a block of colour, thus creating the illusion of a frame.	In a film, the director creates a sequence of shots across frames and scenes to produce coherence between action, setting and the unfolding plot.

REFLECTION STRATEGY 3.14

- The purpose of this Reflection Strategy is to provide opportunities to practice applying the codes and conventions of the spatial semiotic system.
- It is easier when first trying to apply the spatial semiotic system to start analyses with a text delivered via paper or digital technologies before moving on to one delivered live. Use some of the texts that you selected for the previous Reflection Strategies or Theory into Practice strategies.
- Analyse the roles the codes and convention of the spatial semiotic systems play individually and in combination with semiotic systems in the text.
- Investigate how effective the spatial codes and conventions are at contributing to the achievement of the communicative purpose of the text.
- Compare how the spatial semiotic system is used in narrative and other genres, such as documentary, explanation or argument.
- Find examples of the spatial codes and conventions being used to achieve salience and identify how salience is achieved.
- Find examples of the codes and conventions being used to achieve cohesion and identify how cohesion is achieved.
- Consider using the codes and conventions in different ways and evaluate the effectiveness or lack of effectiveness that would be achieved through using the codes in different ways. For example, try using a centre margin layout rather than a top and bottom one, or different distances. Try different layouts and framing to draw attention to or separate aspects of the text. Consider the impact of your changes and their communicative effectiveness.

THEORY INTO PRACTICE 3.7

- The purpose of this Theory into Practice is to assist students to develop their understanding of the codes and conventions of the spatial semiotic system through inquiry.
- You may wish to audiotape any of the lessons you teach from this Theory into Practice activity for future reference and analysis.
- Use the ideas for investigation in Reflection Strategy 3.13 to plan and frame inquiry-based lessons. In these lessons, students take major responsibility for identifying questions they would like to investigate regarding the use of the spatial semiotic system and planning their investigations.
- Encourage investigations that explore the codes and conventions of the spatial semiotic system from both a consumption and production perspective.
- Ensure your planning and implementation of these lessons provides adequate time for students to share and discuss their investigation process and their findings.
- Add findings to the individual and class references that have been built around investigation of the five semiotic systems.

Introducing metalanguage for the codes and conventions of the five semiotic systems across the year levels

Curriculum documents provide detailed scope and sequence charts for the introduction of knowledge, skills and metalanguage for many areas of a literacy curriculum, but to date many focus mainly on language. While some documents acknowledge the need to teach students to comprehend and compose multimodal texts, a detailed scope and sequence for teaching the skills, knowledge and metalanguage necessary to accomplish this is often missing, particularly for those semiotic systems other than the linguistic. At present the Australian Curriculum English acknowledges the visual by including a 'thread' on Visual Language in the sub-strand 'Expressing and Developing Ideas' of the 'Language Strand' of the curriculum. (There are five 'threads' in this sub-strand that detail sentence and clause level, word level grammar, vocabulary and spelling.) However, the inclusion of particular codes in the Visual Language thread would seem to be somewhat random, as the examples are far from comprehensive and codes for the gestural and spatial semiotic systems (e.g. gaze and layout) are included among the visual without reference to their relationship to other semiotic systems. Within the Text Structure and Organisation 'sub-strand' of the Language Strand is a 'thread' called Concepts of Print and Screen that acknowledges multimodal texts. Interestingly, there is also a thread in this sub-strand on text cohesion that only specifies linguistic cohesive devices (Australian Curriculum English, 2015).

The balance in the Australian Curriculum English in all strands is heavily weighted towards the linguistic. While Anstey and Bull acknowledge this is very important, it is not sufficient to equip students for a multiliterate and multimodal future. Furthermore, it does not assist individual systems, schools and teachers to address multiliteracies and multimodal texts. At present it is up to these systems, schools and individual teachers to interpret the curriculum from a multiliterate and multimodal perspective, make links with other curricula such as the Arts (Dance, Drama, Media Arts, Music, Visual Arts) and work with specialist teachers of these curricula in order to develop a multiliterate classroom and **pedagogy**. Gardner (2017) compared the English Curricula of Australia and England and commented on the similarities and differences. He concluded that while both documents are more focussed on language than other semiotic systems (as revealed in an initial analysis of the most frequently occurring words), the Australian curriculum acknowledged that English and language is a social construct, acknowledged the multimodal nature of text and focussed upon understanding and use in context, while the English Curriculum from the U.K. had a more static picture of English and language use, focussing on skills and knowledge.

Anstey and Bull (2011a) developed a scope and sequence for the metalanguage of the semiotic systems for the second edition of the *STEPS Viewing Map of Development*. Since then they have introduced teachers to this sequence and teachers have used it in their action learning projects when introducing the semiotic systems to students as part of developing a multiliterate pedagogy. The results of these projects have been quite astounding in terms of the capabilities of students when given a language for talking about text and opportunities to conduct investigations into and produce multimodal texts. The students' ability to explain their decision-making and thought processes about producing a text increased dramatically. As one teacher reported on her year 2 (age 7) students' investigations into colour and line and their subsequent application of this knowledge to illustrating emotions:

> Here they were explaining to me that they had used dark colours like blue and purple and grey but then mixed up specific colour by adding black to make the picture more scary.... Then they

explained how they remembered about line and added zig zag lines to make it even more frightening.... I could not believe how they just took the knowledge and ran with it and how clear their explanations were.

(Excerpts from 'Kate's' oral report of her progress during a
whole school action learning project)

It is important to note that the development of student learning observed by Kate and many other teachers in the Action Learning Projects was the result of the teachers' carefully planned and enacted pedagogy. Teachers found that it was important to balance **focussed learning episodes** where students are introduced to particular knowledge, strategies and metalanguage associated with the semiotic systems and multimodal texts with opportunities for students to investigate multimodal texts and the ways in which semiotic systems are used. These independent or group investigations by students enabled them to broaden and develop new understandings about codes and conventions themselves and the ways in which they might be used. As Jan Mansfield stated in her action learning report:

... by providing focussed learning episodes where students are aware of what they are learning, why they are learning and how they can participate in the lesson they can gain a good understanding of the effect of colour in visual texts.

(Mansfield, 2014)

The focussed learning episodes provide the foundational knowledge and understanding that is essential to enable students to explore and transform their knowledge and understandings about the codes and conventions and how the ways they might be might be used to communicate meaning in various multimodal texts. In Transcript One, an example of Jan's first **utterance** at the beginning of a focussed learning episode in her classroom is provided:

TRANSCRIPT ONE

1 T: The learning intention for today's lesson is you will understand how the placement of colours in a visual text affects the meaning. We will do this by looking at harmonious and discordant colours. (*Teacher asks a student to add this learning intention to the colour display board.*) We need to know this because it is really important to know why we look at certain places in a text, whether it is a picture book or an ad on a billboard or in a magazine, on a website. Ok. I know that before I read about colour theory I wasn't aware of how colour placement is used to make me look at certain parts of the visual text. This explains a lot about advertising and how advertisers draw attention to certain things.

We are going to read a picture book called *Tuesday*...(Mansfield, 2014)

Note that Jan clearly identified the learning focus of the lesson, why this learning was important and where it might be used. Jan also identifies herself as a learner, someone who is still investigating and applying this knowledge herself. She is demonstrating the characteristics of a multiliterate person. Later in the focussed learning episode, having modelled some analysis of harmonious and discordant colours in the book being read, Jan asks the students to engage in some analysis. In Transcript Two, it can be seen that Jan is teaching the students how to listen and build upon each other's knowledge and justify their statements, once again encouraging the practices and thinking of a multiliterate person. She also provides specific knowledge and understanding and the opportunity to 'try out' this new knowledge in the supportive, scaffolded environment of a focussed learning episode. Note in utterance 1 she says 'No hands up. One person start' as she encourages students to listen and build upon each other's comments while she listens to their talk and carefully guides the conversation, scaffolding their investigations in this initial learning about harmonious and discordant colours.

TRANSCRIPT TWO

1T: Any comments about the book? No hands up. One person start.

2S: On that page there, the thing, the bit that really catches my eye is the red chimley [*sic*].

3T: So why? Look at your colour wheels, look at the red and look at the other colours on the page and see why the red may have caught Z...'s eye? Look at your colour wheel B...

Groups discuss the questions

4T: Ok Z...?

5S: The colour of the chimney is close to red and yellow and they are primary colours and primary colours stand out.

An interesting answer Z... Let's look at the page some more. What are the main colours on the page? Hands up.

6S: Greens and blue.

7T: Have a look where the greens and blues are on your colour wheel.

Discussion in groups

8T: Right. K... how do you describe where blue and green are on the colour wheel?

9S: Right next to each other.

1OT: Terrific. Colours that are next to each other on the colour wheel are called harmonious colours...(Mansfield, 2014)

In Chapter Four there is another quote from Jan Mansfield's report that shows one of the exploratory experiences she designed for students (see Chapter Four). It demonstrates the use of **dialogic talk** as students developed new understandings about the placement of colours on the colour wheel, the colours present or not present on the colour wheel, discordant colours and intensity of colour.

Building upon the work of Anstey and Bull (2011a), feedback from teachers in action learning projects and further development of the codes and conventions of the five semiotic systems, Bull and Anstey have now developed a scope and sequence table for the introduction of a metalanguage to aid students' development of concepts associated with the codes and conventions of the five semiotic systems across

preschool to year 12. It is presented in Table 3.15, however, two essential points of discussion and explanation precede the presentation of the table. These are:

1   The scope and sequence has a pedagogical intent, as the six phases in the sequence each engender
    a particular focus on the learning that would take place during that phase.
2   While the phases are related to age groups and year levels across primary and secondary school,
    they should not be taken as absolute.

Auditing of students' current knowledge, understandings and metalanguage should be undertaken before
identifying terms and concepts to be introduced. Furthermore, where a school-wide curriculum is being
implemented there would need to be some thought given as to how the concepts would be introduced across
year levels in a school that has previously not undertaken a school-wide approach to teaching the semiotic
systems. Table 3.15 is a guide, an effort to provide systems, schools and teachers with a scope and sequence
that can be audited and modified in consultation with their current English Curriculum and the other relevant curricula areas such as the Arts. Some thought should be given to planning across the curriculum
and teaching among general and specialist teachers, using common vocabulary or addressing the fact that
some codes and terms may be different across curricula but mean the same thing. It is a complex undertaking and could easily become the focus of a school-wide action learning cycle where teachers at various
levels undertake individual action learning projects that will ultimately inform a school-wide approach. This
was the focus undertaken by one school that Anstey and Bull worked with, each teacher at each year level
focussing on the same small group of codes and identifying the levels of complexity students were capable
of at each year level. From these individual teachers' action learning projects, the school had information
that was used to develop a school-wide sequence. The implementation of the sequence was more effective
because all staff had participated in its development, and had a common language and level of knowledge
from this experience and the sharing of information during their individual action learning projects.

Explanation of the six phases of the metalanguage sequence

A year level and chronological age has been provided for each phase which approximates application
in an Australian setting. This information can then be used to facilitate the application of the sequence
across other states, systems and countries.

Foundation phase (preparatory year and year 1, ages 5 and 6)

As the term foundation suggests, the pedagogical focus in this phase is to introduce students to basic
concepts associated with the codes and conventions of the five semiotic systems and provide opportunities for students to engage with them across a variety of text types and delivery systems. While the
introductory and foundational nature of the learning at this stage will mean there will be more focussed
learning episodes, demonstrations and modelling, the inquiry model should still inform much of the pedagogy in this phase. Students should have opportunities to investigate the application of codes and
conventions in texts and use the metalanguage to discuss their investigations and findings in groups,
pairs and individually. Investigations of text should occur across all disciplines or subject areas in order to
develop understandings that literacy informs all aspects of life and learning. Students should be encouraged to collect and bring to school examples of the codes and conventions used in texts from their lifeworlds (e.g. brochures, posters, advertising, on paper, apps and websites) and talk about them, comparing
and contrasting them with other examples that have been found. Opportunities to apply knowledge

about the codes and conventions in the production of multimodal texts should also be provided through joint construction with the teacher, together with group, paired and individual tasks. It is also important to audit the planning and content of this phase in terms of balance between consumption and production of text, and balance across all technologies (live, paper and digital), all text types and curriculum areas. Planning and content should also be relevant to the students' lifeworlds.

Developing phase (years 2 and 3, ages 7 and 8)

As implied by the name of the phase, students will be further developing their understanding from the foundation phase but developing new knowledge as well. A similar approach to pedagogy would be used at this stage, although there would be a greater emphasis on investigation and application when previous learning from the foundation phase is revised and extended. Revision and extension is an important aspect of students' learning as they move through the sequence, as students need to develop more sophisticated understandings about the codes and conventions, their use and the ways in which semiotic systems work together in a text. This is why a focus on inquiry is essential to students' learning in every phase. Assessing students' current understanding and application of those items identified for revision and extension should inform how the revision and extension takes place. It is also important to audit the planning and content of this phase in terms of balance between consumption and production of text, and balance across all technologies (live, paper and digital), all text types and curriculum areas. Planning and content should also be relevant to the students' lifeworlds.

Investigating phase (years 4 and 5, ages 9 and 10)

In this phase and in subsequent phases, there are fewer new terms; the focus is more on revision and extension. Assessing students' current understanding and application of those items identified for revision and extension should inform how the revision and extension takes place. The goal of this phase is to develop an increasing level of sophistication in the investigation and application of the codes and conventions. Some metalanguage is replaced with 'correct' terminology as students are now at a stage where they can better understand more abstract terms, for example, 'see through' from the foundation phase is replaced with 'transparent'. At this point, pedagogy will focus on increasing the level of complexity of students' inquiry and application by examining not just the range of ways codes and conventions might be used but the ways in which choices about their use might be influenced, guided or limited. For example, students might specifically examine how particular codes and conventions and semiotic systems are applied similarly and differently in different text types, or how the choice of technology limits or expands use of semiotic systems or codes. They may also start investigating the influence of context and audience on the selection of semiotic systems, codes and conventions. These investigations would apply to both the consumption and production of texts and engage students in critical evaluations of texts. It is also important to audit the planning and content of this phase in terms of balance between consumption and production of text, and balance across all technologies (live, paper and digital), all text types and curriculum areas. Planning and content should also be relevant to the students' lifeworlds.

Synthesising phase (years 6 and 7, ages 11 and 12

In Australia, this phase would at the end of primary or elementary school years. It is important at this point to assess students' understanding and application of knowledge and revise and extend any areas necessary. While revision and extension of existing knowledge is still essential, the codes and conventions that are introduced at this point require a more critical analysis of texts as they focus on sophisticated aspects of those codes introduced to date. For example, in the spatial semiotic system the analysis of the effect of *angles* as an aspect of *distance* between people and objects represented is introduced. At this point students should be amalgamating the knowledge, skills and understandings from previous years and incorporating it into their daily encounters, producing and consuming multimodal texts in their lifeworlds and across all curriculum areas. Their inquiries and investigations should focus on integrating information about the relationships between all the semiotic systems in a text and considering how meanings are being produced through these relationships. Students should engage their critical literacy skills by comparing the ways in which semiotic systems are combined in texts and drawing conclusions about their effectiveness in producing meaning that is aligned with the goals of the text, the identified audience and context. These investigations should be applied when consuming or producing text. Such inquiries and investigations assist students in synthesising their knowledge and understandings as the name of the phase indicates. It is also important to audit the planning and content of this phase in terms of balance between consumption and production of text, and balance across all technologies (live, paper and digital), all text types and curriculum areas. Planning and content should also be relevant to the students' lifeworlds.

Accomplished (years 8, 9 and 10, ages 13, 14 and 15)

As the title of this phase implies, there is little new information in this phase, and students at this level should be accomplished in their knowledge, skills, understandings and application of the codes and conventions of the five semiotic systems in multimodal texts across all platforms of delivery. Therefore it is imperative that careful assessment of students' accomplishments take place and inform planning, teaching and pedagogy. In particular, this assessment should address their accomplishments in relation to:

- Consumption and production of text
- All technologies (live, paper and digital)
- All text types
- All curriculum areas
- The students' understanding of the relevance of this knowledge to their lifeworlds.

This should not be interpreted as subjecting students to a round of exhaustive testing; rather investigations and tasks should be devised that would enable students to demonstrate application of their skills, knowledge and understanding. Both group and individual inquiries should be devised and students themselves should also demonstrate their ability to investigate texts by identifying planning and completing an inquiry of their own.

In short, this phase is one in which planning and teaching should address any areas that are identified where students are less than proficient. These areas may apply to all students, a group or individuals, and revision and extension in these areas should be addressed at the whole group, smaller group or individual level, as appropriate. For those students who are identified as generally proficient, opportunities should be provided for them to move on to the innovative phase.

Innovative phase (years 11 and 12, ages 16 and 17)

The focus of this phase is students using the knowledge, skills and understandings they have acquired in innovative ways. That is, they should engage in projects and investigations that employ critical and creative use of the codes and conventions of the five semiotic systems to consume and produce texts:

- Across all technologies (live, paper and digital),
- Across all text types,

- Across all curriculum areas,
- That demonstrate students' understanding of the relevance of this knowledge to their lifeworlds.

The focus of the projects should be student driven, and inquiry based, where students identify an issue they feel they could research and improve in relation to multimodal texts. The issue may involve a particular age group, type of text, communication issue, community issue or way of using the semiotic systems, but must be one that will involve them individually or in groups researching the issue, consulting with those involved and then coming up with an innovative solution and the creation of a multimodal text demonstrating and justifying that solution.

ACTION LEARNING TASK 3.2

- The purpose of this Action Learning Task is to review your Action Learning Plan and consider whether you wish to make any revisions to it, based upon your reading of this chapter.
- If you had previously identified one of the items referring to the semiotic systems on the Matrix as a focus of your project, then you may wish to refine the scope of your project, perhaps focussing upon one semiotic system and only one technology at this point. It is important to keep your action learning plan small and tightly focussed, otherwise it will become difficult to make progress and feel a sense of movement towards your goal.

ACTION LEARNING TASK 3.3

- The purpose of this Action Learning Task is to examine either the audiotape of a lesson you made for Action Learning Task 3.1 or another that you made as you were reading and reflecting upon this chapter and conducting the Theory into Practice tasks.
- Review your Action Plan and any revisions you have made as a result of reading this chapter. Identify the audiotape you feel is most relevant to your action learning plan and prepare to use it as your baseline data on how you currently teach the identified focus area and goal you wish to achieve.
- Transcribe the lesson and analyse it in terms of the categories of talk and **phase structure** presented in Tables 1.3 and 1.4 in Chapter One.
- Having analysed the lesson, identify areas for improvement or change based upon your goal and make further revisions to your action learning plan in terms of professional reading, pedagogy, practice and planning.
- Plan how and when you will undertake your next steps in these four areas. Chapter Four will provide further information on classroom talk and developing a dialogic pedagogy and will help you further refine and implement these aspects of your action plan.

Table 3.15 A suggested sequence for introducing metalanguage and describing the functions of the codes and conventions for the five semiotic systems and focussing the related pedagogy across all school years

Semiotic System/ Phase	Foundation Preparatory and Year 1 Ages 5 and 6	Developing Years 2 and 3 Ages 7 and 8		Investigating Years 4 and 5 Ages 9 and 10	
	Introduce	Introduce	Revise and Extend	Introduce	Revise and Extend
VISUAL	**Colour** • Colour • Colour wheel • Placement • Go together (harmonious) • Clash (discordant) • Light (tone) • Dark (tone) • Pure • Mixed • Warm • Cool • Happy • Sad • See-through (transparent) • Solid (opaque) **Texture** • Touch/feel **Line** • Line • Thick • Thin • Heavy • Light • Straight • Curved • Jagged • Real • Imaginary	**Line** • Diagonal • Horizontal • Vertical **Shape** • Visual outline • Symbol **Point of View** • Top down • Bottom up • Eye level **Editing** • Editing • Sequence • Speed • Real speed • Sped up • Slow motion	**Colour** • Colour • Colour wheel • Placement • Go together (harmonious) • Clash (discordant) • Light (tone) • Dark (tone) • Pure • Mixed • Warm • Cool • Happy • Sad • See-through (transparent) • Solid (opaque) **Texture** • Touch/feel **Line** • Line • Thick • Thin • Heavy • Light • Straight • Curved • Jagged • Real • Imaginary	**Colour** • Harmonious • Discordant • Tone • Mood • Emotion • Transparent • Opaque **Texture** • Texture **Line** • Right angled **Juxtaposition** • Juxtaposition **Focus** • Focus • Soft • Hard **Lighting** • Degree • Soft • Harsh	**Colour** • Colour • Colour wheel • Placement • Go together (harmonious) • Clash (discordant) • Light (tone) • Dark (tone) • Pure • Mixed • Warm • Cool • Happy • Sad **Texture** • Touch/feel **Line** • Line • Thick • Thin • Heavy • Light • Straight • Curved • Jagged • Diagonal • Horizontal • Vertical • Real • Imaginary

(Continued)

Table 3.15 (Continued)

Semiotic System/Phase	Foundation Preparatory and Year 1 Ages 5 and 6	Developing Years 2 and 3 Ages 7 and 8		Investigating Years 4 and 5 Ages 9 and 10	
	Introduce	Introduce	Revise and Extend	Introduce	Revise and Extend
	Shape • Shape **Point of View** • Bird's-eye • Worm's-eye • Eye level **Framing** • Close-up shot • Medium shot • Long shot **Lighting** • Lighting • Bright • Dull		**Shape** • Shape **Framing** • Close-up shot • Medium shot • Long shot **Lighting** • Lighting • Bright • Dull		**Shape** • Shape • Visual outline • Symbol **Point of View** • Top down • Bottom up • Eye level **Framing** • Close-up shot • Medium shot • Long shot **Lighting** • Lighting • Bright • Dull **Editing** • Editing • Sequence • Speed • Real speed • Sped up • Slow motion

(Continued)

Semiotic System/ Phase	Synthesising Years 6 and 7 Ages 11 and 12		Accomplishing Years 8, 9 and 10 Ages 13, 14 and 15		Innovating Years 11 and 12 Ages 16 and 17
	Introduce	Revise and Extend	Introduce	Revise and Extend	Revise and Extend
VISUAL	**Colour** • Intensity • Dilute • Strengthen **Line** • Quality • Vector • Vectorality **Lighting** • Direction of lighting • Top • Bottom • Side • Front • Back • Spotlight	**Colour** • Colour • Colour wheel • Placement • Pure • Mixed • Warm • Cool • Harmonious • Discordant • Tone • Mood • Emotion • Transparent • Opaque **Texture** • Texture • Touch • Feel **Line** • Line • Thick • Thin • Heavy • Light • Straight • Curved • Jagged • Diagonal • Horizontal • Vertical • Right angled • Real • Imaginary	**Colour** • Saturation **Texture** • Tactile memory **Line** • Implied • Actual **Point of View** • Point of view • Positioning the viewer • Angle of view **Framing** • Framing • Context • Characterisation • Cropping **Editing** • Transitions • Fading • Dissolving • No transition • Parallel cutting • Split screen • Inserts • Pacing (fast or slow)	**Colour** • Colour • Colour wheel • Placement • Pure • Mixed • Warm • Cool • Harmonious • Discordant • Tone • Mood • Emotion • Intensity • Dilute • Strengthen • Transparent • Opaque **Texture** • Texture • Touch • Feel **Line** • Line • Thick • Thin • Heavy • Light • Quality • Straight • Curved • Jagged • Diagonal • Horizontal	**Colour** • Colour • Colour wheel • Placement • Pure • Mixed • Warm • Cool • Harmonious • Discordant • Tone • Mood • Emotion • Intensity • Dilute • Strengthen • Saturation • Transparent • Opaque **Texture** • Texture • Touch • Feel • Tactile memory **Line** • Line • Thick • Thin • Heavy • Light • Quality • Straight • Curved • Jagged

(Continued)

Table 3.15 (Continued)

Semiotic System/ Phase	Synthesising Years 6 and 7 Ages 11 and 12		Accomplishing Years 8, 9 and 10 Ages 13, 14 and 15		Innovating Years 11 and 12 Ages 16 and 17
	Introduce	Revise and Extend	Introduce	Revise and Extend	Revise and Extend
		Shape · Shape · Visual outline · Symbol **Juxtaposition** · Juxtaposition **Point of View** · Top down · Bottom up · Eye level **Framing** · Close-up shot · Medium shot · Long shot **Focus** · Soft · Hard **Lighting** · Lighting · Bright · Dull · Degree · Soft · Harsh **Editing** · Editing · Sequence · Speed · Real speed · Sped up · Slow motion		· Vertical · Right angled · Vector · Vectorality **Shape** · Shape · Visual outline · Symbol **Juxtaposition** · Juxtaposition **Point of View** · Point of view · Top down · Bottom up · Eye level **Framing** · Close-up shot · Medium shot · Long shot **Focus** · Soft · Hard **Lighting** · Lighting · Bright · Dull · Degree · Soft · Harsh · Direction of lighting · Top · Bottom · Side · Front · Back · Spotlight	· Diagonal · Horizontal · Vertical · Right angled · Actual · Implied · Vector · Vectorality **Shape** · Shape · Visual outline · Symbol **Juxtaposition** · Juxtaposition **Point of View** · Point of view · Top down · Bottom up · Eye level · Positioning the viewer · Angle of view **Framing** · Close-up shot · Medium shot · Long shot · Framing · context · Characterisation · Cropping **Focus** · Soft · Hard **Lighting** · Lighting · Bright · Dull · Degree

(Continued)

Semiotic System/Phase	Synthesising Years 6 and 7 Ages 11 and 12		Accomplishing Years 8, 9 and 10 Ages 13, 14 and 15		Innovating Years 11 and 12 Ages 16 and 17
	Introduce	Revise and Extend	Introduce	Revise and Extend	Revise and Extend
				Editing • Editing • Sequence • Speed • Real speed • Sped up • Slow motion	• Soft • Harsh • Direction of lighting • Top • Bottom • Side • Front • Back • Spotlight **Editing** • Editing • Sequence • Speed • Real speed • Sped up • Slow motion • Transitions • Fading • Dissolving • No transition • Parallel cutting • Split screen • Inserts • Pacing (fast or slow)

(Continued)

Table 3.15 (Continued)

Semiotic System/ Phase	Foundation Preparatory and Year 1 Ages 5 and 6		Developing Years 2 and 3 Ages 7 and 8		Investigating Years 4 and 5 Ages 9 and 10	
	Introduce		Introduce	Revise and Extend	Introduce	Revise and Extend
AUDIO	**Sound effect** **Voice** **Music** **Volume and Audibility** • Loudness • softness • silence **Pitch** (at present only use terms high and low) • High • Low **Pace** • Fast • Slow **Rhythm**		**Pitch** (introduce term) **Expression** (to be used for the term modulation) **Rhythm** • Rhythm patterns	**Sound effect** **Voice** **Music** **Volume and Audibility** • Loudness • Softness • Silence **Pitch** • High • Low **Pace** • Fast • Slow **Rhythm**	**Pace** • Pace • Pause **Timbre** **Harmony** • Melody, melodic **Discord** • Dissonance **Motifs** • Musical phrases **Key** • Major • Minor	**Sound effect** **Voice** **Music** **Volume and Audibility** • Loudness • Softness • Silence **Pitch** • Pitch • High • Low **Expression** **Pace** • Fast • Slow **Rhythm** • Rhythm patterns

(Continued)

Semiotic System/ Phase	Synthesising Years 6 and 7 Ages 11 and 12		Accomplishing Years 8, 9 and 10 Ages 13, 14 and 15		Innovating Years 11 and 12 Ages 16 and 17
	Introduce	Revise and Extend	Introduce	Revise and Extend	Revise and Extend
AUDIO	**Modulation** (introduce term) **Projection** (voice) **Articulation** (voice) **Intonation and Stress** (voice) **Pace** • Phrasing	**Sound effect** **Voice** **Music** **Volume and Audibility** • Loudness • Softness • Silence **Pitch** • Pitch • High • Low **Expression** **Pace** • Pace • Fast • Slow • Pause **Rhythm** Rhythm patterns **Timbre** **Harmony** • Melody, melodic **Discord** • Dissonance **Motifs** • Musical phrases **Key** • Major • Minor	No new terms	**Sound effect** **Voice** **Music** **Volume and Audibility** • Loudness • Softness • Silence **Modulation** • Expression **Projection** (voice) **Articulation** (voice) **Intonation and Stress** (voice) **Pitch** • Pitch • High • Low **Pace** • Pace • Fast • Slow • Pause • Phrasing **Rhythm** Rhythm patterns **Timbre** **Harmony** • Melody, melodic **Discord** • Dissonance **Motifs** • Musical phrases **Key** • Major • Minor	**Sound effect** **Voice** **Music** **Volume and Audibility** • Loudness • Softness • Silence **Modulation** • Expression **Projection** (voice) **Articulation** (voice) **Intonation and Stress** (voice) **Pitch** • Pitch • High • Low **Pace** • Pace • Fast • Slow • Pause • Phrasing **Rhythm** Rhythm patterns **Timbre** **Harmony** • Melody, melodic **Discord** • Dissonance **Motifs** • Musical phrases **Key** • Major • Minor

(Continued)

Table 3.15 (Continued)

Semiotic System/ Phase	Foundation Preparatory and Year 1 Ages 5 and 6	Developing Years 2 and 3 Ages 7 and 8		Investigating Years 4 and 5 Ages 9 and 10	
	Introduce	Introduce	Revise and Extend	Introduce	Revise and Extend
SPATIAL	**Framing** • Frames • Bringing together • Separating	**Position** • Position • Placement • Layout • Foreground • Background • Importance **Distance** • Distance • Space • Close • Distant **Framing** • Framing • Directing attention • Real (frames) • Imaginary (frames)	**Framing** • Frames • Bringing together • Separating	**Position** • Left right (old new)	**Framing** • Frames • Bringing together • Separating • Framing • Directing attention • Real (frames) • Imaginary (frames) **Position** • Position • Placement • Layout • Foreground • Background • Importance **Distance** • Distance • Space • Close • Distant

(Continued)

Semiotic System/Phase	Synthesising Years 6 and 7 Ages 11 and 12		Accomplishing Years 8, 9 and 10 Ages 13, 14 and 15		Innovating Years 11 and 12 Ages 16 and 17
	Introduce	Revise and Extend	Introduce	Revise and Extend	Revise and Extend
SPATIAL	**Position** • Top bottom • Centre margin **Distance** • Obtuse angles • Acute angles • Front on angles **Framing** • Implied (frames)	**Framing** • Frames • Bringing together • Separating • Framing • Directing attention • Real (frames) • Imaginary (frames) • Left right (old new) **Position** • Position • Placement • Layout • Foreground • Background • Importance • Left right (old new) **Distance** • Distance • Space • Close • Distant	**Framing** • Group identity (absence of framing stresses this) • Individuality (presence of framing stresses this) **Position** • Salience (replacing importance)	**Framing** • Frames • Bringing together • Separating • Framing • Directing attention • Real (frames) • Imaginary (frames) • Implied (frames) **Position** • Position • Placement • Layout • Foreground • **Background** • Importance • **Left right (old new)** • **Top bottom** • **Centre margin** **Distance** • Distance • Space • Close • Distant • Obtuse angles • Acute angles • Front on angles	**Framing** • Frames • Bringing together • Separating • Framing • Directing attention • Real (frames) • Imaginary (frames) • Implied (frames) • Group identity (absence of framing stresses this) • Individuality (presence of framing stresses this) **Position** • Position • Placement • Layout • Foreground • Background • Importance • Left right (old new) • Top bottom • Centre margin • Salience (replacing importance) **Distance** • Distance • Space • Close • Distant • Obtuse angles • Acute angles • Front on angles

(Continued)

Table 3.15 (Continued)

Semiotic System/ Phase	Foundation Preparatory and Year 1 Ages 5 and 6	Developing Years 2 and 3 Ages 7 and 8		Investigating Years 4 and 5 Ages 9 and 10	
	Introduce	Introduce	Revise and Extend	Introduce	Revise and Extend
GESTURAL	**Appearance** · Tall · Short · Clothes · Costume · Hairstyle · Jewellery · Make-up **Head Movement** · Nodding · Shaking **Facial Expression** · Mouth · Eyes · Eyebrow position · Smile · Frown · Squint **Body Language** · Body movement · Head · Arms · Legs · Hands · Feet	**Proximity** · Distance · Space **Body Position** · Body position · Face-to-face · Away · To the side **Appearance** · Appearance · Props · Slight · Heavy · Height · Weight · Build **Facial Expression** · Facial expression · Grimace **Posture** · Posture · Rigid · Upright · Leaning	**Appearance** · Tall · Short · Clothes · Costume · Hairstyle · Jewellery · Make-up **Head Movement** · Nodding · Shaking **Facial Expression** · Mouth · Eyes · Eyebrow position · Smile · Frown · Squint **Body Language** · Body movement · Head · Arms · Legs · Hands · Feet	**Body Contact** · Body contact · Touch **Body Position** · Angle **Head Movement** · Angle · Tilt **Facial Expression** · Nostrils flared **Gaze and Eye Movement** · Eye level · Bottom up · Top down · Offer · Demand	**Appearance** · Appearance · Tall · Short · Clothes · Costume · Hairstyle · Jewellery · Make-up · Props · Slight · Heavy · Height · Weight · Build **Head Movement** · Nodding · Shaking **Facial Expression** · Facial expression · Mouth · Eyes · Eyebrow position · Smile · Frown

(Continued)

Posture
- Standing
- Sitting
- Slumped
- Lying

Gaze and Eye Movement
- Look
- Length of look

Posture
- Standing
- Sitting
- Slumped
- Lying

Gaze and Eye Movement
- Look
- Length of look

- Squint
- Grimace

Body Position
- Body position
- Face-to-face
- Away
- To the side

Body Language
- Body movement
- Head
- Arms
- Legs
- Hands
- Feet

Posture
- Posture
- Standing
- Sitting
- Slumped
- Lying
- Rigid
- Upright
- Leaning

Gaze and Eye Movement
- Look
- Length of look

Proximity
- Distance
- Space

(Continued)

Table 3.15 (Continued)

Semiotic System/Phase	Synthesising Years 6 and 7 Ages 11 and 12		Accomplishing Years 8, 9 and 10 Ages 13, 14 and 15		Innovating Years 11 and 12 Ages 16 and 17
	Introduce	Revise and Extend	Introduce	Revise and Extend	Revise and Extend
GESTURAL	**Proximity** • Proximity • Personal space **Gaze and Eye Movement** • Gaze • Eye movement • Focussed • Unfocussed • Scanning • Directed gaze • Angle of gaze	**Appearance** • Appearance • Tall • Short • Clothes • Costume • Hairstyle • Jewellery • Make-up • Props • Slight • Heavy • Height • Weight • Build **Head Movement** • Nodding • Shaking **Facial Expression** • Facial expression • Mouth • Eyes • Eyebrow position • Smile • Frown • Squint • Grimace **Body Position** • Body position • Face-to-face • Away • To the side **Body Language** • Body movement • Head	**Kinesics** • Kinesics (replacing the term, body language)	**Appearance** • Appearance • Tall • Short • Clothes • Costume • Hairstyle • Jewellery • Make-up • Props • Slight • Heavy • Height • Weight • Build **Head Movement** • Nodding • Shaking **Facial Expression** • Facial expression • Mouth • Eyes • Eyebrow position • Smile • Frown • Squint • Grimace **Body Position** • Body position • Face-to-face • Away • To the side **Body Language** • Body movement • Head • Arms • Legs	**Appearance** • Appearance • Tall • Short • Clothes • Costume • Hairstyle • Jewellery • Make-up • Props • Slight • Heavy • Height • Weight • Build **Head Movement** • Nodding • Shaking **Facial Expression** • Facial expression • Mouth • Eyes • Eyebrow position • Smile • Frown • Squint • Grimace **Body Position** • Body position • Face-to-face • Away • To the side **Kinesics** • Kinesics • Body language • Body movement • Head

(Continued)

Semiotic System/Phase	Synthesising Years 6 and 7 Ages 11 and 12		Accomplishing Years 8, 9 and 10 Ages 13, 14 and 15		Innovating Years 11 and 12 Ages 16 and 17
	Introduce	Revise and Extend	Introduce	Revise and Extend	Revise and Extend
		• Arms • Legs • Hands • Feet **Posture** • Posture • Standing • Sitting • Slumped • Lying • Rigid • Upright • Leaning **Gaze and Eye Movement** • Eye level • Bottom up • Top down • Offer • Demand **Proximity** • Distance • Space		• Hands • Feet **Posture** • Posture • Standing • Sitting • Slumped • Lying • Rigid • Upright • Leaning **Gaze and Eye Movement** • Look • Length of look • Eye level • Bottom up • Top down • Offer • Demand • Gaze • Eye movement • Focussed • Unfocussed • Scanning • Directed gaze • Angle of gaze **Proximity** • Proximity • Distance • Space • Personal space	• Arms • Legs • Hands • Feet **Posture** • Posture • Standing • Sitting • Slumped • Lying • Rigid • Upright • Leaning **Gaze and Eye Movement** • Look • Length of look • Eye level • Bottom up • Top down • Offer • Demand • Gaze • Eye movement • Focussed • Unfocussed • Scanning • Directed gaze • Angle of gaze **Proximity** • Proximity • Distance • Space • Personal space

(Continued)

Table 3.15 (Continued)

Semiotic System/ Phase	Foundation Preparatory and Year 1 Ages 5 and 6	Developing Years 2 and 3 Ages 7 and 8		Investigating Years 4 and 5 Ages 9 and 10	
	Introduce	Introduce	Revise and Extend	Introduce	Revise and Extend
LINGUISTIC	**Parts of Speech** • Word • Noun • Pronoun • Verb **Punctuation** • Capital letters • Full stops • Question marks • Exclamation marks • Statements • Questions • Commands **Phrases, Clauses and Sentences** • Sentence • Simple sentence **Cohesive Devices** • Written text • Spoken language • Repetition • Contrast	**Parts of Speech** • Adjective • Adverb • Concrete, proper and abstract nouns • Articles • Tense **Punctuation** • Contractions • Apostrophes • Commas **Phrases, Clauses and Sentences** • Compound sentence • Clause • Subject • Predicate **Cohesive Devices** • Word associations • Synonyms • Antonyms • Paragraphs	**Parts of Speech** • Word • Noun • Pronoun • Verb **Punctuation** • Capital letters • Full stops • Question marks • Exclamation marks • Statements • Questions • Commands **Phrases, Clauses and Sentences** • Sentence • Simple sentence **Cohesive Devices** • Written text • Spoken language • Repetition • Contrast	**Parts of Speech** • Preposition **Punctuation** • Quotation marks • Dialogue • Titles • Reported speech **Phrases, Clauses and Sentences** • Noun group • Word group • Phrases • Adverbial and prepositional phrases • Direct and indirect speech, interjections **Cohesive Devices** • Pronoun reference • Text connectives	**Parts of Speech** • Word • Noun • Pronoun • Verb • Adjective • Adverb • Concrete, proper and abstract nouns • Articles • Tense **Punctuation** • Capital letters • Full stops • Question marks • Exclamation marks • Statements • Questions • Commands • Contractions • Apostrophes • Commas **Phrases, Clauses and Sentences** • Sentence • Simple sentence • Compound sentence • Clause • Subject • Predicate **Cohesive Devices** • Written text • Spoken language • Repetition • Contrast • Word associations • Synonyms • Antonyms • Paragraphs

Semiotic System/ Phase	Synthesising Years 6 and 7 Ages 11 and 12		Accomplishing Years 8, 9 and 10 Ages 13, 14 and 15		Innovating Years 11 and 12 Ages 16 and 17
	Introduce	Revise and Extend	Introduce	Revise and Extend	Revise and Extend
LINGUISTIC	**Punctuation** • Apostrophes (to denote possession) **Phrases, Clauses and Sentences** • Noun and adjective groups • Principal and subordinate clause • Conjunctions	**Parts of Speech** • Word • Noun • Pronoun • Verb • Adjective • Adverb • Concrete, proper and abstract nouns • Articles • Tense • Preposition **Punctuation** • Capital letters • Full stops • Question marks • Exclamation marks • Statements • Questions • Commands • Contractions • Apostrophes • Commas • Quotation marks • Dialogue • Titles • Reported speech	**Parts of Speech** • Modality • Nominalisation **Punctuation** • Colons • Semicolons • Dashes • Brackets **Phrases, Clauses and Sentences** • Embedded clauses **Cohesive Devices** • Overviews • Initial paragraph • Concluding paragraph • Topic sentences • Indexes • Site maps • Substantiation (of claims) • Lexical cohesion • Ellipsis	**Parts of Speech** • Word • Noun • Pronoun • Verb • Adjective • Adverb • Concrete, proper and abstract nouns • Articles • Tense • Preposition **Punctuation** • Capital letters • Full stops • Question marks • Exclamation marks • Statements • Questions • Commands • Contractions • Apostrophes • Commas • Quotation marks • Dialogue • Titles • Reported speech	**Parts of Speech** • Word • Noun • Pronoun • Verb • Adjective • Adverb • Concrete, proper and abstract nouns • Articles • Tense • Preposition • Modality • Nominalisation **Punctuation** • Capital letters • Full stops • Question marks • Exclamation marks • Statements • Questions • Commands • Contractions • Apostrophes • Commas • Quotation marks • Dialogue

(Continued)

Table 3.15 (Continued)

Semiotic System/Phase	Synthesising Years 6 and 7 Ages 11 and 12		Accomplishing Years 8, 9 and 10 Ages 13, 14 and 15		Innovating Years 11 and 12 Ages 16 and 17
	Introduce	Revise and Extend	Introduce	Revise and Extend	Revise and Extend
		Phrases, Clauses and Sentences • Sentence • Simple sentence • Compound sentence • Clause • Subject • Predicate • Noun group • Word group • Phrases • Adverbial and prepositional phrases • Direct and indirect speech, interjections **Cohesive Devices** • Written text • Spoken language • Repetition • Contrast • Word associations • Synonyms • Antonyms • Paragraphs • Pronoun reference • Text connectives		• Apostrophes (to denote possession) **Phrases, Clauses and Sentences** • Sentence • Simple sentence • Compound sentence • Clause • Subject • Predicate • Noun group • Word group • Phrases • Adverbial and prepositional phrases • Direct and indirect speech, interjections • Noun and adjective groups • Principal and subordinate clause • Conjunctions **Cohesive Devices** • Written text • Spoken language • Repetition • Contrast • Word associations • Synonyms • Antonyms	• Titles • Reported speech • Apostrophes (to denote possession) • Colons • Semicolons • Dashes • Brackets **Phrases, Clauses and Sentences** • Sentence • Simple sentence • Compound sentence • Clause • Subject • Predicate • Noun group • Word group • Phrases • Adverbial and preposition-al phrases • Direct and indirect speech, interjections • Noun and adjective groups • Principal and subordinate clause • Conjunctions • Embedded clauses **Cohesive Devices** • Written text • Spoken language • Repetition • Contrast

(Continued)

Semiotic System/ Phase	Synthesising Years 6 and 7 Ages 11 and 12		Accomplishing Years 8, 9 and 10 Ages 13, 14 and 15		Innovating Years 11 and 12 Ages 16 and 17
	Introduce	Revise and Extend	Introduce	Revise and Extend	Revise and Extend
				• Paragraphs • Pronoun reference • Text connectives	• Word associations • Synonyms • Antonyms • Paragraphs • Pronoun reference • Text connectives • Overviews • Initial paragraph • Concluding paragraph • Topic sentences • Indexes • Site maps • Substantiation (of claims) • Lexical cohesion • Ellipsis

Conclusion

The purpose of this chapter was to build upon information about the codes and conventions of the five semiotic systems (linguistic, visual, gestural, spatial and audio) and provide further definition and exploration of the codes and conventions, together with a suggested sequence for their introduction to students. It was asserted that semiotic systems are social and culture specific resources and therefore subject to change and that pedagogy around the semiotic systems should encourage this understanding. The influences on meaning making were explored, in particular the role of the literacy identity of both consumer producer of the text.

It was emphasised that the semiotic systems do not operate in isolation in a multimodal text and that it was important to explore how the semiotic systems, their codes and conventions, together with other resources contribute to the meanings conveyed. The inquiry model was recommended as a way of devising pedagogies that would encourage and facilitate such explorations into multimodal texts by students and teachers. Finally, along with the metalanguage and terms that might be used to discuss frame, conduct and share findings from these explorations, a focus for pedagogy was suggested to build knowledge and understandings about literacy as a process of problem solving and inquiry and foster the knowledge skills and processes to facilitate the development of independent and innovative inquiry and problem solving skills was suggested.

4 Developing dialogic talk and dialogic pedagogy: Designing multiliterate classrooms

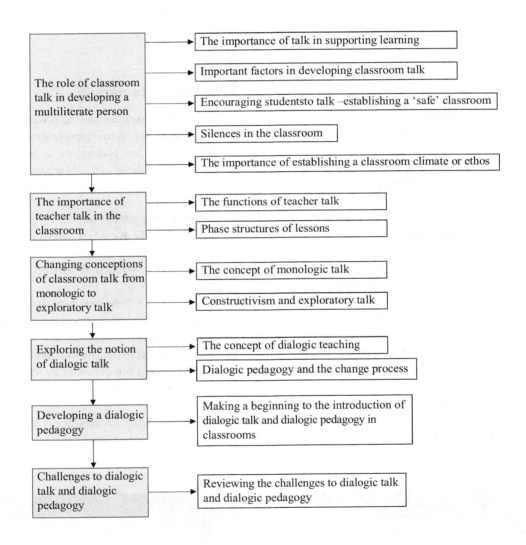

In this chapter the role of classroom talk in developing a multiliterate person will be explored and the factors that support and encourage the development of students' talk will be discussed. The importance of establishing a **safe classroom** where students feel confident to talk, and where a classroom climate that encourages the development of students' talk has been created, will be examined. The part that the **functions of teacher talk** and the phase structure of lessons play in understanding the effect of teacher talk will be considered. The concepts of **monologic, exploratory** and **dialogic talk** will be introduced, and the part that the constructivist approach to teaching plays in the development of these different types of talk will be analysed. The concept of dialogic pedagogy will be explored and how it is affected by the responses of teachers to changes in pedagogy will be examined. Finally, the challenges arising from the introduction of dialogic talk and dialogic pedagogy into the classroom will be identified, and the ways in which teachers might respond to the challenges will be discussed.

The role of classroom talk in developing a multiliterate person

Two of the major themes of this book are (1) to elaborate the concept of **multiliteracies** and **multimodal texts** and (2) to investigate classroom practices and teacher pedagogies. It is important now to explore how classroom talk can support the development of multiliteracies and address both practices and pedagogies. As previously outlined in Chapter One, Anstey and Bull (2006), Anstey (2009) and Bull and Anstey (2010b) proposed a set of characteristics of a multiliterate person. They suggested that in order to be multiliterate, an individual must:

a   Be flexible and able to deal with change – be analytical and reflective problem solvers, be strategic, creative and critical thinkers who can engage with new texts in a variety of contexts and audiences;

b   Have a repertoire of literate knowledge and practices – understand that new texts that have differing purposes, audiences and contexts will require a range of different behaviours that draw on a repertoire of knowledge and experiences;

c   Understand how social and cultural diversity effects literate practices – know that experiences and culture influence and produce a variety of different knowledges, approaches, orientations, attitudes and values that will influence the interpretation and occurrence of literate practices;

d   Understand, and be able to use, traditional and new communication technologies – understand the semiotic systems and recognise that the increasing variety of new texts are delivered by paper, live and digital technologies, and realise that purpose, audience and context determine which semiotic systems and which technology is appropriate;

e   Be critically literate – understand that in every literate practice it is necessary to determine who is participating and for what reason, who is in a position of power, who has been marginalised, what is the purpose and origin of the texts being used and how are these texts supporting participation in society and everyday life.

REFLECTION STRATEGY 4.1

- The purpose of this Reflection Strategy is to determine what part the five characteristics of a multiliterate individual play in the teaching and learning practices in your classroom.
- Review your lesson planning for the last 2–3 weeks to see which, if any, of the characteristics are present in the goals, outcomes or objectives you have specified.

- Check the designs of strategies you have taught and the activities that your students have engaged in to establish which, if any, of the characteristics your students have had access to.
- Decide how you are going to address the characteristics and which one you are going to begin with.

It is appropriate to examine the five characteristics of a multiliterate person and consider the role of classroom talk in their development.

Characteristic (a): An important consideration in this characteristic is that students need to become analytical and reflective problem solvers and be strategic, critical and creative thinkers. Because students do not develop these skills automatically, they need to be taught explicitly. Explicit teaching requires demonstrations and modelling by the teacher that largely rely on teacher talk. As has been previously argued in earlier chapters, successful learning is built upon student involvement in the learning process, a factor that has become increasingly important as concepts about literacy have changed. A careful case was also made in Chapter Two to involve students in the **inquiry** process in order that they became actively involved, and participated, in their own learning. It follows that students should be engaged in talk about these skills rather than just listening to the teacher explaining them. Such talk might take the form of teacher–student discussions at a whole class or individual level, or student-to-student talk in collaborative group situations. Classroom talk therefore becomes an essential feature of learning the skills of a multiliterate person. It is then a logical, further step that when students engage with a variety of new texts that these texts should be multimodal.

Characteristic (b): In order to be multiliterate, students will need to acquire a repertoire of different knowledges and practices. This will include the realisation of the value of engaging in classroom talk in an active and informed way in order to develop new knowledge and new practices. Students will also need to develop an understanding that, in a multiliterate environment, texts can no longer be limited to paper but must include texts that are produced by live and digital technologies. In other words, students (and their teachers) need to appreciate that texts are no longer monomodal but multimodal.

Characteristic (c): The important consideration here is that students will need to understand that their fellow students are highly likely to come from different social or cultural backgrounds. Every background will potentially bring with it differentiated ways of talking, each needing to be equally valued and accepted by both students and teachers. These different types of talk will impact on the nature of classroom talk, who gets to speak, who is marginalised and who is silenced.

Characteristic (d): There are a number of considerations to be accounted for in this characteristic of a multiliterate classroom. First, students and teachers will need to have a detailed knowledge of **semiotic systems**, particularly the audio, spatial and gestural, since each of these can influence the meanings that are conveyed through talk. As has been previously discussed in Chapter Three, elements in the semiotic systems such as **volume** and **tone** in audio, **proximity** in spatial, and arm or hand gestures in gestural can affect the meanings that are conveyed in classroom talk. Second, paper, live and digital technologies have an impact on how talk is used to convey meanings in the **production** and **consumption** of multimodal texts. Lastly, students and teachers need to understand that purpose, audience and context are determining factors in the selection of which semiotic system and which technology is appropriate to convey particular meanings through classroom talk.

Characteristic (e): Because this characteristic addresses how to be critically literate, it explores questions of choice. Who gets to talk, or who is allowed to talk, are important considerations that affect the quantity and quality of classroom talk. In some classrooms, the position of power is held by the teacher, so that most talk is teacher talk and there is little opportunity for student talk. Some students, because they are more extroverted than others, will get to talk more frequently and more often than their introverted fellow students. Some students may also be chosen to answer by their teachers more often than others. The social and cultural backgrounds of students come into play here, where some students are less likely to engage in classroom talk. In each case, some students will be marginalised, some disempowered and some silenced, so that not only will they be less likely to engage in classroom talk, but they will be less successful in participating in society and everyday life.

The preceding discussion demonstrates a strong relationship between the concept of multiliteracies and what it is to be multiliterate, and the nature of classroom talk. This has an obvious impact on how important classroom talk is to learning in a multiliterate classroom, who gets the opportunities to learn through talk, and who has the power to make their talk an important part of learning.

ACTION LEARNING TASK 4.1

- The purpose of this Action Learning Task is to revisit the Multiliteracies Matrix and the Action Learning Proforma that were the tools described in Chapter One.
- As a way of designing your Action Research project, you specified which items from the Matrix you were selecting to form the basis of your classroom research. This enabled you to structure your research using the Action Learning Proforma. In the light of the preceding discussion about how the five characteristics of a multiliterate individual impinge upon classroom talk, it would be useful to revisit the Matrix to decide whether you want to select different items in the light of the knowledge you have acquired about what it is to be multiliterate and classroom talk.
- If you have changed the items you selected from the Matrix, it is necessary to redesign your project on the Action Learning Proforma.
- You will need to adjust the planning, practice and pedagogy items on the Proforma, which means that you may also need to change your evaluation strategies and perhaps the expected outcomes of your research.

The importance of talk in supporting learning

In the last two to three decades there has been an increasing amount of research into the value of talk in classrooms and the role it plays in learning. As Alexander (2005a, p.1) stated when discussing the emerging **pedagogy** around talk, 'It is a pedagogy which exploits the power of talk to shape children's thinking and to secure their engagement, learning and understanding'. This view is supported by Wolfe and Alexander (2008, p.2) in the preface to their paper in which they suggested that research about talk '... begins by establishing the context for debate about the relationship between talk, learning and pedagogy'. Further, they reported (2008, p.2) that there was an increasing body of evidence demonstrating that '... children learn more effectively, and intellectual achievements are higher, when they are actively engaged in pedagogic activity, through discussion, dialogue and argumentation', a view earlier espoused by Mercer and Littleton (2007). The research on the importance of talk in the development of learning has not been confined to the discipline of English or lessons about literacy. The value of talk in science is addressed in the Discourse Primer for Science Teachers as part of the Ambitious Science Teaching project conducted by the National Science Foundation in Washington, DC. This report ('Discourse Primer', 2013, p. 4) suggested, in exploring the question of why talk is so important for learning, that talk is a form of thinking and 'Students who get practice at this become better learners, both individually and as a class. It is sobering to think that in many classrooms, students sit, nearly silent, as their teachers do all the talking'. The report also suggested that talk makes students' thinking visible and reveals conceptual understandings about the nature of learning. Edwards and Jones (2001), Solomon (2009) and Herbel-Eisenmann and Cirillo (2009) reported similar findings about the value of talk in mathematics lessons as did Mortimer and Scott (2003) and Dawes (2008) in science lessons. These conclusions, in referring to the importance of talk in the conduct of science and mathematics lessons, indicate the interdisciplinary nature of talk that pervades the whole curriculum.

AUDITING INSTRUMENT 4.1

- The purpose of this Auditing Instrument is to investigate your approach to teaching and learning in your classroom.
- To determine what part talk plays in the way you approach the teaching and learning in your classroom, you need to establish how often talk features in the way you design the structure of your lessons.
- You also need to review the strategies and activities that students are engaged in to measure what exposure your students are getting to participate in talk.
- To what extent in the design of your lessons and strategies does talk feature in your construction of your literacy pedagogy?

Important factors in developing classroom talk

The development of classroom talk relies on both teachers and students understanding the important part that it plays in learning. There are, however, some widely held beliefs and attitudes about talk that can interfere with this process of learning through talk. Because talk is understood to be universal, there is an underlying, or common sense, belief that everyone will successfully learn to talk as part of the natural process of growing up. These beliefs are then sometimes applied in classrooms to explain how classroom talk develops in school. The problem, of course, is what understandings are transferred to the classroom in the belief that talk is a 'natural' act. As Booth and Thornley-Hall (1991, p. 7) stated, 'Not too long ago a teacher's worth was measured by the silence in the classroom', and they concluded (1991, p. 7) that 'Generally, children in school have not been given time to hypothesize and talk themselves into understanding, to think out loud'. These two scenarios, proposed almost three decades ago, point to the fact that classroom talk does not just happen and is far from a natural act. Classroom talk could be more accurately described as an unnatural act. As Booth and Thornley-Hall (1991, p. 7) further suggested, classroom talk involves students groping towards meaning where talk is '... marked by frequent hesitations, rephrasing, false starts, and changes in direction'. The idea that classroom talk is an unnatural act has been taken up more recently by Wolfe and Alexander (2008), who described talk as uncomfortable. This idea was taken from Lefstein (2006, p. 6), who stated that talk was involved with '... competition, argument, struggle to be heard, persuasion ... and power relations', an opinion that was repeated by Lefstein and Snell (2014, p.18), who went on to suggest that talk was rarely cooperative or orderly.

These ideas suggest that classroom talk is not only unnatural, but also difficult. This conflicts with another belief that suggests that because most children are proficient speakers by the time they come to school, they will find classroom talk easy. The idea that classroom talk can be difficult to engage in is perhaps best summed up by Littleton and Mercer (2013, p.19) who reported that 'Talk is messy stuff, and does not fit neat categorizations'. Despite these ideas, there is strong support for the centrality of talk for engaging students in learning (Mercer & Littleton, 2007; Alexander, 2008a; Mercer & Hodgkinson, 2008; Howe, 2010; Simpson, Mercer & Majors, 2010; Littleton & Mercer, 2010, 2013). This strong support for the value of classroom talk in learning does not seem to translate into classroom practice. As Alexander (2005b, p. 2) suggested, '... talk which in an effective and sustained way engages children cognitively and scaffolds their understanding is much less common than it should be'. This position is supported by Littleton and Mercer (2013, p.96), who suggest that '... many students, perhaps most, do not know how to talk and work together effectively'. However, as Littleton and Mercer report, most teachers assume that students have the strategies to do so. There is little doubt that students need to learn how to talk to reason together, and as Littleton and Mercer (2013, p.96) suggest, '... they may never accomplish this unless they are helped to do so by their teachers'.

REFLECTION STRATEGY 4.2

- The purpose of this Reflection Strategy is to find out what opinions the other teachers in your school hold, particularly about the value of talk.
- Suggest to other teachers that it would be useful for you to discuss with them whether they believe that talk is a natural act, since almost all students are competent speakers by the time they arrive at school.
- Have further discussions with your fellow teachers about how often students exhibit fluency in their talk and how frequently students display hesitancy when they are meaning making through talk. It might be useful to gather opinions from all the staff and not just those who are teaching the same year level as you.
- Collect strategies from teachers throughout the school relating to how they teach their students to work in groups.

Because the promotion of classroom talk is so critical to student learning, it is useful to explore the potential advantages of talk.

- *Talk makes thinking visible.* Talk is not just about sharing with others what you know. It can also be about talking your way into meaning and attempting to make your ideas explicit. Through talk, reasoning, formulation and elaboration of ideas and critical thinking can be made visible so that you and others will know what you have learnt and what you still need to learn. In this way talk makes thinking public and enables both teacher and student to engage in conversations that contribute to greater understandings.

- *Talk produces a repertoire of ideas that can be shared between student and student and between student and teacher.* Students can benefit from understanding how other students think, and teachers can assess the quality and quantity of their students' learning. This allows students to understand how others formulate their ideas and provides opportunities for the resolution of disagreements and potential issues.

- *The more talk becomes a normal part of classroom practice, the more likely it is that those students who are silent will be recognised.* Students may be silent, or silenced, because they are introverts or because they have been overwhelmed by the extroverts in the classroom. There may be linguistic, social or cultural factors in play that result in some students not engaging in classroom talk. Identifying silenced or marginalised students is only the beginning. There may be any number of reasons why students are not talking, and it is up to teachers to diagnose the causes of such silence. Teachers may modify the amount of their talk in order to give students more opportunities to participate. Sometimes a rearrangement of classroom organisation will promote more talk. Alternatively, increasing the amount of group work may make it less intimidating for students or ensuring that there is a mixture of introverts and extroverts in each group. Establishing ground rules for classroom talk also has the potential to increase opportunities for reluctant students to talk.

- *Confining the focus on talk to literacy or English lessons has the potential to limit some students' willingness to engage in talk.* Students will be more likely to engage in talk if they are interested in the subject matter. Shifting talk to other subject areas provides the opportunity to engage in discipline-specific talk and permits the learning of specialised language. Students can benefit from greater understandings in talk-rich contexts in disciplines such as science and mathematics as much as they can in English.

 AUDITING INSTRUMENT 4.2

- The purpose of this Auditing Instrument is to investigate what contributes to silence in your classroom.
- As you teach a series of lessons, take particular note of which students remain silent in your lessons.
- Is it always the same students who remain silent?
- Do particular students tend to remain silent only in whole class lessons or also in small group activities as well? Why might this be so?
- Do some students tend to remain silent only in certain subjects and not others? What might be the possible reasons for this?
- Make an audiotape recording of one of your lessons to see how often, or if, you allow your students opportunities to talk by remaining silent yourself.

Encouraging students to talk – establishing a 'safe' classroom

In the research by Bull and Anstey (2004, 2005b, 2007, 2010b, 2014), many of the teachers involved in the various projects reported some difficulty in getting students to talk in classroom lessons except when they were called upon to answer direct questions posed by their teachers. The difficulties appeared to increase with the age of students, as teachers who were working with students in the higher year levels experienced the greatest difficulties. The participants in the projects frequently hypothesised that the students' reluctance to talk was a result of their experiences in previous year levels where there was a predominance of teacher talk. Interestingly, those participants in the projects who were teaching students at the preschool, prep and year 1 levels (ages 4 to 6 in Australia) reported that the problem was to get the majority of students to stop talking, or at least to stop talking all at once. Given that upwards of 150 teachers drawn from state, independent and Catholic schools were involved in the research by Bull and Anstey accounting for some 3,000 students, it would appear that this is a common occurrence across many schools. What these teacher comments would seem to indicate is that somewhere between entering school and reaching the higher year levels most, although not all, students have been silenced.

The issue centres around what steps can be taken to encourage students to talk. Earlier in this chapter the potential advantages of talk were discussed. If teachers explore the advantages of talk in their classrooms, then it is likely that students will begin to realise that engaging in talk will support their thinking and learning. There are, however, other steps that teachers can take that will begin to construct a classroom climate that will create the conditions for classroom talk to develop. Bull and Anstey proposed a number of pedagogical moves that teachers can instigate that will promote student talk. These pedagogical moves included:

- Making a tape recording of a lesson and then listen to how much you talk and how often the students initiate talk
- If the lesson tape indicates a monopoly of teacher talk, take some steps to reduce the amount of teacher talk
- Reviewing how many whole class lessons you give and replace some of these lessons with a variety of grouping strategies
- Developing a change in your pedagogy that encourages students to be responsible for, and actively construct, their own learning (refer to Chapter Two on the inquiry process for some strategies)
- Reviewing your questioning procedures to determine how much time you allocate between questions to give your students time to reflect.

Silences in the classroom

It is interesting to note that there are two types of silences in a significant number of classrooms. First, there is the silence related to the absence of student talk that has already been discussed in this chapter. Second, there is the silence, or lack of it, related to those occasions when teachers purposefully pause (that is cease talking). In the research by Bull and Anstey (2004, 2005b, 2007, 2010b, 2014), many of the participants, after listening to their taped lessons, reported that they rarely ceased asking questions in their whole class lessons. The participants suggested that they were sometimes using questioning to advance to the next stage of the lesson, which indicated that their purpose in asking questions was to get through the lesson rather than assessing student learning. It is likely that some, if not most, students will learn this 'game' of 'doing school' and begin to realise that there are some teacher questions that do not need to be answered (you only have to listen to students role-playing the role of the teacher to realise how well they have learnt the rules of the game). What the participants in the research came to realise was that some of their teaching strategies were causing the student silences. The participants also came to understand that if they asked a question and got no student response, they quickly asked a further question, or series of questions, until they received a response. Bull and Anstey termed this as an 'intolerance for silence', where many of the participants' taped lessons demonstrated that there was a marked tendency for teachers to fill in the silences. This is somewhat of a paradox, where on the one hand teachers can become concerned about the lack of student talk, while on the other hand they fill in the silences with teacher talk. What is of further interest is that in listening to the tapes of their lessons, the participants came to realise the importance of allowing students time to think, or reflect, by taking a step back and creating space and a safe environment for student talk.

AUDITING INSTRUMENT 4.3

- The purpose of this Auditing Instrument is to explore how, or if, you create opportunities for the students in your class to talk.
- Make an audiotape of one of your lessons and then listen to it to determine if there is a balance between teacher and student talk.
- You may also wish to convert the tape to a transcript and count the number of exchanges between student and teacher; how often you give feedback, both positive and negative, to the students; how often you ask a follow up question to a student after they have provided a response; and how frequently you build on students' answers.
- Measure how long you pause after each question to provide students with enough time to reflect.

The importance of establishing a classroom climate or ethos

The research of Bull and Anstey indicated that an important part of encouraging classroom talk is to establish a classroom climate where there is a balance between teacher and student talk. Both Alexander (2003b, 2004a) and Wolfe and Alexander (2008) referred to the importance of what they termed establishing a classroom ethos that they felt was the foundation necessary to be in place before embarking on attempts to encourage classroom talk. As Wolfe and Alexander (2008, p.7) reported, students '… are often unaccustomed to having a voice of their own', so establishing the right conditions for encouraging classroom talk is essential for success. Alexander (2003b, 2004a) had earlier pointed out that the difference between those teachers who were successfully implementing the establishment of classroom talk and those who were experiencing difficulties was whether care had been taken to achieve an appropriate classroom ethos. As previously discussed, part of creating a supportive ethos or climate is to establish an environment where students feel safe to engage in classroom talk. Such a safe classroom is one where students know that their comments are sought after and valued by their teacher and fellow students. Productive and substantive conversations are only likely to take place when students feel confident in going public with their thoughts. This involves an element of risk taking on the part of students, particularly when advancing ideas that they are not sure of. This is the antithesis of classrooms where teachers ask questions they frequently know the answers to, and where students only answer questions when they believe they have the correct answer. Part of establishing a safe classroom is supporting students to gain enough self-confidence to begin to ask questions themselves and to critique, but not ridicule, the ideas of others. Such critiques require students to listen carefully to other opinions and to take up, and comment on, the ideas of their fellow students. This has led to the call from many researchers in the areas (Mercer, 2000; Alexander, 2003b, 2004a and Wolfe & Alexander, 2008) for the establishment of ground rules for talk that have ideally been generated by both teachers and students. This type of approach to classroom talk draws on earlier work by Vygotsky (1978), who advanced the notion that people learn best when engaging in social interaction with others, and by Nystrand (1997), who argued that people did not learn only by using spoken or written language, but also by participating in discussions of ideas with others. More recently, Wolf, Crosson and Resnick (2006, p.20) concluded that the quality of classroom talk had a positive relationship with '... listening to others, questioning other's knowledge, and exploring one's own thoughts'.

REFLECTION STRATEGY 4.3

- The purpose of this Reflection Strategy is to establish the type of classroom climate present in your room.
- Have you intentionally attempted to create a classroom climate conducive to student talk, and if so, how have you gone about doing this?
- What strategies have you put in place that encourage students to talk about how safe (confident) they are in providing answers without feeling that they might be ridiculed for giving an incorrect response?
- How often do the students in your class listen respectfully to the answers of other students and follow up those answers with further comments?
- What ground rules for talk have you established in your classroom? In what way did your students have some say in determining the rules?

As the foregoing discussion suggests, the value of classroom talk is that it builds a secure foundation for student learning and understanding. It can then, as Myhill et al. (2006) pointed out, be regarded both as a context where talk becomes a product of students' learning and a process that supports student learning and understanding. As Edwards and Mercer (1987, p.20) stated earlier, classroom talk '... is one of the materials from which a child constructs a way of thinking'. It is important, then, to understand the conditions that support the development of classroom talk as both a product and process.

The importance of teacher talk in the classroom

A considerable body of research has indicated that classroom talk has been dominated by teacher talk (Edwards, 2003; Alexander, 2003b, 2004a, 2005a, 2008a; Myhill, 2006; Bull & Anstey, 2004, 2005b, 2007, 2010b; Edwards-Groves, Anstey & Bull, 2014). This is in part due to the belief that there is a

'... perceived correlation between whole class teaching and high attainment' (Myhill et al., 2006, p. 4). This belief has been exacerbated in the U.S., the U.K. and Australia by the development of a national curriculum, by increasing calls for teacher accountability and the support that high-stakes testing has attracted from various levels of government. These developments have resulted in a version of teaching that has framed classroom communication as based on

> ... a great deal to get through, the pace of transmission is likely to be fast. This privileges the teacher's talk, producing not only a great deal of exposition but also a predominance of questions to which the answers are likely to be short and readily 'marked'.

> (Edwards, 2003, p. 39)

The pressure to deal with content has led teachers to a reliance on continually asking questions and redirecting questions as a way of progressing the lesson. As Edwards (2003, p. 39) suggested, by way of an alternative strategy, 'The pressure to evaluate the consequent answers is so pervasive that there is much to be gained from sometimes replacing them with statements that invite rejoinders, elaboration or disagreement or that even admit perplexity'. There is, therefore, much to be gained from changing the nature of teacher talk as a way of influencing how classroom talk is conducted.

The functions of teacher talk

As has been discussed earlier in this chapter, classroom talk can be monopolised by the teacher so that teacher talk dominates and controls the communication. However, a preponderance of teacher talk is not always undesirable. When new or complex knowledge and concepts are being introduced, there is a necessary increase in teacher talk required to deal with these new ideas in such a way that students will understand them. Such explicit teaching lays the foundations for learning so that the teacher can introduce modelling and demonstrations in later lessons. In order to be explicit, teachers need to appreciate that teacher talk is not a unitary process, but rather there are different types or categories of talk that have different purposes. The research by Anstey (1993b, 1998, 2003) and Anstey and Bull (2004) identified seven categories of teacher talk that were spread across three *functions of talk*. These are outlined in Table 4.1.

In Table 4.1 it can be seen that the seven categories of talk are related to different actions or strategies enacted by the teacher that result in distinctive types of teacher talk that, in turn, has different functions. As an example, the category of classroom management talk can result in the reinforcement of classroom or school rituals, such as 'Pens down' or 'Turn around Mandy', which are focussed on organising students. Such categories of talk are necessary for the effective operation of lessons but have little to do with actual literacy learning but rather how to organise the students to be ready to learn. The two heavy black lines in the table separate the three functions of teacher talk. The function of 'Doing Literacy' essentially addresses knowledge about literacy and practice exercises where students are engaged in tasks but are given no information about how, or why, the tasks might be useful. In the final two categories of teacher talk, students are provided with information about the processes that are involved in literacy learning and how, or why, they might be useful. Table 4.1 illustrates that different categories of teacher talk have different functions that produce different degrees of literacy learning. Given the emphasis throughout this book on critical literacy, problem solving and critical thinking, it is evident that the earlier categories of teacher talk described in Table 4.1, classroom management and literacy management, do not produce the same level of deep understanding about literacy learning present in the process and utility

Table 4.1 Definitions for analysing the functions of teacher talk (developed from Anstey (1993b, 1998, 2003) and Anstey and Bull (2004)

Category/Type of Talk	Description Questions or Statements That Focus On:	Example	Focus and Function of Talk
Classroom Management	• Physical, social and organisational management • School rituals	• Turn around Mandy • Pens down • Get out your …	**Organisation**
Literacy Management	• Management of literacy tasks and lesson • Functional aspects of literacy not teaching about literacy	• Read the first page • Write … • Look at the cover	
Reconstruction Restatement	• Construct, reconstruct paraphrase or rephrase oral written or pictorial text • Repeat students' answers • Confirm a correct answer – but no more • Require literal thinking • Provide implicit modelling	• Mary ran away (paraphrasing text) • John said Mary is frightened (repeating student answer) • Yes, right, well done • I would write … • I think there are two ideas	**Doing Literacy**
Elaboration Projection	• Require inferential thinking, • Require drawing on own experience or knowledge from previous lessons	• Why might he do that? • What can you tell me about …	
Informative	• Provide information or definitions about literacy • Do not provide explanations about how to use the information to complete the task	• Every sentence has a verb • Usually the first sentence in the paragraph provides the main idea	
Process	• Focus on cognitive aspects of task, decision-making processes • Explicitly model cognitive activity and thinking processes	• What is a better strategy than guessing? • How would you work that out? • I am writing … because …	**Learning What, How, When and Why about Literacy**
Utility	• Explain how the strategies or process might be useful in other situations • Explain why it is useful to be able to do this	• It is useful to do … because … • You skim to work out whether there is useful information present • Why do we use paragraphs?	

Adapted from Anstey in Bull & Anstey, 2003, p.114

categories. Nor do these earlier categories prepare students to function successfully in contemporary society. Nevertheless, in order for the process and utility categories of teacher talk to be developed, the other five categories need to be adequately dealt with. It is the issue of balance that is crucial. A lesson, or series of lessons, that contain a preponderance of the organisation function of teacher talk is undesirable as are lessons that focus on the doing literacy function to the exclusion of the how, when and why function. It is important to point out that not all seven categories of teacher talk will be present in every lesson, nor is there a particular order in which the categories need to occur. Nevertheless, it would be expected that lessons would be more likely to produce in-depth student learning when there was a minimum of classroom and literacy management talk and where teachers used more informative, process and utility talk. In her study, Anstey (1993b) categorised over 14,000 teacher **utterances** from twenty-five individual teachers and classified them into the types and functions of teacher talk. The research results from Anstey (1993b, p.129) indicated that 43 per cent of teacher talk involved organising students (classroom and literacy management) with only 3 per cent process talk and 1 per cent utility talk. What these results suggest is that the majority of the students in these twenty-five classrooms were 'doing school' or 'doing literacy' and few were engaged in literacy learning.

AUDITING INSTRUMENT 4.4

- The purpose of this Auditing Instrument is to determine the types of teacher talk you are using and not just how much you talk.
- In Auditing Instrument 4.3, you made an audiotape of one of your lessons. If you have not already done so, make a transcript of the first 5–10 minutes of your lesson.
- How many of your utterances involved classroom or literacy management?
- How many of your utterances were directed towards students engaging in doing school, that is following the routines established by you, and how much literacy learning talk were you using?
- Did you tell the students what the lesson was going to be about, that is establishing the purpose of the lesson, and did you tell them why the lesson was important? How would this affect the likely success of the lesson?

The teachers who participated in the Action Learning Cycle projects outlined in Chapter One were required to tape record a literacy lesson, produce a transcript of the lesson and then analyse the categories of talk that they used in the lesson. The majority of the participants across all of the projects undertaken by Bull and Anstey (2004, 2005b, 2007, 2010b, 2014) reported a marked reliance on the categories of classroom management and literacy management talk. Most of the participants were surprised by these results and also somewhat disturbed by them because they had not realised that they spent so much time organising their students and so little time on teaching them about literacy. Another surprising result of their analyses was that few of the teachers reported that they had addressed the processes of literacy learning, and even fewer reported that they had discussed with their students why they were engaging in particular activities and how they were useful. These results were a replication of the earlier research by Anstey (1993b). An encouraging outcome of the projects was that once the participants understood the different categories of teacher talk and had analysed their lessons, they were able to successfully overcome the imbalances in subsequent lessons. It became evident that when participants became aware of the different categories of teacher talk, they were able to plan their lessons differently, change their literacy pedagogy and vary their categories appropriately to successfully address the issue of student literacy learning. What also became evident was that knowledge of the different categories of teacher talk was fundamental to successful teaching and learning about literacy. (Further information about the functions of teacher talk can be found in Chapter Four of the complementary volume *Foundations of Multiliteracies: Reading, Writing and Talking in the 21st Century*.) What became evident during the ALC projects was that participants needed to understand not only which categories of teacher talk to incorporate in their lessons, but also when in their lessons each category of talk would be most effective.

ACTION LEARNING TASK 4.2

- The purpose of this Action Learning Task is to return to the Multiliteracies Matrix and the Action Learning Proforma discussed in Chapter One.
- Now that you are familiar with the functions of teacher talk, you may wish to reconsider which item, or items, you selected from the pedagogy section of the Matrix.
- You may wish to redirect your attention to particular types of talk and change, or adapt, your research to allow you to study your use of teacher talk.
- If you do reorient your research and modify your planning, pedagogy and practice, then you will need to adapt the direction of your research, amend your evaluation procedures and change the type of evidence you will attempt to gather.

Phase structure of lessons

The research by Anstey (1993b, 1998, 2003) and Anstey and Bull (2004) indicated that knowledge of the categories of teacher talk was, by itself, insufficient. They reported that timing was also crucial, that is in which part of the lesson would engaging in a particular category of teacher talk be most effective. They proposed a series of what they termed phases of lessons, where each phase had a particular focus that was related to teacher talk or teacher activity. **Phase structure** was based on the idea that learning episodes or lessons usually had a sequence of activities that required particular types of teacher talk and student learning behaviour. As Anstey (2003, p.116) suggested,

> ... each time students move to a new phase of a lesson... they are required to behave and interact slightly differently. Therefore, in order to participate successfully in the literate practices of a lesson and learn, students need to be able to recognise the phase structures.

Anstey also suggested that students needed to be able to identify when **transition** occurred from one phase to the next and that teachers needed to be aware of the phase structure of their lessons and ensure that the phases were appropriate and in a logical sequence to support student learning. As can be seen in Table 4.2, lessons have the potential to vary considerably in the number of phases incorporated and also in the combinations of phases used in any particular learning episode. Table 4.2 represents the ten phases initially proposed by Anstey (1993b, 1998, 2003) and further developed by Anstey and Bull (2004).

It is important to point out that, as with categories of teacher talk, it is not expected that every lesson will contain all ten phases, nor is there an ideal sequence of phases that are necessary for successful

Table 4.2 Possible lesson phases (developed from Anstey (1993b, 1998, 2003) and Anstey and Bull (2004)

Phase	Focus and Function of the Phase	Example Statements or Description of Activity
Attention	How the lesson commences, e.g. gaining students' attention and organising for class and materials. It is not the introduction to the learning aspects of the lesson.	*Boys and girls, who's ready? My, that is good to see.*
Focus/Refocus	**Focus** usually occurs at the beginning of the lesson, when the teacher's tone and language identifies the learning focus of the lesson. Some information may be imparted.	*Now today we are going to talk about the structure of stories.*
	Refocus may occur at other times in the lesson when the teacher revises the overall learning focus of the lesson or identifies a new learning focus.	*So far we have been exploring the structure of stories, but now we are going to look particularly at the complication and resolution.*
Guided Implementation	Where teacher and students identify, practise, or implement the knowledge which is the focus of the lesson. The activity is guided by the teacher, for example explaining or modelling first and then engaging students in joint construction. Specific aspects of Guided Implementation:	
	(a) **Identifying** Identifying examples of new knowledge, skills or strategies. May include writing on whiteboard or students writing.	*Teacher leads students in identification of main idea in paragraph.*
	(b) **Practice** Using new knowledge, skills or strategies previously identified in a different combination or context.	*Teacher leads students in finding main idea in a new paragraph and making notes about the main idea.*
	(c) **Transferring** Applying new knowledge, skills or strategies previously identified and practised in a different context. Apply the knowledge skills or strategies to the completion of a new task.	*Teacher leads students in using notes taken about main idea to construct a paragraph.*
Report	Students display or present finished work/task. No commentary by teacher.	*Students read answers or completed work to class as requested by teacher.*
Display	Teacher displays/presents/reads aloud/models task he or she has completed.	*Teacher might show work and say 'When I was looking for information on this topic the first thing I did was…'*
Unguided Implementation	Same as Guided Implementation, but student must perform on own. Same sub-categories as for Guided Implementation. Independent student-driven or student-led work.	*As for Guided Implementation examples except student led or done by student independently.*

(Continued)

Table 4.2 (Continued)

Phase	Focus and Function of the Phase	Example Statements or Description of Activity
Review	Teacher reviews knowledge, skills and strategies presented in previous phases at a general level. It is not a complete reworking or re-teaching of examples but a review of what has been done and learned. Students may be asked to participate in, or lead, the review. A review can occur at any time in a lesson and may occur several times.	*Teacher might use flowing phrases in such a phase:* *'Now what we have learned so far...'* *'First we found out that...'*
Presentation of Text	Teacher reads text to students, or students read text. Random exchanges between teacher and students may occur during this phase.	*Reading of story to class as part of a shared book activity.*
Coda	Occurs at end of lesson. Teaching aspect of lesson has concluded, but teacher or students may continue exchanges in some way related to topic or content of lesson.	*Discussing dogs or pets after reading and discussing a passage about dogs in previous lesson phases.*
Transition Out	Signals end of lesson and tidying up or reorganisation of class for subsequent lessons.	*Usually signalled by activity and teacher instructions such as 'Put your materials away'.*

Adapted from Anstey in Bull and Anstey (2003, p.117)

student learning. However, it would be expected that most lessons would have a focus phase early in the lesson where the teacher tells the students what the lesson is about. What would also be anticipated is that most lessons would have a review phase where the teacher revises what they have taught (and what the students may have learnt). Anstey (1993b, p.104) reported that the occurrence of the focus phase was 4 per cent and the review phase 4 per cent. This is a particularly concerning result because, as indicated in Table 4.2, both the focus and review phases can occur a number of times throughout a lesson and at any time in the lesson. This is because there is no justifiable pedagogical reason why the focus phase always has to occur only at the beginning of the lesson or that the review phase should only occur at the conclusion of the lesson. A teacher might focus and refocus students' attention a number of times during a lesson (particularly when engaging students in new activities throughout the lesson) or review what has been taught at the conclusion of each activity. As with the different types or categories of teacher talk, the participants in the ALC projects reported similar results for the focus and review phases, as was found in Anstey's original research. As before, once teachers had completed the analysis of their initial lessons, they were then able to redress this imbalance in ensuing lessons. What is encouraging about the results from Anstey's (1993b) research is that 34 per cent of the teacher utterances in the twenty-five lessons that she taped were present in the guided identification and guided practice phases. A similar result was reported by the participants in the ALC projects. Students were being given significant amounts of guidance about how to engage in, and practice, particular strategies. What appears to be critical is that teachers need to possess an in-depth knowledge of both the different categories of teacher talk and the distinctive phases of lesson structures.

AUDITING INSTRUMENT 4.5

- The purpose of this Auditing Instrument is to determine which phases you are using.
- In Auditing Instrument 4.3, you made an audiotape of one of your lessons. If you have not already done so, make a transcript of your lesson.
- How many of the ten phases did you employ in your lesson?
- Do you need to change the phase structure of your lesson? How might you accomplish this? Why does the phase structure of your lesson need to change?
- Did you tell the students when each phase ended and another began?
- How did you determine why each phase was necessary?
- Was there a clear relationship between the phase type and the learning objective of that phase?
- Have your findings affected the likely success of the lesson, and if so, how would you approach the structure of your lessons in the future?

It is important to understand that there is a relation between categories of teacher talk and the phases to be found in lesson structures. Different categories of teacher talk will be more powerful if they are associated with particular phases in lesson structure. As an example, the utility category of teacher talk can occur at any point in a lesson, but it has the potential to be more effective as a teaching point if it occurs at a focus phase at the beginning of the lesson. It will also be potentially more useful to students in their literacy learning if they are informed about the reason for the lesson at the outset. Similarly, informative and process talk are more likely to be effective if they are incorporated into the guided implementation phase of a lesson. Given that Anstey (1993b) found seven phases of lesson structure and ten categories of teacher talk in her research, there are at least seventy possible combinations when considering both phase and talk, given that multiple types of talk might occur in each phase and any or all of the phases might be present in a lesson. Some of these combinations would be largely ineffectual, for example attempting to implement classroom and literacy management categories of teacher talk in either the coda and transition out phases. However, what these potential combinations suggest is that teachers not only need to be aware of the categories of teacher talk and the phase structure of lessons, but also how to make teacher talk more effective by incorporating it into the appropriate phases. What these considerations indicate is that teachers need to give careful thought about to the nature of the talk in their lessons. Teacher talk is far from a natural act that is intrinsic to classrooms, nor is it an instinctive quality that good teachers are born with. Teacher talk is an unnatural act that is context specific to the classroom. Teachers need to become aware of these considerations if they are going to adequately support students in their literacy learning and in their learning in other disciplines.

REFLECTION STRATEGY 4.4

- The purpose of this Reflection Strategy is to determine in which phases you are using particular functions of talk.
- Review the transcript of the lesson you made for Auditing Instrument 4.5 to establish which phases you are using in conjunction with which functions of teacher talk.
- You need to make judgements about whether your use of the functions of teacher talk is appropriate to the phase and learning purpose of that phase.
- If changes need to be made, how might this be achieved? Why were the changes you made necessary?

It is important to realise that classroom talk is not just a matter of how and when teachers talk to their students. What is also important is how, or if, students get to talk to their teachers or fellow students in the classroom, and if there are opportunities for students to initiate talk.

THEORY INTO PRACTICE 4.1

- The purpose of this Theory into Practice is to support discussions about the purposes of using a variety of different functions of teacher talk and different phases of lessons.
- Instigate a series of discussions with other teachers throughout your school in order to confirm that there is a school-wide approach to studying functions of talk and structuring phases of lessons.
- The following questions might be useful in guiding discussions:
  o How often are teachers making audiotapes of their lessons?
  o Has the staff a uniform approach to the analysis of transcripts?
  o What experiences can be shared about which functions of talk are more successful in which phases of lessons?
  o Is there any evidence that has been gathered in the school to measure whether there is any appreciable growth in student learning?
  o In what ways have teachers reported that their pedagogy has become more effective?

Changing conceptions of classroom talk: from monologic to exploratory talk

Teacher talk can be just a matter of the teacher talking to, or at, the students who are expected to listen passively. This type of teacher talk resembles a monologue where students' only opportunity to talk is to answer questions posed by the teacher. In describing this type of communication, Edwards (2003, p. 38) stated that 'Teachers direct the talk by doing most of it themselves, combining lengthy exposition with many questions, allocating the right or obligation to answer those questions and evaluating the answers'. As Myhill et al. (2006, p. 4) concluded, 'This privileges the teacher's talk, producing not only a great deal of exposition but also a predominance of questions'. This type of question and answer interaction has become known as an **IRE** sequence, which involves an initial teacher question (I) followed by a student response (R) and culminating in an evaluative comment (E) from the teacher. (The IRE sequence is also sometimes referred to as IRF, where the F denotes feedback.) As Edwards (2003), Bull and Anstey (2004, 2005b, 2007, 2010a, 2014) and Edwards-Groves, Anstey and Bull (2014) and many others have concluded in their research, this type of sequence is a common form of teaching exchange in a significant number of classrooms and is often, as Cazden (1988) earlier pointed out, the default position that teachers engage in when in a stressful situation. (Further information about the IRE sequence can be found in Chapter Four of the complementary volume *Foundations of Multiliteracies: Reading, Writing and Talking in the 21st Century*.) Apart from putting limitations on the amount talk, and who gets to talk, this type of interaction can also lead to a situation where a single right answer can be accepted '... as representing a class-wide understanding and single wrong answer as a common failure to get the point' (Edwards, p. 38).

The concept of monologic talk

The concept of teacher monologues began to be referred to as **monologic talk**. Nystrand et al. (1997), in their investigation of over 100 U.S. classrooms, found an overwhelming number of lessons where the teaching was based on monological instruction which they defined as teacher-to-student transmission of knowledge through the use of IRE exchanges. Lefstein and Snell (2014, p. 14) defined monologue as a situation where only one person speaks, and in an educational setting where '... the teacher speaks most of the time, controls the topic and allocation of the floor, mediates all pupil–pupil communication, and primarily recognizes those pupil ideas that advance the teacher's own agenda'. This type of teacher talk is sometimes referred to as 'recitation script' (Wells, 2001; Barnes, 2008). Monologic talk can have a negative impact on classroom communication because it can potentially silence students by not giving them the opportunities to talk. It can also effectively marginalise some students because, in IRE sequences, some students' answers will be preferred over others by virtue of the fact, as Lefstein and Snell (2014) have pointed out, their answers do not follow the teacher's agenda. As Lobato et al. (2005, p. 103) concluded, this 'teaching by telling' positions the teacher as the source of all knowledge and communicates to the students that there is only one acceptable answer or solution to the question. However, monologic talk has been seen as essential by some writers such as Wells (1993), Cazden (1988) and Alexander (2008a) because it can support student learning if new work is being introduced or if the conceptual level of the lesson is high. In these cases, explicit instruction, through the use of monologic talk, is needed to support student learning and has the potential to lead to the development of discussion.

IRE sequences can also serve a useful purpose depending on the type of questions that the teacher asks. Probing questions or prompts (e.g. "What do you mean by that?") can encourage students to make their thinking public, or visible, to other students because they allow students the space to initiate talk. These probing questions can be followed up by pressing questions (e.g. "Can you give an example?") where the teacher further questions particular students to explain their reasoning through talk. Re-stating student answers (e.g. "Is this what you meant?") gives students the opportunity to comment on teacher talk by making follow-up suggestions. These types of questions support students to make logical arguments through talk. Therefore, teachers need to be aware that it is not only a matter of asking questions such as those that relate to the various levels of difficulty to be found in Bloom's taxonomy, but also asking the type of questions that create opportunities and space that promote student talk. Teachers can create space not only by taking a step back from monopolising classroom talk, but also by rearranging classroom space. As Alexander (2005a, p. 6) suggested, the teacher, by arranging desks in a horseshoe or square so that each student can see and interact with all others and with the teacher, can '... provoke a very different kind of talk, and a different relationship, to that signalled by having separate desks in rows facing the front'. Wells (2001, p. 4) suggested that this type of talk led to what he termed 'co construction rather than transmission' that would develop '... personal initiative and responsibility, adaptable problem-posing and -solving skills, and the ability to work collaboratively with others'. He further stated that in order to achieve these changes, schools and classrooms needed to become more democratic, more critical and more willing to listen respectfully to the opinions of others. A particular approach to teaching and learning is required in order to achieve these types of changes.

Constructivism and exploratory talk

Following the ideas proposed by Wells (2001) and Alexander (2005a), what was being suggested was a movement away from monologic talk to developing a type of talk that allowed students to become involved in the construction of, and accept responsibility for, their own learning. They saw students identifying problems and becoming problem solvers through collaborative learning. These ideas were originally established by Barnes et al. (1969) and Barnes (1976) and later followed up by Barnes (2008, 2010). Barnes proposed that learners should be actively involved in their own learning rather than being passive receivers of information from their teachers. Barnes (2008, p. 2) proposed that students involved in active learning would be '... attempting to interrelate, to re-interpret, to understand new experiences and ideas' and be actively constructing new ways of understanding. As Barnes (2008, p. 2) reported, this view of learning has come to be termed **constructivism**, where '... each of us can only learn by making sense of what happens to us in the course of actively constructing a world for ourselves'. In his view, this constructivist view of learning required teachers to, among other things, set up situations and challenges that encouraged students to relate new ideas to existing understandings in order to modify earlier learning. Earlier Wells (2001), in exploring the constructivist view, saw this position as involving the construction and reconstruction of knowledge in collaborative achievement. He suggested that '... knowledge is only truly known when it is being used by particular individuals in the course of solving specific problems; and then it is open to modification and development as it is reconstructed to meet the actual demands of the situation'.

What has been explored by the preceding writers requires a significant shift, or in Barnes's (2008, p. 3) words a radical change, in teachers' views about the nature of teaching and learning. One of the ways of making this radical shift from teacher exposition to a focus on student understanding is the idea of trying out new ways of thinking and understanding to open up new possibilities. As Barnes (2008, p. 4) suggested, 'The readiest way of working on understanding is often through talk, because the flexibility of speech makes it easy for us to try out new ways of arranging what we know'. Barnes (1976) originally proposed what he called **exploratory talk** as a way of students approaching new ideas. Barnes suggested that owing to the fact that it involved exploring new ideas, this type of talk was hesitant and incomplete and required an element of risk taking on the part of students because it was concerned with sorting out ideas – hence the term exploratory. When discussing the nature of exploratory talk, Edwards (2003, p. 38) suggested that this type of talk occurred when both '... teachers and pupils see the possibility of conclusions unexpected, and certainly unplanned, when talk began'. This does suggest that both teachers and students will need to be comfortable with a certain degree of uncertainly and risk taking. However, as Edwards (2003, p.40) concluded, the advantage of this approach is that 'Teachers and pupils take explicit account of what others have said, so that their speech is responsive as well as expressive'. As has been previously discussed in this chapter, students will only be confident to engage in this type of exploratory talk if the teacher has taken the time to set up a supporting classroom climate or ethos. As Barnes (2008, p.5) pointed out, students will only engage in exploratory talk if they feel at ease and are confident that they will not be contradicted in a hostile manner or belittled. Barnes was also quick to point out that exploratory talk was different to what he called presentational talk, which he suggested was commonly used in classrooms where teacher talk was dominant. He reported that in these classrooms students were called upon to engage in activities such as morning talks, giving reports and debates so that teachers could evaluate them rather than use exploratory talk to talk their way into meaning. Recently Littleton and Mercer (2013, p.113) have defined exploratory talk as representing reasoning in social contexts where the purpose of the talk is to support a group of people, or students, to achieve a collective solution to a shared problem. They also report that exploratory talk is sometimes referred to as accountable talk (see Wolf et al., 2006), although they suggested that accountable talk bore a strong resemblance to their own definition of exploratory talk (Littleton and Mercer, 2013, p.16).

THEORY INTO PRACTICE 4.2

- The purpose of this Theory into Practice is to discover whether constructivism and exploratory talk are being actively explored in your school.
- Have a series of discussions at the whole school level that address constructivism and exploratory talk. The following questions might be useful in guiding the discussions:
  o   What approach to pedagogy are you implementing in your classroom?
  o   What do you understand by the term constructivism?
  o   In what ways do you think constructivism might support exploratory talk?
  o   What do you see as the advantages in introducing exploratory talk into your classroom?
  o   What, if anything, do you see as challenging about introducing exploratory talk into your classroom?
  o   Can you encourage exploratory talk without using the constructivist approach?

Earlier research by Mercer (1995, 2000) and Dawes et al. (2000) explored the development of a range of social modes of thinking that were related to the establishment of understanding through talk. Dawes, Mercer and Wegerif proposed what they termed three forms of argument that were based on three types of talk that were earlier defined by Mercer (1995, p.104). These types of talk were based on the need for students to explain and justify their decision-making to fellow students and grew out of the original work of Barnes (1976). Mercer (1995, 2000) defined three types of talk that have been adopted and adapted by other researchers:

- **Exploratory talk** – characterised by constructively engaging with each other's ideas in a critical but supportive manner growing out of reflecting on the reasoned arguments advanced by other learners. The result of such talk is that knowledge is shared and made public so that individual's thinking and reasoning becomes visible.

- **Cumulative talk** – represents a cooperative undertaking where students build on each other's ideas in order to arrive at a consensus. Exchanges of this type of talk usually confirms and elaborates on the contributions of others.
- **Disputational talk** – is competitive and involves disagreements where participants are usually unwilling to accept the ideas of others. It usually results in individual rather than collaborative decision-making and is based on exchanges that are built upon assertions rather than reasoned argument.

These types of talk have become the subject of a considerable amount of research. Wolfe and Alexander (2008) explored these three types of talk in their exploration of how a consideration of argumentation can inform the development of a pedagogy for a changing world. In order to adopt these types of talk, Wolfe and Alexander (2008, p.1) suggested that '… teachers may need to reconfigure their roles in order to guide rather than control the processes of inquiry and knowledge production'. This view aligns with the approach explored earlier in this chapter where a shift away from monologic talk and teacher exposition was being recommended. Similar conclusions were reached by Edwards and Jones (2001) when investigating the role of exploratory talk in mathematics. They concluded (2001, p. 23) that this type of talk established '… the role of helping each other and has the effect of reducing the degree to which extremes of intellectual conflict occur, thus improving the effectiveness of the collaboration'. Edwards and Jones (2001, p.23) also suggested that these improved students' confidence in offering solutions and expressing opinions. Littleton and Mercer (2013) also investigated the three types of talk in their studies of the occurrence of talk in social situations. They suggested (2013, p. 22) that 'Exploratory Talk can be described as a cultural tool for reasoning collectively' and that it embodied the principles of '… accountability, clarity, constructive criticism and receptiveness to well-justified proposals'. They felt the focus of cumulative talk was more directed towards maintaining solidarity and trust rather than seeking the best possible outcomes that were aligned with exploratory talk. Because cumulative talk was concerned with solidarity and trust, Littleton and Mercer (2013, p.21) stated that it required '… the constant repetition and confirmation of partners' ideas and opinions'. They therefore proposed that both exploratory and cumulative talk were concerned with the achievement of consensus. In contrast, they interpreted disputational talk as competitive and defensive where '… ideas are asserted rather than shared, differences of opinion are emphasized not resolved' and where talk was dominated by assertions and counter-assertions and a lack of cooperation.

REFLECTION STRATEGY 4.5

- The purpose of this Reflection Strategy is to explore the types of talk you have encountered in your classroom.
- How familiar are you with exploratory, cumulative and disputational talk?
- How useful do you think these types of talk on students' literacy learning?
- In what ways have you studied student, or learner, talk in your classroom?
- How might study of the use of these three types of talk in your classroom assist in achieving a multiliterate pedagogy?

It is tempting to conclude that the research into these three types of talk indicates that useful progress can be made by focussing only on student talk. However, this would ignore the significant amount of research exploring the role of the teacher in encouraging student talk. As has been suggested earlier in this chapter, the work of Wolfe and Alexander (2008) explored the necessity of teachers changing their role from a controller of interaction to a guider in order to support student inquiry. In addition to this, the work of Alexander (2003a, 2004a, 2005a, 2005b) and Bull and Anstey (2004, 2005b, 2007, 2010b, 2014), as has been previously discussed, emphasised the importance of the teacher establishing an ethos or climate that was conducive to the encouragement of student talk. It is clear that the teacher has a crucial role to play in setting up the conditions that support students in their use of exploratory and cumulative talk and minimising the occurrence of disputational talk.

Exploring the notion of dialogic talk

The discussion of teacher talk in this chapter has focussed primarily on IRE sequences and monologic talk. The concept of monologic talk as teacher exposition relates to a monologue by the teacher where students receive information passively and there is no explicit interaction between teacher and student. IREs represent a type of teacher–student interaction where the students do not get to initiate talk but merely answer questions posed by the teacher. Authentic two-way interaction only occurs when student-to-student, teacher-to-student and student-to-teacher talk takes place. This type of talk has come to be referred to as *dialogic* and has been defined by Lefstein and Snell (2014, p.14) as a form of interaction '... which typically involves two or more interlocutors freely exchanging ideas, listening to one another, affording one another equal opportunities to participate, addressing one another's concerns and building upon one another's contributions'.

The shift from monologic to dialogic talk involves a radical change in the power relationships in a classroom whereby teachers have created the space, and students have been confident to use this space, to construct authentic interactional talk. Mills (2011, p.80), in discussing the nature of talk in multiliterate classrooms, proposed that these types of spaces were created in classrooms where

> Dialogic spaces of authorship were created that shared interactions between teacher, students and their designs. In this socially produced space, the participants collaborated and reflected on the ideas of others, viewing their peers and the teacher as coparticipants and sources of complementary skills and experiences.

As Alexander (2005a, 2005b), Littleton and Mercer (2013), Edwards-Groves, Anstey and Bull (2014) and many others have pointed out, there is a positive relationship between dialogic talk and increased literacy learning. Some classrooms and schools, because of their incorporation of dialogic talk into everyday learning, particularly literacy learning, may create advantage for their students. It follows that some students, because of the presence of dialogic or reasoned discussions in their homes, may arrive at school with a distinctive advantage over their fellow students. Interestingly, this proposition is similar to the arguments put forward by Bernstein (1960, 1961, 1962, 1964, 1971), Cazden (1967, 1970, 1972, 2015), and Gee (1990, 1992, 2004) about the advantages of learning particular **codes** or discourses in the home or community. (For a detailed discussion of these issues see Chapter One.) It may also be, as Littleton and Mercer (2013, p.95) pointed out, that school may represent the only opportunity for some students to experience dialogic or reasoned discussions. As Michaels et al. (2002, p.27) earlier suggested, 'Very few students come to school adept at constructing well reasoned arguments. Very few students are used to supplying well-grounded evidence to support any claims that they might make'. There are, therefore, important advantages for students to be exposed to dialogic talk because it supports their literacy learning. Similarly, dialogic teaching allows teachers to encourage students to assume responsibility for their own learning and also to create a classroom environment where students can engage in problem formulation and problem solution following the constructionist approach recommended by Barnes (1976, 2008, 2010).

The concept of dialogic teaching

Simplistically stated, dialogic teaching occurs when teachers encourage students to engage in dialogic talk. One of the distinct advantages of dialogic teaching is that it provides a framework for teachers to introduce the constructionist approach or, as it is sometimes referred to, the discovery method, problem-based learning or the inquiry approach. It is important for teachers who wish to implement dialogic talk to be able to construct a supportive environment that will enable students to engage in this type of talk. At the same, teachers need to develop the skills to implement the necessary strategies to support dialogic talk and recognise when dialogic teaching and learning is successfully taking place. The questions in Table 4.3, adapted from Lefstein and Snell (2014, p.15), provide an initial framework for teachers to consider when thinking about the implementation of a dialogic pedagogy.

These types of questions have formed the background to a great deal of research into dialogic teaching. Central to the concept of dialogic teaching has been the research by Alexander (2001a, 2001b, 2003, 2004a, 2004b, 2005a, 2005b, 2008a, 2008b, 2010), who investigated talk in England (Yorkshire and London), France, India, Russia and the U.S. Part of Alexander's research was concerned with establishing criteria for dialogic teaching. Table 4.4 addresses these criteria and has been adapted from Alexander (2005b, p.14).

Table 4.3 Initial framework for the implementation of a dialogic pedagogy

Questions	Concept or Topic Addressed by Question
Which students get to talk, to whom and how often?	Equity and participation
Which students talk to other students or to the teacher?	Interaction
When students talk to each other, or to the teacher, what is the quality of the thinking skills and processes that are made visible?	Focussed discussion or inquiry learning
To what extent are the students listening to each other and basing their talk on the extension of other student's ideas?	Respect
Are there students who are extroverts who dominate the talk, and are there other students who have been silenced or marginalised as a result of this?	Notions of equality, individual differences and participation
Which students' ideas are being subjected to critical examination and which are not?	Community of learners

Table 4.4 Criteria for establishing dialogic teaching

Criteria	Description of Criteria
Collective	Students and teachers engage in learning tasks together in a group or whole class situation.
Reciprocal	Students and teachers share and respect each other's ideas and address alternative opinions and viewpoints.
Supportive	In a positive classroom climate, students feel confident to express their ideas without fear of embarrassment or making mistakes in order to achieve shared understandings.
Cumulative	Students and teachers extend their own and each other's ideas in order to construct meaningful inquiries and coherent thinking.
Purposeful	Teachers implement and direct classroom talk with specific objectives in mind.

The ideas and approaches about dialogic teaching represented in Tables 4.3 and 4.4 have been drawn from a number of different sources that suggest that emerging conceptions of dialogic talk are constructed when:

- Teachers and students develop understandings through engaging in shared inquiries that are based upon sustained discussions and collaboration (Bruner, 1996);
- Dialogue is developed through open-ended questioning by the teacher and the use of exploratory talk by the students (Wells, 1999);
- Interaction in the classroom is supported by reciprocal communication between students and teachers and between student and student that involves the sharing of ideas and opinions (Palincsar & Brown, 1984 and Mercer, 2000);
- Talk is reciprocal, collective, cumulative and supportive (Alexander, 2008b).

Dialogic talk, according to Myhill (2005) and Myhill et al. (2006), encourages students to adopt certain roles and behaviours and is more likely to transpire when students have a common purpose, value each other's talk, tolerate uncertainty, share opinions and **points of view** and gather evidence to underpin ideas.

Alexander used these ideas as a foundation for his seminal research in what has become known as his Five Nations Study (2001a) and in his research in Yorkshire (2003, 2004a) and London (2005a). The Five Nations research gathered evidence that suggested that teachers across all the nations were primarily engaged in IRE sequences and reported the following findings (adapted from Alexander, 2001a):

- Instruction was predominantly based on IRE sequences.
- There was little, if any, evidence of exploratory talk.
- Teachers used frequent questioning either to achieve progress through the lesson or to address student participation.
- Questions were content focussed.
- Open-ended questioning was infrequent, with closed questions predominating.
- There was little evidence of teachers use of pause to give students the opportunity to reflect.

- Teacher feedback to the students was mostly concerned with giving praise rather than addressing students' responses.
- The lessons focussed on students supplying the 'correct' answers to teachers' questions.
- Teacher questioning did not address understanding.

REFLECTION STRATEGY 4.6

- The purpose of this Reflection Strategy is to determine whether the findings in Alexander's Five Nations Study could be applied to your classroom.
- It would be too complex to explore all nine of these findings in your classroom at the same time. Review all the findings and identify any that you know apply to the talk in your classroom.
- Using an analysis of a transcript of one of your lessons, take each of the other findings in turn to identify if it is present consistently throughout the lesson. Any lesson may occasionally contain one of these types of talk, so it is important to identify if it occurs frequently. It may be useful to study a number of your lessons over time to get an accurate idea.
- Alternative to the transcript analysis approach, you may prefer for a colleague to run a series of observations over a number of lessons.

Both Alexander (2001b) and Wells (2001) reported disappointment, not only in the predominance of teacher talk in IRE sequences, but also in the effect that this was having on student learning due to the lack of opportunity for student-initiated talk. The *Talking Our Way Into Literacy* project (1996, p.136) had earlier reported that the effect of IREs on student talk was that 'Most of the student contributions were single words or incomplete sentences'. This effect on student learning was further highlighted in a study carried out by Smith et al. (2004) that reported that only 10 per cent of teacher questions were open and that, on average, students' responses had a duration of 5 seconds and were limited to three words or fewer in 70 per cent of cases. The research results from both the Alexander and Smith et al. studies indicate that there is an urgent need for teachers to become aware of the role that IREs play in their classrooms and the balance between student- and teacher-initiated talk. It may be, as Cazden (1988) concluded much earlier, that the ubiquitous occurrence of IRE sequences is due to teachers using it as a default position when faced with stressful situations such as a troublesome class or the introduction of new work. It may also be, as Smith et al. (2004) and Moyles et al. (2003) suggested, the result of the standards drive in many countries that has encouraged many teachers to adopt more traditional patterns of teacher talk. While IREs may limit students' learning in particular ways, nevertheless a case can be made for their use in situations such as the introduction of a complex sequence of ideas (see Wells, 1993, Cazden, 2001, Alexander, 2003b, 2004a). The major concern with the Five Nations Study results was that the IRE sequence was the only one being used. Interestingly, both Alexander and Myhill et al. (2006) reported that there was an important difference in the way British teachers used IREs from those teachers in Russia. They suggested that students in England responded to teachers' questions by carefully waiting for their turn to reply to the teacher. In contrast, students in Russian classrooms tended to reply to teachers' questions by talking to fellow students and not directly to the teacher. In this way, Russian students brought problems to the rest of the class to seek collaborative solutions, whereas in British classrooms solutions were more likely to be resolved through one-on-one interactions between student and teacher. It would appear that, following these reports, it can be critical how teachers implement, and students reply, to IRE sequences. Therefore, the problem may lie not only in the IRE sequence alone but also in the way that IRE sequences are conducted. As Alexander (2001a) suggested, Russian teachers' frequent use of questions to elicit extended responses from students led to higher levels of student attainment when compared to students in international studies.

Later, Alexander reported on his research in Yorkshire and London where teachers were involved in dialogic talk and dialogic pedagogy. These findings, presented below, are adapted from Alexander (2003b, 2004a, 2005a) and illustrate a significant shift in the quality and quantity of talk in these British classrooms. These findings are particularly compelling when compared to those from the Five Nations Study that included British classrooms.

- There was a significant increase in discussions about talk by both teachers and students.
- Classroom discussions were supported and guided by the establishment of rules or protocols for engaging in talk.
- There was a predominance of open-ended questioning by the teachers and fewer examples where they were seeking a specific response.
- There were fewer examples of hands up, or competitive bidding, in favour of sustained discussions and nominating particular students to provide answers.
- Teachers used pauses more frequently in order to allow students more time to reflect rather than provide quick responses.
- Exploratory talk was more common and there were fewer occasions when students attempted to compete with each other and 'guess what was in the teacher's head'.
- Teachers used more questioning sequences to extend students' answers and encourage them to engage in critical thinking.
- Student-to-teacher exchanges were becoming longer and student-to-student exchanges were becoming more frequent.
- Students were listening more carefully and respectfully to each other and talking to each other rather than at each other.
- There was more confidence being shown by the students to engage in exploratory talk and less hesitancy in tentative responses.
- The interaction in the classrooms was becoming more inclusive, which led to greater involvement by the less able students and the quiet students in the middle.
- The reading and writing of all students, especially the less able, was benefitting from a greater emphasis on talk.
- Student responses to teachers' questions were becoming more extensive.
- There was more questioning from the students and more student-to-student interaction leading to less control of discussions by the teachers.

The conclusion from these two sets of findings suggests that implementing dialogic talk and pedagogy results in a significant improvement in student learning. These trends in the data identified by Alexander indicate that it is well worth the effort to change classroom talk and teacher pedagogy. However, these changes do indicate a radical adjustment in teacher pedagogy and in the balance between teacher talk and learner talk. Alexander (2005a) qualified the results from the Yorkshire and London studies by reporting that this radical change in talk and pedagogy proved to be a problem for some teachers. He indicated (2005a, p.16) that '... there is a growing gap between those teachers who are achieving real change and those whose interaction has shifted rather less'. He reported (2004, 2005a) that this difference could be partly explained by the fact that some teachers attempted to implement both dialogic talk and dialogic pedagogy before adequately establishing a supportive classroom ethos or climate. Further, Alexander stated that following the completion of the Yorkshire and London studies at that point, the proportion of teachers who had comprehensively and consistently implemented the changes was 'fairly small'. In addition, Alexander concluded that allowing students time to offer extended answers was becoming more common, but many teachers were not following up on students' answers with further questioning. Rather than using further questions to provide 'informative' feedback, teachers were still tending to provide 'minimal and judgemental' feedback. Thus, a proportion of teachers were still struggling with the balance of teacher talk and learner talk.

Similar findings were reported by Bull and Anstey (2004, 2005b, 2007, 2010b, 2014), who concluded that teachers in their research required intensive support from outside experts and on-site advisors for periods of 2 to 3 years to successfully fulfil the conditions for dialogic teaching. They also reported that an important factor in supporting teachers to change their pedagogy was a knowledge of the change process.

Dialogic pedagogy and the change process

If teachers are to make radical changes in their pedagogy, then it follows that some understanding of the change process and how it operates would support teachers in their efforts to successfully manage change. As has been previously discussed in Chapter One, much of the research that looks at the nature of change and how teachers deal with it is based on the work of Fullan (2001, 2002, 2004, 2005, 2007, 2008). Much of the research conducted by Fullan and others has indicated that change is a complex, and often a challenging and uncomfortable, process. In their work, Bull and Anstey (2004, 2005b, 2007, 2010b, 2014) reported that the simple act of informing teachers about the complex nature of change tended to reduce the amount of stress that teachers were feeling, particularly when they realised that struggling with change was a normal part of the process that everyone experienced. They also found, following the suggestion of Hendricks (2002), that change was more likely to occur when teachers worked collaboratively so they encouraged teachers in their Action Learning Cycle (ALC) projects to form a community of learners. (For more information on the ALC projects, see the previous discussion in Chapter One.) Bull and Anstey concluded that this was an effective technique for moderating teacher stress about change, a conclusion that was reinforced by the amount of positive teacher comment about the value of a community of learners reported across all ALC projects. Further to this, Bull and Anstey, following the work of Fullan, reported that informing teachers that the change process involved a series of highs (where individuals felt very positive about change) and lows (where individuals felt very challenged) also assisted teachers in dealing with change. In addition, Bull and Anstey (2010b), along with Edwards-Groves and Ronnerman (2013), reported that change in dialogue, pedagogy and practice was more likely to occur if high expectations about the amount of teacher change were a feature of expectations about teacher learning.

All of these factors that impinge upon change led Anstey and Bull to develop various tools that would support teachers in dealing with the change process. First, an important part of the ALC was construction of a transcript by individual participants of one of their literacy lessons. In order to analyse their transcripts, participants were provided with detailed information about the functions of teacher talk and phases of lessons (see Chapter One of this book and also Chapter Four of the complementary volume *Foundations of Multiliteracies: Reading, Writing and Talking in the 21st Century*). This knowledge supported teachers to make changes to their talk by addressing the functions of teacher talk that were not a feature of their transcript. It provided further knowledge about which phases they were currently not incorporating in their lessons and which phases were more appropriate to include particular functions of teacher talk. With this knowledge, teachers were provided with a number of techniques to use to make significant changes in the manner which addressed the teaching and learning of literacy in their classrooms.

Second, by providing access to the Multiliteracies Matrix, participants were provided with information about the semiotic systems, contexts for literacy learning, and the pedagogies of multiliteracies. This enabled them to design strategies that would promote change in their lessons and pedagogies. Third, participants were introduced to the Action Plan Proforma as a method of designing strategies that would promote changes in their teaching and pedagogy and provide them with the tools to assess the success, or otherwise, of the changes. Fourth, in each ALC project, Bull and Anstey (2010b) provided the space and time for participants to form a community of learners where discussion focussed on the change process and how it could be managed. (Further information about the Multiliteracies Matrix, the Action Learning Proforma and the community of learners can be found in Chapter One.) What became clear, through reviewing the outcomes of the ALC projects, was that if teachers were to be expected to make radical changes in their pedagogy, such as the adoption of a dialogic pedagogy, then specific design strategies needed to be developed to support teachers. It was not enough to make them aware of a dialogic pedagogy and expect them to successfully implement it. Most, if not all, teachers can benefit from a knowledge and understanding of the change process.

Finally, there are different cultures in schools that can be characterised in particular ways. Some schools, because they hold clearly identified and well-specified goals and have shared understandings about how students learn, are able to negotiate consensus about different approaches to teaching. These types of schools are therefore more open to change and are more likely to respond positively to, and adopt, new pedagogies and novel practices. Conversely, there are schools that struggle to reach consensus and, because they are quite content to remain as they are, are far less able to engage in the change process. The former types of schools are more likely to be excited at the prospect of change, while the latter interpret change as threatening. There have been a number of attempts to classify schools according to the characteristics they exhibit and how they respond to change. One such classification is that proposed by Gossen and Anderson (1995) following on from the work of Barth (1990) and Glickman (1993). The following classifications and characteristics have been adapted from Gossen and Anderson (1995, pp. 117–146):

- Conventional schools – traditional climate that can tend to be competitive, teachers operate in silos where they teach in isolation and do not cooperate with fellow teachers, schools are regarded as a place of work rather than a professional community;

- Congenial schools – a social climate where friendship is valued, the teachers are conflict averse so when a difficult issue arises there tends to be silence and the discussion is left to another time or is ignored, belonging to a group of likeminded teachers is valued;
- Collegial schools – not averse to vigorous debate or disagreements, open to shifts in pedagogies and examination of practices, cooperative sharing of values, ideas and differences, listens while others are talking.

An alternative topology of school cultures was proposed by Stoll and Fink (1996) and Stoll (1998). The following cultures of schools and characteristics were adapted from Stoll (1998, pp.10-11).

- Moving culture – focussed on enhancing students' progress, teachers cooperate to respond to change, specific statements of standards that are supported by clearly identified goals;
- Cruising culture – appears to be effective but powerful statements of standards inhibit change, school usually situated in an affluent area, not preparing students to adequately deal with change, students are achieving in spite of the quality of teaching;
- Strolling culture – school is neither effective or ineffective and is therefore inadequately dealing with change, not dealing with future needs of students, goals not clearly defined leading to lack of student progress;
- Struggling culture – teachers aware of lack of progress, expending considerable effort on student progress that is largely unproductive, have the will but not necessarily the skills to succeed, often identified by outsiders as failing leading to lack of motivation;
- Sinking culture – feeling of failure leading to isolation, loss of faith in ability to achieve improvement, tendency to blame others, inability of staff to change, schools often in disadvantaged areas leading to attributing of failure to parents or students, staff require significant support that includes considerable action.

It is important to realise that the culture of the school can have a marked effect on the likelihood that staff will be able to respond to change in a meaningful manner and therefore any **transformation** of practices would be more likely to occur in some schools and not others. However, it was not the intention of either Gossen and Anderson (1995) or Stoll and Fink (1996) to suggest that these various cultures would be found operating uniformly through a particular school. Some schools will exhibit some, but not all, characteristics of a particular culture. It is likely that some schools that exhibit the characteristics of a sinking or conventional culture will have pockets, or subcultures, of a moving or collegial culture within the school. It also depends on who is categorising the school, where different teachers or outsiders might classify the school in diverse ways. There may also be some occasions when schools might undergo change in culture because of factors such as change in staff, principal or students, or when a teacher or group of teachers attends a professional learning and development session that changes their perspective. However, as a result of investigating the culture of the school, a different approach to the transformation of practices within the school may be instigated. Interestingly, those teachers who participated in the ALC projects conducted by Bull and Anstey (2004, 2005b, 2007, 2010b, 2014) frequently reported that being aware of the various cultures of schools enabled them to understand how and why change was taking place in their school, or why it was not occurring in the manner that they had predicted. It then became possible for the participants to target support in the particular areas of their school where it was needed.

REFLECTION STRATEGY 4.7

- The purpose of this Reflection Strategy is to explore the concept of school cultures.
- Using either the Gossen and Anderson or the Stoll and Fink categories, have a discussion with other teachers to see if there is common agreement about the type, or types, of cultures present in your school.
- It may be useful to conduct a similar discussion with the whole school to obtain a broader perspective.
- Following these discussions, it might be informative to achieve some consensus about what effect this is having on the school.

Developing a dialogic pedagogy

One of the major concerns in developing a dialogic pedagogy, as explored by both Alexander (2008a) and Twiner et al. (2014), is how to affect the transformation from a pedagogy that is focussed on IRE sequences to one that concentrates on co-construction between students and teachers. As has already been discussed in this and in preceding chapters there is a repertoire of dialogic teaching practices that supports the development of a dialogic pedagogy as suggested by Alexander (2005a, p.11) and Lefstein and Snell (2014, p.8). These explicit talk moves have been adapted from the work of Alexander (2008b), Churchill et al. (2011) and Edwards-Groves, Anstey and Bull (2014) and are summarised below. Dialogic pedagogy was most likely to occur when the teacher:

- Allows space and time for *sustained dialogue* or discussion between student and teacher or between student and student. This enables students to clarify and develop their own thinking rather than the teacher passing quickly on to the next student (as in IRE sequences).
- Creates opportunities for *extending thinking* and asks probing questions so that students build on the answers of other students and incorporate evidence to support their answers.
- *Challenges students' thinking* by establishing capacities to encourage students to identify bias, propaganda, marginalisation and ideologies (particularly in the digital world) in order to justify their own responses and create their own arguments.
- Encourages students to engage in *active listening* by listening to the contributions of fellow students and their teachers and accepting the ideas and opinions of others.
- Allows for *wait time*, where silence gives the students time to reflect and construct an answer that they feel comfortable with, and are confident in, sharing. This creates an opportunity for students to formulate and rehearse their responses.
- Continues to ask *open-ended, guided and extending questions* that encourage dialogue and higher levels of critical thinking, rather than closed questions.
- *Vacates the floor* by minimising the amount of teacher talk and by reconfiguring the classroom space. By placing students in pairs or small groups, the teacher creates opportunities for students to

talk, thereby allowing them to take more responsibility for their own learning as well as the chance to listen attentively to the thoughts of other students.

- *Provides feedback* that is informative rather than judgemental. The teacher addresses the answers given by the students in order to explore how the students constructed a particular response or answer. In this way, the teacher supports students' learning and reasoning as well as attempting to deal with any confusion or misconceptions.
- Engages in *purposeful reflection* about students' learning is order to determine if the desired learning outcomes have been achieved. Students need to be taught the skills of reflection explicitly so that they can independently reflect on their learning and become active learners.

Incorporating these explicit, dialogic teaching practices into the literacy classroom creates a foundation for the adoption of a dialogic pedagogy. As has been argued previously, students and teachers need to engage in collaboration and in various communities of learners in order to participate successfully in the 21st century. Dialogic pedagogy is particularly suited to this type of approach because it is, above all else, a participatory and democratic form of teaching and learning because it caters for both teacher and student in the learning process. As Wolfe and Alexander (2008, p.6) stated, 'Dialogic pedagogies are premised on the ability of students *and* teachers to establish reciprocal relationships through language and other means'. It also is a pedagogy for diversity because it allows both teacher and student to initiate classroom talk. Further, it encourages students to explore their individual ideas by making their talk visible and by creating contexts that allow students to be hesitant and to advance ideas that are only partly formed. Dialogic pedagogies value the concept of teachers and students being co-constructors of classroom talk and is therefore a more equitable, dynamic and active process. As Lefstein and Snell (2014, p. 20) suggested, 'Dialogic pedagogy can help initiate pupil-citizens into democratic participation by cultivating norms and rational deliberation and by facilitating pupils' acquisition of argumentation and public speaking skills'. They further suggested (2014, p. 21) that 'Dialogic pedagogy is seen by many as a more culturally appropriate and sensitive way for teachers to manage classroom life through negotiation with pupils'. As concluded by Lefstein and Snell (2014) and Nystrand et al. (1997, 2003), the result of implementing a dialogic pedagogy in the classroom or school is improvement in student learning and better learning outcomes. Perhaps the best recommendation for adopting a dialogic pedagogy is reported by Lefstein and Snell (2014, p. 21) when they stated that 'We engage in dialogue because we want everyone to have opportunity to develop and express their unique voice'. It is important to note that none of these researchers is suggesting that dialogic talk or dialogic pedagogy should be used all the time. Other researchers such as Mortimer and Scott (2003), Mercer and Littleton (2007), Walsh (2011) and Twiner et al. (2014) have called for a balance between explicit instruction and dialogic pedagogy, for as Twiner et al. (2014, p.104) maintain, there are ' . . . benefits of interweaving authoritative periods of instruction with opportunities for dialogic interaction'.

In order to establish dialogic talk, and to support the implementation of a dialogic pedagogy, many classrooms have instituted rules for engaging in talk. Littleton and Mercer (2013) suggested a list of ground rules and also reported on those instigated by Dawes (2010, 2011) that have been adapted in the following list. They are representative of ground rules established in the classrooms of the participants in the ALC projects reported by Bull and Anstey and would need to be reworded in order to be appropriate for a particular year level.

- All appropriate information is shared among the students and between the students and teacher.
- All students are expected to contribute ideas to discussions and all ideas are accepted as germane.
- Everyone's ideas and opinions are treated with respect.

- All students are expected to give reasoned responses and provide evidence for their views.
- Alternative ideas and opinions are considered carefully and subject to negotiation.
- The group attempts to reach consensus before a decision is made.

Ground rules such as these are meant to give direction to the teachers when implementing a dialogic pedagogy and to both students and teachers when engaging in dialogic talk. Lefstein and Snell (2014) suggested that dialogic structures can indeed be translated into explicit rules that both teacher and student can follow. However, they added a word of caution that following a set of ground rules for dialogic talk, as with following any set of rules, does not guarantee that students or teachers will be fully engaged in dialogic talk. To support this assertion, Lefstein and Snell (2014, p. 16) suggested that in a group of students where ideas are being negotiated, a consensus may be achieved by everyone expressing views that they think others want to hear resulting in only one perspective being voiced. They suggested that to overcome this problem, different approaches to dialogue, such as thinking together through reasoned inquiry, might be used. Further, they concluded that this would enable participants in dialogic talk to engage in critical thinking about episodes of talk rather than evaluating the extent to which exchanges might be counted as dialogic. As always, it becomes a matter of how thoroughly dialogic pedagogy is being implemented, taking into consideration that establishing a set of ground rules for dialogic talk does not, by itself, guarantee that dialogic pedagogy will be successfully implemented.

Because adoption of a dialogic pedagogy represents such a radical shift in teacher pedagogy, it is useful to revisit the preceding discussion about dialogic pedagogy. The following points represent key understandings advanced by the writers and researchers in the field. In summary, dialogic pedagogy is:

- A participatory and democratic form of teaching and learning that encourages collaborative learning that can best occur in a community of learners (Littleton & Mercer, 2013);
- Ideally suited to meet the cultural and civic demands of the 21st century (Lefstein & Snell, 2014);
- Premised on the establishment on the ability of students and teachers to establish reciprocal relationships through talk (Wolfe & Alexander, 2008);
- A pedagogy for diversity because it allows both teacher and student to initiate classroom talk (Edwards-Groves, Anstey & Bull, 2014);
- Designed to support students to advance ideas that are hesitant and only partly formed through making their talk visible (Alexander, 2005b);
- Based on the concept of teachers and students being co-constructors of classroom talk and is therefore a more equitable, dynamic and active process (Edwards-Groves, Anstey & Bull, 2014);
- A more culturally appropriate and sensitive way for to engage in negotiation with students (Lefstein & Snell, 2014);
- Likely to improve students' literacy learning (Nystrand et al., 2003; Alexander, 2005b; Lefstein & Snell, 2014; Edwards-Groves, Anstey & Bull, 2014);
- More likely to succeed if there is a balance between explicit instruction and dialogic pedagogy (Mortimer and Scott, 2003; Mercer and Littleton, 2007); Walsh, 201; and Twiner et al., 2014);
- Supported by the introduction of a set of ground rules for talk (Dawes, 2010, 2011; Littleton and Mercer, 2013; Lefstein & Snell, 2014).

Much of the strength of dialogic pedagogy lies in its emphasis on cooperative learning, the co-construction of ideas and establishing reciprocal relationships through talk in an effort to improve student learning. In their recent research on talk, Littleton and Mercer (2013) investigated the process of thinking together and developed the concept of what they termed interthinking, which they concluded scaffolded students' literacy learning. They defined interthinking as '... using talk to pursue collective intellectual activity. It represents an important and distinctive strength of human cognition, whereby people can combine their intellectual resources to achieve more through working together than any individual could do on their own' (Littleton & Mercer, 2013, p. 111). This is a very useful concept that highlights the value of cooperative learning in small groups as a way of supporting many of the tenets of dialogic pedagogy that have been discussed in this chapter. As was suggested earlier in this chapter, a beginning can be made in the introduction of dialogic talk and dialogic pedagogy by changing the organisation of classrooms to permit students to learn in small groups. However, Littleton and Mercer (2013, p. 96) qualify their position on learning in small groups by maintaining that '... many students, perhaps most, do not know how to talk and work together effectively, but teachers assume that they do'. They further suggest that 'To put it simply students need to learn how to talk to reason together... and they may never accomplish this unless they are helped to do so by their teachers'. These ideas give important direction to teachers on how to begin the process of introducing dialogic talk and dialogic pedagogy into their classrooms.

Making a beginning to the introduction of dialogic talk and dialogic pedagogy in classrooms

In their work with teachers in the ALC projects, Bull and Anstey (2004, 2005b, 2007, 2010b, 2014) found that one of the outcomes that came out of this research, reported in Bull and Anstey (2010b), was that the success of making a beginning with dialogic talk was influenced by the size of the group of teachers who were involved from a particular school. They found that when teachers participating in an ALC project came from a network of schools, sometimes there was only one representative from a particular school whose role it was to return to their school to support other teachers to implement dialogic talk. These 'lone' teachers proved to have less success with introducing dialogic talk in their own classroom, and great difficulty in supporting fellow teachers to engage with the task of beginning an effective program of dialogic talk. As the size of the participating groups grew, teachers tended to have greater success and fewer challenges. This was an expected outcome because the teachers who were part of a group had the opportunity to form a community of learners to share their successes and discuss the challenges they were dealing with. On occasion, Bull and Anstey were asked to implement an ALC project for the whole school that involved all teachers including the principal and other administrative staff. These projects proved to be the most successful, and in feedback sessions with the participating staff this was attributed to a larger community of learners in which to share ideas, or the increased likelihood that teachers could form smaller communities where they had the opportunity to select the membership of the group themselves. Participants also reported that a whole school approach had an added benefit because they were able to construct a sequential program that could be implemented at each year level. In this way, they suggested that they were able to determine what the students in their class had learned in their previous classes and what was to be expected of them at the next year level.

In order to support participants directly, Bull and Anstey recommended a number of strategies that encouraged participants to begin the process of implementing dialogic talk and dialogic pedagogy in their classrooms and schools. There were three of these strategies – vacating the floor, wait time and reducing competitive bidding – that the participants reported as most useful in establishing an appropriate classroom that was conducive to implementing a dialogic pedagogy.

- *Vacating the floor.* The proponents of dialogic talk consistently argue that learner talk should be of equal importance to teacher talk and should be valued by both teachers and students. While

IRE sequences predominate in the classroom, teacher talk will always overshadow learner talk. Continuous use of IREs allows no space for students to participate in talk because they are too focussed on providing responses to teacher questions. In order to provide opportunities for students to initiate talk the teacher needs to take a step back, or vacate the floor, as suggested by Perrott (1988), Cazden (2001) and Godinho and Shrimpton (2003). Studies of children's talk behaviour outside of school, such as Heath (1983), reported that many children were quite happy to engage in talk and also ask enumerable questions. Yet, when those children become students in school, talk is curtailed and they no longer get to ask the questions. As Edwards-Groves, Anstey and Bull (2014, p.13) reported, 'Vacating the floor has come to be seen as one of the most significant factors in encouraging students to engage in exploratory talk and to take on some responsibility for shaping meaning through talk'. Godinho and Shrimpton (2003, p.38) supported this position and went on to maintain that vacating the floor afforded students the chance to be more analytical while teachers could still retain the roles of mediator and facilitator and promoted a 'collaborative inquiry approach'. They also reported that in classrooms where teachers were making little or no effort to vacate the floor, students struggled to remember important points in discussions. Godinho and Shrimpton (2003) concluded that many teachers found this pedagogical move quite difficult. On the other hand, as previously discussed in this chapter, a rearrangement of classroom organisation can create greater possibilities for learner talk, but this does rely on students being explicitly taught how to work in groups and how to reason with others (Littleton & Mercer, 2013). Bull and Anstey (2004, 2005b, 2007, 2010b, 2014) reported that a knowledge of the effect of IREs, in itself, can assist teachers to make the change, particularly in combination with the analysis of lesson transcripts. Interestingly, both Bull and Anstey (2004, 2005b, 2007, 2010b, 2014) and Alexander (2005b, p.15) reported that, in the case when videotapes of classroom lessons were recorded, students (and teachers) were capable of sophisticated discussions about the nature of interaction and talk in the lessons and how it was being conducted. Their research also indicated that when students and teachers had a language to talk about talk, a **metalanguage**, then the process of vacating the floor became more attainable. Finally, as discussed earlier in this chapter, some teachers are more open to change than others.

- *Wait time.* The process of vacating the floor can be facilitated by the introduction of wait time. Simply, wait time occurs when teachers pause after asking a question before seeking a response from students. However, the process is not that simple, because a significant proportion of teachers have an intolerance for silence. If a teacher question elicits no immediate response, there is a common tendency for teachers to immediately ask a further questions or questions. Bull and Anstey (2004, 2005b, 2007, 2010b, 2014) suggested to the participants in their ALC projects that when they asked a question, they should count silently to five before seeking a response. Most teachers found this inordinately difficult and required 2 to 3 weeks of practice before they felt comfortable with the amount of wait time. Bull and Anstey then increased the length of wait time to ten seconds, and participants had difficulties similar to those they had experienced with 5-second wait times. The crucial point about implementing wait time is that it allows teachers time to observe their students and make judgements how they are reacting to questions and to decide if the students appear to be following the discussion. Perhaps of more importance is that wait time allows students time to reflect on the questions and construct a meaningful answer, rather than try to guess what is in the teacher's head. This process is facilitated if the teacher expects that, when a student provides a response, that they will need to provide a reason why they have given a particular answer. It is also crucial that students understand what is required of them during periods of wait time otherwise they may come to the conclusion that their teacher has forgotten the purpose of the lesson or has simply 'lost it'. Students, as well as teachers, need to understand what is involved in reflection, what roles to adopt, and why it is important in the creation of meaning making.

- *Reducing competitive bidding.* It is almost a universal practice in classrooms that students raise their hands when signalling that they know the answer to a question posed by the teacher. Sometimes this becomes a competition among students who wave their arms around, or call out, in a bid to be chosen to provide a response. This striving to 'choose me' has become known as competitive bidding. Usually, only students who know the answer raise their hands while the other students remain quiet. Studies of classroom interaction suggest that, in many classrooms, the same group of students continue to be chosen by the teacher to answer the questions while the same group of students are comfortable to remain silent and let them do the work. The former group of students are involved in the lesson and are making conscious attempts to learn what the teacher is endeavouring to teach while the latter group tends to drift through the lesson and remains disengaged and largely uninvolved. Bull and Anstey (2004, 2005b, 2007, 2010b, 2014) further suggested to the participants in their ALC projects that they attempt to reduce, or eliminate, competition bidding by instructing students not to raise their hands. The participants of the projects reported that students found this very difficult and that the older the students, the more trouble they had in complying. Unsurprisingly, the older the student, the more 'unlearning' they had to do to eradicate past practices. What the 'no hands up' policy essentially does it that it puts students on notice that anyone can be chosen to answer a teacher question, everyone needs to have an answer ready, and they need to be able to explain why they arrived at that particular answer. The result of this pedagogical move is that no student gets to monopolise the talk and everyone is expected to engage in talk. This strategy, combined with vacating the floor and wait time, increases the likelihood that dialogic talk will begin to develop. The participants in the ALC projects found that, in order to support the development of these three strategies, that the establishment of ground rules for talk was necessary. Ground rules became important to encourage the development of attentive listening, respect for the ideas and opinions of others, and commenting on, and extending, other students' thoughts.

The following transcript was prepared by Jan Mansfield (2014) from an audiotape that she made of one of her literacy lessons. Jan was a participant in the ALC project reported by Bull and Anstey (2014). The class was a combined year 5/6 class of 10- and 11-year-old students in a public school in a medium-size country town. She had been introducing the students to the codes and conventions of the visual semiotic system and in this lesson the students were working in groups conducting further investigation of harmonious and discordant colours in a range of picture books. Each utterance is numbered to enable analysis and discussion of the transcript.

1 S1:   Mrs M. look at the grey hair on the old lady. Why does that stand out?

2 Mrs M: Where is grey on the colour wheel?

3 S1:   It isn't on the colour wheel.

4 S2:   Grey is used to add to other colours – isn't that making a shade of a colour?

5 S3:   That is when you add black

6 S1:   But grey is like black, it isn't a primary or secondary colour. It isn't on the colour wheel.

7 Mrs M: We could look up what you call the colour grey, but yes it does stand out, so it is a contrast to the other colours.

8 S1:   That is like the colours that stood out in *The Violin Man*.

9 S2:   Yes, what did we learn about colours from *The Violin Man*? *(S2 grabs their English book off their desk)*
Intensity, that was in *The Violin Man*.
(S3 gets The Violin Man from the book shelf.)

10 S1:   Yes, the green was an intense colour, that was intense. The grey hair on the lady is more intense than the other colours...
(Later when all the groups reported back...)

11 S1:   *(Shares their discussions about the grey hair and finishes the report with this utterance.)*
... so not only discordant colours stand out, it can be the intensity of a colour that can make it stand out.

There are a number of interesting features in this transcript that relate to the previous discussion about dialogic talk. In utterance 1 the students in a small group invite Jan to join in their discussion. This illustrates not only that the students are initiating talk and asking the question, an important feature of dialogic talk, but also that the power relationship in the classroom has shifted. The students are controlling the discussion through managing how the group operates.

In utterance 2 Jan gets to ask a question but immediately in utterance 3, student 1 makes a response that is almost a reprimand. There is no response from Jan, or from other students, about utterance 3 indicating that this is not a problem but just a normal part of how the classroom talk is conducted. It is difficult to imagine that such a series of utterances would occur in a classroom where monologic talk was predominant.

In utterances 4, 5 and 6 the students continue their discussion about colour without reference to Jan. This is not to suggest that Jan is no longer part of the discussion but rather a member of the group who is listening but not talking. An important feature of the students' talk is that they are building on each other's answers in order to advance their learning as part of a community of learners. This illustrates an important aspect of dialogic talk where there is less teacher talk and more learner talk.

In utterance 7 Jan makes a suggestion that is taken up by the students in utterances 8, 9 and 10. These latter utterances again demonstrate students building on each other's comments to advance their understanding of the intensity of colour.

Utterance 11, which occurs towards the end of the lesson, summarises the learning that has occurred in the lesson. Not only is it an accurate summary of the learning that has taken place, but it also illustrates the level of sophistication of the student's talk. This reflects another important dimension of dialogic talk, that it results in significant increase in student learning.

These results are similar to those reported by Bull (2003) when he was working with year 2 students in a class of 7-year-old students in a regional city in Queensland, Australia. What this indicates is that age is no barrier to engaging in dialogic talk.

AUDITING INSTRUMENT 4.6

- The purpose of this Auditing Instrument is to investigate the application of the strategies vacating the floor, wait time and reducing competitive bidding.
- Make an assessment of which of these strategies you are currently using. It may also be useful to see if other teachers are using them.

- If you are not currently employing any of the strategies, then it is advisable to introduce one at a time over a period of weeks. Ensure you discuss with students the reasons for this change and their role during wait time.
- There is no obvious one to start with, and it is a matter of individual choice as to which one you feel most comfortable with.
- After a period of time, review the strategies and determine how successful they are. Don't forget to involve your students in this determination.

Many of the participants in the ALC projects reported that implementing dialogic talk and dialogic pedagogy was not an easy process and required a considerable time to establish. However, almost without exception, participants reported significant increase in literacy learning and often commented that they were continually surprised at what the students were capable of, and that students' learning in general far exceeded their expectations. An unexpected result of implementing dialogic talk was that many participants reported that they, and their students, had regained their excitement about learning. The participants often reported on being reinvigorated in their profession and frequently commented that 'I can never go back'. While this discussion provides a very positive picture of dialogic talk and dialogic pedagogy, it would be remiss not to discuss some of the challenges that were faced by Bull and Anstey and others.

Challenges to dialogic talk and dialogic pedagogy

When reading this section on challenges to dialogic talk and dialogic pedagogy, it is important to realise that the selection of the word 'challenges' was deliberate and was preferred over the word 'negatives', which would represent a comparison to the discussion in the previous section. The discussion to follow is intended to make those teachers who are contemplating introducing dialogic talk into their classrooms aware that there are certain issues that need to be addressed. These challenges should not be understood as negatives and interpreted as reasons why dialogic talk should not be introduced. The focus of the following discussion is directed towards identifying issues that teachers need to address in order to successfully change their pedagogical stance.

- *Challenge One.* The study investigating talk in schools and homes carried out by Freebody and Ludwig (1998, p. 7) found that teachers associated the need for a skill-based approach to literacy pedagogy with students in what they termed disadvantaged schools. Conversely, the teachers associated a less structured or whole language approach to literacy pedagogy with students from advantaged or rich backgrounds. Additionally, Freebody and Ludwig (1998, p. 7) reported that some parents were less positive about their supportive role in the home because of what they interpreted as differences between home and school pedagogies. Further, Freebody and Ludwig (1998, p. 65), in response to the prevalence of IRE sequences in the classrooms being observed, suggested that students were constructed as 'doing literacy' rather than being given the opportunity to be co-constructors of literacy pedagogy, a tendency that had earlier been identified by Anstey (1993b).
  Response. Teachers' beliefs about the requirement for a skill-based pedagogy for disadvantaged students needs to be challenged because there is no definitive research that establishes this relationship. Nor is there any definitive research suggesting a relationship between whole language

approaches to pedagogy for advantaged students. Rather it is a matter of varying pedagogical approach according to the nature of what is to be taught or learnt. Teachers also need to become aware of the relationship of home and school, adopt pedagogical approaches that value both home and school, and be aware of the literacy identities of their students. Finally, as has been previously discussed, teachers need to minimise the IRE sequences in their teacher talk.

- *Challenge Two.* The *Talking Our Way Into Literacy* (1996, p.137) project reported that teachers rarely gave negative feedback to students when they exhibited a lack, or incorrect knowledge of, content. Conversely, the project found that teachers gave both positive and negative feedback to students about behaviour. One of the outcomes of this difference in feedback is that students may, and often do, associate success in literacy learning with behaviour rather than content knowledge. In a similar vein, Alexander (2005b, p.16) reported that teacher feedback to students was often minimal and judgemental rather than informative.

  Response. If teachers record one of their lessons and then construct a transcript, it is possible to focus on when, or if, they provide feedback, when it is positive or negative feedback, and whether the feedback is directed towards behaviour. The preparation and analysis of transcripts is not a new idea for, as Heap (1982, p. 409) reported almost four decades ago, '... we suggest that teachers audiotape and relisten to their own lessons ... the exercise will aid the teacher in developing the distance from his or her role performance that allows one to see and evaluate oneself as others might'. Interestingly, both Alexander (2005b) and Bull and Anstey (2014) reported that students were capable of sophisticated analysis of talk and interaction of videotapes of lessons. Alternatively, teachers can invite a colleague into their classroom to observe when and how they provide feedback. It is useful if the teacher can provide a checklist to assist their colleague in observing the feedback.

- *Challenge Three.* As reported by Twiner et al. (2014, p.104), there are benefits in balancing authoritative periods of instruction with opportunities for dialogic interaction. They suggested that '... at times the content is beneficially provided by the teacher, and at other often unexpected times it is more beneficially explored dialogically by and with the pupils'. Teachers therefore need to implement a variety of pedagogical approaches that incorporate both teacher and learner talk.

  Response. Teachers need a thorough knowledge of dialogic talk and pedagogy and an understanding of when to employ them and when to engage in explicit instruction. This balance can be established through the preparation of a transcript or observation by a colleague similar to the response to Challenge Two. Teachers also need to make sure that they have created a classroom climate that that provides opportunities for students to engage in dialogic talk.

- *Challenge Four.* Edwards (2003, p. 39) reported that 'Intervening to answer questions or provide information useful for getting past a sticking-point requires not only the self-restraint not to take the discussion over, but also the willingness to listen to what is being said rather than merely listening for whatever best promotes the teacher's pedagogical agenda'. Teachers may, because of pressure to cover the curriculum or of uncertainty about new content knowledge, be likely to use a considerable amount of teacher talk in particular lessons. Whatever the reason for significant amounts of teacher talk, it is important for teachers to be aware of the balance of teacher talk and learner talk. This is not to suggest that there is something inherently bad about teacher talk for there are times when it is appropriate. However, there should also be times when learner talk is more appropriate. Alexander (2005b, p.17) maintained that teachers were striving to extend their repertoire of teacher talk but were giving less attention to student talk.

Response. Preparation of a transcript or observation by a colleague will determine whether appropriate types of talk are present in a particular lesson. It may be useful if the teacher is aware of, and is attempting to employ, the 'vacating the floor' strategy discussed earlier in this chapter. There may also be some benefit if the teacher visits other classrooms to observe how fellow teachers are addressing the issue.

Challenge Five. Alexander (2005b, p. 8) commented on what he saw as an important distinction between dialogue and conversation that was also reported by Wolfe and Alexander (2008). Alexander maintained that '... the end point of conversation may not be clear at the outset', and it may consist of a sequence of unrelated exchanges where participants talk at, rather than to, each other. He saw dialogue, on the other hand, as having a clear intension and a specific end point and having a meaningful sequence of exchanges. As Wolfe and Alexander (2008, p. 8) reported, conversation is more relaxed and may lead nowhere.

Response. Just because students are talking to one another, or to the teacher, does not mean that anyone is engaging in dialogic talk. It is important that teachers can appreciate the distinction between conversation and dialogue. Teachers need to listening attentively to student talk to determine whether it is meaningful and is addressing the desired outcomes of the lesson. There can be a tendency for teachers to accept student talk in the belief that it is leading to appropriate interaction when what is actually happening is that the purpose of the lesson has been derailed. Sometimes students engage in conversation intentionally in order to subvert the lesson and sometimes teachers misunderstand student conversation as evidence that the objective of the lesson has been met. It is therefore crucial that distinctions are made between meaningful dialogue and directionless conversations even if, at times, conversations are pleasant and engaging.

- *Challenge Six*. When the focus of the teacher is directed towards students engaging in dialogic talk, then there are advantages in students initiating talk. However, this places the teacher in a somewhat ambivalent position for, as Wolfe and Alexander (2008, p. 9) suggested, there are '... huge demands on teachers required to steer pedagogic content whilst ensuring that children's contributions are woven into the unfolding discourse'. Wolfe and Alexander (2008, p. 9) further suggested that the attempt to balance teacher and learner talk '... raises questions concerning the extent to which they should stand back and permit children to explore ideas unassisted and when and how to intervene with new information'. When to accept students' contributions and when, and how, to intervene are questions that pertain to a range of lessons, but because dialogic pedagogy emphasises negotiating co-construction and joint responsibility for learning, these two issues become of central concern. This question of balance of teacher talk with learner talk concerned Lefstein and Snell (2014, p.170), who referred to it as a dilemma and suggested that '... taking a peripheral position can empower pupils to engage, take control of the conversation and communicate with another directly, but can also lead to disintegration of the discussion'. For them the dilemma centred around how to challenge students' ideas or opinions without overpowering their talk and dominating the discussion.

Response. Part of this issue of intervention can be overcome if the teacher has introduced the strategies of vacating the floor and wait time. Vacating the floor results in less teacher talk and reduces the opportunities for the teacher to intervene while, at the same time, providing more opportunities for learner talk. The introduction of wait time allows students more time to reflect and create meaningful responses to teacher questions. Building on these ideas, it is important that teachers consider the purpose for which they are engaging in dialogic talk. Lefstein and Snell (2014, pp.14–18) suggested that dialogic talk could focus on the interaction between students and teachers.

However, they proposed that it could also focus on thinking together, on the interplay of the talk of one student with another, on critique of each other's ideas or on the power relationships between student and student or student and teacher. What these different foci allow teachers to do is to target one purpose in a particular lessons or sequence of lessons making it more likely that intervention can be achieved without affecting discussion.

- *Challenge Seven*. Lefstein and Snell (2014, p.18) stated that '... few of us are happy to have our ideas refuted, and most prefer winning to losing an argument. Partly for this reason, discourse is rarely the cooperative, orderly and attentive affair commonly evoked by the word 'dialogue'. Some participants may try to dominate the dialogue or silence or marginalise others and behave in a way that Lefstein and Snell term non-dialogically. Ideally, according to Lefstein and Snell (2014, p. 18), 'To approach another dialogically is to enter into a relationship of respect, mutual concern and solidarity'. Such a relationship, they suggested, needs to be based on participants having equal rights and similar opportunities to participate in dialogic talk. Power relationships are critical in determining who gets to talk and when. Cain (2012, pp. 51–57) concluded that power in relationships can be related to a number of factors including the balance between extroverts, who get their talk valued, and introverts, whose talk is to a large extent ignored.

  Response. One way to achieve a balance between the more argumentative and marginalisation aspects of dialogic talk and the more cooperative features of mutual concern and respect is to generate ground rules for talk. A set of ground rules was developed earlier in this chapter as an example of general rules that could be adapted for any year level. The establishment of any ground rules is more likely to succeed if they are the result of cooperative negotiation between students and teacher. It is unlikely that students will fully commit to any rules unless they feel they have had some power during any discussion to authenticate them.

- *Challenge Eight*. As with any approach to the teaching and learning of literacy, teachers are always faced with a choice of which pedagogy is the right one to adopt for their students. An example of such a choice is whether to instigate a skill-based or a whole language pedagogy. Rather than opting for one or other of these pedagogies, many teachers choose to embrace both approaches so they can select which pedagogy is appropriate for the literacy learning in a particular lesson or phase of a lesson. In the case of monologic or dialogic pedagogies, the choice is a similar one.

  Response. As both Alexander (2005b) and Lefstein and Snell (2014) have suggested, it is not a question of either monologic or dialogic talk, but rather a question of the degree to which they are adopted. The majority of participants in the ALC projects reported by Bull and Anstey (2004, 2005b, 2007, 2010b, 2014) had rejected the idea of a forced choice between one pedagogy and another because it encouraged them to drop what they were currently implementing in favour of the next new approach. The approach that the participants adopted was to critically analyse any new development to judge whether there were elements contained in it that could be meaningfully integrated with their current pedagogy.

Reviewing the challenges to dialogic talk and dialogic pedagogy

It is important to realise that the eight challenges discussed above are not to be interpreted as problems with the notion of dialogic talk, or as reasons why dialogic talk and dialogic pedagogy are too difficult to implement. Each of the questions and responses were designed to address the nature of pedagogy and how pedagogical change might be managed by teachers. The intention is to provide a framework, as with the Multiliteracies Matrix outlined in Chapter One, that will support teachers to reconsider their pedagogical position and provide them with strategies that will underpin reflection about the transformation of current practices.

The research that investigated dialogic talk and dialogic pedagogy clearly demonstrated that there were significant increases in students' learning, particularly literacy learning, and that teachers' pedagogical approaches became more effective. There were also substantial benefits for less able students, and students in the middle, due to the interactive nature of dialogic talk that led to more inclusive classrooms. Considerable improvements occurred in reading and writing for all students, especially the less able, because of the greater emphasis on classroom talk. Students also listened more carefully and respectfully to each other's responses as teachers' questions moved away from a preponderance of IRE sequences and asking closed, rather than open, questions. Students' answers became longer and were more likely to exhibit the characteristics of reflection, critical thinking and illustrate a willingness to provide intuitive responses rather than always focussing on providing the correct answers.

In short, the benefits of engaging in dialogic talk mainly accrue to the students. In contrast, the challenges to dialogic pedagogy focus on the need for teachers to review their pedagogical approach in order to enable them to support their students more effectively. These trends indicate that a move towards dialogic talk and dialogic pedagogy is highly desirable for both students and teachers.

ACTION LEARNING TASK 4.3

- The purpose of this Action Learning Task is to conduct a further review of your action research project.
- Go back to the selection of items you made on the Multiliteracies Matrix to see if you want to make any adjustments. You may now be attracted to the idea of implementing a dialogic pedagogy or exploring dialogic talk. It is quite normal to make adjustments to the direction of your research as you begin to finalise the details.
- If you have made adjustments to your Matrix, then it follows that you will need to make adjustments to your Action Plan Proforma, particularly in the planning, pedagogy and practice sections.
- It can be quite useful to discuss your research with other teachers, particularly if they are also involved in action research. Another perspective can be very informative.

Conclusion

In this chapter the importance of classroom talk in developing a multiliterate person was explored together with those factors that supported the development of student or learner talk. Establishing a safe classroom environment where students feel free, and have the confidence to talk, was recommended. The importance of instituting a supportive classroom environment before introducing dialogic talk was recommended. A detailed examination of the role of the functions of teacher talk and the phase structure of lessons in the study of teacher talk was presented. Monologic, exploratory and dialogic talk were explained in detail and the part that the constructivist approach to teaching and learning plays in the development of these types of talk was analysed. The concept of dialogic pedagogy was established and the radical shift in pedagogy that it necessitated was explored. A discussion of how teachers responded to the change process that was involved in such a radical shift in pedagogy, together with the effect that the culture of the school has on response to change, was presented in detail.

Finally, the challenges that may arise from the introduction of dialogic talk and dialogic pedagogy into the classroom were presented together with possible teacher responses to the challenges. This discussion focussed on the changes in student or learner talk brought about by the introduction of dialogic talk, and the necessary changes in teacher pedagogy required by a dialogic pedagogy.

5 Investigating the reading process in multiliterate classrooms: Consuming multimodal texts

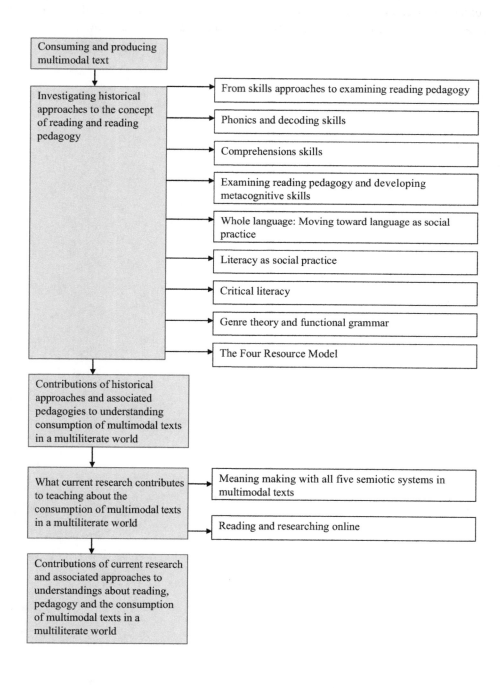

The focus of this chapter is reading text in a multiliterate world, or, using the term which has previously been discussed, consuming text. It will begin by reviewing previous approaches to the teaching of reading with the aim of understanding how these approaches might be reinterpreted and applied in a digital age of multimodal texts and constant change. An examination of current research about the teaching of reading will follow. This will be accompanied by an investigation of the concept of reading in terms of multimodal texts and a range of technologies. Skills, strategies and processes that inform the consumption of text will be examined in online and offline contexts. The links between the consumption of text, problem solving and **inquiry** will be explored, including the application of research skills across all technologies and discipline areas. The implications for pedagogy will be discussed, particularly the role of talk around texts and balancing **focussed learning episodes** with student-centred **inquiry-based teaching**.

Consuming and producing multimodal texts

In Chapter Three the **consumption** and **production** of text in a multiliterate world was discussed as designing, and the similarities between the processes of designing as producer and consumer of text were discussed. It is important to acknowledge the links between reading and writing and the fact that in many situations the act of consuming a text is accompanied by writing, before, during or after reading. The more students know about texts and how to consume them, then the more they know about how to produce a text that will fulfil their desired purpose. For the purpose of examining the teaching of reading and writing in detail, the two processes are written about in separate chapters (Chapters Five and Six), with reference made to interrelated skills, processes and strategies when appropriate. It is recommended that the two chapters be read together and that the reader consider the implications of what they are reading for both reading and writing as they read. Should the reader wish to access further information about the links between reading and writing before reading on, Chapter Three of the complementary volume *Foundations of Multiliteracies: Reading, Writing and Talking in the 21st Century* explores them in detail.

A suggested strategy for reading this chapter

When discussing the similarities between the consumption and production of text in Chapter Three, a figure was produced to represent this process as **design**. It has been reproduced here as Figure 5.1. It is recommended that after reading each major area of research that is discussed, the reader examine the information in terms of Figure 5.1 and consider what is necessary but not sufficient about this research and **pedagogy** for consuming and producing (designing and **redesigning**) texts in a multimodal, multiliterate world. The following questions may guide this reflection. How does the research that informs this approach and ensuing pedagogy and practice:

- Inform understandings about the role of purpose when consuming a text?
- Contribute knowledge, skills and processes that become part of a **repertoire of resources** aiding consumption of multimodal texts?
- Provide knowledge, skills and strategies that inform the **synthesising** process of meaning making (combining, recombining and reworking selected resources to make meaning)?
- Provide knowledge, skills and strategies that inform the recording, preservation and dissemination of meaning making from the text?
- Develop understanding about the consumption as the transforming and **transformation** of meaning?

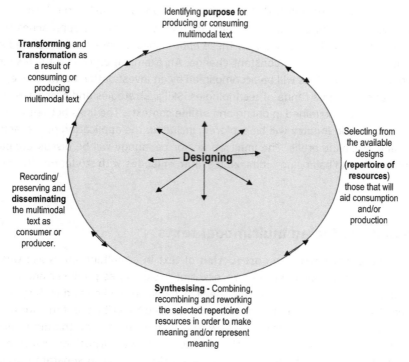

Figure 5.1 Consuming and producing multimodal text in a multiliterate world

ACTION LEARNING TASK 5.1

- The purpose of this Action Learning Task is to review your decision-making to date regarding your Action Plan and consider how this chapter might inform parts of it, for example, focussing your goal and selection of items from the matrix you completed in Chapter One, planning for data collection or using it as part of your data collection on your professional reading.
- If you are waiting to finalise your Action Plan, review the items on the Multiliteracies Matrix that you are thinking about choosing and consider how this chapter might help you refine knowledge and any ideas you have about your goal or desired outcome or data collection.
- If you have already completed your Action Plan and are now in the process of seeking specific knowledge or data gathering, skim the chapter and its headings and consider whether it might inform any of these areas. For example, the sections on talk around text, planning and pedagogy may help you with data collection or with your knowledge about the selected pedagogy item, or the discussions about balancing aspects of reading comprehension may inform the planning part of your Action Plan.

Investigating historical approaches to the concept of reading and reading pedagogy and how they inform the concept of multiliteracies

It is appropriate at this point to look at the history of teaching reading and the research that has informed it. It is only by examining what has come before in previous times and contexts, together with current research and contexts, that informed, defensible decisions can be made about how to teach reading. Unfortunately, there is a tendency for state departments of education and those that legislate curriculum content, assessment and the provision of 'compulsory' professional learning for teachers to present content, assessment and professional learning in a research vacuum, neither acknowledging what has come before nor examining its value in current contexts and how it might be used together with new ideas and research. The media often exacerbates the problem by publicising particular approaches to the exclusion of others without careful evaluation. When other points of view and evidence are submitted, they receive little or no acknowledgement or very biased reporting. This often results in pendulum-like swings from one approach (or extreme) to another, the dismissal or ignoring of previous learning and research, and misinformed and biased 'wars' in the media regarding the merits of the new over the old. Because the arguments for change are not persuasive and the 'wars' do not help or inform teachers' decision-making and teachers themselves are not involved in the research and decision-making, teachers become confused about what action to take and may simply continue to do what they were doing (Schoenfeld & Pearson, 2009; Kim, 2008). Freebody (2011, p. 8) suggested this question of the relationship between research, professional development and everyday teaching practices, who plans, executes and disseminates research and professional learning, and what research is valued and disseminated, is critical and must be examined. Addressing this issue is essential to achieving the best professional learning for teachers and the best educational outcomes for students. Freebody cited the example of small-scale experiments on the teaching of phonics receiving large amounts of media attention, inferring that teachers who did not follow the recommended methods from this study were not competent. In addition, Freebody (2011, p. 10) referred to the fact that some commissioned reports that inform decision-making regarding curriculum content and teaching are highly biased, omitting extensive research and distilling arguments to simply choosing between alternative approaches, rather than making careful and thorough informed research-based recommendations. Kim (2008) made similar comments about the relationship between research, professional development and everyday teaching practices, advocating an increase in the role of teachers in contributing to the implementation of research around new ideas by conducting further research through trialling, collecting data and contributing to the analysis and conclusions.

From skills approaches to examining reading pedagogy

Currently there is a trend in English-speaking Western countries such as Australia, the U.S. and U.K. to return to a more skills-based approach to the teaching of reading. See Gardner (2017) for a comparison of curriculum documents in Australia and the U.K. and the conclusions drawn, and Comber (2012) for a discussion of the reasons behind a move towards a more reductionist approach to teaching of literacy in Australia and Canada. The consequence is a reliance on levelled readers with limited vocabulary and little depth in structure and complexity and thus little facility for developing comprehension because of the focus on developing decoding skills. The balance between decoding (often realised as phonics instruction) and comprehension in early years education has become so weighted towards decoding that some researchers have questioned whether comprehension is actually being explicitly taught in the early years (Freebody, 2011, p. 9). This approach is not limited to young readers. Struggling older readers are often retaught decoding skills using basal readers that are not intellectually stimulating (Arizpe and Styles, 2003 pp. 93-96). Woolley (2010, pp. 108-109) suggested that repeating the teaching of decoding (specifically phonics) with struggling readers was often based on assumptions and testing that did not adequately examine the students' understandings about, and practices with text, when reading. Repeating strategies and materials that have not enhanced these students' reading skills previously does not seem appropriate. Strangely, the teaching of reading has reflected these characteristics before and then moved on, based on research that indicated a heavy emphasis on phonics instruction alone might not be the best approach. Reading the next section that traces the development of skills methods and the teaching of reading post-Second World War to the 1980s may seem familiar to the reader. It certainly indicates a need to think more about what research has indicated over time and what reading actually entails in the 21st century and beyond and most importantly, the implications for reading pedagogy.

Phonics and decoding skills

Interestingly there was no large-scale research into the teaching of reading until the advent of the Second World War, when the reading ability of the men and women entering the armed services was found to be very low and there was a necessity to know the best way of improving their reading skills rapidly. Given that many people at this time did not stay at school beyond primary years and the previous lack of research, the low level of reading was not surprising.

Up until this time reading was largely taught in a didactic way focussing on decoding, that is, the translation of the written word into oral sound. Much of the research that informed this focus on decoding examined visual perception skills. This included identifying how the eye moves across the page when reading, how often the eye pauses and fixates on a part of the page and how often the eye returns or repeats fixations (Buswell, 1922; Gilbert, 1953, 1959). This research led to the development of pre-reading programs designed to enhance students' visual and auditory perception, the conclusion being that if students can perceive the alphabetic symbols on the page and the sounds associated with them more efficiently, their decoding will be enhanced. The focus was on visual and audio discrimination, memory and sequencing, that is, being able to discriminate between sounds and **symbols** and remember them in sequence. This was followed by the teaching of word attack skills that could be divided into phonic analysis and structural analysis. Phonic analysis was concerned with simple symbol sound relationships and association, while structural analysis was concerned with common combinations of sounds such as digraphs and diphthongs. Hierarchies of these skills were developed for teachers to plan and sequence the teaching of decoding.

These skills are still taught in similar sequences, though the teaching practices may vary from rote memory and application to more investigative approaches where students and teacher engage in guided inquiry about groups of words and draw conclusions about their structure. Kalantzis et al. (2016, p. 256) characterises these two methods as synthetic phonics and analytic phonics. In many ways, these terms reflect the pedagogical advantages and disadvantages of such approaches. The term *synthetic* phonics suggests something that is contrived, and such an approach does encourage the use of contrived texts rather than authentic ones and consequently teaching out of context. The term analytic suggests a focus on the development of strategies in such a way that their purpose and utility become evident and the transfer of the knowledge gained is more likely. The adherence to one or the other approach exclusively would not be help-ful to students as both skills and strategies are necessary. Nevertheless, in terms of the linguistic semiotic system, teaching phonic analysis as a system for decoding is necessary but it is not sufficient.

Other researchers (Thorndike, 1917; Bransford & Franks, 1977) found that it was not decoding skills alone that aided reading, but the reader's ability to relate what they were seeing and the associated sounds to previous experiences, for example, remembering individual words and sequences of words they have seen before. Thus, a focus on cognition, later referred to as comprehension, and the acknowledgement of prior knowledge, emerged in the teaching of reading. This led to the inclusion of additional skills about decoding. Together with phonic analysis, students were taught sight vocabulary (sometimes referred to as a look and say method), recognising a word as a whole rather than breaking it into sounds, configuration cues focussing on the **shape** of the word to remember it and the use of other cues to assist decoding, such as pictures cues. As students progressed through school they also learned to syllabify words and examine the Latin or Greek roots of words to give them clues when decoding and making meaning. Despite recognition of cognition as important to reading, a hierarchical or bottom up approach to reading prevailed at this point, suggesting that perception and decoding skills preceded being able to comprehend and should be focussed on first, to ensure success. This view of reading as presented in Figure 5.2.

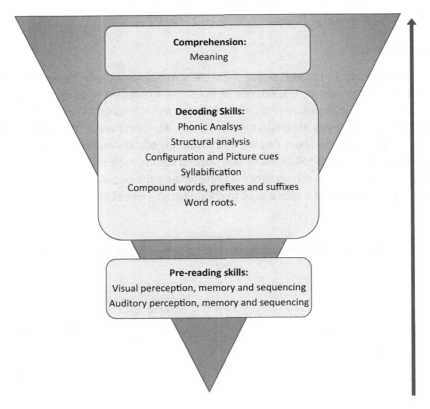

Figure 5.2 A hierarchical or bottom-up theory of reading instruction

Adapted from Anstey and Bull (2004, p.130)

This hierarchical, bottom-up or skills approach to the teaching of reading prevailed in the U.K., U.S. and Australia until the mid-1970s. It was accompanied by teaching materials, often developed and distributed by the state. These consisted of items such as alphabet and phonic charts and carefully sequenced sets of readers that gradually introduced simple sight words and word groups that reflected the level of decoding and phonic analysis being taught. Thus, a state-wide, systematic introduction to reading was accomplished. The advantages of this were that teaching was consistent and systematic, covering content in a carefully sequenced way throughout the school and state. However, the disadvantages were an emphasis on decoding rather than meaning and that this approach did not cater to individual differences or variation in social and cultural background. The scenes and activities shown and written about in the readers were largely the province of white, middle class, urban children in conventional families. For example, mother, father, girl and boy, pet dog and/or cat were depicted in a clean, new, detached house with a garden in which swings and trees provided places to play. Clearly these social and cultural settings would be unfamiliar to many students. Furthermore, the careful sequencing of skills in the readers led to a limited vocabulary presented in short, repetitive sentences. Figure 5.3 presents a fictitious example that would be typical of content and layout on a double-page spread.

The language of these books was artificial and did not represent the oral language of students or the language of their everyday lives. Therefore, transferring these reading experiences to the authentic reading experiences of everyday life could be difficult for many students. See Anstey and Bull (2004 pp.108–139) for a full discussion of the skills approach to reading.

Comprehension skills

Early research on meaning in reading began with the exploration of how to define comprehension behaviour and the development of taxonomies of skills. For example, the early definition of comprehension by Bloom et al. (1956) as translation, interpretation and extrapolation was further developed by Banton Smith (1965) as four levels of comprehension: literal, interpretative or inferential, critical and creative, and associated skills. These levels and Bloom's taxonomy of thinking skills inform many curriculum documents and reading programs today, but as was pointed out in Chapter Two, the issue is whether they are used to inform planning and teaching about reading for genuine purposes, with authentic texts, and a range of technologies and contexts, or are used to create taxonomies of skills to be 'covered' and tested.

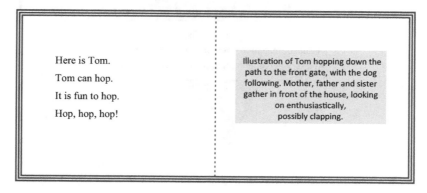

Figure 5.3 A fictitious example of a skills approach reader

During this period there was also interest in the use of reading skills in specific situation. As early as the 1940s, some researchers identified that in secondary schools when readers were reading different types of texts their success in comprehending varied (Hall & Robinson, 1945, Robinson & Hall, 1941). Researchers concluded that reading skills needed to be taught from preschool to secondary school and that there needed to be specific instruction on reading for information in other discipline areas. Concomitant with the skills and pedagogical focus of the times, hierarchies of skills were identified and taught, largely in isolation. Because these skills were designed to aid students in reading and learning in other disciplines, they were termed research skills. Four main areas were identified: locating, organising, evaluating and reporting. Table 5.1 identifies the four areas of research skills and examples of the types of skills that might be taught in each area.

As can be seen in Table 5.1, while the categories of research skills are still relevant, the focus is on using paper technologies for research, which is appropriate for the times they were first identified and used in schools. While many of these skills are still necessary they are not sufficient and more recent research focusses on the use of research skills with multimodal text and technologies. These will be discussed in detail later in this chapter. The hierarchical and skills focus of the pedagogy around research skills at this time meant they were seldom taught in context as part of the inquiry process (see previous discussion of the relationship between research skills and inquiry in Chapter Two of this volume). Therefore, the utility of these skills was not always apparent to students and the transfer from the learning and practice of skills in isolation to actual research and inquiry was not always easy for them.

The work of Thorndike (1917), who drew parallels between reading and problem solving, and others in the early 1970s led to a change in focus from perception of words to how meaning is made when reading. During the period 1970 to the late 1980s there was a period of well-funded, in-depth research

Table 5.1 Early concepts of research skills

Area of Skills	Example of Skills
Locating: used to find a source of information	• Identifying fiction and non-fiction text • Using the Dewey decimal system to locate a suitable text • Using the table of contents and indexes to locate relevant information in the text
Organising: skills needed to aid note-taking and outlining information for reporting	• Skimming and scanning for information • Identifying the main ideas • Taking short and long notes • Taking notes from several sources • Grouping information in notes and organising them into an appropriate sequence • Converting the notes into paragraphs
Evaluating: used to check the authority and authenticity of sources	• Identifying appropriate sources of information – checking publication date, authority of author • Selecting appropriate information to answer the question, complete the report • Detecting bias
Reporting: use to share the information with others	• Using writing skills to write report • Planning and rehearsing oral presentation skills • Planning and using audio-visual equipment for presentation

into reading as a cognitive process, focussing on meaning making, comprehension and the pedagogy of reading. This period of research is now sometimes referred to as the golden age of comprehension (Yopp-Edwards, 2003, cited by Freebody, 2011, p.10) and much of this research is relevant to, and can still inform, the teaching of reading today. During this period there was further, more focussed investigation of the concept of prior knowledge and its role in reading comprehension. Smith (1978) distinguished between outside the head knowledge, which he grouped into visual and non-visual information and inside the head knowledge, such as understandings about the topic, semantics, syntax and text types. Goodman (1976) and Smith (1978) concluded that the combination of outside the head and inside the head knowledge enabled the reader to sample the text and make links and interpretations based on prior knowledge and that reading was not a carefully sequenced and structured bottom-up process that progressed from letters to words to whole text and then meaning.

Pearson and Johnson (1978) took these ideas further concluding that the brain collects information and sorts and links it into semantic maps and that if readers access these maps prior to reading, then it will make their reading more efficient and enhance their comprehension. Their work led to a whole body of research on activating prior knowledge and eventually **metacognition** that has previously been discussed in Chapter Three and addressed in more detail in Chapter Three of the companion volume *Foundations of Multiliteracies: Reading, Writing and Talking in the 21st Century*. From the work of Goodman, Smith, Pearson and Johnson and others, there emerged an alternative view of reading as top down rather than bottom up. It was suggested that a reader tries to make sense of their reading from the moment they encounter a text rather than commencing with decoding before considering meaning. A diagrammatic representation of this view of reading is presented in Figure 5.4.

This debate between top-down and bottom-up approaches to reading still continues and has been intensified by the categorisation of further research in literacy that informed particular approaches that rose to prominence in the late 1980s and 1990s into two groups. These developments will be discussed shortly, but first the merits of the contrasting versions of the reading process that emerged in the 1970s and early 1980s should be addressed in terms of how they might inform **multiliteracies** and **multimodal texts**.

There is much that is relevant and can inform teaching about the consumption of multimodal texts as indicated by the use of italics in the following discussion. Discussion of multiliteracies in this book and its companion volume have focussed on reading as a *problem solving process*, but also indicated the *need for knowledge and skills* to enable problem solving. Purpose and context have been identified as helpful in focussing the activation of prior knowledge (*inside the head and outside the head knowledge*) and then using it in creative and new ways if necessary (*sampling and making links*). The role of *metacognition* has been identified as necessary to enhance problem solving and the strategic use of skills and knowledge when encountering texts that are new, in contexts that may be unfamiliar and delivered by a range of technologies. With regard to whether one or other of the approaches (*top down or bottom up*) is 'better', it can be seen that, particularly in a multimodal world of constant change, both are necessary, and the decision about which will be employed when will depend upon the individual's knowledge and experience, their purpose in reading, the context in which they are reading and the technologies involved. Any or all of these factors may mean that the reader will need to draw upon basic decoding skills, reading word by word and combining that with any prior knowledge, because so much about the text is unfamiliar. Consider, for example, a multimodal text that contains a dense scientific explanation of a process, using a lot of specialist scientific vocabulary, accompanied by a diagram and possibly some photographs or film.

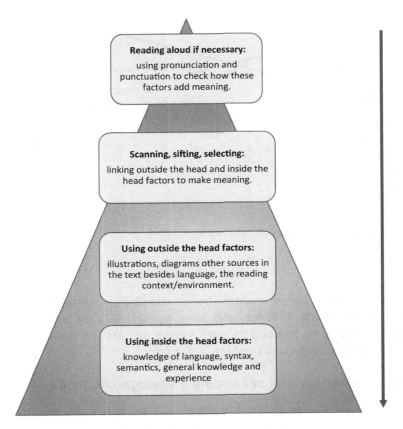

Figure 5.4 A top-down or meaning-focussed approach to reading

Adapted from Anstey & Bull (2004, p.130)

Unable to decode the seemingly unfamiliar words immediately, the reader might use strategies to sample the text using the images and photographs to activate any knowledge they already possess. They might then listen to the video to hear the scientific vocabulary which may be familiar, but has not previously been seen written down. They may also draw on word attack skills and Latin and Greek roots and their broader vocabulary in order to make sense of the written words. But to begin with they will rely on other semiotic systems to assist their meaning making while drawing upon their linguistic decoding skills to try and decode and make meaning of the linguistic text. During the process they will use metacognitive skills to monitor their strategies and refocus them if necessary. In other words the relative use of decoding and comprehension skills will depend on a range of factors. Figure 5.5 summarises what the relative use of decoding and comprehensions skills might be when taking into account the characteristics of text in the 21st century.

The conclusion in terms of the application of bottom-up or top-down theories and its relevance to consuming text today is that both provide skills, strategies and knowledge that can be drawn upon at

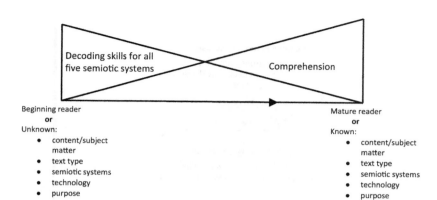

Figure 5.5 Relative use of decoding and comprehension skills

particular times and a multiliterate person would use both, strategically to achieve their reading purpose. However, it is inappropriate to think of them as alternative approaches to the teaching of reading, only one of which should be used. To do, so would be to think about the teaching of reading in precisely the way discussed earlier as being unhelpful to teachers.

Examining reading pedagogy and developing metacognitive skills

The pedagogy that translates the research into practice is the key to how this research might inform today's goal of helping students become multiliterate. The reader has to be strategic and therefore the pedagogy surrounding the teaching of reading must emphasise strategy rather than only rote learning of skills followed by their application to reading. Interestingly research by Durkin (1978-1979) conducted in the late 1970s drew a similar conclusion and informed much of the research that followed. After observing reading lessons in twenty-four fourth-grade classrooms across thirteen different school districts, she found that less than 1 per cent of the time allocated to reading was actually spent *teaching how to read and comprehend*. The pattern of 'teaching' in these classrooms was for students to read a text and then answer questions about it; in other words they were *tested rather than taught*. Durkin's research is still regarded as groundbreaking because it refocussed the research in reading on pedagogy, identifying what helped reading comprehension and how to teach it.

A focus on the role of metacognition and how to teach identified skills and strategies that aid comprehension and how to teach them followed (for a detailed discussion of metacognition, see Chapter Three in this volume and Chapter Three in the complementary volume *Foundations of Multiliteracies: Reading, Writing and Talking in the 21st Century*). Paris et al. (1984) conducted research in classrooms to aid students in developing strategies that taught them to use skills in strategic ways. Both skills and strategies are necessary; the critical aspect is how they are taught and that students' knowledge and use of both skills and strategies is assessed to further inform teaching. The work of Pearson and Gallagher (1983) around the pedagogy of teaching reading comprehension was groundbreaking and has influenced pedagogy to this day. As discussed in Chapter Two, the proposed Gradual Release of Responsibility Model suggested that responsibility of learning and teaching moves from teacher dominated to student dominated. It was suggested that this be achieved by moving the focus of pedagogy from teacher modelling to teacher and students working collaboratively and finally to students working independently. In Chapter Two this model was used as the basis of a pedagogy for inquiry learning which the authors believe informs multiliterate approaches to pedagogy.

The work of the researchers of the 1970s and 1980s is highly relevant and can inform current research into, and pedagogy around, the consumption of multimodal texts delivered by a range of technologies in 21st-century contexts. Such research has been happening since the 1990s and is ongoing (see for example, Shapiro & Niederhauser, 2004, and Coscarelli & Coiro, 2014, who examine the application of metacognitive strategies to reading and researching online) and will be the focus of later sections in this chapter.

REFLECTION STRATEGY 5.1

- The purpose of this Reflection Strategy is to examine your current planning and practice and consider what aspects of the preceding discussion you feel are present or absent from your current approach to teaching reading.
- How much emphasis is there on decoding in your current practice? Do you teach decoding or codebreaking of all semiotic systems? If so, what is the balance between them?
- How much emphasis is there on comprehension in your current planning and practice?
- Do you actively teach skills and strategies of comprehension – for example metacognitive strategies?
- Do you teach comprehension at different levels (e.g. literal, interpretative or inferential, critical or creative), or is one level emphasised more than others?
- Do you teach reading across all disciplines, text types and technologies? What is the balance?
- Examine your answers and consider what has informed them, why you have made the decisions to approach the teaching of reading in this way.
- Having reflected upon your approach to the teaching of reading, would you change it in any way? If so, how and why? If not, why not?

AUDITING INSTRUMENT 5.1

- The purpose of this Auditing Instrument is to gain insight into the way your students perceive reading and how they approach reading. It will provide data that can inform your teaching practices.
- Ask your students the following questions or, if they are older and can write easily, then present the questions in written form as a questionnaire. Be sure to tell your students that this is not a test; you are trying to find out how to teach reading better and help them with their reading.
  - o   What do you think makes a good reader?
  - o   What do good readers *know* that makes them good readers?
  - o   What do good readers *do* that makes them good readers?

- o What do you *think about* before you start reading a text?
- o What do you *do* before you start reading a text?
- o What do you *do* when you come to a word that you don't know?
- o What do you *do* when what you are reading does not make sense to you?
- o What do you *think about* while you are reading a text?
- o What do you *do* when you are reading a text?
- o Do you always think about and approach reading a text the same way? If not, what do you do differently and why?

- Construct a table of the answers students give for each question, grouping similar answers together in such a way that you can count them.
- Add up the different groups of answers for each question and see which ones are most prevalent.
- Is there a trend among the answers to a particular view of reading, and how it is done?
- Examine your answers in Reflection Strategy 5.1. Do you feel the students' answers closely reflect how you have suggested you teach reading? Are there areas of disagreement? What do you feel are the reasons for those, and what do you think you might do about this?

AUDITING INSTRUMENT 5.2

- The purpose of this Auditing Instrument is to audit your actual practice when teaching reading and see how well it matches the beliefs about how you practice teaching reading that you identified in Reflection Strategy 5.1.
- Audiotape your next reading lesson.
- Listen to it with a view to finding how well it reflects what you believe to be your approach to teaching reading.
- Your practice in this lesson may have been influenced by your reading in this chapter and others, however you may still identify areas of mismatch between your beliefs and practice. If you do, think about how you may address these differences between belief and practice.

ACTION LEARNING TASK 5.2

- The purpose of this Action Learning Task is to consider whether your findings from Reflection Strategy 5.1 and Auditing Instruments 5.1 and 5.2 may provide ideas for revising and refining your Action Plan or data collection for your Action Learning Plan.

- Consider your findings in Reflection Strategy 5.1 and Auditing Instruments 5.1 and 5.2:
  - o   Do you need or want to revise your action learning plan?
  - o   If so, what part(s) do you need or want to address?
  - o   How will you go about this?
  - o   Do your revisions mean that you will need to modify or refine your data collection and analysis methods?
  - o   Do you want to use the data from Reflection Strategy 5.1 and Auditing Instruments 5.1 and 5.2 as part of your data collection, for example as baseline data?

Whole language: moving towards reading as a social practice

In the late 1980s a new theory of how to approach the teaching of reading, a whole language approach, emerged. It spanned two countries: the U.S. through the work of Ken and Yetta Goodman (K. Goodman, 1987, 1989; Y. Goodman, 1989) and Australia through the work of Cambourne (1988). Proponents of this approach argued that the oral and written modes of language were similar and that the processes engaged in when producing and comprehending language were different but parallel. The conclusion was that all students acquire oral language before they come to school, except in the case of severe physical or neurological damage, and therefore study of the conditions under which they acquire language should inform the teaching of reading and writing written language when they arrive at school. Research focussed on examining the interactions of adults and children in a variety of settings to identify how children acquired oral language in home and play settings.

Cambourne (1988) concluded that there were particular conditions present in these settings and that if these conditions were present in the classroom then reading instruction could be more effective. These conditions were identified as immersion, demonstration, responsibility, use, approximation and response. In many ways Cambourne's conclusions inform ideas about the teaching of multiliteracies that have previously been discussed, for example, immersion in a range of authentic texts, demonstration or modelling of skills strategies and processes, providing opportunities for students to take responsibility and try out their strategies, using mistakes as a way of learning. In addition, as most of the interactions observed were oral whole language research also provided insight into the role of talk in learning. The identified conditions for learning provided insight into the types of talk and interaction that aid particular types of learning. Given the research into **dialogic talk** discussed in Chapter Four, considering creating these conditions through dialogic talk would seem to be useful.

Luke et al. (1989) critiqued whole language and suggested that using research based on home experiences may foreground middle class Anglo-Saxon child-rearing practices, advantaging some students over others. This critique is useful when considering a multiliterate approach to literacy pedagogy. One of the key understandings about multiliteracies, is that literacy is socially and culturally based and therefore basing teaching strategies on practices of the home is flawed because students' and home and community experiences will be very different (Luke et al., 1989).

The other major criticism of whole language was the assumption that oral and written language are both 'natural' and therefore it is inappropriate to transfer conditions for learning oral language to the learning of written language. Moorman et al. (1994, p.24) suggested that 'reading and writing are cultural artefacts, tools developed to solve problems and create shared meanings' and are therefore not natural. While this is a valid criticism in terms of transfer, the role of talk and interaction in learning generally is a valuable insight into how learning occurs.

Finally, there were critiques of the classroom strategies that emerged from whole language approaches, particularly the shared book experience and retelling (Brown & Cambourne, 1987). As these strategies are still widely used in classrooms with multimodal texts, it is important to investigate the critiques. Concerns were raised that if the purpose of the shared book experience was not explicitly identified then students could simply see the shared book activity as entertainment and even 'mindless chanting' (Unsworth, 1988; Baker & Freebody, 1989a). Another concern was that the question and answer sequences conducted during the shared book experience could be random, again not reinforcing specific learning outcomes. These concerns are legitimate and because Shared Book is still a widely used strategy must be addressed. Anstey & Bull (2010b) observed the reading lessons of every classroom in Anon Primary School from preparatory to year 7. Every lesson started with the shared book strategy and the questions followed the same pattern, regardless of the learning purpose and text type. Frequently there was no reference to a specific learning outcome at the beginning of the shared book lesson. This meant that students engaged in procedural display, that is, going through the expected patterns of behaviour, rather than actively engaging in learning, particularly as the same patterns of interaction around text were occurring from preparatory years to year 7. The school-wide use of this approach intimated that there was a belief among the teachers that, regardless of learning outcome, the same strategy will achieve it. When questioned about this the teachers indicated that this was not their belief, but they had decided to adopt 'shared book' as a school-wide approach to promote continuity of learning. At the time, there was a significant push among publishers offering professional development to promote shared book reading materials and one state in Australia had adopted shared book as its state-wide approach to reading. This is a very good example of the issues referred to earlier about the relationship between research, professional development and everyday teaching practices, who plans, executes and disseminates research and professional learning, and what research is valued and disseminated. It also demonstrates that a strategy based in research that is well intended can be implemented inappropriately. The identified conditions for learning in Anon state school were not being implemented in the talk around text or the shared book reading experience, and this was only discovered by examining the talk in the classrooms. The role of talk in learning is critical, and monitoring how it is occurring in classrooms provides insights that can inform teaching practices. The issue is the pedagogy, as was discussed in relation to skills approaches and decoding and phonics.

Despite the critiques, there are aspects of the whole language approach that are useful in current contexts, provided teachers are mindful when planning for teaching and talk around text. The research on dialogic talk presented in Chapter Four can help guard against some of the issues raised in these critiques, particularly those concerned with the classroom strategies generated from whole language. Table 5.2 summarises Cambourne's conditions for learning in terms of how they might be realised in a multiliterate classroom.

Table 5.2 A summary of Cambourne's conditions for learning and possible implications for practice in a multiliterate classroom

Cambourne's Conditions for Learning		Implications for Multiliterate Classroom Practices
Immersion		Students should engage with a range of authentic text types, that are transmitted by a range of technologies and utilise various combinations of the semiotic systems. These texts should be engaged with for different purposes and in different contexts.
Demonstration		Reading and writing strategies and processes should be modelled with a range of authentic text types, transmitted by a range of technologies and utilising various combinations of the semiotic systems. Modelling these strategies and processes should include a range of different purposes and contexts in which they might be used.
Responsibility	These conditions must be present during **Engagement**	Students should be given opportunities to try out their learning, taking responsibility for the selection and use of strategies, reviewing their success.
Use		Students should engage with authentic texts and settings.
Approximation		As a result of taking responsibility and reviewing and discussing the success of chosen strategies, students develop an understanding that approximation and making mistakes helps learning.
Response		Teacher responses to students' work should provide relevant feedback, praising both success and reinforcing what was successful about it. Similarly, approximations and errors should be responded to in ways that facilitate further learning by providing explanations and praising good decisions by the student.

REFLECTION STRATEGY 5.2

- This Reflection Strategy is linked to the critique regarding the use of whole language strategies. Its purpose is to examine your planning and practice for reading, identify strategies you use frequently (e.g. you may use shared book, read and retell, story maps, hot potato, or think-pair-share) and review why you use those strategies.
- Examine your planning for the teaching of reading for the last month. Identify the most frequently used strategies and the desired learning outcome or goal that was specified for which those strategies were employed.
- Compile a summary of your findings in tabular form. If you cannot find a specified learning outcome for a strategy, note this as 'no specified learning goal'.
- Were some strategies dominant, and what were the reasons for their selection and use? (e.g. Is every use linked to the same desired learning outcomes, are you implementing a particular theory about the teaching of reading?)

- Identify the least used strategies and the reasons for their selection and use. (e.g. Is every use linked to the same desired learning outcomes, are you implementing a particular theory about the teaching of reading?)
- How often do you explain to students why a particular strategy is being employed and how it will help them in reading? How often do you ask students to think about and discuss the utility of the strategy?
- What does this analysis tell you about your planning and practice around the teaching of reading?
- Does what you found surprise you? Does it match your beliefs about the teaching of reading? Is there anything you might do in response to your findings?
- Think about these strategies in terms of their application to multimodal texts and a multiliterate approach to teaching reading:
  o Do they embody and support the development of reading multimodal texts and becoming a multiliterate person?
  o Do you use these strategies in other discipline areas? Explain your reasons for this decision.
  o Do you use these strategies across various technologies? Explain your reasons for this decision.
  o Do you use these strategies across all semiotic systems? Explain your reasons for this decision.
- Is the use of these strategies aiding or inhibiting your approach to teaching reading around multimodal texts?
- Are there any changes you might make as a result of your analyses regarding your approach to teaching reading around multimodal texts?

AUDITING INSTRUMENT 5.3

- The purpose of this Auditing Instrument is to gain insight into the way your students perceive the strategies you use in your classroom. It will provide data that can inform your teaching practices.
- Compile a list of the most frequently used strategies from your analyses in Reflection Strategy 5.2.
- Either orally or in questionnaire form, ask your students to:
  o Identify the strategies they like most and the reason(s) they like them.
  o Identify the strategies they think *are the most useful and help them with reading* and the reason(s) for this.
  o Identify what each strategy *helps them with*, when reading and give an example of when they might use it.

- Collate your results and think about:
  - o The difference/similarities between strategies students like and those they find useful and their reasons. What does this tell you about your teaching of reading strategies?
  - o Whether students could identify or explain how each strategy helped them with their reading, and what this tells you about your teaching of reading strategies.
- Are there any changes to your planning and/or practice you might make as a result of these investigations?

AUDITING INSTRUMENT 5.4

- The purpose of this Auditing Instrument is to audit your actual practice when teaching reading strategies.
- Audiotape the next lesson in which specific strategies are introduced, used or revised.
- Listen to it with a view to gaining more insight into the results of your investigations in Reflection Strategy 5.2 and Auditing Instrument 5.3, that is how you teach and conduct talk with your students around the use of reading strategies.
- Your practice in this lesson may have been influenced by your reading in this chapter and others, however it may help you make changes to your planning and practice you identified.

ACTION LEARNING TASK 5.3

- The purpose of this Action Learning Task is to consider whether your findings from Reflection Strategy 5.2 and Auditing Instruments 5.3 and 5.4 may provide ideas for revising and refining your Action Plan or data collection for your Action Learning Plan.
- Consider your findings in Reflection Strategy 5.1 and Auditing Instruments 5.1 and 5.2:
  - o Do you need or want to revise your action learning plan?
  - o If so, what part(s) do you need or want to address?
  - o How will you go about this?
  - o Do the revisions to your action plan mean that you will need to modify or refine your data collection and analysis methods?
  - o Do you want to use the data from Reflection Strategy 5.1 and Auditing Instruments 5.1 and 5.2 as part of your data collection, for example as baseline data?

Literacy as social practice

The critiques of whole language heralded a new phase in research about, and practices in, the teaching of reading during the 1990s and early 21st century, the concept of reading as **social practice**. The concept of literacy (and reading) as social practice has been discussed extensively in Chapters One and Two of the complementary volume *Foundations of Multiliteracies: Reading, Writing and Talking in the 21st Century* and was reviewed in Chapter One of this volume. Therefore, discussion in this section will focus mainly on the main ideas and implications for the teaching of reading. The main concepts of literacy as social practice can be summarised as follows:

- Literacy is practiced daily by all individuals in all parts of their life, for example civic, social, cultural and workplace contexts. It is practiced through live, paper and digital technologies.
- Literacy is not a neutral practice, every text and interaction conveys views, beliefs and values about the world and how it is perceived by the participants in the interaction.
- Literacy can empower or disempower particular social groups.
- Literacy is practiced differently and aspects of it are valued differently among different social and cultural groups.

Research around the concept of literacy as social practice resulted in three major influences regarding the teaching of reading:

- The development of the concept of critical literacy and its application to all texts, contexts, disciplines and technologies;
- The development of the genre approach and functional grammar, which though largely concerned with the teaching of writing also influenced the teaching of reading;
- The development of the Four Resource Model as an approach to the teaching of reading based on the notion of reading as a social practice.

Critical literacy

The recognition that no text is neutral and that therefore text can be empowering or disempowering depending upon people's literacy skills and practices, led to a focus on reading pedagogies that developed critical literacy skills. Freebody, Luke and Gilbert (1991) suggested that as texts are a product of sociocultural, political and economic influences, they contain messages and associated attitudes and beliefs about, among other things, gender, ethnicity and socioeconomic status. Their concern was that the implicit and explicit messages in such texts would result in the construction of a particular picture of the world (a reality) that may or may not be accurate. Therefore, Luke and Gilbert together with other researchers suggested that reading pedagogy must enable students to deconstruct and reconstruct the meanings of texts. Students needed to become critical readers.

Luke (in Unsworth 1993, p. 35) summarised the concept of critical literacy in terms of students' interactions with texts in their lifeworlds. He suggested that texts that are used in powerful social situations, such as religious settings, schools, libraries or family settings, help students build up a picture of the world and that, because the texts are used in powerful settings, the messages they contain may be seen as acceptable, and even endorsed, by society. Luke's concern was that without the necessary critical literacy skills, students would simply accept these messages and current inequalities and injustices would be maintained. Luke's concerns are even more relevant today as the accessibility of the internet and social media increases the range of beliefs, attitudes and values with the potential to influence students' views of the world.

Anstey and Bull (2004, pp. 62-63) and Knobel and Healy (1998) suggested that students should be taught to question texts in order to identify the ideologies, beliefs and values they represent and then consider whether these ideologies should be challenged or investigated further before acceptance of them. They suggested the questions might focus on:

- The values and attitudes being represented;
- Whether the values and attitudes presented are consistent throughout the text or whether contradictions occur;
- Who is represented and who is not, sometimes referred to as gaps and silences in the text;
- Whether particular practices are being shaped and valued;
- How the text relates to the students' own values, culture and place in society;
- The authority and authenticity of the text.

The development of critical literacy pedagogies led to concerns that students might simply learn to 'do tricks with texts' as they identified such things as stereotypes about families, gender and ethnicity (Rowan, 2001, p. 58). Rowan and others (Lankshear et al., 1997, p. 60, Barton et al., 2000, p. 8) suggested that pedagogies around critical literacy should be viewed in the social context in which they have developed, in order that students understand that the goal of being critically literate was to be empowered to take action. For example, if students investigated a local store's toy catalogues and found gender stereotypes in the colours, layout and captions accompanying particular toys, then they should be encouraged to think about how these ideas might be challenged and take action. As a result of their investigations, students might write to the toy store, present their findings and make constructive suggestions about action the store could take to prevent the maintenance of these stereotypes. Thus, students would be active citizens taking responsibility and designing their social future, concepts that are essential to a multiliterate person.

One of the most influential places in which live, paper and digital texts are used is the school. However, it is possible that the selection and use of texts marginalises some students and advantages others because there is a gap between the literacies of home and school (Hannon, 1995, p. 14). Therefore, it is important that schools need to know more about their school community and investigate the literacies and literate practices of home and community. An example of the influence of the research on critical literacy and literacy as a social practice was The Literate Futures Reading Project, a state-wide professional development program implemented between 2002 and 2005 in Queensland, Australia. It required all schools to conduct an audit of their home, school and community literacies and literate practices and use the information from this audit to develop a whole school literacy plan, particularly focussed on the teaching of reading. It can be seen that the concepts that underpin critical literacy are highly relevant to, and inform, multiliterate reading practices and a multiliterate pedagogy. For further information about critical literacy see Chapters One, Two, Four and Five in the complementary volume *Foundations of Multiliteracies: Reading, Writing and Talking in the 21st Century*. Chapter Four provides the most detail and Chapter Five examines it in relation to teaching children's literature.

AUDITING INSTRUMENT 5.5

- The purpose of this Auditing Instrument is to consider the texts currently used regularly in your classroom and whether they include texts from your students' home and community.
- Conduct an audit of the texts used in your classroom so far this year. How many of them came from your local community – for example community notices, the local newspaper, local brochures and advertising, websites and blogs for local community groups and businesses?
- How often do you ask your students to bring in texts or show on the internet the texts they use regularly? (e.g. the texts they are using at home or in their lifeworlds such as community, cultural or sporting groups). Do you ever use these texts as a focus for teaching reading or strategies at school?
- As a result of your audit and reflecting upon the section on reading as a social practice and critical literacy would you change your selection and use of texts in the classroom in any way? If so, how?

Genre theory and functional grammar

The concerns about equity and the mismatch between the home and community literacy experiences of students and those of their school experiences, led to researchers investigating how such potential inequities for some students might be addressed. Researchers such as Martin (1993) and Martin and Rothery (1993) suggested a functional approach to the teaching of literacy, to ensure students were specifically taught about the structure and grammar of the kinds of texts that would aid their success in school across all disciplines. It was based upon the systemic-functional linguistics developed by Halliday (1975, 2004) and proposed the teaching and use of functional grammar rather than traditional grammar. Teacher and students would investigate and analyse the social function of particular genres of text (the context in which they were used together with their purpose), the generic structure of the text (its stages or parts) and its grammar (the clauses, sentences, phrases and words). The pedagogy for such investigations focussed on modelling and deconstruction, followed by joint construction and independent construction (Kalantzis et al., 2016). Generally, its focus initially was on writing texts. However, as the investigations involved reading and analysing texts in order to know more about them, there were specific links with, and influences on, the teaching of reading. The genre approach to pedagogy recommended a sequence of modelling, collaborative investigation and independent writing. This sequence reflects the work of Pearson and Gallagher (1983) discussed earlier and is a positive aspect of this approach.

Proponents of the genre approach claimed to address the shortcomings of whole language approaches which they said foregrounded middle class language and text. However, they also suggested that whole language approaches failed to explicitly teach about text structure and grammar (see Kalantzis et al., 2016, pp. 146–160 for a detailed explanation of this critique). This debate still rages and as stated previously is not useful. Once again it comes down to the translation of research into practice through professional development and pedagogy. There were certainly classrooms where poor translation of whole language resulted in a lack of explicit teaching and the reading and writing of a limited range of genres, but there were others where explicit teaching occurred alongside the sort of investigations and analysis that are advocated by proponents of a genre approach. Similar observations could be made about the range of pedagogical practices in classrooms where teachers implement genre approaches – the suggested sequence of instruction can become formulaic if not accompanied by explicit exploration and discussion of a variety of texts implementing genres in a variety of ways, including the combination of several genres in one text.

Nevertheless, the functional approach provides a framework for investigating a range of genres in context and therefore contributes to a multiliterate approach to the teaching of reading and a multiliterate pedagogy. It also provided a metalanguage around text structure that is particularly useful for informing a multiliterate approach to reading and a multiliterate pedagogy. While the early work was focussed solely on language, more recently these ideas have been applied to multimodal texts, particularly the visual and audio semiotic systems (see for example, Kress & van Leeuwen, 2006; Callow, 2013; Barton & Unsworth, 2014). These ideas and their application to other semiotic systems will be discussed in detail later in the chapter.

AUDITING INSTRUMENT 5.6

- The purpose of this Auditing Instrument is to examine how much your practices around the teaching of reading embed the ideas about reading as social practice, critical literacy and genre theory.
- Examine your selection of texts that you use to teach reading. Do they represent a range of disciplines as well as a range of technologies?
- What is the range of text types (genres) present?
- Do you actively teach and discuss the text structure and grammatical features of different text types (genres) as part of your reading program, or is this more a part of your writing program?
- Do you examine the role of all five semiotic systems in different text types, for example the role and characteristics of visual material in scientific texts or procedural texts?
- What pedagogies and types of talk happen around the discussion and analysis of different text types? Is it more oriented to didactic teaching of the structure, or are there investigations conducted by the students where they share findings and draw conclusions that become part of their knowledge about genre or text types?
- How much of your reading comprehension program is concerned with teaching critical literacy skills and actively using them with local texts?
- Having considered all these questions, how well balanced is your reading program in terms of genres and pedagogy? Do you feel the need to make changes, and if so, how will you go about them?

AUDITING INSTRUMENT 5.7 (THIS COULD ALSO BE USED AS AN ACTION LEARNING TASK)

- The purpose of this Auditing Instrument is to compare your perceptions about how you teach reading against your practice.
- Audiotape a lesson in which the major focus is teaching about reading a text type used in another discipline (e.g. science or history), and then audiotape a lesson in which the main focus is teaching critical literacy skills.
- Listen to each lesson and consider the following:
  - o Did you identify the learning purpose, why these skills are important and where they might be used?
  - o Did you examine the role of all five semiotic systems in the text types or during application of the critical literacy skills?
  - o What pedagogies and types of talk happened around the discussion and analysis of the text type or the text used to develop critical literacy skills?
  - o Was there a balance between **monologic talk** and dialogic talk? Did the dialogic talk include disputational and investigative talk?
  - o How well do you feel either of these lessons fulfils the goals of a multiliterate approach to the teaching of reading? Are there aspects you would like to change, and if so, how might you go about this?
- Identify one thing you would like to change, plan for these changes and audiotape the lesson in which you attempt these changes. (You may find re-reading or referring back to Chapter Four useful when you do this.)
- Review this lesson and how these changes were addressed. What helped or hindered the implementation of these changes, and how might you address these issues? Repeat the process with other aspects identified for change.

Asking better questions about the teaching of reading: the Four Resource Model

The concept of reading as a social practice and observations of the debates around how to teach reading in the late 1980s and early 1990s led Luke and Freebody (1999a, 1999b) to suggest that rather than asking the question 'What is the best way to teach reading?' and descending into 'reading wars' such as those that were currently going on regarding skills, whole language and genre approaches, the more informed question was 'What are the kinds of reading practices and positions schools should value, encourage and propagate?' (Luke & Freebody in Muspratt, Luke & Freebody, 1997, p. 213). They then examined the social practices of reading in terms of what reading was used for in various aspects of life. Freebody and Luke believed that by focussing on use rather than trying to identify skills and texts, no particular culture, practice or text would potentially be excluded, or included, when planning for the teaching of reading

(Anstey, 2002b). In this way, concerns about balance, equity and power raised by researchers examining literacy as social practice could be addressed. Having identified the uses of reading Freebody and Luke then posed the question, 'What do students need to know and be able to do?' in order to read. They identified four practices of reading that would be needed to engage in as readers. Readers would need to become codebreakers, meaning makers, text users and text analysts (Luke & Freebody, 1999a, 1999b; Freebody & Luke, 2003). More detail regarding the Four Resource Model as a pedagogical framework can be found in Chapter Two of the complementary volume, *Foundations of Multiliteracies: Reading, Writing and Talking in the 21st Century*.

Recently Bull and Anstey were participating in a conversation among some teacher leaders regarding planning for teaching reading with multimodal texts and digital technologies. The teacher leaders were anxious to provide their teachers with a framework for planning that would help them to balance their planning and teaching across semiotic systems text, types and technologies but would also address the decoding and comprehensions skills of reading. The Four Resource Model came up as a planning framework, and several people immediately rejected it as too old and not relevant to multimodal texts and technologies. Yet if the model is examined carefully it is easy to see how these changes in reading and the consumption of texts can be addressed. Because the Four Resource Model focusses on *use*, the necessary resources (what students need to know and be able to do) can be added and modified as texts and technologies change. The pedagogy can then be developed with a focus on the processes and thinking strategies necessary to facilitate those resources and practices. Figure 5.6, adapted from the work of Anstey (2002b, p.29), demonstrates the application the Four Resource Model to the consumptions of text in terms of design, multimodal texts and multiliteracies.

Contributions of historical research and associated approaches to understandings about the consumption of multimodal texts in a multiliterate world

In order to consider how previous approaches inform teaching reading and the consumption of text today, it is useful to review what students need to know and be able to do in current and future multimodal and multiliterate worlds.

In Chapter One the characteristics of a multiliterate person were identified as follows. A multiliterate person needs to:

- Be flexible and able to deal with change – be an analytical and reflective problem solver, be a strategic, creative and critical thinker who can engage with new texts in a variety of contexts and audiences;
- Have a repertoire of literate knowledge and practices – understand that new texts that have differing purposes, audiences and contexts and will require a range of different behaviours that draw on a repertoire of knowledge and experiences;
- Understand how social and cultural diversity effects literate practices – know that experiences and culture influence and produce a variety of different knowledges, approaches, orientations, attitudes and values that will influence the interpretation and occurrence of literate practices;
- Understand, and be able to use, traditional and new communication technologies – understand the **semiotic systems** and recognise that the increasing variety of new texts are delivered by paper, live and digital technologies, and realise that purpose, audience and context determine which semiotic system and which technology is appropriate;

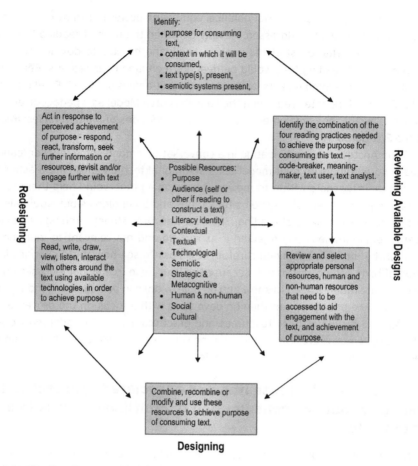

Figure 5.6 Applying the Four Resource Model to the consumption of text in terms of design, multimodal texts and multiliteracies

- Be critically literate – understand that in every literate practice it is necessary to determine who is participating and for what reason, who is in a position of power, who has been marginalised, what is the purpose and origin of the texts being used and how these texts are supporting participation in society and everyday life.

It was also suggested that the following understandings about texts were essential:

- All texts are consciously constructed and have particular social, cultural, political or economic purposes.
- Texts will continue to change as society and technology changes.
- All texts are multimodal.
- Texts can be interactive, linear or non-linear.
- Texts may be intertextual.

- Texts are tending to become more screen-like as design and designing become more central to the production of texts.
- Texts can be created by the consumer using the links in digital texts to produce **hypertexts**.
- The social and cultural background of individuals influences the production of, and engagement with, text.
- A text may have several possible meanings.
- The consumer interacts with the text to actively construct the meaning of the text.
- The complexity of multimodal texts means that consumers have to consciously differentiate the focus of their attention across the semiotic systems.
- No text is neutral.

At the beginning of this chapter a suggested approach for examining the historical approaches was recommended. It was suggested that after reading the description and discussion of each major area of research and the associated approaches, pedagogy and practices, the reader should re-examine Figure 5.1 and consider a series of questions. The major question was 'What is necessary but not suffi-cient about this research and pedagogy for consuming and producing (designing and redesigning) texts in a multimodal, multiliterate world?' The minor questions focussed on examining the historical research and approaches in terms of the stages on Figure 5.1. How does the research that informs this approach and ensuing pedagogy and practice:

- Inform understandings about the role of purpose when consuming a text?
- Contribute knowledge, skills and processes that become part of a repertoire of resources aiding consumption of multimodal texts?
- Provide knowledge, skills and strategies that inform the synthesising process of meaning making (combining, recombining and reworking selected resources to make meaning)?
- Provide knowledge, skills and strategies that inform the recording, preservation and dissemination of meaning making from the text?
- Develop understandings about consumption as the transforming and transformation of meaning?

Consideration of these questions together with the characteristics of a multiliterate person and under-standings about text inform Table 5.3 that provides a summary of such investigations. The reader may wish to annotate it with their own findings.

It is important to realise that the recommended process for analysing the historical review of research and associated approaches, pedagogy and practice represents a similar process to the consumption of text presented in Figure 5.1 and Figure 5.5. In terms of these figures, previous research findings, their applications and recommended pedagogies become the resources educators can draw upon when developing policy, curriculum, pedagogy, classroom practice or further research. When reviewing these resources, educators are examining 'available designs' in terms of the questions they have, or problems they want to resolve or investigate regarding teaching about the consumption of text in a multimodal world. The historical and current research and associated approaches and pedagogy can be reviewed, analysed, critiqued and redesigned, according to the specific purpose of the inquiry and then action can be taken. Thus, teachers and educators engage in and replicate the very processes they are trying to teach their students. Teachers and educators employ the inquiry model discussed in Chapter Two when they are making decisions about their pedagogy and practice. They then conduct action learning in their classrooms, as described in Chapter One, in order to investigate the decisions taken and then continue the process as new research and ideas became available. Such educators are reflective, flexible, can cope with change and have a repertoire of resources available to draw upon. If educators cannot, or will not, engage in the processes of inquiry, reflection and action learning, then they cannot adequately model and teach these processes to their students or empathise with the issues students face as they learn how to engage in these processes. A multiliterate pedagogy requires teachers who are developing the characteristics of a multiliterate person, who can continuously engage in and take responsibility for con-ducting inquiry and action learning. Education systems should support development and implementation of inquiry and action learning processes for teachers as a matter of policy and professional learning.

Analysis of Table 5.3 informs how the history of literacy teaching, in particular the teaching of read-ing, can inform current pedagogy and practice. The understandings about text and characteristics of a multiliterate person and multiliterate pedagogy provide a context against which to examine the summary in Table 5.3. In terms of how the research and associated approaches, pedagogy and practice *can inform and contribute* to current understandings about text and multiliteracies the following can be identified:

- Contributions to the foundations of multiliteracies in terms of understanding
    - o   Reading as problem solving
    - o   That the reader/consumer must take responsibility for the process
    - o   The role of inquiry and research skills in assisting consumption of texts across disciplines and throughout all years of schooling
    - o   That literacy is a social practice and therefore authentic contexts and texts are important to pedagogy around the consumption of texts
    - o   That it is necessary to acknowledge the social, cultural and economic influences on the literacies and literate practices of students in the school community
    - o   The role of cognition and metacognition in developing multiliterate practices
    - o   The need to be critically literate
- Specific aspects of pedagogy and frameworks for planning that can inform a multiliterate pedagogy, specifically
    - o   Cambourne's conditions for learning
    - o   Gradual Release of Responsibility model
    - o   Four Resource Model
    - o   Model for teaching about genres/text types
- Provision of resources for consuming multimodal texts and engaging in multiliterate practices
    - o   Various taxonomies and hierarchies of necessary skills in codebreaking, cognition and research skills
    - o   Specific strategies for engaging in metacognition and activating prior knowledge (resources)
    - o   Metalanguage for talking around text, for example, features of text types, the linguistic semiotic system, and some of other semiotic systems
- Recognition of the role of talk and talk around text (including deconstruction and analysis) as part of learning about the consumption and production of text

The following challenges and cautions were identified and the implications for each are discussed.

- Many of the approaches, because of the times in which the research was conducted only provide information for the linguistic semiotic system and paper technologies.

Table 5.3 How the history of research about reading and the associated approaches, pedagogy and practices inform the teaching of reading and consumption of multimodal texts and a multiliterate pedagogy

Research and Associated Approaches, Pedagogy and Practice	Comments in Terms of Teaching About the Consumption of Multimodal Text and a Multiliterate Pedagogy
Phonics and Decoding: Skills approach Identified reading as a set of linguistic decoding skills to be mastered in hierarchical order, particularly in terms of perceptual skills and phonics.	Informs, because it: • Contributes linguistic resources useful in code-breaking practices. • Identifies the **codes** and **conventions** of linguistic text, and concepts about paper text that need to be learned. • Assists in identification of skills necessary to early reading development. Potential challenges: • Concomitant with the times, it focussed on paper texts and linguistic semiotic system – needs to include codes and conventions of other semiotic systems and characteristics of texts delivered via other technologies. • Focusses on behaviour and skills rather than on literacy as a social, cultural and cognitive practice. • Takes no account of social and cultural, background of students. • Does not always emphasise the combining and recombining of skills in different ways for different purposes and contexts with paper and digital text. • Need to balance synthetic and analytic approaches. • Can lead to decontextualised teaching of skills unrelated to the lifeworlds with limited range of text types that are not authentic.
Early approaches to cognition and comprehension Defined reading in terms of cognition, translation, interpretation and extrapolation (Bloom, 1956) and different types/levels of comprehension, literal, inferential, creative and critical (Banton Smith, 1965). Recognised reading in disciplines required different skills which led to identification of four areas of research skills (locating, organising, evaluating and reporting).	Informs, because it: • Focussed attention on different types of meaning making. • Identified a hierarchy of thinking skills. • Recognised need for, and identification of, research skills. • Identified the need to teach reading across all disciplines. Potential challenges: • Concomitant with the times, it focussed on paper texts and linguistic semiotic system – needs to be developed and applied to multimodal texts, multiple semiotic systems and technologies. • Because of the decontextualised teaching of skills, focusses on behaviour and skills rather than on literacy as a social, cultural and cognitive practice. • Associated pedagogy and practice meant translation to lifeworlds was limited,

(Continued)

Table 5.3 (Continued)

Research and Associated Approaches, Pedagogy and Practice	Comments in Terms of Teaching About the Consumption of Multimodal Text and a Multiliterate Pedagogy
Metacognition Recognised that if prior knowledge or schema about the content is consciously activated it helps meaning making. Identified metacognition as the conscious control of thought processes (thinking about one's thinking) and developed strategies and pedagogies such as reciprocal teaching to aid metacognition. Contributed the Gradual Release of Responsibility Model of pedagogy (Pearson and Gallagher, 1983).	Informs, because it: • Contributes to the idea of reading as a problem solving process that is key to a multiliterate pedagogy. • Informs further research and application of metacognition to other semiotic systems and technologies. • Provides a pedagogy that focusses on the reader taking responsibility by identifying the resources required to complete a task, the employment of those practices, and monitoring the use of them, modifying if necessary (Gradual Release of Responsibility Model). • Can help readers actively reflect on how their lifeworlds influences their meaning making. • Can provide resources that are useful to all of the four reading practices identified by Freebody and Luke. • Can provide resources that are useful to the four areas of research skills. Potential challenges: • Concomitant with the times, it focussed on paper texts and linguistic semiotic system – needs further research and application to include codes and conventions of other semiotic systems and characteristics of texts delivered via other technologies. • Needs to take account of literacy as a social and cultural practice and that therefore students from diverse backgrounds will have diverse prior knowledge and schemas.
Whole language approach Focussed on the whole text and meaning before the learning of skills in context (whole to part rather than part to whole). Identified conditions for learning which can be reproduced in the classroom. Focussed attention on talk as a key part of learning.	Informs, because it: • Informed classroom pedagogy in terms of using authentic texts and contexts for learning. • Provided conditions for learning that are useful for planning pedagogy (immersion, demonstration, modelling, engagement, response, expectations and responsibility). Potential challenges: • Can lead to implicit rather than explicit teaching practices that advantage some groups and disadvantage others. • Can lead to reinforcement of the dominant sociocultural values and genres if notion of literacy as social practice and the importance of making connections between home, school and community are not addressed. • Can result in the repetitive use of a small group of strategies (e.g. shared book and read and re-tell) that become decontextualised and lead to students engaging in procedural display rather than learning.

Research and Associated Approaches, Pedagogy and Practice	Comments in Terms of Teaching About the Consumption of Multimodal Text and a Multiliterate Pedagogy	
Literacy as Social Practice – Critical Literacy Based on the following premises: • Literacy is constructed by through and around the social practices of home, community and workplace. • Literacy is not neutral: it constructs our world and we are constructed by it. • Particular literacies are valued by particular parts of society, therefore individuals and groups may be dominant or marginalised. • Schools are sites where literacy is practised and therefore potentially empower or disempower students (text selection, pedagogy, authorising meaning).	Informs, because it: • Acknowledges the relationships among social, economic and technological change and how literacy, and the ways it is used and practiced, evolves. • Provides knowledge and skills that enable producers and consumers to question the source, authority and authenticity of texts and identify potential, gaps and silences in texts. • Informs both consumption and production of texts. • Informs all four reading practices of the Four Resource Model. • Informs the four areas of research skills. • Provides knowledge and skills that enable teachers and schools to examine the use of texts and the practices around them and identify balance/imbalance, authenticity and relevance in terms of the homes and communities surrounding the school.	Potential challenges: • May not address all semiotic systems, text types and technologies. • Pedagogy may encourage analysis over action and may not be applied to authentic texts and contexts, for example community issues.
Genre approach A structured, explicit and functional approach to the teaching of literacy, focussing on the structure and grammar of texts across all disciplines. Examined purpose of texts and social contexts in which they were used. Pedagogy recommended modelling and deconstruction, followed by joint construction and finally independent construction.	Informs, because it: • Provides resources for use in consumption and production of text. • Provides a metalanguage useful for talking about text. • Provides resources that aid in all practices of the Four Resource Model. • Provides resources that aid in use of research skills. • Recent work includes application to audio and visual semiotic systems. • Provides a pedagogy similar to Gradual Release of Responsibility, therefore emphasising the need for the consumer/producer to take responsibility and control.	Potential challenges: • Concomitant with the times, it was originally developed it focussed on paper texts and linguistic semiotic system – needs further research and application to include codes and conventions of all five semiotic systems and characteristics of texts delivered via other technologies. • Recommended pedagogy can result in repetitive superficial pedagogical practices that do not address social context of texts, individual learning needs or community links. • Does not always acknowledge that some texts contain several genres within them and that genres are not always 'pure'. • Debate regarding the use of functional or traditional approach to grammar is not constructive. Either can inform this approach.

(Continued)

Table 5.3 (Continued)

Research and Associated Approaches, Pedagogy and Practice	Comments in Terms of Teaching About the Consumption of Multimodal Text and a Multiliterate Pedagogy
Four Resource Model Examined the purpose for which reading is used in everyday life and the ways in which it is practiced, to identify the reading practices and resources that can inform the teaching of reading. Identified codebreaker, meaning maker, text user and text analyst practices.	Informs, because it: • Focusses on practices and resources and can therefore respond to change. • Embedded in concept of literacy as social practice but can acknowledge contributions of psycholinguistic research on cognition and metacognition as contributing resources and practices. • Can be applied to all semiotic systems, text types and technologies. • Can inform pedagogy and planning, ensuring balanced approach to teaching about the consumption of text. • Encourages talk around text. Potential challenges: • Requires continuous review and renewal to accommodate changes in practice, technologies, semiotic systems and texts. However this can also be seen as an advantage as it ensures it is embedded in current social practice. • The four reading practices can be interpreted as a hierarchy rather than a balanced approach across every level of schooling and every discipline. • Pedagogical practice associated with the Four Resource Model may teach the practices separately instead of in relation to one another, therefore leading to a representation of reading process that is not authentic and does not emphasise use in context.

Implications: This does not mean they should be rejected (e.g. the decoding skills identified in the skills approach). The codes and conventions necessary to decode other semiotic systems need to be identified and incorporated into planning and pedagogy for the consumption of multimodal texts. Other skills identified are still relevant, for example, thinking skills, levels of comprehension and research skills. Nevertheless, their application to other technologies, particularly the consumption of online and offline texts must be further investigated. In addition, it is necessary to audit curricula, planning and practice in schools and classrooms to ensure balance among technologies, semiotic systems and online and offline texts.

- Many of the approaches do not acknowledge literacy as social practice and do not provide guidelines for responding to social and cultural differentiation among students.

Implications: The combination of skills approaches, a lack of acknowledgement of social and cultural variation and its influence on texts and literate practices, can mean that students do not have the opportunity to engage with authentic texts and contexts when learning about the consumption of texts. Consequently, students do not have exposure to a wide range of vocabulary, text types, and technologies making it difficult to firstly, see the relevance of what they are learning and secondly translate and apply their learning into lifeworld contexts. Therefore, it is necessary to identify the texts and literate practices, social and cultural backgrounds of the school community and then audit curricula, planning and practice in schools and classrooms to ensure this information is informing the selection of texts, pedagogy and practice of the classrooms. Note that this does not mean text selection and content of the curriculum should be limited to reflect only the school community, but that the curriculum and practice acknowledges difference and makes learning relevant.

- The largest area of potential challenges and cautions relates to critiques of associated pedagogies. The concerns related to:
  o Implicit rather than explicit teaching of skills because of the overuse of particular strategies
  o The repetitive use of strategies leading to decontextualised learning and students engaging in procedural display rather than learning
  o The application of strategies and frameworks without careful attention to potential challenges or flaws
  o The necessity for balancing synthetic and analytic approaches to the learning of codebreaking skills such as phonics
  o Balancing focussed learning episodes with inquiry and investigation of texts and the consumption of texts.

Implications: Pedagogy around teaching about the consumption of text needs to be continuously reviewed and investigated to ensure good strategies do not become bad strategies because of the ways they are enacted in the classroom. Ritualised repetitive strategies and behaviour, decontextualised learning, a lack of authentic texts, are the antithesis of a multiliterate pedagogy that develops multiliterate adults. In Chapters Two and Four the inquiry model and research on talk and dialogic pedagogy provide very clear guidelines for avoiding these potential challenges. Chapter One identified action learning as a way of investigating practice to ensure beliefs match practice. Careful detailed planning, frequently audited to ensure balance among texts and technologies, variation among teaching strategies and practices and response to social and cultural difference are necessary to ensure effective pedagogy around consumption of multimodal texts.

What current research contributes to teaching about the consumption of multimodal texts in a multiliterate world

Current research on the consumption of multimodal texts focusses on many of the challenges identified in previous research; meaning making with all five semiotics systems, the similarities and differences between reading online and offline, reading as problem solving and the use of metacognitive skills with all semiotic systems and technologies, developing online research skills and changing pedagogy, particularly the ways in which classroom talk occurs around meaning making with multimodal texts. These areas will be explored in the remainder of the chapter.

Meaning making with all five semiotic systems in multimodal texts

Since 2000 there has been an enormous body of work in developing ways of analysing, meaning making, and developing metalanguage to talk about text that comprises multiple semiotic systems (Kress, 2000, 2003, 2010; Kress & van Leeuwen, 2006; Anstey, 2002a; Anstey & Bull, 2016; Bull & Anstey, 2010a; Cope & Kalantzis, 2000, 2015; Unsworth, 2001; Barton & Unsworth, 2014; Kalantzis et al., 2016; Callow, 2013). Much of this has been reviewed in Chapter Three, together with an explanation of the codes and conventions of all five semiotic systems and recommendations for teaching strategies. A sequence for introduction across primary and secondary schooling with a recommended pedagogical focus for each phase – foundation, developing, investigation, synthesising, accomplished and innovative, was also provided. The importance of developing curriculum, content, pedagogy and practices that balance all five semiotic systems and texts delivered via live, paper and digital technologies was emphasised and the reader was cautioned to ensure that codebreaking focussed on all semiotic systems, including an emphasis on meaning making, with authentic texts and contexts. In the complementary volume *Foundations of Multiliteracies: Reading, Writing and Talking in the 21st Century*, Chapter Three introduced the semiotic systems and their role in multimodal texts and Chapter Four explored them using children's literature.

At this point it is appropriate to examine the ways in which current research has explored meaning making and comprehension of multimodal texts and recommendations for pedagogy around meaning making or comprehension.

The question arises, does meaning making or comprehension operate differently or require different ways of thinking and interacting when engaging with multimodal texts that constitute multiple semiotic systems? The comprehension models discussed earlier in this chapter have focussed on hierarchies of thinking skills (Bloom), levels of comprehension (Banton Smith), and the practices and resources necessary to engage in these uses (Freebody and Luke). All can be applied to multimodal texts provided students have the tools to break the codes of all semiotic systems present. Current research on meaning making has focussed on two areas: comprehending with multimodal texts comprising multiple semiotic systems and comprehending online (which by definition, includes multimodal texts). The remainder of this chapter examines this research and identifies the implications for pedagogy around the consumption of text.

Kress and van Leeuwen (1990, 2006) used the work of Halliday (1973), who examined language from a systemic linguistic perspective, to develop a system for examining the visual aspects of text in order to make meaning. (As previously discussed, Halliday's work also informed the development of functional grammar and genre approaches.). Kress and van Leeuwen suggested that it was necessary

Table 5.4 Using the metafunctions of language to interpret visual text using Kress and van Leeuwen's definitions*

Metafunction	Explanation of Meaning Conveyed Through Its Use	Examples of Codes and Conventions in the Visual That May Convey This Meaning
Ideational	Representing relationships among participants (people and things represented in the image)	**Vectors, juxtaposition, framing**
Interpersonal (sometimes referred to as interactive)	Representing social relationship between the person who produced the image and the person consuming the image and positioning the consumer to view the visual in a particular way	Gaze, **point of view**, angle
Textual	Representing relationship between the elements on the screen or page, for example between image and language	Left right, top bottom

* Some of the codes that Kress and van Leeuwen identified as visual, Bull and Anstey (2010a) have since identified as part of the spatial and gestural semiotic system.

to look at the metafunctions of the system being used (linguistic or visual) and how they were being realised through the visual codes and conventions (1990, p. 21). They later elaborated on this in more detail (Kress & van Leeuwen, 2006). Table 5.4 provides an example of how Kress and van Leeuwen's system might be applied.

Callow (2013) also used the work of Halliday to identify how semiotic resources are being used to convey meaning. However, he used Halliday's terms of **field, tenor and mode**, identifying (but not using the terminology of) their metafunctions. He defined them as follows: field (describing what is happening), tenor (how the consumer relates or interacts with it) and mode (how the design and layout build meaning). This is potentially confusing if trying to apply both the work of Kress and van Leeuwen and Callow. Nevertheless, Callow (2013, p.14) provided a framework that focusses on the questions a consumer might ask about the meaning making focus of field, tenor and mode and is potentially useful for classroom discussions around text. Table 5.5 provides an example based on Callow's work and how it might be applied to discussion about the cover of a piece of children's literature. The following purpose for this discussion has been identified, using Callow's framework to aid predicting what the book might be about. QR Code 5.1 provides a link to an image of the cover for Emily Gravett's book *Mine!* that should be viewed in order to fully understand the analyses in Table 5.5.

QR Code 5.1 Cover of *Mine!* by Emily Gravett (2016) (www.emilygravett.com/books/bear-and-hare-mine)

Callow's framework, particularly the use of questions to stimulate a discussion in which students can draw upon their knowledge of the codes and conventions of the visual and linguistic semiotic

Table 5.5 Applying Callow's framework to the cover of a picture book

Purpose of Analysis: Predicting what 'Mine!' might be about.		
Metafunction	**Focus of Meaning Making**	**Application to Cover of Mine!**
Field: What is happening on the page or screen	Representation of characters and things through visual and linguistic semiotic systems, together with the context in which the action is taking place.	Linguistics: The title of the book is *Mine!* The characters are named as Bear and Hare. Visual: Bear and Hare are both grasping the jar and appear to be pulling it in opposite directions.
Tenor How do I as consumer interact and react to what is happening?	The way in which the visual and linguistic semiotic systems provide codes and conventions that enable the consumer to form reactions that may be related to emotions, attitudes, authenticity of text or feelings of empowerment (or otherwise) towards the text.	Visual: The **facial expression**, angle of the animals' bodies and their **body positions** remind the viewer of the emotions shown when little children are fighting over a toy. Linguistic: *Mine!* reminds the reader that children fighting over a toy often say this. The reader can relate to the ideas presented here very easily because of their experiences with young children.
Mode How does the design and layout of the text help meaning making?	How are cohesion and **salience** used in the visual and linguistic aspects of the text to aid meaning making?	Linguistic: The word 'Mine' is larger than all other words, and is multicoloured unlike all others, suggesting it provides more information about the subject of the book. Centring of words in white space at top of cover draws attention to them, suggesting they should be read first. Top bottom layout of the words and image add possible meaning – 'Mine!' (top) represents the 'ideal' of rabbit and hare to possess the jar and its contents, but the image (bottom) shows the 'real' which is them fighting to make the jar their own (mine).
Conclusions after analysis: The meanings conveyed through the codes and conventions of the visual and linguistic text reinforce one another and suggest a fight over something. Therefore, the book might be about Bear and Hare fighting over things because they don't want to share.		

systems to make meaning, is very useful. However, it is imperative that real purposes should guide any such discussion and students should be encouraged to justify their observations and conclusions. Students need to be made aware of why such strategies are useful and practice them with other texts and in other contexts. This process would need to be modelled and conducted in a classroom climate in which students had developed appropriate listening and speaking protocols, ways of listening and talking with one another that foster exploration and learning. This would ensure discussions are conducted in productive ways, focussing on learning how to mean with multimodal texts rather than procedural display. Refer to the principles of dialogic talk discussed in Chapter Four to assist with this aspect of implementation. Such discussions, using Callow's framework, foster the idea of meaning making and the consumption of text as a problem solving process where questions, and drawing upon known or accessing unknown resources to guide the inquiry, are the responsibility of the consumer. It also fosters the idea that several meanings may be available, depending upon the resources brought to the text by the consumer and the purpose for accessing the text. The framework could be further developed and used with paper, live or digital texts and other semiotic systems, although Callow (2003) did not extrapolate to other semiotic systems.

The challenge or caution that should be considered with the application of such a framework is the same as many of those identified in the preceding section on historical research and approaches. The framework could simply become a ritual, similar to read and retell, shared book or analysis of genres. This is why it is necessary to use the framework to aid the fulfilment of real purposes and ensure dialogic talk takes place around it. Furthermore, it should be just one of a range of strategies and frameworks that can be drawn upon and used when appropriate to the task and/or learning purpose.

REFLECTION STRATEGY 5.3

- The purpose of this Reflection Strategy is for you to apply your understandings about the codes and conventions of the five semiotic systems presented in Chapter Three to the meaning making frameworks developed by Kress and van Leeuwen and Callow that have just been presented.
- In Table 5.6 the three ways of constructing meaning are presented in the first column together with a brief definition. In the remaining columns sample questions that might be drawn upon by the consumer when engaging with a text are provided, together with examples of the codes and conventions that might be drawn upon to investigate them.
- Review the information presented in Chapter Three on metacognition and the codes and conventions of the semiotic systems, together with the explanations of the work of Kress and van Leeuwen and Callow in this chapter, particularly Tables 5.4 and 5.5.
- Add to the questions and semiotic systems that might be drawn upon. The purpose of this revision and application is to assist you in planning for dialogic talk around texts when exploring meaning making as a problem solving process of inquiry with your students. The more detail you can add, the better this table will work as a resource when planning.
- You may find it useful to actually engage with a multimodal text to assist you in the process of elaborating the table. You could use a fiction text such as a picture book and a non-fiction text such as a science or history text to investigate whether the focus of questions and codes and conventions might be similar or different and whether all of them would be used or just a selection.

Table 5.6 A resource for planning pedagogy and practice around meaning making with multimodal texts

Ways of Constructing Meaning	Sample Questions (Metacognitive Prompts)	Sample Codes and Conventions That Might Be Useful
Ideational Meaning Representing events, objects, participants and their context.	What is happening? Where is it happening How is it represented? Who is involved?	Gestural: Linguistic: use of adjective and verbs Visual: top down point of view Audio: Spatial:
Interpersonal and Interactive Meaning Relationships being constructed between participants and objects in the texts and between producer and consumer through text.	Where am I positioned to view what is happening? How are the participants and objects positioned in relation to one another? How does the positioning influence my meaning making?	Gestural: gaze Linguistic: conjunctions Visual: Audio: Spatial: **distance** between participants
Textual Meaning How the layout indicates value of information provided.	What is attracting my attention and how is this being achieved? What can I see easily? What is partly obscured or absent? How do the semiotic systems work together? Is the text coherent?	Gestural: Linguistic: Audio Visual: Colour, vectors Spatial: framing

THEORY INTO PRACTICE 5.1

- The purpose of this Theory into Practice strategy is to develop some pedagogy and practice from the work you have undertaken in Reflection Strategy 5.3.
- One of the challenges identified among many of the approaches to reading comprehension was that some pedagogy became ritualised and learning goals were implicit rather than explicit, making it difficult for students to translate their learning to reading or consuming text in their lifeworlds. The role of purpose context and drawing upon a variety of resources when consuming texts has been emphasised, particularly in Chapter Three and this chapter. The ideational, inter-personal, textual framework is a resource for approaching text that may be useful to students in some situations. The questions can become metacognitive prompts or may even become part of a strategy students develop – another resource. The identified codes and conventions may or may not be relevant to every situation, but they can also be a resource. Students need to develop the ability to draw upon all these resources when appropriate.
- Identify ways in which you can teach about these resources as investigations, rather than the ritual of oral questioning.
- Review Chapters Two and Four on Inquiry and Dialogic Talk and consider how you might incorporate these ideas into lessons about how to use the resources in Table 5.6. Focus on problem solving and inquiry, on students developing and using their metalanguage around texts, and on metacognitive strategies that might be developed around these concepts.
- Plan a lesson sequence around authentic texts and contexts.

Cope and Kalantzis (2000, pp. 211-217), when first elaborating the concept of meaning making as designing, proposed a way of thinking about meaning making that could be applied across all semiotic systems (linguistic, visual, audio, spatial and gestural). Once again their work derived from Halliday (1975, 2004). They suggested that the meaning maker should engage with the text in terms of the following dimensions: representational (Who and what is being represented?), social (How are those in the text and those using the text connected?), organisational (How do the meanings present work together?), contextual (How do the meanings relate to the context in which it is being used?) and ideological (What interests and meanings are being promulgated?). They provided examples of how the codes and conventions of the semiotic systems might aid the consumer of the text in examining the text in these ways. More recently, Kalantzis et al. (2016, pp. 239-243) proposed a grammar for multimodal meaning as a framework to examine meaning making in texts that can be applied with students over a series of lessons. Table 5.7. interprets this framework and how general questions might be focussed as a way of making meaning of a text.

Table 5.7 A grammar for multimodal meaning adapted from Kalantzis et al. (2016, p. 242)

Level and Definition	Sample Questions to Focus on at This Level	Sample Questions That May Relate to Specific Semiotic Systems Present
Reference What is there/represented.	What or who is the subject or subjects of the text and what is represented? How is it represented?	What is represented by each semiotic system? What are the dominant codes and conventions present in that representation (e.g. particular colours, sound effects, vocal qualities, music)? Do some semiotic systems provide more information than others (e.g. descriptive adjectives (the linguistic) or the **texture** and line of the visual)?
Dialogue How the text is connected to the consumer.	How are you as consumer connected to this text? Are the subjects of the texts interrelated and how are these relationships demonstrated?	What semiotic systems provide clues about the relationships between subjects in the text and how do they achieve this (e.g. aspects of gesture such as gaze and body position)?
Structure How the text is structured	How is the text structured? What makes it cohere (or not)? How do those features aid meaning making?	Do the semiotic systems operate in the structure of the text in complementary, reinforcing or hierarchical ways? Do particular codes and conventions in the semiotic systems provide salience or cohesion (e.g. conjunctions in the linguistic, line in diagrams in the visual)?
Situation Context in which text is found and used.	What are the contexts in which this text might be found and used? How does this influence meaning making?	Does the context mean that particular aspects of the semiotic systems are being used in specialised ways (e.g. diagrams in an explanation to aid building a book case)?
Intention Purpose of text in terms of bias, authenticity, gaps, silences, potential influence.	What is the author of this text trying to achieve, what is their intent? Who produced the text and what are their credentials? Who do they represent?	Are particular semiotic systems (for example, the visual) providing a message that is reinforcing one point of view (e.g. colour schemes, cropping of images)?

The work of Kress and van Leeuwen (2006), Callow (2013) and Kalantzis et al. (2016) indicates the complexity of meaning making with multimodal text and provides frameworks that assist the consumer of the text in self-questioning and questioning of the text as they pursue their purpose with the text. They are all useful resources for both consumers and producers of texts, provided they are used strategically according to purpose.

Hartman et al. (2010, pp.131–164) conducted an extensive review and analysis of research on comprehension with print. They suggested reading comprehension or meaning making had developed from a dyadic (reader-text interaction) or triadic (reader-text-task) conception of comprehension to what they term a tetradic conception. Within the tetradic conception they firstly contrasted a reader-text-task-context conception with a reader-text-activity-context conception. They distinguished between task and activity in reading comprehension, suggesting that often reading is accompanied by the activity of writing in order to achieve the desired purpose, particularly when reading for information. They also acknowledged that sociocultural context and the student's own experiences influence how the student will use the context. The focus on use in this explanation is concomitant with the ideas of Luke and Freebody (1997, 1999a, 1999b) and (Freebody & Luke, 2003), where use and purpose become the reasons for engaging particular practices and selecting resources to achieve the reading comprehension outcome. Hartman, Morsink and Zheng also identified a reader-text-author-context in the tetradic conception, suggesting that the author will be drawing on many texts when consuming a text. These might include other texts read on the topic when reading for information, for example comparing content and ideas with those in the current text, or drawing on what the consumer already knows about text in general and this text type in particular. In other words, Hartman, Morsink and Zheng identified the consumption of text as being intertextual, even when consuming just one text. In addition, they suggested that the consumer adopts a variety of roles or stances while reading a text, for example locating information desired, comparing that with previous knowledge, or operating as a critic when considering the relative authenticity and potential bias of the text. They concluded that readers could not be described as singular and single minded but should be constructed as plural or protean readers (Hartman et al., 2010 p.137). These are important understandings, particularly as they foreground reader responsibility, the active consumption of text, the importance of metacognitive skills and the construction of reading as utilising a set of resources that are related to the reading practices in use, as Luke and Freebody suggested in the Four Resource Model. Finally, Hartman, Morsink and Zheng pointed out that the intertextual view of reading related to context and use meant that taking on different stances as a reader may not be done as an individual but as one of many readers, because the reading purpose and context may require interaction with others (e.g. in the workplace clarifying the meaning of a letter with a colleague, discussing a film review with friends to aid decision-making about which movie to attend, or simply sharing the plot of a story read for pleasure with a classmate). In these situations, there are multiple texts (oral and written) and multiple authors of text. The notions of meaning making and the consumption of text constituting intertextual reading, taking different stances as you read and reading not being an isolated or individual task, are all consistent with the concept of a multiliterate individual and understandings about text necessary to becoming multiliterate. The review of the literature on reading comprehension and subsequent description of four concepts of reading conducted by Hartman et al. (2010) can be used to inform and shape pedagogy to develop concepts about consuming text in the 21st century. It also emphasises the necessity for students to develop flexibility through engagement in the consumption of a range of authentic texts and authentic contexts. In particular, Hartman et al. (2010) highlighted the complexity of consuming text. They indicated that it was not isolated or singular but plural or protean, requiring the consumer to constantly monitor and change strategies and ways of engaging throughout the process, including engagement with others and other texts. Their review went on to discuss the implications for reading online, which will now be discussed.

Reading and researching online

As has been discussed, recent research has addressed the complexities of reading with multimodal texts and reading for changing purposes and contexts. However, as many researchers have also indicated (Hartman et al., 2010; Leu et al., 2011; Coiro, 2003, 2005, 2011; Coscarelli & Coiro, 2014), the complexities of reading online require not only using comprehension skills that apply to offline reading, but the further development and application of offline, together with the development of new skills and processes. Coiro (2014, p.30) suggested that online reading comprehension and using the internet for learning comprised four challenges for students. These four challenges can be summarised as:

- Understanding and using the new skills and practices required online
- Developing a 'digital wisdom' about learning how to learn online
- Understanding it is expected and necessary to actively participate and contribute as part of a community in the digital world
- Developing positive attitudes and resilience when using the internet for learning.

Anstey and Bull (2018) have previously identified reading multimodal texts and operating as a multiliterate individual as necessitating the possession and application of complex problem solving skills. In Chapter Two of this volume, the role of inquiry as the basis of becoming multiliterate was explored. The research on online reading constructs it as a problem solving process in two ways: firstly, the actual process of reading online involves inquiry and problem solving multiple times over multiple texts, authors and readers; secondly, the purposes of online reading are often about inquiry or problem solving. Leu et al. (2011, p.7) identified five stages of online reading comprehension, constructing it as problem-based inquiry over multiple sources. The stages are described as identifying important questions, locating information, critically evaluating information, synthesising information and communicating information. As can be seen, these are almost identical to the processes involved in designing identified in Figure 5.1. Leu et al. (2011) also cite McVerry (2007) and Zawilinski (2009), who suggested that online reading, writing and discussion is almost inseparable from problem-based inquiry. Coiro (2011, 2014) also concluded that online comprehension skills and research skills are almost inseparable and should be the responsibility of every teacher, not just the technology teacher or the librarian. She suggested that online reading comprehension could be framed as web-based inquiry and involve skills and strategies that help locate, evaluate, synthesise and communicate information (Coiro, 2011, p.354). An important aspect of reframing online comprehension in these ways is that the processes of reading/consuming and writing/producing are used together, and therefore many of the skills and processes are shared.

Leu et al. (2011) identified three specific differences between online and offline reading which mean that very specific online skills must be developed. Firstly, they emphasised the self-regulated nature of online reading, in that the consumer of the text chooses what to read, what to take from it and where to go next, composing their own individual text or hypertext as they go. Secondly, they pointed out that because of this self-directed individual and idiosyncratic process, no two consumers of text will construct the same text in order to solve their problem. Finally, they suggested that the interactive nature of online reading meant that it can be, and often is, a collaborative social practice. They cited research that indicated that when inquiry is conducted collaboratively online, it can lead to important learning gains. This research has important implications for pedagogy around online reading and the development of research skills.

Hartman et al. (2010 p.139) suggested that there are 'family resemblances' among the skills for offline and online meaning making when it involves lower level processes and is conducted in isolation. However, these resemblances dissipate when higher level processes are engaged online, and offline reading skills and processes are 'refeatured' as they migrate online. They suggested that the core issue that makes the consumption of text online more complex is that all the elements of comprehension offline suddenly become multiplied and more complex when online. When reading online, not only are there more texts available, made of more elements and semiotics systems, but there are more authors and potentially, more readers. This is because the online experience may also involve others in the room, and online, creating another group of texts, text types and semiotic systems. Hartman et al. (2010) suggested that reading comprehension online is dynamic and the possibilities of combinations and numbers of text, author, task, activity, reader relationships is almost infinite. Rather than describing it as a dyadic, triadic, tetradic or hexadic concept, it becomes 'n-adic', where 'n' is unknown until the actual consumption of text has occurred. It cannot be mapped in advance because it mutates as it occurs (Hartman et al., 2010, p.150). As Coiro (2014) stated, such complexity requires a positive attitude and resilience, as well as specific knowledge, skills and processes about using the internet.

This description of online reading fits very well with a multiliterate concept of literacy and understandings about text identified as necessary earlier in this chapter. The role of metacognition and self-regulation becomes paramount when reading online. Not only are there more combinations of reader, text, semiotic systems, author, task and activity available, but multiple comprehension tasks and stances (reader roles) occur more rapidly. Short and different comprehension tasks occur before and after every click of the mouse or touch of the screen. Therefore, strategies are necessary to make more informed decisions about 'clicking'. Coiro (2003, p.463) suggested that while some tasks on the internet require the use of offline skills in new ways, others demand new and different skills, particularly when the online tasks involve research and inquiry and collaborative work among online and offline participants.

Similarly, Hartman et al. (2010, p.146) suggested that when reading online, the offline metacognitive strategies of knowing what, knowing how and knowing when need to be supplemented by three new groups of metacognitive strategies. They refer to these as knowing who, locational knowledge and goal knowledge. Knowing who is described as strategies that enable students to understand how to identify the authenticity, origins and credibility of authors online – in other words, having critical literacy strategies that are specific to online contexts. Locational knowledge refers to the fact that when reading online it is sometimes difficult to work out 'where you are' in a text. In a two-dimensional paper text, chapter headings, tables of contents, indexes and the actual physical thickness, page size and layout of the book provide clues about where the reader is in the text. However, online text is three-dimensional and it is possible to get 'lost in space' as clicking moves the consumer both within and across sites. Therefore, it is necessary to know and understand the conventions of websites and how this knowledge can help the consumer make informed decisions about where they have been and where they are going online. For example, tabs, home pages, site maps and drop-down menus are just some of the conventions that help orient the consumer. Goal knowledge is constructed as 'knowing why' an aspect of metacognition that Anstey and Bull (2018) also suggested should be added to metacognitive skills, with the advent of multimodal texts using new technologies. Essentially in an online context this means that the consumer has to ensure their choices about where to go next or what to click on, are informed by their original purpose for consuming text, problem solving or researching online. The screen is filled with distractions, advertising, videos, and clickable words and objects that look enticing. Therefore, it is necessary to plan before commencing a search, identifying a purpose and breaking it down into smaller goals, then constantly referring back to the planned purpose and goals during the research process. It may be necessary to cross off goals as they are reached or refine and/or add new goals to the plan as the research process unfolds.

Coiro (2003, 2005) examined students' locating skills online and was concerned that many students lacked skills to make informed decisions about how and where to search for the information they required. This effectively prevented them from achieving their research purpose before they had started. Other researchers have referred to these skills as gatekeeping skills, because without them the gate to learning, researching, problem solving and comprehending online is shut. Offline, these research skills would be referred to as locating skills such as using catalogues to locate books or journals in which information might be found and then using indexes, previewing skills, headings and subheadings to locate information in the text. Such offline skills are still necessary and some overlap with online locating skills but are presented and used differently. Internet searches rather than catalogues are the starting point for most online searches, but as Coiro (2005) pointed out, without specific knowledge about how search engines work and what website addresses indicate about a source and website structure, students can click aimlessly and access sources indiscriminately. Coiro suggested that it is important that students think about and make predictions about which websites they might explore before even touching the technology. Understanding how to use keywords to narrow a search, terms such as URL and search engine and how parts of the URL can indicate something about the source, its authenticity and reliability are essential skills to locating information appropriate to the research purpose.

Having located a site, students need to assess whether the information they want is there and where they might locate that information. Offline this would involve previewing the text, looking for keywords or images, scanning headings and subheadings. While some of these are available online (e.g. keywords, headings), skimming every page of a website is not efficient. However, knowing how to find menu choices, exploring dynamic features, popup menus and scroll bars will help predict the location of information. In order to check the reliability of the source, the date the website was last updated can be sought. Students can also check the site's creator, site maps and 'about' sections to help decide whether it is a reliable source. Knowing how to bookmark or otherwise organise the sites found so they can be returned to and examined in full for later consumption and note-taking is also part of this process. This allows students to better organise the next stages of the research process, further checking of the bias, credibility and gaps or silences in the site and note-taking (paper or digital), organising and synthesising information for reporting. These are the equivalent of offline skimming, scanning and evaluating skills and help predictions and decision-making about where to search next. They involve metacognitive and self-regulation skills. But as Hartman et al. (2010) pointed out, every one of these is done in seconds, before the next click, over and over – short, sharp comprehension tasks that repeatedly involve literal, inferential and critical literacy skills, hence the need to employ the additional metacognitive skills of knowing who, location knowledge and goal knowledge and build positive attitudes and resilience.

Research by Coiro et al. (2014) indicated that when students worked collaboratively in pairs on inquiry tasks, their interaction and talk about the task, together with the levels of thinking employed, influenced their ability to accomplish the task. These findings and other research by Sekeres et al. (2014) with primary school students indicate that an important part of teaching students about using the internet for inquiry is not only teaching them knowledge and strategies but also about providing opportunities where students can engage in productive dialogue as they try out, evaluate and revise their choices in order to develop both cognitive and metacognitive skills. Talking through choices provides an opportunity to engage in critical thinking and analysis of the strategies being used. As Coiro et al. (2014) concluded, their findings encourage the design of instructional scaffolds to foster productive dialogue and strategic reading during online inquiry, or in any online reading or writing. This reinforces the discussion of the role of dialogic talk to foster learning that was discussed in Chapter Four.

THEORY INTO PRACTICE 5.2

- The purpose of this Theory into Practice task is to access an article that provides four strategies for helping students develop online research skills and use these ideas to develop appropriate lessons for students in your year level and discipline area.
- Use QR Code 5.2 to access an article by Julie Coiro. Think about the strategies she has developed to assist students with conducting research online.
- Identify a research task your students are about to engage in and consider whether they have the necessary skills to engage in it effectively. Use the four areas Julie Coiro has identified as a guide for your reflections.
- Using the ideas in the article and your reflections on your students and the research task they are about to engage in, modify existing lessons, or plan new or additional lessons, to address the areas you have identified.
- Focus on modelling and engaging students in metacognitive skills and strategies and self-monitoring and regulation. Note that Coiro's activities ask students to justify their decision-making, an important aspect of understanding the reasons for developing specific strategies, self-monitoring and self-regulation.

QR Code 5.2 Julie Coiro article
(www.ascd.org/publications/educational-leadership/oct05/vol63/num02/Making-Sense-of-Online-Text.aspx)

One of the most challenging aspects of teaching online comprehension and research skills is assessing students' ability. As Coiro (2011, p. 374) pointed out, given online comprehension and research require high levels of strategic thinking and decision-making traditional methods of assessing comprehension such as multiple choice would not provide information about the how these processes are being carried out. The fact that students find information is not indicative of the employment of good online reading comprehensions and research skills. In order to assess students' skills it is necessary to find ways to examine the thinking processes behind their decision-making. Some of the strategies in the article available through QR Code 5.2 provide such information. Examining students' talk as they discuss what they are doing and why as they search is also useful. In a classroom where dialogic talk is a feature of learning developing observational assessment methods in these situations would be useful.

Contributions of current research and associated approaches to understandings about reading, reading pedagogy and the consumption of multimodal texts in a multiliterate world

A summary of the contributions of current research and associated pedagogies has been provided in Table 5.8. It has been developed in the same way as Table 5.3 which summarised the historical review of research and associated approaches to the teaching of reading. Consideration has been given to the major question associated with Figure 5.1 and the contributing questions presented at the beginning of this chapter, together with the characteristics of a multiliterate person and understandings about text.

Analysis of Table 5.8 identifies further contributions to the body of knowledge about the consumption of multimodal texts, particularly in the area of online research and reading. The contributions can be summarised in three areas:

- Contributions to the foundations of multiliteracies and understandings about consuming multimodal texts:
  o Reinforcement of consumption and production of text as dynamic
  o Further information about the way meanings are conveyed in multimodal texts
  o Further information about the knowledge, skills and processes that are common to both the consumption and production of text
  o The construction of both online and offline reading as inquiry
  o Consumption of text as intertextual and interactive (collaborative) rather than individual
  o Understandings about the idiosyncratic nature of reading online
  o Understandings about the need for a positive attitude and resilience when reading and research-ing online
  o Understanding that locating skills and knowing about how the internet works are gatekeeping skills when reading online
  o Consumers engage in multiple stances/roles and engage in multiple acts of comprehension while consuming text online.
- Specific aspects of pedagogy and frameworks for planning that can inform multiliterate pedagogy:
  o A spiral sequence for introducing the codes and conventions of the five semiotic systems with recommended foci for pedagogy as the sequence is introduced
  o Metafunctional framework for analysing text
  o Grammar of multimodal meaning framework for analysing how meaning is conveyed in text

Table 5.8 How current research and the associated approaches, pedagogy and practices inform the teaching of reading and consumption of multimodal texts and a multiliterate pedagogy

Research and Associated Approaches, Pedagogy and Practice	Comments in Terms of Teaching About the Consumption of Multimodal Text and a Multiliterate Pedagogy
Development of a metalanguage and initial set of definitions for the codes and conventions of the five semiotics systems Included the development of a recommended spiral sequence for introduction and a focus for pedagogy designed to increase students' depth of understanding and application of the codes and conventions as they move through school (Bull & Anstey 2010, Anstey & Bull, 2016).	Informs because it: • Provides a metalanguage and initial set of definitions for all five semiotic systems that can be modified as social, cultural and other changes influence them. • Enables the discussion, analysis and application of understandings about how the semiotic systems, their codes and conventions, contribute meaning to a multimodal text. • Provides knowledge and understandings that can be applied to both the consumption and production of text. • Provides an initial guide for introduction throughout school. Potential challenges: • The codes and conditions of the five semiotic systems, together with their metalanguage, must be taught and used strategically to inform real reading purposes with authentic texts. This is to ensure the identification of codes and conventions does not become a mindless repetitive activity leading to procedural display. • Metalanguage and definitions must be continuously informed by social and cultural context and social, cultural and technological change. • Must be taught in such a way that the semiotic systems, their codes and conventions are understood to be dynamic not static. • The pedagogical sequence and curriculum used in schools should seek a balance among all five semiotic systems and their use in paper, live and digital texts. • Pedagogy must balance focussed learning episodes with an inquiry approach to the analysis of texts, using authentic texts and contexts. • Students must be given opportunities to apply their knowledge in creative ways through the consumption and production of texts (changing focus of pedagogy throughout school). • The sequence of introduction must be informed by assessment of students' knowledge and needs and community context, rather than implemented without question.
A metafunctional approach to meaning making Using an approach based on field, tenor and mode and the **ideational, interpersonal and textual metafunctions** as a way of analysing and identifying how meaning is conveyed through the linguistic and visual semiotic systems in a multimodal text (Kress & van Leeuwen 1990, 2006, Callow 2003).	Informs because it: • Provides a framework for analysis that focusses on what is represented and how the representation conveys meaning. • Enables the consumer to develop purpose-appropriate questions to aid metacognition when consuming a text. • Encourages active consumption of text. • Has the potential for application to all semiotic systems, text types and technologies. Potential challenges: • The framework must be taught and used strategically to inform real reading purposes with authentic texts to ensure it does not become a mindless repetitive activity leading to procedural display. • Need to extrapolate to all semiotic systems (this has begun; see Barton & Unsworth, 2014). • Need to ensure balance across text types and technologies – paper, live and digital texts. • Should be seen as one of many resources available to aid the consumption and production of text.

Research and Associated Approaches, Pedagogy and Practice	Comments in Terms of Teaching About the Consumption of Multimodal Text and a Multiliterate Pedagogy	
Grammar of multimodal meaning Framework for analysis of text based around reference, dialogue, structure, situation and intention (Kalantzis et al., 2016).	Informs because it: • Has the potential for application to all semiotic systems, text types and technologies.	Potential challenges: • The framework must be taught and used strategically to inform real reading purposes with authentic texts to ensure it does not become a mindless repetitive activity leading to procedural display. • Need to ensure balance across text types and technologies – paper, live and digital texts. • Should be seen as one of many resources available to aid the consumption and production of text.
Dyadic, triadic, tetradic and hexadic concepts of reading offline (Hartman, Morsink & Zhang, 2010). Review of constructions of reading offline as combinations of reader-text-task-activity-context.	Informs because it: • Focusses on the roles of the consumer and what might be involved in the process. • Acknowledges that multiple texts are used and drawn upon when consuming (e.g. prior knowledge of content or about texts) – reading as intertextual. • Acknowledges the consumer must take multiple stances/roles during the process of consuming text. • Identifies the consumer as plural or protean reader – consumption of text is not an individual process. • Acknowledges reading or consumption of text may not be an individual process. It may require interaction with others and will therefore involve multiple texts and multiple authors.	Potential challenges: • More useful as a way of reviewing the emphasis of teacher pedagogy (e.g. reader-text, reader-text-context, reader-text-task-context) and informing the planning and implementation of pedagogy and practice, than as a tool for students to use.
Reading online (Leu et al., 2011, Hartman, Morsink & Zheng 2011, Coiro, 2003, 2005, 2011; Coscarelli & Coiro, 2014). Constructing reading/consumption of text and researching online as inquiry (locating, evaluating, synthesising and communicating). Reading as 'n-adic', where 'n' is unknown because of the infinite possibilities. Necessity for planning in advance, self-direction and self-regulation. Inclusion of attitude and resilience as important to successful online reading.	Informs because it: • Confirms the dynamic nature of consuming and producing text and the interrelationship of consuming and producing. • Identifies shared consumption and production processes and skills. • Identifies online locating skills as gatekeeping skills – necessity of understanding how the internet works. • Recognises the idiosyncratic nature of online read-ing and therefore the need for self-regulatory and metacognitive skills, including additional metacognitive skills for online inquiry. • Acknowledges the collaborative nature of reading and researching on line with online and offline participants. • Identifies the necessity for a positive attitude towards the internet and resilience.	Potential challenges: • Developing pedagogy and dialogue around reading and researching online that develops these skills in purposeful and authentic contexts. • Developing pedagogy around texts and reading paths that are largely unknown because of the idiosyncratic nature of reading and researching online. • Ensuring a consistent approach to teaching about the internet and its associated metalanguage throughout the school, across year levels and disciplines. • Developing pedagogy around reading and researching online that is largely skills and process and attitude focus based rather than content based (e.g. developing self-regulation, metacognitive skills and strategies, resilience, positive attitudes). • Developing a pedagogy around online consumption of text that focusses on inquiry with all text types and semiotic systems that may be available.

- o   Dyadic, triadic, tetradic, hexadic and n-adic concepts of reading that can be used as frames for analysis of teaching practice and planning pedagogy and practice
- o   An inquiry framework for reading and researching online – locating, evaluating, synthesising and communicating (Leu et al., 2011)
- Provision of resources for consuming multimodal text and engaging in multiliterate practices:
  - o   Definitions and metalanguage for the codes and conventions of the five semiotic systems
  - o   Metafunctional framework for analysing how meaning is conveyed in multimodal text
  - o   Grammar of multimodal meaning making for analysing how meaning is conveyed in multimodal text
  - o   Specific online inquiry and research skills
  - o   Additional metacognitive skills necessary for online reading.

In contrast to the review of historical research and approaches to the consumption of text, current research presents few potential challenges and addresses many of those challenges identified in the historical research. The research addresses multimodal texts and the issues associated with the presence of multiple semiotic systems, together with the ways in which the consumption of text delivered by paper and online technologies require both similar and different skills and processes. Further there is an acknowledgement that literacy is a social and cultural practice and will continue to change. There is great emphasis on students becoming active, responsible and resilient learners who can plan for the consumption of text, and use metacognitive skills and strategies to self-regulate during the process. The concept of literacy as a problem solving process involving inquiry has been emphasised.

The potential challenges are in the same major area of challenges regarding the historical research: pedagogy. As with the historical approaches, the greatest pedagogical challenges are ensuring:

- Any frameworks or strategies used to teach about the consumption of text are taught strategically to inform real reading purposes with authentic texts.
- Balance among text types, technologies (paper, live and digital) semiotic systems and disciplines.
- Pedagogy and practice does not become repetitive leading to procedural display.
- Students are given opportunities to take responsibility for planning and selecting strategies and then reviewing the success of their plan.
- A balance between explicit teaching in focussed learning episodes with dialogic talk that encourages inquiry, problem solving and reflection.
- Metalanguage is introduced and used consistently for talking about all aspects of text and technology.
- Students engage in collaborative inquiry and research both online and offline.
- That talk around text and its consumption focusses on modelling and discussion of metacognitive skills and strategies, self-direction, and self-regulation and resilience.
- That the links between consumption and production processes with text are made explicit and actively taught when students engage in both processes during inquiry and research online and offline.

Given the findings of the review of historical and current research, the emphasis on examining and reflecting upon pedagogy and practice around reading seem essential. However, it is necessary to have a set of principles, knowledge and understandings that can inform beliefs and enable the development of a set of principles about the teaching of reading to guide reflection about and examination of practice.

The two Action Learning Tasks that follow are designed to assist in taking the findings of this chapter and developing a set of beliefs and guiding principles to inform planning, pedagogy and practice in the readers' classroom or school. These beliefs and principles would also inform reflection on, and analysis of, teaching practices, including classroom talk. Literacy and literate practice is socially and critically based and one of the strong recommendations about teaching reading has been the use of authentic purposes, texts and contexts to teach reading. Therefore, the beliefs and principles must be informed by not only the careful evaluation of the research in terms of multiliteracies and understandings about text, but knowledge of the school and staff, the system of which it is part, its students and the school community.

ACTION LEARNING TASK 5.4

- The purpose of this Action Learning Task is to use the information in this chapter together with knowledge of the students, school and community in which the school is situated, to develop an appropriate set of beliefs and principles to guide the planning, pedagogy and practice around the teaching of reading in your school. If the teaching of reading is a school or personal focus in your action plan, then this task may be useful as a way of reflecting upon and taking action as a result of professional reading about the teaching of reading.
- Make a copy of the characteristics of a multiliterate person and the understandings about text presented in this chapter, together with Tables 5.3 and 5.8.
- Examine them side by side and identify aspects of Tables 5.3 and 5.8 that relate to particular characteristics and understandings. Use any other techniques or strategies that you find useful to conduct this analysis.
- Next consider the characteristics of your students, the school, the community, the system and curriculum and how they relate to or inform the information you have been collating. Consider also your own background, experiences and general beliefs about teaching generally and the teaching or reading in particular that might inform these considerations.
- Extrapolate from these considerations a set of the beliefs you feel would inform the teaching about reading and consumption of multimodal texts in your school. Then try to develop a set of principles about planning, pedagogy and practice that will help you translate your beliefs when planning for the teaching of reading and inform your pedagogy and practice. It may be useful to think in terms of the following:
  o 'If I believe ... about the teaching of reading, then I need to...'. For example, 'If I believe that understanding the purpose of reading is important for students to work out appropriate strategies to fulfil that purpose, then I must ensure my planning always has a purpose for the reading my students will engage in and my teacher talk should facilitate students discussing the link between purpose and strategy selection'.
- Clearly there might be several 'then statements' for each 'belief statement'.
- It will take a considerable time, reflection and discussion with colleagues to begin this process and then revise, reorganise and refine it. However, if it is done carefully and revised regularly

as new research and approaches to reading become available, then it will be an effective tool to inform planning pedagogy and practice (including talk) around the teaching of reading in your classroom. It can also inform any analysis of your planning and teaching practice. If done as a whole school, it will lead to a consistent approach to planning, pedagogy and practice around the teaching of reading across the school.

- Refer back to Chapter One on Action Research, Chapter Two on Inquiry, Chapter Three on Dialogic Talk and Chapter Four on the Semiotic Systems may then be useful to inform translation of the beliefs and principles into practice.

ACTION LEARNING TASK 5.5

- The purpose of this Action Learning Task is to audit the commonly used strategies, activities and tasks that you use to teach research and reading. It is important to review commonly used strategies to ensure awareness of the original learning purpose, relevance to current understandings about the teaching of reading and exactly when and why they might be used. This in turn would inform the talk that is conducted around the activity to ensure its utility is clearly discussed with students.

- Review your planning for the preceding unit of work and list the strategies, activities, and tasks that you have used. Audit the list in terms of how often they are used and reflect upon the variation in use. Why are some used more frequently and some not?

- Retrieve any school-based resources that have been developed, such as lists of strategies and activities that teachers are encouraged to draw upon. Audit the list against your analyses of the strategies you use most frequently and consider the match and mismatch in terms of use.

- Go back to the copy of the characteristics of a multiliterate person and the understandings about text presented in this chapter, together with Tables 5.3 and 5.8, and examine the strategies being used in terms of how they facilitate these ideas about the teaching of reading.

- If you have begun to develop your beliefs and principles, examine the strategies in terms of whether they facilitate pedagogy and practices that would implement these beliefs and principles.

- Generate lists of strategies that would facilitate pedagogy and practices around the teaching of research skills, reading and the consumption of multimodal texts that would implement these beliefs and principles.

- For each strategy, identify the learning purposes about reading that it would fulfil. Use this list together with the identified learning purposes as a resource for planning the teaching of reading as a way of ensuring your beliefs and principles are matched by your planning, pedagogy and practice.

Conclusion

At the beginning of the chapter, the issue of how research on reading can be transferred to the classroom was discussed. It was suggested that teachers need to be provided with the opportunity to add to the body of research by conducting **action research** on reading in their own classrooms to evaluate the implications of the research for classroom practice. It was suggested that this cycle of action research was necessary not only to add to the research, but also to ensure teachers examine and reflect upon their practice and whether it reflects their knowledge and beliefs about the teaching of reading. The research on reading was reviewed against the concept of producing and consuming multimodal text presented in Figure 5.1 and the contributing questions, together with the characteristics of a multiliterate person and understandings about text. The results of this analysis were then summarised in Tables 5.3 and 5.8, providing a basis for consideration of the utility of the research and associated approaches and practices for teaching about the consumption of text.

As has been shown, the research and approaches to the teaching of reading and the consumption of multimodal texts is large and will continue to grow and inform pedagogy. Further, the challenges of teaching reading are as much about the *implementation* of the research and its associated strategies and approaches in the classroom as they are about any *shortcomings* of the research itself. In summary, regardless of choices made about approach or strategy to teach reading, it is the *pedagogy, practice and classroom talk* around the consumption of text that will determine success in helping develop multiliterate students who can consume multimodal text for different purposes, in different contexts and using a variety of technologies.

6 Investigating the writing process in multiliterate classrooms: Producing multimodal texts

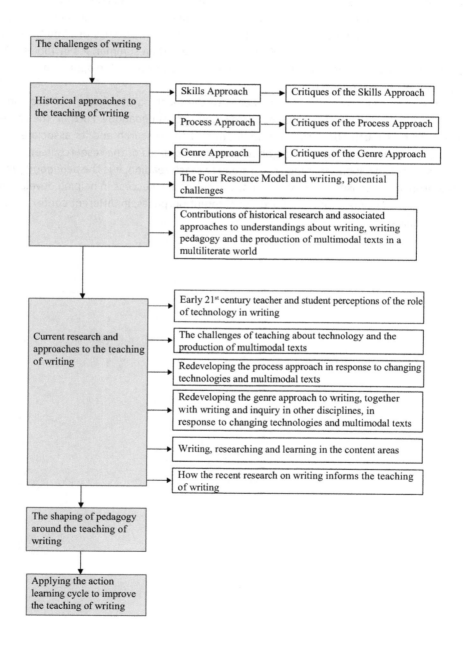

The challenges of writing

Historical approaches to the teaching of writing
→ Skills Approach → Critiques of the Skills Approach
→ Process Approach → Critiques of the Process Approach
→ Genre Approach → Critiques of the Genre Approach
→ The Four Resource Model and writing, potential challenges
→ Contributions of historical research and associated approaches to understandings about writing, writing pedagogy and the production of multimodal texts in a multiliterate world

Current research and approaches to the teaching of writing
→ Early 21st century teacher and student perceptions of the role of technology in writing
→ The challenges of teaching about technology and the production of multimodal texts
→ Redeveloping the process approach in response to changing technologies and multimodal texts
→ Redeveloping the genre approach to writing, together with writing and inquiry in other disciplines, in response to changing technologies and multimodal texts
→ Writing, researching and learning in the content areas
→ How the recent research on writing informs the teaching of writing

The shaping of pedagogy around the teaching of writing

Applying the action learning cycle to improve the teaching of writing

The focus of this chapter is writing, that is producing **multimodal text**. It will begin by briefly discussing what writing is and the challenges involved in producing text, particularly in a multiliterate world. This will be followed by a brief revision of the connections between consuming and producing text, previously discussed in Chapter Three of the complementary volume *Foundations of Multiliteracies: Reading, Writing and Talking in the 21st Century* and in Chapter Five in this volume. These connections will be further explored at appropriate times throughout the chapter, particularly the ideas that both reading and writing involve **inquiry** and problem solving. The contributions of historical research to the teaching of writing will be explored, together with the associated pedagogies. Following this current research and approaches will be examined. Finally, the role of **pedagogy** will be discussed, and how **action research** in classrooms can inform pedagogy about producing multimodal texts in the 21st century. As advised in Chapter Five, it is highly recommended that Chapters Five and Six be read together as they inform one another. It is also recommended that Chapter Three, which focussed on the role of the semiotic systems in both the consumption and production of multimodal text, be accessed and reviewed as it informs both Chapters Five and Six.

ACTION LEARNING TASK 6.1

- The purpose of this Action Learning Task is to reflect upon what you currently know and believe about the teaching of writing.
- Write a few sentences about:
  o   Why you think it is important to teach writing,
  o   What aspects of writing you think are important to teach,
  o   What approach to teaching writing you currently use and why you have chosen this approach.
- As you read each section of this chapter, return to these statements and add comments about anything you might add, change or keep the same.
- There will be an Action Learning Task at the end of this chapter that will focus on your original statements and the comments you have made as you read.

The challenges of writing

A piece of writing or text is produced to communicate a message to an audience. The producer of the text selects from the available **semiotic systems** and technologies to design a text with a particular purpose, context and audience in mind. Kalantzis et al. (2016, p. 284) referred to this process as producing an artefact for use in communication. However, as they pointed out, the consumer of the text and the producer of the text may never be in the same place and time. Consequently, it may not be possible for the producer to clarify or assist the consumer in comprehending the producers' intended meaning.

Therefore, crafting a text to communicate that intended meaning is a complex and exacting process that involves many levels of inquiry, problem solving and decision-making and revision in order to achieve it. Even then, the social and cultural background of the consumer, together with the context in which the text is consumed, will influence the meanings made. While advances in technology mean that texts can be produced and shared instantaneously with larger audiences, it also increases the options and therefore the decision-making among the available semiotic systems, their **codes** and **conventions** and technologies. Being able to plan and create a text using selected semiotic systems and technology to achieve an intended purpose is empowering and enables students to become agents of change in their communities (Lipscombe et al., 2015). The importance of being able to take responsibility, respond to change and take control of life through writing and producing multimodal text is part of being multiliterate in the 21st century.

THEORY INTO PRACTICE 6.1

- The purpose of this Theory into Practice activity is to assist students in understanding that because the producer of the text and the consumer of the text may never be in the same place and time, it may not be possible to clarify or assist the consumer in making the intended meaning. This understanding is critical to students developing an understanding that the production of text is a complicated process in which decisions must be strategic and revision will be necessary to achieve their communicative purpose.
- Students will work in pairs. One person will write a set of instructions that the other person in the pair will then have to follow while the producer of the text looks on but is not allowed to help in any way. The writer must not be watched by the person who will follow the instructions when the writer is creating the text. Similarly, the person who will have to follow the writer's instructions cannot hear you give instructions to the other person, or they will know what they have to do before seeing the instructions. You will have to organise this in a way that suits your classroom context.
- The students producing the text should first draw a simple house (or select something simple that is appropriate to your class and context), ensuring their partner does not see it. Then on separate piece of paper they should write instructions using words and images to enable a person to draw the same picture of a house. (NB: The writer cannot provide a picture of the final drawing of the house as part of the instructions.)
- Once instructions are written, the writer should hide their picture and give their partner the instructions and a pencil and paper so they can use them to draw the house. Emphasise to students that the consumer must follow the instructions exactly as they are written; the goal is to see how good the instructions are. The writer (producer) cannot assist the reader (consumer). Once the consumer has finished the drawing as best they can, the producer should show them their original drawing.
- Ask the students to discuss in pairs what worked and didn't work in the instructions and make a list of each. Then ask the students to use the list to jointly revise the instructions if necessary.

- As a whole class, discuss how the producers felt when the consumer was having difficulty following the instructions and how the consumers felt when they were having trouble with the instructions.
- Ask the pairs to share their lists of what worked and what didn't and to discuss what their lists tell them about writing a text, particularly instructions.
- Finally, ask the students to think about how, when they produce a text, most often the consumer will not have access to them to clarify meaning. Ask them what they have learned from this activity that will help them in future when producing a text.
- Using these discussions, together with the students, jointly construct a set of guidelines for writers to remember when writing.

Historical approaches to the teaching of writing

Skills approach

Similar to the teaching of reading, early approaches to the teaching of writing (around the 1950s) were skill based and the associated pedagogies resulted in the skills of writing being taught separately from the practice of writing. The focus was first on the development of skills (handwriting, spelling, punctuation and grammar) before consideration of meaning. Curriculum documents at the time specified that satisfactory achievement in writing for the first year of school was the ability to write one simple sentence (with correct spelling, grammar and punctuation). The expectation was that students would progress in sequenced steps of increasing complexity – from single, simple sentences to paragraphs, combining sentences and finally to a complete 'composition' (Walshe, 1981; Anstey & Bull, 2004; Lipscombe et al., 2015).

The assessment of writing focussed on neatness and accuracy, and writing activities included writing from dictation (a spelling test), handwriting, punctuation and grammar exercises. A composition session, usually once a week, required students to write on a given topic and to finish it within a given time, at which point the writing was collected and assessed with a focus on the surface features of spelling, grammar and punctuation. The topics reflected the dominant sociocultural values of the time (mainly those of the Anglo-Saxon middle class). For example, in the 1960s and '70s childhood was idealised and creativity nurtured, and students were asked to recount personal experiences or write imaginatively. As these descriptions indicate, there was no attention to teaching the structure of a text or the processes of writing. In many ways writing was taught by testing. Similar to early approaches to reading, these approaches were very much a reflection of the role of writing in the community and workplaces at that time and who undertook writing in those settings. Similar to early approaches to reading, the teaching of writing was a bottom-up approach as represented in Figure 6.1.

Critiques of the skills approach

While teaching the skills of writing was and is necessary, the shortcomings of the skills approach were in its pedagogy. As would be expected, this approach favoured students who came from backgrounds that closely mirrored the language of the dominant social class and culture, that informed the language and

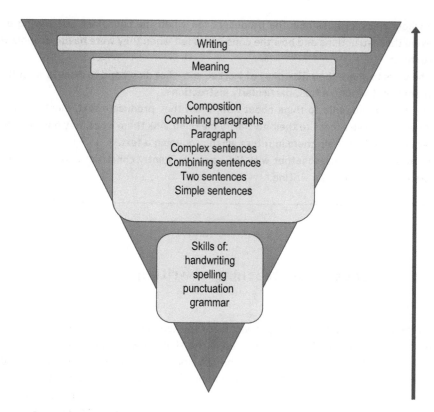

Figure 6.1 A hierarchical or bottom-up theory of writing instruction

Adapted from Anstey and Bull (2004, p.170)

behaviours of the classroom. It did not assist students from different social and cultural backgrounds as their language and home behaviour were dissimilar to those of school and they had to first make sense of 'school' language and behaviour in order to learn. For a full discussion of the issues of social and cultural class and schooling, see Chapter Two in the companion volume *Foundations of Multiliteracies: Reading, Writing and Talking in the 21st Century*.

Furthermore, the actual teaching of writing in the skills approach was largely implicit. This was because the teaching of writing separated skills lessons from the actual act of writing, or composition as it was called, and teaching was dominated by testing rather than instruction. Students were left to make the connections between the skills lessons and how the skills might assist them in writing themselves. For students who did not come from the dominant social class and culture and who did not find implicit teaching suited their learning style or background, the pedagogy of the skills approach was not appropriate. Many of these critiques have issues in common with critiques of the skills approach to reading. It is useful to refer back to these criticisms that were presented in Chapter Five and consider them in relation to the skills approach to writing, before moving on to the next section. Reflection Strategy 6.1 facilitates this process.

REFLECTION STRATEGY 6.1

- The purpose of this Reflection Strategy is to consider the similarities between the **consumption** and **production** of text (reading and writing) and identify what the skills approaches to the teaching of reading and writing have in common.
- Figure 5.1, previously presented in Chapter Five, has been reproduced as Figure 6.2 below. Use it to revise your understandings about the similarities between the process of designing and redesigning text when consuming (reading) and producing (writing) texts.
- Re-read the section on the skills approaches to reading in Chapter Five and identify similarities between the skills approach to reading and the skills approach to writing. Consider the reasons for these similarities, not only in terms of the times and context and knowledge available, but also in terms of the similarities between reading and writing.
- Consider the implications of the critiques of skills approaches to reading and writing for your current approach to teaching writing. Examine your planning for the teaching of writing. How closely does your approach approximate a skills approach? What are the similarities and differences to your approach?
- How does a skills approach to the teaching of writing fit with multimodal texts and a multiliterate pedagogy? What is necessary, but not sufficient?

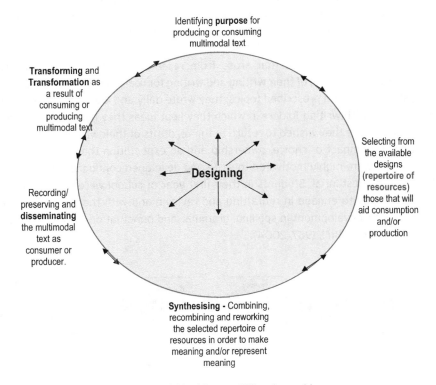

Figure 6.2 Consuming and producing multimodal text in a multiliterate world

Process approach

In the 1980s researchers began to examine the ways in which 'real' writers write, that is those who write extensively in their profession. They then documented the tasks and processes in which the writers engaged (Graves, 1983; Murray, 1982, 1985). Their discoveries turned the skills approach upside down. Professional writers were focussed on their writing purpose and intended audience and were therefore concerned with meaning throughout the process. They revised and rewrote several times in order to ensure that the writing would achieve the intended purpose, that is in order to get the meaning right. When the writing was close to the desired outcome, they would attend to surface features – handwriting or keyboarding, spelling, punctuation and grammar – prior to publication. They knew these surface features were important for publication because without these conventions being applied appropriately, their meaning and purpose would not be clear. Although this process could be represented as a top-down process, when researchers interpreted the writing process in terms of teaching writing, early representations of the process were linear, as shown in Figure 6.3. As can be seen, the process was interpreted as having three stages (pre-writing, writing and post-writing) and particular foci and strategies were identified for each stage (Walshe, 1981).

One of the most significant differences between the skills approach and the process approach was the assumption made about students' ability to write when they entered school. While the skills approach assumed students could not write until they mastered the skills, the writing process assumed students could write, would have reason to write and would want to write, and therefore encouraged writing from the day students entered the classroom. At this point in time many researchers documented the progress of students' attempts at writing from both before they entered school and when they entered the classroom (Clay, 1978; Calkins, 1983; Temple et al., 1988). The findings emulated the findings of investigations into professional writers, in that students identified purposes for writing and wished to convey meaning. In addition, 90 per cent of students believed they could write when they arrived at school while only 15 per cent believed they could read (Graves in Walshe, 1981).

The associated classroom practices that arose from research into the writing process approach focussed on students taking control of their writing and writing for real purposes and audiences. Students were no longer asked to write on prescribed topics; they wrote daily and identified topics of their choice. Students were provided with writing folders in which they kept ideas they had for future writing, drafts they had abandoned (in case they wished to return to them), drafts of their writing and completed pieces prior to publication. The impact of choice, ownership and an expectation they could write on students was very positive; they were highly motivated to write and developed confidence. Their development in writing ability was also substantial. Students in their first year of school were writing much more than one sentence, were happy to engage in redrafting and revising and with the aid of **focussed learning episodes** related to their development in spelling, grammar and punctuation, and mastered appropriate skills (Anstey, 1986; Anstey & Bull, 1987, 2004).

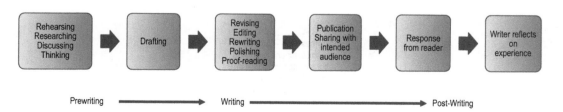

Figure 6.3 An early linear representation of the writing process

As more educators began to implement and research the teaching of a process approach to writing, the representation of the process evolved further. There were three main changes to the previous representation:

- Recognition that the writing process is recursive rather than linear, that writers may commence at various points in the cycle and move back and forth among them as needed.
- The conference became a key form of feedback to students from others (not always the teacher) as part of the process.
- Any feedback to students should focus on meaning first and surface features second.

These changes informed a new diagrammatic representation of the writing process, as shown in Figure 6.4.

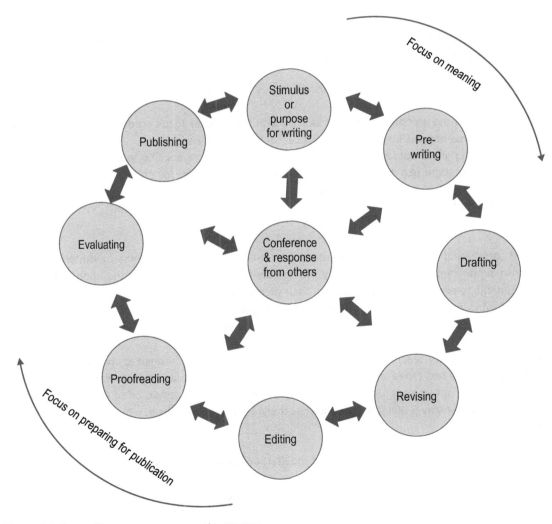

Figure 6.4 The writing process as a recursive process

Representing the writing process as recursive rather than linear emphasises how the process might vary depending upon purpose, audience and context. A writer might start at various stages, and repeat stages as necessary, travelling back and forth around the cycle until satisfied the piece is ready for publication or use. Not all stages would be engaged in every time a person writes. A shopping list, where the audience is oneself, would not require a response from others or revision or editing in terms of surface features, as long as it was intelligible to oneself, though a person might reorganise the final list in terms of which items would be purchased first. Similarly, a piece of writing that is therapeutic, for example a poem about the death of a loved one, may never be revised or published once the therapeutic purpose is satisfied. However, in settings such as a workplace, reports or a persuasive piece suggesting changes to procedures must be accurate, as would a set of health and safety instructions. In such settings, due to the purpose and context, responses from others, possibly including the intended audience for the writing, during revision and proof reading for accuracy prior to publication, would be essential.

The position of the conference or response in the centre of Figure 6.4 represents how the conference or response became central to teaching in the writing process. Hornsby (1988, pp. 1-15) identified four different types of conferences, all of which had a teaching role, but occurred at different stages of the writing process and fulfilled different purposes. Hornsby suggested:

- Individual conference be used for addressing issues that a student felt were preventing them from moving on;
- Group conferences among five or six students with the teacher focus on drafts and how they are moving towards addressing purpose, audience, context and direction;
- Small teaching group conferences address a shared issue where specific teaching of a strategy or skill might be taught (e.g. how to prepare an outline in the pre-writing stage, or a punctuation skill such as the use of quotation marks for speech);
- Publishing conferences, sometimes referred to as author's chair, where students present their published piece to a real audience for response.

The most challenging aspects of the conference were managing time, as numbers of students required a response simultaneously. How to actually run the conference, for example using open questions to enable students to explain where they were in their piece of writing and identify any issues or problems they were having, was also challenging. Graves (1983) suggested that it was necessary to have questions that identified the purpose of the conference, follow-up questions to narrow the focus of that purpose or issues and questions that focussed on the process and progress.

Another challenge for teachers was that because students were encouraged to choose their own topics and therefore the text types or genres, sometime this meant that students never varied topics or text types. As a result of a three-year longitudinal study of the classroom application of the writing process, Anstey (1986) and Anstey & Bull (1987) found that there were several ways in which this problem might be addressed:

- Developing a literature program as part of the literacy curriculum that provides students with many examples of different text types and genres;
- Writing in other subject areas and teaching writing in these contexts - for example writing science reports, an exposition of an event in history, instructions for making something in art;

- Teacher modelling or demonstrating different text types or topics they have written or are currently writing (demonstrating process and text type features);
- Innovating on text, where teacher and students rewrite a text they have been reading or studying and changing an aspect of it, for example rewriting a fairy tale from a different **point of view** or in a different time or setting.

Critiques of the process approach

Critiques of the process approach to writing emerged during the 1990s. Many of the critiques were similar to the critiques of the whole language movement that was also dominating approaches to the teaching of literacy and reading at the time. Hammond (1996) was concerned that the teaching of the process approach was largely implicit because of the incidental nature of conferences and identification of students' instructional needs arising from the conferences. Rivalland (1989) suggested that students from different social and cultural groups would be disadvantaged because they were not used to implicit teaching practices and would not have the same resources to draw upon as students from the dominant social and cultural class. Kamler (1992) reported on research in two classrooms, one of which was a process writing classroom. Her conclusions were that students were not developing knowledge of a range of genres because they always chose their own topics and many did not have sufficient knowledge and experience of other genres to choose from. She also suggested that if all teaching arose from students identifying their writing problems, then again some students would not have the knowledge and resources to do so and thus they would not make progress.

A final concern was that process writing classrooms focussed more on narrative than other text types or writing in other curriculum areas and that narrative was the least used genre or text type for learning in school, the workplace and community. This critique reinforced concerns about a lack of attention to the sociocultural background of students when implementing the writing process, potentially limiting their ability to grow and develop in a process writing classroom.

These were valid criticisms as in both Australia and the U.S. the writing process movement was not curriculum mandated, it was a more grass-roots adoption among teachers. Up to this time writing had not been a focus in curriculum documents and it was only during this period that the focus of curricula began to change and explicitly include and acknowledge the connections between talking, listening, reading and writing (Turbill et al., 2015, p. xiii). As reported by Turbill et al. (2015), teachers' learning about the writing process was supported by conferences, publications and professional learning provided through professional associations and academics conducting research in the areas during the 1980s. Therefore, teachers' knowledge about, and ways of implementing the approach, varied greatly, depending upon their access to professional reading and professional development. Consequently, some students were in classrooms where explicit learning episodes were conducted as part of the writing process in order to provide comprehensive skills development and information about text types and other resources students could draw upon as they engaged in, and learned about, the processes of writing. Other students were in classrooms where the writing process existed as the sole way teaching of writing, and still others were in classrooms that still used a skills approach. These variations provided the seed for debates that have continued to this day and spread across the U.S., U.K. and Australia and diverted attention from the informative and positive aspects of the approach that were demonstrated in the carefully documented research reported by Graves (1981, 1983), Calkins (1983), Walshe (1981) and Murray (1982). Valid critique, rather than informing further careful research and professional learning, became the tool that led to negative systemic changes in the teaching of writing, which will be discussed in detail later in this chapter. While the 1980s and early 1990s were periods of significant and positive change in the pedagogy informing all aspects of literacy (see Chapter Five for details of the simultaneous developments in whole language and the teaching of reading), it also heralded as a turning point as debates about the 'right way to teach reading and writing', the beginnings of political interference around the teaching of literacy generally, and high-stakes national testing emerged.

REFLECTION STRATEGY 6.2

- The purpose of this Reflection Strategy is to consider the similarities between the consumption and production of text (reading and writing) and identify what the whole language approach to the teaching of reading and the process approach to the teaching of writing have in common.
- Re-examine Figure 6.2 and revise your understandings about the similarities between the process of designing and redesigning text when consuming (reading) and producing (writing) texts.
- Re-read the section on whole language approaches to reading in Chapter Five and identify similarities between the whole language approach to reading and the process approach to writing. Consider the reasons for these similarities, not only in terms of the times, context and knowledge available, but also in terms of the similarities between reading and writing.
- Consider the implications of the critiques of whole language and process writing for your current approach to teaching writing. Examine your planning for the teaching of writing? How closely does your approach approximate a process approach? What are the similarities and differences between a process approach and your approach?
- How does a process approach to the teaching of writing fit with concepts about multimodal texts and a multiliterate pedagogy? What is necessary, but not sufficient?

Genre approach

As was discussed in Chapter Five, the genre approach emerged as a result of concerns that whole language approaches and process approaches exacerbated any mismatch between students' social, cultural and community background and the literate practices of the school. Researchers such as Martin (1993) and Martin and Rothery (1993) suggested that the combination of mismatches between student sociocultural background and school, together with a lack of explicit teaching about the genres that were prevalent in particular disciplines, meant that for some students, particularly those in what they termed 'disadvantaged schools', reading, writing, and therefore learning, was inhibited.

Martin (as reported by Derewianka, 2015) examined the social purposes for using writing, that is how writing is used to achieve particular goals. He related this to the school curricula and identified what he described as five genres prevalent in school curricula. These were describing, arguing, reviewing, recounting and storytelling. He demonstrated that these genres were structured in particular ways and these features could be explicitly taught to students which would help them when reading and writing in other curriculum areas, ensuring all students had access to the power of reading, writing and learning. As Unsworth (2015, p. 267) summarised,

> In the case of curriculum area reading and writing it was clear that developing effective subject specific literacy learning necessarily entailed for many students the need for explicit teaching of the linguistic forms that constructed and communicated knowledge in the particular subject area.

Genre theorists were also concerned that the pedagogy of process and whole language approaches was too child centred and embedded in self-directed, discovery learning. They felt that the role of the teacher was becoming unbalanced, moving too far towards being a facilitator of the process and concentrating less on providing explicit instruction about the skills and knowledge necessary to enact the process successfully. However, as Derewianka (2015, p. 71) pointed out in a review of the origins of genre theory, teachers are generally not either traditional or progressive, but take on a variety of roles throughout the day. Nevertheless, as has been previously discussed, in some cases this was a valid criticism of classroom practices around the process approach.

Genre theorists translated their concerns and research about the types of texts used in various curricula into a more structured approach to teaching writing, based on scaffolding students' learning. Their approach was very similar to the Gradual Release Model (Pearson and Gallagher, 1983) previously discussed in detail in Chapter Two, and also referred to in Chapter Five. The genre approach took students through a carefully sequenced cycle of learning episodes that led students from immersion in and analysis of the genre through episodes that facilitated approximation of the genre, to finally gaining independent control of the genre. As discussed in Chapter Five, their work also drew heavily on Halliday's theory of functional linguistics (Halliday, 1973, 2004) and therefore interpreted **field, tenor and mode** as a way of focussing the exploration of genres. The focus of field was identified as the expression and development of ideas, mode was identified as focussing on text structure and organisation and tenor was identified as focussing on language for interaction. (See the section on genre theory in Chapter Five for a full discussion of these concepts.) Unsworth (2015, pp. 267-269) reported on a range of approaches that emerged as a result of early work in genre by Martin and Rothery (1993). He cited the Teaching and Learning Cycle (Rose & Martin, 2012) as one interpretation of a genre approach in the classroom, and accelerated learning pedagogies (Cowey, 2005) as another. All retained the focus on equity of access for all students to learning by developing knowledge and understanding about the genres of texts in a range of contexts and for a variety of purposes. Figure 6.5 draws upon the various approaches taken by genre researchers to provide a graphic representation of the cycle developed by genre theorists for teaching writing.

Critiques of the genre approach

While genre theory emerged in Australia, its influence has spread to the U.K. and U.S. and there has been considerable debate about its approach. While most acknowledge the need for understanding about text types and the specific ways of writing in various disciplines, critiques have largely focussed on the pedagogy associated with the approaches and the definitions of genres. Shand and Konza (2016) detailed the main arguments and debates around genre theory and their summary informs the following discussion.

Rosen (2011, 2013) raised concerns regarding the addition of genre theory to the U.K. National Literacy Strategy and its potential to be rigid and arbitrary in its implementation. His particular concern was that by assigning categories to texts they become fixed and invariable in the minds of students, and therefore their social origins and the fact that they will evolve and change would not be acknowledged.

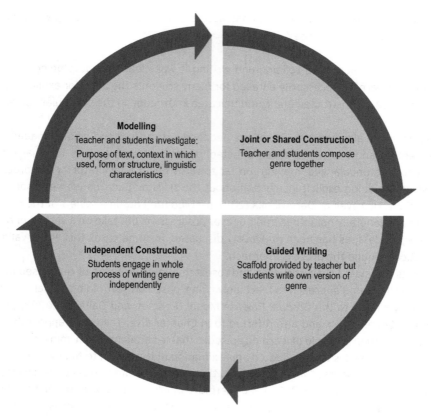

Figure 6.5 A representation of the genre approach to writing

Doecke and Breen (2013) were similarly concerned that classifying and categorising language denies the dynamic origins and development of language. There was a general concern that students would see the construction of text as simply filling in the gaps that corresponded to the structure of the genre. Yet, as has previously been discussed, researchers of genre approaches were basing their theory and research in Halliday's view of language, that is heavily embedded in its social origins language. This theory of language is far from static and acknowledges that language and its structures will continue to evolve and change as society changes. So how is it that these critiques of the genre approach as promoting a static view of language emerged?

Again, this concern arises from the pedagogy that emerged as genre theory was implemented. Some classrooms provided worksheets outlining the generic structure of the genre as a scaffold students could use during the guided writing stage of learning about a genre. The scaffold on its own was not necessarily poor pedagogy. It was the way the talk was conducted around the scaffold and in the previous modelling, demonstration and joint construction of text that would potentially develop understandings about text as static rather than dynamic. These critiques are particularly important because they address one of the major beliefs underpinning a multiliterate pedagogy, that text is dynamic rather than static and that pedagogy, and particularly talk, around text should encourage a dynamic understanding of text. This was discussed extensively in Chapter Three (see Figure 3.1).

REFLECTION STRATEGY 6.3

- The purpose of this Reflection Strategy is to consider the similarities between the consumption and production of text (reading and writing) and identify what the genre approach to the teaching of reading and writing have in common.
- Re-examine Figure 6.2 and revise your understandings about the similarities between the process of designing and redesigning text when consuming (reading) and producing (writing) texts.
- Re-read the section on genre approaches to reading in Chapter Five and identify similarities between the genre approach to writing. Consider the reasons for these similarities, not only in terms of the times, context and knowledge available, but also in terms of the similarities between reading and writing.
- Consider the implications of the critiques of genre approaches to reading and writing for your current approach to teaching writing. Examine your planning for the teaching of writing. How closely does your approach approximate a genre approach? What are the similarities and differences between a genre approach and your approach?
- How does a genre approach to the teaching of writing fit with concepts about multimodal texts and a multiliterate pedagogy? What is necessary, but not sufficient?

The Four Resource Model and writing, potential challenges

In Chapter Five the development of the Four Resource Model was discussed as a response to debates about the 'best' way to teach reading. Given the debate that arose regarding process or genre approaches to the teaching of writing, it is appropriate to revisit it and examine how it might refocus thinking around the pedagogies associated with the teaching of writing. The similarities between reading and writing and the necessity to read or consume text as part of the writing process indicate that The Four Resource Model can be applied to producing text. Producing a text is a process of using available designs to **design** and **redesign** text to achieve a particular purpose for a specific audience and context. Figure 6.6 has been developed by reworking Figure 5.6 from Chapter Five to demonstrate how the Four Resource Model can be applied to the production of text. For more information about the Four Resource Model, refer to the appropriate section in Chapter Five of this volume and Chapter Two of the complementary volume *Foundations of Multiliteracies: Reading, Writing and Talking in the 21st Century*.

Contributions of historical research and associated approaches to understandings about writing, writing pedagogy and the production of multimodal texts in a multiliterate world

In order to consider the contribution of historical approaches to the teaching of writing in a multiliterate world, it is necessary to review the characteristics of a multiliterate person that a multiliterate pedagogy is endeavouring to develop and to consider the characteristics of texts that a multiliterate person must understand in order to produce and consume them.

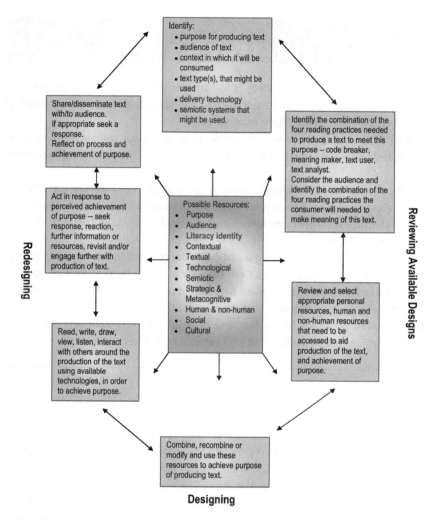

Figure 6.6 Applying the Four Resource Model to the production of text in terms of design, multimodal texts and multiliteracies

In Chapter One the characteristics of a multiliterate person were identified as follows. A multiliterate person needs to:

- Be flexible and able to deal with change – be analytical and reflective problem solvers, be strategic, creative and critical thinkers who can engage with new texts in a variety of contexts and audiences;
- Have a repertoire of literate knowledge and practices – understand that new texts that have differing purposes, audiences and contexts and will require a range of different behaviours that draw on a repertoire of knowledge and experiences;
- Understand how social and cultural diversity affects literate practices – know that experiences and culture influence and produce a variety of different knowledges, approaches, orientations, attitudes and values that will influence the interpretation and occurrence of literate practices;

- Understand, and be able to use, traditional and new communication technologies – understand the semiotic systems and recognise that the increasing variety of new texts are delivered by paper, live and digital technologies, and realise that purpose, audience and context determine which semiotic system and which technology is appropriate;
- Be critically literate – understand that in every literate practice it is necessary to determine who is participating and for what reason, who is in a position of power, who has been marginalised, what is the purpose and origin of the texts being used and how these texts are supporting participation in society and everyday life.

It was also suggested that the following understandings about texts were essential:

- All texts are consciously constructed and have particular social, cultural, political or economic purposes.
- Texts will continue to change as society and technology changes.
- All texts are multimodal.
- Texts can be interactive, linear or non-linear.
- Texts may be intertextual.
- Texts are tending to become more screen-like as design and designing become more central to the production of texts.
- Texts can be created by the consumer using the links in digital texts to produce **hypertexts**.
- The social and cultural background of individuals influences the production of, and engagement with, text.
- A text may have several possible meanings.
- The consumer interacts with the text to actively construct the meaning of the text.
- The complexity of multimodal texts means that consumers have to consciously differentiate the focus of their attention across the semiotic systems.
- No text is neutral.

It is also useful to review historical approaches in terms of how they might inform a pedagogy that teaches the consumption and production of text as a process of design. Review Figure 6.2, which has been previously presented and depicts the processes of producing and consuming text as a process of design.

REFLECTION STRATEGY 6.4

- The purpose of this Reflection Strategy is to review the historical approaches to the teaching of writing in terms of developing multiliterate individuals, developing a multiliterate pedagogy, developing concepts about multimodal texts, understanding the consumption and production of text as design.
- Draw up a table in which you can compare and contrast historical theories and approaches to the teaching of writing.

- Re-read the characteristics of a multiliterate person and understandings about multimodal text and use this knowledge to review the approaches in terms of the following general question: 'What is necessary but not sufficient about this research and pedagogy for producing (designing and redesigning) texts in a multimodal, multiliterate world?'
- Use the following minor questions to examine the historical research and approaches in terms of the stages on Figure 6.2. How does the research that informs this approach and related pedagogy and practice:
  - Inform understandings about the role of purpose, audience and meaning when producing a multimodal text?
  - Contribute knowledge, skills and processes that become part of a repertoire of resources that aid the production of multimodal texts?
  - Provide knowledge, skills and strategies that inform the **synthesising** process of production (combining, recombining and reworking selected resources to make meaning)?
  - Provide knowledge, skills and strategies that inform the recording, preservation and dissemination of a multimodal text?
  - Develop understandings about the production of text as the transforming and **transformation** of meaning?
  - Contribute to the development of understandings about the relationships between the consumption and production of multimodal text?
- Examine your analyses and think about how they might inform your current methods of teaching writing. Are there aspects of your pedagogy that you would change in any way, and if so, how would you go about this?

Table 6.1 provides a summary of the historical approaches to the teaching of writing, together with a commentary that identifies how they might inform a multimodal and multiliterate pedagogy and the challenges they might present to implementing a multimodal and multiliterate pedagogy.

Analysis of Table 6.1 indicates that historical approaches to the teaching of writing can inform a multiliterate pedagogy, however it also identified potential challenges. The following challenges and cautions were identified and the implications for each are discussed.

- Many of the approaches, because of the times in which the research was conducted only provide information for producing texts using the linguistic semiotic system and paper technologies.

   Implications: This does not mean they should be rejected. It simply highlights the need to incorporate the semiotic systems, their codes and conventions into planning and pedagogy about the production of multimodal texts. It is also necessary to audit curricula, planning and practice in classrooms and across the school to ensure balance among technologies, and semiotic systems in the writing program.

- Many of the approaches do not acknowledge literacy as **social practice**, or if they do, do not always use pedagogies or provide guidelines for responding to social and cultural differentiation among students.

   Implications: The skills, process, genre and Four Resource Model approaches, despite the original intent of some, may all fail to emphasise the social origin of literacy when implemented, depending

Table 6.1 How the history of research about writing and the associated approaches, pedagogy and practices inform the teaching of writing and production of multimodal texts and a multiliterate pedagogy

Research and Associated Approaches, Pedagogy and Practice	Comments in Terms of Teaching About the Production of Multimodal Text and a Multiliterate Pedagogy
Skills approach Identified writing as a set of linguistic skills to be mastered in hierarchical order, particularly in terms of spelling, grammar and punctuation. Skills taught separately to composition lesson.	Informs, because it: • Provides knowledge base for writing - grammar, punctuation, spelling. Potential challenges: • Concomitant with the times, it focussed on paper texts and only the linguistic semiotic system - needs to include codes and conventions of other semiotic systems and characteristics of texts delivered via other technologies. • Decontextualised teaching of skills limiting understanding of their role in writing. • Focusses on skills rather than on literacy as a social, cultural and cognitive practice. • Takes no account of social and cultural background of students. • Tests rather than teaches writing by using composition as approach.
Process Approach Identified the processes of writing and focussed on purpose, audience and clarifying meaning of the writing through drafting, revision and response from others, prior to editing and attending to surface features of punctuation, spelling and grammar. Initially depicted as a linear process but moved to a recursive cycle as better representing the process.	Informs because it: • Encouraged the student to take control of the process, which increased motivation, engagement in whole process and development. • Taught about the processes necessary to achieve the writing purpose. • Focussed on purpose, audience and meaning which had previously been ignored. • Taught skills in context. Potential challenges: • Concomitant with the times, it focussed on paper texts and only the linguistic semiotic system - needs to include codes and conventions of other semiotic systems and characteristics of texts delivered via other technologies. • Lack of consistent pedagogy because it was a grass roots movement and access to professional learning varied greatly. • Potential issues with pedagogy balancing implicit and explicit teaching. • Did not account for variation in students' social and cultural background, which potentially disadvantaged students whose home and community were different to literacies of the school. • Did not teach a variety of genres or explicitly teach structure of other text types.

(Continued)

Table 6.1 (Continued)

Research and Associated Approaches, Pedagogy and Practice	Comments in Terms of Teaching About the Production of Multimodal Text and a Multiliterate Pedagogy
Genre approach A structured, explicit and functional approach to the teaching of writing, focussing on the structure and grammar of texts across all disciplines. Examined purpose of texts and social contexts in which they were used. Pedagogy recommended a teaching cycle of modelling and deconstruction, followed by joint construction and finally independent construction.	Informs, because it: • Provided resources about the structure of different text types or genres for use in production of text. • Focussed on writing in other discipline areas and the text types or genres related to those disciplines. • Informed both reading and writing, and therefore learning. • Provided a metalanguage useful for talking about text. • Provided resources that aided in use of research skills. • Provided a pedagogy similar to Gradual Release of Model, therefore emphasising the need for the producer to take responsibility and control. Potential challenges: • Concomitant with the times it was originally developed, it focussed on paper texts and only the linguistic semiotic system – needs further research and application to include codes and conventions of all five semiotic systems and characteristics of texts delivered via other technologies. • Recommended pedagogy could result in repetitive superficial pedagogical practices that do not address authentic texts, social context of texts, individual learning needs or community links. • Pedagogy could develop a static rather than dynamic view of language and literacy. • Did not always acknowledge that some texts contain several genres within them and that genres are not always 'pure'. • Debate regarding the use of functional or traditional approach to grammar is not constructive. Either can inform this approach.
Four Resource Model Examined the purpose for which reading is used in everyday life and the ways in which it is practiced, to identify the reading practices and resources that can inform the teaching of reading. Identified codebreaker, meaning maker, text user and text analyst practices. Can be used to guide the reading the producer engages in during the writing process. Can help the producer think about the reading practices their writing will require of the consumer/audience of their text, thus informing the producer's decisions during the process of writing. Informs the links between consumption and production of text.	Informs, because it: • Focusses on writing as a process of design and redesign. • Emphasises the links between reading and writing. • Focusses on practices and resources and can therefore respond to change. • Embedded in concept of literacy as social practice but can acknowledge contributions of psycholinguistic research on cognition and metacognition as contributing resources and practices. • Can be applied to all semiotic systems, text types and technologies. • Can inform pedagogy and planning, ensuring balanced approach to teaching about both the production and consumption of text. • Encourages talk around text that focusses on processes, practices and purposes for writing and reading. Potential challenges: • Requires continuous review and renewal to accommodate changes in practice, technologies, semiotic systems and texts. However, this can also be seen as an advantage as it ensures it is embedded in current social practice. • The four reading practices can be interpreted as a hierarchy rather than a balanced approach across every level of schooling and every discipline. • Pedagogical practice associated with the Four Resource Model may teach the practices separately instead of in relation to one another, therefore leading to a representation of reading process that is not authentic and does not emphasise use in context. • Can be seen as only applying to reading, rather than examining the links between reading and writing.

upon how carefully pedagogy and talk around texts is planned and monitored. A lack of acknowledge-ment of social and cultural variation among students, and a failure to examine the social and cultural community students are part of outside the school, can mean that students do not have the opportu-nity to engage with authentic texts and contexts in the classroom when learning about the production of texts. Consequently, students do not have exposure to a wide range of vocabulary, text types, and technologies making it difficult to firstly see the relevance of what they are learning and secondly translate and apply their learning into lifeworld contexts. Therefore, it is necessary to audit curricula, planning and practice in schools and classrooms to ensure this information about the school commu-nity is informing the selection of texts, pedagogy and practice of the classrooms. Note that this does not mean text selection and content of the curriculum should be limited to reflect only the school com-munity, but that the curriculum and practice acknowledges difference and makes learning relevant.

- Similar to historical approaches to the teaching of reading, the largest area of potential challenges and cautions relates to critiques of the pedagogies associated with the different approaches to teaching about the production of text. The concerns related to:
  o   Implicit rather than explicit teaching of skills because of the overuse of particular strategies;
  o   The repetitive use of strategies and teaching cycles, leading to decontextualised learning and a static view of texts and literacy;
  o   Balancing focussed learning episodes with encouraging students to take control of their learning;
  o   Ensuring pedagogies associated with the analysis of texts use authentic texts and contexts and address variations among texts that result from social and cultural and technological change;
  o   Focussing on understanding text types or the teaching of skills to the exclusion of attention to the writing process.

  Implications: Pedagogy around teaching about the production of text needs to be continuously reviewed and analysed to ensure good strategies do not become bad strategies because of the ways they are enacted in the classroom. Ritualised repetitive strategies and behaviour, decontextualised learning and a lack of authentic texts are the antithesis of a multiliterate pedagogy that develops multiliterate adults. In Chapters Two and Four, the inquiry model and research on talk and dialogic pedagogy provide very clear guidelines for avoiding these potential challenges. Chapter One iden-tified action learning as a way of investigating practice to ensure beliefs match practice. Careful, detailed planning, frequently audited to ensure balance among texts and technologies, variation among teaching strategies and practices, and response to social and cultural difference are neces-sary to ensure effective pedagogy around the production of multimodal texts.

As has been previously stated, there is a strong relationship between the consumption and production of text. Therefore it useful to examine the historical approaches to the teaching of reading and consider whether any of these approaches might inform the teaching of writing. Re-examination of Table 5.3 in Chapter Five identifies approaches that are repeated but with a focus on writing and production (the skills approach, genre approach and the Four Resource Model), some approaches that are similar (the whole language approach and the process approach) and some approaches that can most definitely inform pedagogies around the production of text. Early approaches to cognition and comprehension pro-vide insights into the thinking skills that might be used when producing a text (e.g. when researching for writing, planning an outline, synthesising information from several sources for writing, critically analysing your drafts, seeking a response from, or responding to, others' writing). The research on **metacognition** can inform pedagogies around the process of writing, particularly students' taking responsibility, being strategic and self-monitoring. The research on literacy as a social practice and critical literacy is useful in addressing the issues of acknowledging students' social and cultural backgrounds and focussing on literacy and texts as products of society that will continue to change. It also emphasises the importance of using authentic texts and contexts for both the analysis and production of texts. The reader may find it useful at this point to refer back to Table 5.3 and the sections in Chapter Five on early approaches to comprehension and cognition, metacognition, and literacy as social practice (critical literacy) and re-read these sections in with a focus on producing rather than consuming text.

Ivanic (2004) conducted a meta-analysis of approaches arising from the theories and research about the teaching of writing and the pedagogy of writing. She analysed these approaches in terms in terms of:

- Their focus (e.g. the skills approach focussed on the text, creativity and process approaches on the mental process and genre and sociopolitical approaches on the sociocultural and political context of writing),
- Their beliefs about writing,
- Beliefs about learning to write,
- Approaches to the teaching of writing
- Assessment criteria (Ivanic, 2004 p. 225).

As a result of her analyses, she identified six ways of talking about the teaching of writing and referred to them as discourses of writing. The six discourses she identified were a skills discourse, a creativity discourse, a process discourse, a genre discourse, a social practices discourse and a sociopolitical discourse. These six discourses reflect the ideas present in the historical overview about the teaching of writing that has been summarised in Table 6.1. However, it is the way in which Ivanic analysed the approaches that is particularly useful for examining class and school approaches to the teaching of writing and how they might influence the pedagogy around the teaching of writing. Examining personal or school beliefs about writing, beliefs about writing, beliefs about learning to write, approaches to the teaching of writing and methods of writing assessment for consistencies and inconsistencies among them would provide individual teachers and schools with very useful information. For example, these analyses may inform observations and assessments teachers have made about the students' writing development, the ways in which students view writing and what they see as important about writing. It may be that there is a mismatch between what teachers believe they are doing and their practice, including the ways they talk about writing with students. This mismatch may account for students' development and understandings about writing. Such analyses might also indicate ways in which the pedagogy, practice and assessment about writing might be changed or improved. The following Action Learning Task demonstrates one way in which it might be used.

ACTION LEARNING TASK 6.2

- The purpose of this Action Learning Task is to identify consistencies and inconsistencies in the teaching of writing. It can be conducted as an individual and/or as a whole school. This task would provide good baseline data for an action learning project focussed on an aspect of the teaching of writing. It would also provide a way of collecting and analysing data as you change your practices over time and enable you to track changes in your planning and practices around the teaching of writing and students' understandings and beliefs about writing

- You will be using the statement of beliefs about the teaching of writing you completed in Action Learning Task 6.1 during this task, so you may need to access this prior to beginning.
- Audiotape at least one lesson in which you teach writing.
- Draw up a table in which you list the main approaches to the teaching of writing (skills, process, genre, social and cultural aspects of writing). As you listen, tick in the appropriate column how often you talk or engage students in talk about writing that reflects these approaches. For example if you are talking about draft and revisions or planning this would focus on process. If you are talking about the structure of the text, this would focus on genre; if you are talking about where these texts might be used and who might use them, then there is a focus on the sociocultural aspects of text.
- Examine where the ticks are and the balance among them. This gives you an idea about how your talk focusses learning about writing. It may be that the focus is being influenced in the lesson by the learning objective of the lesson and other lessons may vary in focus. You would need to listen to several lessons and examine your planning over time to get a real idea of how your planning, practice and talk in writing lessons is focussing student ideas about writing. It should also be noted that this method of analysis is only intended as a guide to assist in reflection on your teaching practice. A detailed analysis would require transcribing the lesson and identifying language that is related to each of the approaches and then tabulating and calculating balance among all the language of the lesson.
- Examine your planning and assessment for writing and use a table, the same as the one you used to analyse your talk to identify the focus of your planning and assessment.
- Having conducted the analyses of your lesson (or lessons) and examined your planning and assessment, go back to your original statement of beliefs and think about whether your planning and practice matches your beliefs, or the degree to which the match or mismatch occurs. Do these analyses and reflections indicate that you need to change your planning and practice in order to better reflect your beliefs about writing, your beliefs about learning to write, your approach to the teaching of writing and criteria for assessment?
- Ask your students (in written or oral form) what they think writing is about and why you need to be able to write, what good writers can do, how they think they learn to write, and what they think helps them learn to write. Explain that there are no wrong or right answers; you simply want to hear everything they have to say to help you improve your teaching. In this way, they realise they are not being assessed, that in fact you are assessing and reflecting upon your teaching. If you do this orally, simply write down or record everything students say. Be careful when you respond to students' ideas to ensure you give neutral responses, otherwise your data will be influenced by your responses and students will start giving answers they think you want or like. Examine their answers and look for a degree of match and mismatch between your statement of beliefs and their answers. Re-examine your analyses of your talk, planning and assessment and look at the degree of match and mismatch between the students' beliefs and understandings about writing and your practice.
- Consider any changes you may wish to make to the ways in which you teach writing as a result of this series of action learning tasks.

Current research and approaches to the teaching of writing

Research on the teaching of writing in the 21st century commenced with a focus on the increasing use of technology when writing, in particular the development and use of word processing software for writing in schools. It was still largely focussed on the linguistic aspects of writing. However, the focus then moved to the redefining of text as multimodal and moved beyond word processing technology to understanding the technologies that produce multimodal texts. At this point in time, current research has not led to completely new approaches but rather the adaption and enhancement of existing approaches to the teaching of writing by incorporating new understandings about multimodality and technology. As Lipscombe et al. (2015, p. 296) indicated, teaching writing from a multimodal perspective incorporating linguistic text and the affordances of new and changing technologies requires the reworking of concepts from previous seminal work on writing research and pedagogy. In addition to examining the affordances of new technologies, reworking of current approaches has focussed on talk around text and the pedagogy surrounding the teaching of writing. This research focus has addressed many of the concerns regarding historical approaches about talk and pedagogy previously identified. The research has also examined students' perceptions of writing, their use of, and decision-making when using, technology and the implications of this for pedagogy around the teaching of writing.

Early 21st-century teacher and student perceptions of the role of technology in writing

Lenhart et al. (2008) conducted research regarding teens' perceptions of writing and technology using surveys and focus groups. The results presented an interesting dissonance between what students wrote or composed and their beliefs about what constitutes writing. While students composed a lot of texts, they did not consider the writing they did using electronic means, for example texting, emailing and using social media, as 'real' writing. Writing was perceived as something done in school and largely paper based. Overall students believed being a good writer was essential to achieving success. When asked what motivated them to write, students indicated that relevant topics, high expectations and an interested audience, as well as opportunities to write creatively motivated them. This result is particularly interesting, as it reflects the findings of researchers in the 1980s – that providing students with real purposes, an audience and indicating to students a belief that they can write were strong motivators and led to success. Despite the students' belief that writing with technology was not 'real' writing when asked what would assist them in improving their writing, they indicated knowing more about technology and more writing time in class. Their comments indicated that responses from teachers to their drafts was a key factor in assisting them with their writing – again a feature of the findings of research of the 1980s. They also felt that the use of computer-based tools would assist them in their writing. Comments indicated that they felt a lot of the technology they were using outside of school would soon be part of everyone's jobs.

Purcell et al. (2013) reported on a study of 2,462 middle and high school teachers in the U.S. regarding their perception of the impact of digital tools on writing. The study used person-to-person and online focus groups and surveys. The teachers were identified as advanced skills teachers who were regarded as highly competent in the teaching of writing. The results provide insights into perceptions and teaching about writing and technology at the end of the first ten years of the 21st century and a context for examining the research that has followed.

Generally, teachers saw digital tools as beneficial to students writing because students could share writing online, reach a wider audience, write collaboratively and develop creativity and personal expression through social media. However, they were concerned about the impact of technology on students' care with spelling and grammar and the time students would spend on writing. Specific concerns were that students could not differentiate between the need to write formally or informally and didn't understand that different registers and voices were necessary for different purposes, audiences and contexts.

Responses regarding the utility of digital tools assisting with spelling and grammar were almost equally divided in terms of a positive or negative effect. There was a slightly higher belief that students wrote faster and were more careless and were more likely to take shortcuts and put less effort into their writing. Teacher comments indicated that because the students used digital technology in all aspects of their lives, they were used to speed and immediate gratification. Therefore, slowing students down, getting them think critically, analyse and engage in the process of drafting and revising was difficult (Purcell et al., 2013, pp. 62-63).

Teacher comments also indicated that just because students used technology, they did not necessarily understand it and the ways in which it can be used as a tool to assist with their writing. They suggested that students' use of technology in the form of social media was generally superficial and did not involve analytic thinking about how they might use its tools more effectively to communicate their meaning or think critically about the impact of the use of social media. They also rated students' understanding about plagiarism, copyright issues and the use of sources, as 'fair', indicating that the availability of many sources online meant students could easily 'cut and paste' and incorporate work into their writing that was not their own. Most teachers were explicitly teaching about these issues across all subject areas and felt that judging the quality of information was essential to students' learning about writing for the future. These views are concomitant with current research regarding the essential skills in the workplace. In July 2017, The Foundation for Young Australians published the *New Work Smarts Report*, which identified the skills required of workers by 2030 and the implications for schooling. Two of the four essential skills that were identified were problem solving and making judgements and engaging in critical thinking. It was estimated that workers will spend 100 per cent more of their time involved in problem solving and 41 per cent more time on making judgements and engaging in critical thinking (for more detail, see Chapter One in the companion volume *Foundations of Multiliteracies: Reading, Writing and Talking in the 21st Century*).

A further example of the mixed responses of teachers surveyed regarding the impact of technology was that only half the teachers in the survey indicated that the use of technology made it easier to shape and improve students' writing. However, their comments were particularly insightful, concluding that it was not the tool that made teaching writing with digital technology more or less effective but the pedagogy (Purcell et al., 2013, p. 63). These comments foreshadowed the conclusions of much of the research regarding the teaching of writing and technology that has occurred since this survey.

Interestingly, many comments by teachers indicated that they deliberately used pen and paper for writing with students, firstly to slow them down and encourage them to engage in more thinking and planning time, and secondly because high-stakes testing still required the use of pen and paper. Again, their comments foreshadowed more recent research that examined the relationship between high-stakes testing, pedagogy and student learning in writing, which will be discussed later in this chapter. One group of teachers reported that they had examined students' writing in both digital and pen and paper contexts in order to assess whether students performed differently with some aspects of writing depending upon which technology was being used. They used the results to discuss the differences with students and raise their awareness of what they had difficulty with in each context. The teachers also used the results to inform their teaching and specifically address the aspects students were having difficulty with in each context (Purcell et al., 2013, p. 57).

Teachers were also surveyed regarding the types of writing assignments they asked students to complete. The most common writing was journaling and short essays, followed by short responses and opinion pieces, completed on a weekly basis. Interestingly research papers, multimedia assignments, plays and short stories were assigned only about once a year. It should be reiterated at this point that these were the results across teachers in all discipline areas and that some of these types of writing were used more in some disciplines than others (Purcell et al., 2013, pp. 15-16). However, it is interesting that in the 2011-2012 school year creating a multimedia piece incorporating video, audio or images was assigned less often than weekly or monthly by 56 per cent or teachers and not at all by 22 per cent. In addition, when teachers were asked the skills students would need for writing in the future, 23 per cent felt working with audio, video or graphic content was essential, 54 per cent thought it was important but *not* essential, and 22 per cent thought it was somewhat important (Purcell et al., 2013, p. 21). These results regarding students becoming competent in engaging with, and producing, multimodal texts are at odds with all the research regarding the skills knowledge and understandings students need in the future. As early as 1996 The New London Group was indicating the need for students to be multiliterate and multimodal (for more detail, see Chapter One in the companion volume *Foundations of Multiliteracies: Reading, Writing and Talking in the 21st Century*). Interestingly, the teacher perceptions about technology are also different to the previously discussed perceptions of the students surveyed in 2008 who felt that knowing more about technology would help them with their writing and would be a large part of their jobs in the future Lenhart et al. (2008).

Recently the United Nations Educational, Scientific and Cultural Organisation (UNESCO) released Five Laws of Media and Information Literacy (MIL), stating that the reason this step has been taken is:

> We are travelling towards the universality of books, the Internet and all forms of 'containers of knowledge'. Media and information literacy for all should be seen as a nexus of human rights. Therefore, UNESCO suggests the following Five Laws of Media and Information Literacy.
>
> (UNESCO, 2017)

The five laws assert the rights of everyone to access *and create* media information literacy, and acknowledges the fact that the information, knowledge and messages contained are not neutral. They also acknowledge the dynamic aspects of media and information literacy, stating that it cannot all be acquired at one time and that it will continue to evolve (Anstey & Bull, 2018).

The results of the survey by Purcell, Buchanan and Friedrich were published in 2013 but represented the views of U.S. teachers based on their teaching of writing in the 2011-2012 school year. As can be seen, at this point in time writing was still very much focussed on linguistic text and the implications of the impact of technology and emergence of multimodal texts was not yet fully realised. These views were not just present in the U.S. In Australia, Macken-Horarik et al. (2011) provided further insight into the focus of concerns at the time, identifying four challenges facing the teaching of literacy in the 21st century when students have to appreciate, understand and create texts that not only contain language but also images, animations, hyperlinks and sound. They were concerned that knowledge and understanding of the grammars associated with multimodal texts were not adequately explained in the English curriculum and teachers themselves felt their knowledge was inadequate. They cited studies from the U.K., Australia, Canada and New Zealand that indicated teachers either did not have, or felt they did not have, adequate knowledge of even the linguistic grammar to analyse texts and teach students about reading and writing texts (Macken-Horarik et al., 2011, p. 12). The four challenges they identified are summarised below. Note that only the fourth deals with the multimodal aspects of literacy and technology.

- Developing a clear account of knowledge about language for contemporary English.
- Developing a **metalanguage** for talking about language that enables teachers to talk about the relationships between linguistic grammar and the structural features of genres or text types, focussing on *how* language and grammar works in texts.
- Ensuring the knowledge about language for contemporary English and the metalanguage are developed cumulatively and with continuity throughout schooling.
- Developing 'grammatics' and metalanguage for all modes of multimodal communication, which at this point mainly focus on the visual (Macken-Horarik et al., 2011, pp. 12–19).

However, they concluded that

> ... students' literate knowledge know-how can only be enhanced by teachers who can draw in an informed way on relevant aspects of the language and multimodal systems. It is their knowledge that will inform pedagogic decisions and kinds of talk about language and multimodal texts that they can deploy.

(Macken-Horarik et al., 2011, p. 21)

This journal article, like the work of The New London Group (1996), Cope and Kalantzis (2000), Kress and van Leeuwen (2006), Jewitt (2006), Anstey and Bull (2006), Jewitt and Kress (2008) and others, heralded the need to move beyond the linguistic and define a grammar and metalanguage for all modes or semiotic systems and establish this as part of the literacy curriculum and teachers' pedagogy. This became the focus of much of the research about the teaching of writing that has followed.

The challenges of teaching about technology and the production of multimodal texts

Edwards-Groves (2012) research examined the multimodal writing process, indicating that it required understanding writing for the screen as well as the page, knowing and being able to use multimodal literacies and literate practices, understanding design and the five semiotic systems (linguistic, visual, special, gestural and audio) as well as the actual process of writing multimodally. One of the most significant aspects of this research was that it used an action learning model for teachers' professional learning and development, similar to the model that has been described in Chapter One and which is the learning model underpinning this book. The other significant aspect of the research was exploring how to incorporate the necessary learning about technology with teaching about the multimodal writing process. Edwards-Groves's research examined teachers' developing knowledge about technology and how it was impacting their pedagogy around writing. It had been observed before the project commenced that providing hardware and professional development to assist teachers to embed technology in their teaching had failed to impact teachers' pedagogy (Edwards-Groves, 2012, p. 102). Therefore, the project was designed to not only provide professional learning around technology, but also provide opportunities for teachers to discuss and reflect upon their classroom practice, to engage in dialogue around their teaching and to share and discuss what they were trialling in their own teaching. The results indicated that this combination of providing knowledge and providing time for, and encouraging dialogue among teachers about how they were embedding this knowledge into classroom practice, not only changed classroom practice but also indicated the need for changing approaches to professional learning.

One of the most informative aspects of Edwards-Groves's research was that the teachers' professional dialogues and increased collaboration about their pedagogy was reflected in the classroom. Collaborative work and encouraging student dialogue around using technology for writing became a feature of writing pedagogy. The students themselves identified collaboration and dialogue when creating a multimodal text (a video tour of their town) as

- Improving the quality of their multimodal text,
- Facilitating problem solving,
- Aiding efficiency in getting the task done,
- Helping them learn how to be considerate and co-operative when working together. (Edwards-Groves, 2012, pp. 107-108)

Students also recognised that the collaborative work with technology encouraged them to plan more carefully, research, draft, revise and rewrite, and take the time to 'play' with the technology to work out how to use it best in order to achieve the desired outcome. The teachers' reflections on the changes in their pedagogy mirrored many of the students' comments. In particular, they identified the need to provide sufficient time for students to not only engage in the multimodal writing processes of researching, drafting and revising, but also have the time to play with and learn the affordances of the technology they were using (Edwards-Groves, 2012, pp. 106-107).

The changes in teacher pedagogy also reflected the design of the action learning that teachers were engaging in, that is not only did teachers encourage collaborative learning and dialogue around learning, but they also provided explicit lessons on the grammar of the semiotic systems, the developments and use of metalanguage around the semiotics systems, multimodal texts, technology and writing and specific lessons about the technology of producing a multimodal text (e.g. editing a video, website design, uploading digital photos). These explicit lessons provided knowledge and skills to support the students' collaborative work and their dialogue around producing a multimodal text. In other words, as teachers reflected upon how they learned and the features of the professional learning that were assisting them, they transferred this knowledge to their classroom pedagogy.

Edwards-Groves (2012) concluded that one of the important aspects of the shift towards multimodal communication technologies was the fact that it necessitated interactive and collaborative work and communication, and that therefore classroom pedagogies had to reflect this. This conclusion reflects the conclusions of The Foundation for Young Australians *New Work Smarts Report* (2017) which identified the skills required of workers by 2030 and the implications for schooling. Therefore, collaborative work around technology and **dialogic talk** around technology among and between teachers and students is an essential feature of writing pedagogy. It also meant that teachers themselves had to engage in more dialogue and reflection around their pedagogy through collaborative investigation of their classroom practice. In other words, constant engagement in collaborative action learning on a school-wide basis is a necessary feature of professional learning about technology and literacy generally and, as the research of Edwards-Groves (2011, 2012) indicated, writing in particular.

The challenge of teaching about technology as well as teaching about the writing process and the production of multimodal texts has been the focus of much of the writing and research about writing in the 21st century. Barton et al. (2015) conducted two case studies on the teaching and learning activities focussed on writing in two schools. They were particularly interested in teaching around multimodal texts. They identified the need for teacher modelling or providing 'think alouds' about the intricate processes of using and making decisions about multiple technologies and media to produce a text. They also acknowledged the need for students to take ownership of their learning and be able to self-regulate their actions while producing a text. In one of the case studies Barton et al. (2015) identified the skills that students would need to achieve these outcomes. These included being able to collaborate, self-regulate and engage in metacognition, problem solve the actual problems they encounter as they write, and use of information and communication technology (ICT) for both learning and communicating. The latter is a challenge for both teacher and students. As discussed in Chapter Five, Coiro (2003, 2005) identified the use of the internet as a gatekeeper skill, because if students do not have the technology skills to access information to construct their multimodal text, then they cannot even start. Similarly knowing how to manipulate technology is necessary, but students also need to know how to manipulate it to achieve their communicative purpose. This means a knowledge of the codes and conventions of the semiotic systems as well as the technology. For example, knowing how to add an image is necessary, but knowing how to select or compose that image is even more important, because if the image is not serving its communicative purpose, then there is no point adding it. In addition, understanding the spatial semiotic system as it applies to the page and screen is necessary to place linguistic text and the image appropriately to achieve the communicative purpose. Lipscombe et al. (2015) used case studies of students' writing processes with multimodal texts to identify what the process involved and therefore what skills, knowledge and understandings were required. Their findings were very similar to those of Barton et al. (2015). They concluded from their analyses of six children that when planning for the teaching of multimodal texts, which by default means using technology, the following points need to be considered:

- providing pedagogical supports for digital literary text construction
- choice of materials/technology (affordances and limitations)
- multimodality – management of these decisions and effects, and,
- decision making and processes for construction of digital texts.

(Lipscombe et al., 2015, p. 293)

They described the process of using the technology and the multiple semiotic systems to produce a multimodal text as extremely complex and, as was discussed in relation to reading with technology in Chapter Five, involving multiple aspects of decision-making at multiple times during the process. For example, Lipscombe et al. (2015) observed that during the production of one multimodal text students moved between open and closed networks, paper and digital text as they planned and composed, consulted with multiple sources (people and digital), learned new software, evaluated apps and their suitability for use, and as all these processes and decisions occurred moved recursively through the writing process. Time was also a critical factor, given the complexity of the process and decision-making and the need to research both content and apps and learn skills during the process.

A further challenge with teaching writing using technology and creating multimodal texts was identified by Mills and Dreamson (2015), who pointed out that there were social and cultural dimensions to the use of technology and creation of multimodal texts. They pointed out that in white Western culture the linguistic semiotic system is highly valued and foregrounded. However, some cultures value other semiotic systems associated with image, song, dance, and speech, for example storytelling. They indicated that technology and multimodal texts provide opportunities for different cultures and social groups to create texts using the semiotic systems that resonate with their community and to express their cultural and spiritual connections to the world. They used the example of preparatory and year 1 Indigenous students (aged 5 and 6) in South East Queensland retelling the dreaming stories of their totem using images they had created. For these students, the literacy practices were meaningful and relevant to their culture and identity (Mills and Dreamson, 2015, p. 310). Such practices also make for stronger links between home, school and community and empower authors. These issues also focus on the need to not only engage in critical literacy when reading but also when interrogating models of writing and writing.

Unsworth (2015) identified two further challenges regarding teaching about technology and the production of multimodal texts when teaching writing. He referred to the need to examine multimodal texts across the disciplines, identifying how they are structured and constructed. He cited the work of Kress et al. (2001), who demonstrated that images in science, specifically scientific drawings, were constructed through scientific lens and therefore had particular features. As Kress et al. (2001) indicated, scientific drawing was not an artistic impression or a display of the natural features. It needed to be precise and show the scientific features of the items being drawn accurately. The writing accompanying the drawing also had to use the appropriate language and structure for a science report or scientific procedure, depending upon the purpose and content of the writing. As Unsworth pointed out, this adds a further layer of knowledge necessary for the teachers of disciplines and the assessment of students' writing in those disciplines. Anstey and Bull (2013) observed this issue in one of their long-term action learning projects with some teachers from the Catholic Education system in Brisbane, Queensland. A group of teachers of history from a secondary school realised that some students knew and understood the historical concepts and content they were reporting but were unable to use the semiotic systems and their codes and conventions appropriately to convey this through the multimodal text they were required to construct as part of their assessment. The teachers realised the need to analyse the multimodal texts of history they were requiring students to use (consume) and produce, that is identify the multimodal literacies of history. Having identified the features, the teachers then needed to teach students about the codes and conventions of the semiotic systems they were requiring students to use when creating multimodal accounts of historic events. The teachers also realised the need to re-examine their assessment of these texts. In a multimodal world, teachers across all disciplines need to be teachers of literacy and highly literate in, and about, their discipline. As Unsworth (2015, pp. 272-273) concluded,

> [it is]… essential… all teachers… have explicit knowledge about the ways in which genre and grammar are entailed in knowledge building in their disciplines, but it also appears that knowledge about the meaning making resources of images are crucial to understanding the role of this mode in such disciplinary knowledge building.

Perhaps the words 'all five semiotic systems' should replace 'images' in this quote from Unsworth, as so many of the resources used to learn in the disciplines (e.g. film, photographs, maps, diagrams, formulae) as well as the texts student produce involve the visual, spatial, audio gestural and linguistic semiotic systems. In fact, an image may draw upon all these semiotic systems depending upon the technology used to convey it.

It is now appropriate to examine how these challenges of teaching writing using technology and multimodal texts have been addressed in the 21st century through modifying the two approaches that have dominated the teaching of writing, the writing process and genre.

Redeveloping the process approach to writing in response to changing technologies and multimodal texts

A number of researchers have re-examined the writing process movement of the 1980s, seeking to understand its relevance to teaching about the process of writing using changing technologies to produce multimodal texts. Kervin (2015) re-presented the core ideas of the writing process emphasising:

- That time was a key factor and it was important to allow time for all stages of the writing process
- That students were more invested in and motivated about their writing if they had a degree of ownership, for example choosing their own topic
- The need to engage in writing daily
- Relating learning about the mechanics of writing to the real contexts of reading and writing.

Kervin (2015) pointed out that there were many digital tools that assist with different stages of the writing process and facilitate the production of a multimodal text. For example there are apps such as Voice Record Pro for oral rehearsal or planning, Popplet for outlining, Evernote with note-making tools to assist with keeping track of digital research, tools that facilitate the placement of text and images and the addition of interactive elements to a text, online synonym finders to aid vocabulary selection and editing tools for spelling and grammar. There are also apps and software that actually aid the process of creating the text and getting feedback from, or collaborating with, other writers, for example Google Docs, GarageBand, Puppet Pals and Book Creator. Kervin (2015) concluded that part of teaching about the writing process in a multimodal age was incorporating learning about and using these tools. In addition, students need to learn how to review and select the appropriate software and apps to suit their writing purpose. She suggested that students needed to consider whether features of the app would assist in fulfilling the particular aspects of the text that were required. Drawing upon the work of Kervin (2015), students might consider the following questions as they relate to the students' needs. Will this app assist me to produce a text that:

- Achieves my purpose in producing the text?
- Is suited to the characteristics of my intended audience and will facilitate better communication with them?
- Aids organisation of the text in terms of structure appropriate to the text type or genre and layout for paper or screen?
- Incorporates the semiotic systems I need to use – linguistic, visual, audio, spatial and gestural?
- Incorporates the multiple modes I wish to use (e.g. sounds, images and words)?

Kervin (2015) also commented that the availability of multiple modes (the codes and conventions of five semiotic systems) may mean students simply use all of them in their multimodal text without discerning decision-making. Many teachers can probably recall when PowerPoint presentations first emerged in schools and students used all the options available – sound effects, fading screens, multiple slide designs and a range of fonts – all in one presentation. Kervin (2015) pointed out that it was essential that students' decision-making was focussed on selecting and using only those components that suit the purpose and audience of the text, creating coherent and logical relationships among and between those used. As discussed in Chapter Three, when composing a multimodal text decisions should be made about which semiotic systems would be best to combine to achieve the communicative purpose desired for the audience and context and then choose the technologies, apps and software that enable that selection to be combined effectively. For example, decisions may need to be made about if, and how, the linguistic, audio (e.g. sounds and music) and visual (e.g. colour and line in images or diagrams) might be used together with the spatial when designing screen or page. The need for students to develop understandings about how the codes and conventions of the semiotic systems in a multimodal text can be used to show the relative importance of **meaning making elements** and provide coherence throughout a text was addressed in some detail in Chapter Three which focussed on the five semiotic systems. The reader may wish to re-read this chapter for further information and understanding about this aspect of creating multimodal texts.

Lipscombe et al. (2015, p.285) reviewed previous approaches to the teaching of writing and identified the following characteristics of a good writer, which could be applied to the use of technology and construction of multimodal texts:

- Able to use a range of practices and understands that different stages of the writing process vary in importance depending upon purpose, context and audience.
- Understands that they must find out about their audience and make appropriate decisions about their writing based on this knowledge.
- Understands that as a writer they have the power to position readers and persuade them to take on particular points of view and beliefs.
- Makes careful choices about which semiotic systems and technologies they might use, the text type, text structure and the relationships between and among the modes of their multimodal text.
- Knows that the process of seeking and giving critique and feedback during the writing process supports and enhances the recursive nature of the process and achieving their communicative purpose.

An interesting aspect of the influence of technology on the writing process arose from careful observation of students as they engaged with technology during the production of a text. Lipscombe et al. (2015), Edwards-Groves (2011, 2012) and Dix and Cawkwell (2011) all observed that students were more motivated, willing and likely to revise when using technology. Lipscombe et al. (2015) observed students actively seeking responses and further information from peers, technology experts and teachers. In the case of Edwards-Groves's research (2012), student interviews revealed that the additional context of working collaboratively and the talk among students during decision-making facilitated revision. Dix and Cawkwell (2011) reported that teachers found the role of group response and dialogue during sharing and revising as they engaged in writing as part of their professional could be successfully transferred to classroom practice. As discussed in Chapter Four, the role of talk in learning and particularly dialogic talk among, and between, teacher and students is critical to students developing understanding more about the processes they are engaging in and their relevance to learning. The work of Coiro et al. (2014) and Sekeres et al. (2014) cited in Chapter Five also indicated that collaborative work and talk around text and task when accessing the internet for research (for reading or writing) was beneficial.

　　The work of Kervin (2015), Lipscombe et al. (2015) and Edwards-Groves (2011, 2012) indicates that just like reading, the writing process, when enacted with new technologies and the production of multimodal texts, requires high levels of cognition, metacognition, planning and decision-making. Therefore, teaching about the writing process must include the modelling and teaching of these thinking processes and the development of skills and strategies that aid them. Kalantzis et al. (2016) described the writing process as a complex social and cognitive learning process. Their updated model of the writing process incorporated similar stages to earlier and more recent versions (plan, draft, review, revise, publish), and they emphasised the recursive nature of the process. However, they added three dimensions to the process that are particularly useful in illuminating the complexity and interactive nature of the process. They talked about the social dimension, the metalinguistic and design grammar dimension and the cognitive and metacognitive dimension. Their point was that the cycle was not only recursive in terms of the process (e.g. the planning, drafting or revising stages), but at each of these stages these three dimensions were involved and cycled between as well. For example a student is revising and therefore re-examining their text themselves but also seeking response from others in both person-to-person or digital means (social dimension). As they are doing this, they are thinking about the responses and responding to them, self-managing and monitoring, deciding which to take on and which to reject, and reviewing the responses in relation to their overall purpose. In other words, they are engaging in the cognitive and metacognitive dimension. However, in order to engage in the social, metacognitive and metacognitive dimension of their revising, they also need to draw upon their knowledge of all five semiotic systems, the technology they have been using and what they know about design and production of text. They also have to know and understand the terminology being used to describe all these aspects. They are engaging in the metalanguage and design grammar dimension. These three dimensions are being engaged with simultaneously throughout each stage of the writing process.

　　If the complexities of reading and writing online as part of the writing process are added to the dimensions discussed by Kalantzis et al. (2016), then the decision-making during the writing process is potentially endless, meaning that just as in reading, planning the process completely before commencing writing is not possible. In Chapter Five, the work of Hartman et al. (2010) suggested that the task of reading online was dynamic and the possibilities of combinations and numbers of text, author, task, activity, reader relationships almost infinite. They described it as 'n-adic', where 'n' is unknown until the actual consumption of text occurs. The observations of students producing multimodal texts with technology by Kervin (2015), Lipscombe et al. (2015) and Edwards-Groves (2011, 2012) confirm the complexity of the process when technology is added to the production of multimodal texts. Every decision about using technology to produce the text gives rise to myriad other decisions. Just as no two readers will read a text the same way, no two writers will produce a text the same way. Therefore, understanding the process and having strategies for decision-making, having a metalanguage to talk about all the aspects of the writing process and the semiotic systems and technologies involved, together with metacognitive strategies that enable the process are essential. To teach writing as though it is a static rather than a dynamic process is inappropriate. Opportunities for collaboration and dialogic talk around modelling the physical and mental process involved, deconstruction of texts, joint construction of text, play with technology and writing, making errors and taking responsibility are essential.

　　These descriptions of the complexity of the writing process echo the descriptions of the complexity of the reading process discussed in Chapter Five, and much of the knowledge, skills and processes are the same, simply used in different ways. The metalanguage around the semiotic systems, text types and technology is the same except for specialised terms for the writing process like 'drafting'. Many of the cognitive skills such as critical analysis, synthesising, planning and being strategic are the same, as are the metacognitive skills such as self-regulation and self-monitoring. Similarly, the design process and concepts of audience and purpose are all common to both the reading process and writing process. This is why it is essential to engage in dialogue around the two processes to help students understand the relationships between reading and writing and how these skills, knowledges and processes can be employed in both consuming and producing text.

Redeveloping the genre approach to writing, together with writing and inquiry in other disciplines, in response to changing technologies and multimodal texts

As previously discussed in Chapter Five and the early part of this chapter, the research around genre arose from a belief that it was necessary for students to understand the texts of the content areas in order to be able to consume and produce texts that were specific to the disciplines. The knowledge was considered essential to learning in the content areas and being able to engage in research and inquiry in these areas. The initial focus was on the linguistic feature of texts in other disciplines, and this has largely continued to be the case. Unsworth (2015) pointed out that while there has been a large body of research on analysing images and developing a metalanguage around images, the interface of images and linguistic text in multimodal text has not been explored extensively, nor has the teaching of multimodal authoring. Kress and van Leeuwen (2006) examined the placement of images in text, and as previously discussed, Kress (2001) identified the fact that the particular types of images were associated with particular disciplines. However, Unsworth (2015) made an important point and is one of the few researchers who has examined the role of other semiotic systems in multimodal text and has endeavoured to develop an approach to examining the visual and linguistic text and the interrelationships between images and words in picture books. (See the research of Barton and Unsworth (2014) on music and sound in multimodal text reported in Chapter Five and the work of Painter et al. (2013), who developed and applied a social semiotic and multimodal discourse analysis of children's picture books based on systemic functional theory.)

Kalantzis et al. (2016, p. 171) provided an overview of the typical genres in curriculum areas, and researchers such as Derewianka (1990, 2011) and Derewianka and Jones (2016) have provided detailed information on the linguistic and structural characteristics of the linguistic aspects of text types associated with specific disciplines, together with a grammar and metalanguage for analysing them. However, given the ways in which multimodal texts are produced and the technologies employed, limiting analysis of material to the linguistic and images does not provide assistance to students learning to consume and produce multimodal texts. Multimodal texts may employ moving images as well as still images, and these may come from the audio, gesture, spatial, linguistic and visual semiotic systems. They may also use diagrams, table and figures. The overall design of the text may employ particular visual or spatial codes and conventions. Therefore, it is necessary to examine multimodal texts in terms of all five semiotic systems in order to understand how they cohere and make meaning. As discussed in Chapter Five, Bull and Anstey (2010a) and Anstey and Bull (2011a) sought to provide a metalanguage to aid talk around multimodal texts by firstly identifying the five semiotic systems and developing a set of codes and conventions (metalanguage) for use when deconstructing, consuming and producing text. Their work can assist teachers using the genre approach by providing tools for analysis and a metalanguage for use in the modelling and joint construction stages of the genre approach.

Rossbridge with Rushton (2015) adapted the genre approach in order to address multimodal texts. Firstly, they grouped the genres or text types in terms of three social purposes for writing, imaginative, informative and persuasive. They also acknowledged that some text types might be used in several disciplines but would have different characteristics because of the requirements of that discipline, for example recount in fiction and a historical recount. In addition, they sought to respond to the multimodal nature of texts by acknowledging the role of the visual in text. They suggested that it was necessary to analyse and discuss both linguistic (or verbal) and visual choices made in the construction of a text, but their model did not encompass audio aspects of multimodal text. Using the concepts of field, tenor and mode (previously discussed when examining genre approaches to reading in Chapter Five), together with the three-stage genre approach (modelling, deconstruction and joint construction), Rossbridge with Rushton (2015) suggested that the visual text could be analysed in terms of how happenings, interactions and relationships, and design and layout were represented and demonstrated its application to imaginative, informative and persuasive texts. They used a mixture of terminology that derived from the gestural, spatial and visual semiotic systems to conduct these analyses. The absence of a systematic examination of all five semiotic systems, together with the absence of an analysis of the interplay of the elements of the text (e.g. linguistic and visual), limits a comprehensive examination of multimodal text. Nevertheless, the work of Rossbridge and Rushton (2015) demonstrated how the genre approach can be further developed to address the changing nature of multimodal texts and incorporate a more systematic way of examining the codes and conventions of the semiotic systems used both within each element and across the text. Table 6.2 summarises the Rossbridge and Rushton (2015) approach to examining the visual text. It can be seen that in order to realise the foci to explore field, tenor and mode in the visual text, the codes and conventions of several semiotic systems would have to be employed. For example, particular characteristics of the setting may be depicted through visual codes such as colour and the spatial codes of point of view and **framing**. Therefore, it would be useful to apply these analyses in a more systematic way using the metalanguage of all five semiotic systems.

Table 6.2 Summary of the approach Rossbridge with Rushton (2015) developed to analyse the visual text in a multimodal text

Field, Tenor and Mode in Visual Text	Foci for Examining How Visual Choices Realise Field, Tenor and Mode
Field: Happenings	• Participants • How actions are depicted • How setting is depicted • Conceptual or symbolic aspects of happenings
Tenor: Interactions and relationships	• Gaze – to viewer, between participants • **Proximity** between participants • Angles between participants • Colour • Indicators of modality or authenticity of what is depicted
Mode: Design and layout	• **Salience** • Reading path placement • Layout and framing

Writing, researching and learning in the content areas

One of the key issues that has emerged in this section of the chapter that focusses on current research and approaches to the teaching of writing has been how to approach the ramifications of technology and multimodal texts to writing in the content areas. As discussed in Chapter Two, inquiry is a key process for learning in other disciplines or content areas and the consumption and production of multimodal texts by students occurs throughout the process of inquiry. The implications of the use of the internet and consumption of multimodal texts during inquiry in the content areas was discussed in some detail in Chapter Five. However, as identified by teachers and students in the surveys reported earlier in this chapter (Lenhart et al., 2008; Purcell et al., 2013), writing occurs in many forms during the process of inquiry in other disciplines. Students make notes when planning to search the internet identifying key-words and phrase that might help refine the search and then adjusting those notes as they search. They then make notes from the multimodal text identified as useful to their inquiry. Later these notes may be converted to paragraphs or diagrams, flow charts or tables as part of their production of a report on their inquiry or they may select or produce images to incorporate in their multimodal report. The research of Lipscombe et al. (2015), Edwards-Groves (2012) and Kervin (2015), reported earlier in this chapter, indicated that during this process students might use various apps and software to aid their internet searching, note-making, and production of a multimodal text.

Earlier in the chapter, the origins of the genre approach which emerged from researchers' concern about students' ability to write in the genres of the disciplines of the content areas were discussed (Martin, 1993; Martin & Rothery, 1993). Being able to write in the genres or text types of the content areas also requires having the ability to research, process and collate multiple paper and digital sources of information in order to write some of these genres. The process of inquiry and writing and the use of technology at each stage of the process has been the focus of recent research. Coiro has been one of the leading researchers in this area in terms of both the reading and writing processes, as reported in Chapter Five. Most recently in work that focussed on the relationships between writing and inquiry, Kiili et al. (2016) developed an online inquiry tool to facilitate the process. The development of the tool arose from concerns that students had difficulty explor-ing controversial issues or open-ended questions on the internet and then formulating an essay to present supporting arguments and counterarguments. As Kiili et al. (2016) reported, at its simplest level researching and learning online involves locating, evaluating, comparing, contrasting and integrating ideas from multiple sources. However, as students move through the school and begin to explore controversial issues from multi-ple perspectives and viewpoints, inquiry requires a lighter level of critical thinking and analysis as the actual arguments and justifications supporting these different perspectives have to be identified and considered. Therefore, Kiili et al. (2016) investigated the development of digital and instructional scaffolding to aid stu-dents in the process of inquiry. The goal was that students would think critically and deeply about the different points of view and synthesise arguments as they engaged with different sources during their inquiry rather than engage in note-taking from each source and then commence comparing, contrasting, thinking criti-cally and synthesising. The theoretical basis of the tool drew on the five practices that inform problem-based inquiry: generating important questions, locating, evaluating information critically, synthesising and com-municating learned information Coiro (2011). The role of argumentation and deep level understanding was also explored together with transactive reasoning – questioning, explanation, justification and elaboration of ideas. The importance of metacognition and self-monitoring and regulation to all these processes was also acknowledged. Kiili et al. (2016) identified research that indicated when investigating controversial issues and open-ended questions, students had difficulty reporting arguments and counterarguments to justify their conclusions. Therefore, facilitating the identification and synthesising of arguments and counterarguments was identified as an important feature of the tool's development. The tool also facilitated identification of the perspectives that might be taken about the topic (e.g. environmental, political or financial), thus helping students to develop questions from those perspectives to facilitate their reading and note-taking. Most importantly the design of the tool enabled students to put their notes together in such a way that they could view arguments and counterarguments across the screen and then write a synthesis on the far right of the screen. There was also a facility to record the URL for future reference and to rate the authority of the source using traffic lights. As students explored different perspective down the screen, they could compare their information vertically and horizontally. The theory behind designing a tool that facilitated students synthesising arguments during the process was that it would aid students when reviewing their research to plan the writing of the essay, including the presentation of arguments and counterarguments to justify the position they have taken. Kiili et al. (2016) emphasised that it was not the digital tool that aided students' meaning making, but the pedagogy and talk surrounding the introduction of the tool and discussion of the processes and thinking it facilitated. They also pointed out that the tool could be used both collaboratively and individually. Previous research by Coiro reported in Chapter Five (Coiro, 2011, 2014; Coiro et.al., 2014) indicates that the talk around collaborative work with the internet and associated tools (particularly in pairs) aids students' learning. The work of Kiili et al. (2016) once again emphasises the links between inquiry, reading and writing and the fact that pedagogy and talk are just as important to learning to produce and consume multimodal texts as the technological tools that aid the process.

How recent research on writing informs the teaching of writing

As the preceding discussion of recent research has indicated, there have been no new approaches to the teaching of writing developed in response to technological advances and multimodal texts. However, the process approach and the genre approach have been the subject of review and redevelopment in response to the use of technology in writing and the production of multimodal texts.

One focus of research has been the examination of students' and teachers' perceptions about writing, technology and multimodal texts. Surveys of teachers and students up to 2012 indicated mismatches between teacher and student beliefs and perceptions about writing, multimodal texts and technology. This research indicates that it is useful to conduct surveys or discuss with students their perceptions about writing as well as identify the perceptions about writing held by teachers in the school. If there are different understandings about what writing is, its importance, the role of technology and multimodal texts among students and teachers, then it is possible that it is interrupting learning. Research about the social and cultural influences around writing by Mills and Dreamson (2015) reinforced this issue and indicated that understanding the school community, its social and cultural values and beliefs about writing is essential to developing appropriate pedagogy.

A large body of the current research has involved the careful examination of how students go about writing when engaging with technology in the production of multimodal texts. This research identified factors that were beneficial to students learning about the production of multimodal texts and the use of technology in writing. These were:

- Developing understandings about the similarities and difference between writing for page and screen
- Developing metalanguage around technology, the writing process and the five semiotic systems employed in producing multimodal texts
- Providing opportunities for students to learn about the selection and use of appropriate technology such as apps and software when writing

- Teaching metacognitive and self-monitoring and self-regulation strategies specific to the writing process because of the complexity of writing with technology and producing multimodal texts
- Examining the construction of multimodal text in specific disciplines and content areas, actively teaching writing across all content areas
- Developing skills specific to researching, inquiry and writing both online and with other technologies in the content areas
- Providing opportunities for talk around the writing process and the use of technology
- Providing opportunities for collaborative writing, particularly when students are working on inquiry in the content areas and using online resources
- Balancing focussed learning episodes with time to explore and try out new technologies and work out their affordances
- Providing regular time for engaging with writing
- Providing more time for writing because writing with technology and multimodal texts is time-consuming and complex.

REFLECTION STRATEGY 6.5

- The purpose of this Reflection Strategy is to review the table you constructed in Reflection Strategy 6.4, in which you compared and contrasted historical theories and approaches to the teaching of writing, and add any further insights you have gained from the current research.
- Re-read the characteristics of a multiliterate person and understandings about multimodal text provided earlier and use this knowledge to review the current research in terms of the following general question 'What is necessary but not sufficient about this research and pedagogy for producing (designing and redesigning) texts in a multimodal, multiliterate world?'
- Use the following minor questions to examine the current research and approaches in terms of the stages on Figure 6.2. How does current research:
    o Inform understandings about the role of purpose, audience and meaning when producing a multimodal text?
    o Contribute knowledge, skills and processes that become part of a repertoire of resources that aid the production of multimodal texts?
    o Provide knowledge, skills and strategies that inform the synthesising process of production (combining, recombining and reworking selected resources to make meaning)?
    o Provide knowledge, skills and strategies that inform the recording, preservation and dissemination of a multimodal text?
    o Develop understandings about the production of text as the transforming and transformation of meaning?
    o Contribute to the development of understandings about the relationships between the consumption and production of multimodal text?
- Examine your analyses and think about how they might inform your current methods of teaching writing. Are there aspects of your pedagogy that you would change in any way, and if so, how would you go about this?

The shaping of pedagogy around the teaching of writing

Much of the research about the teaching of writing that has been reviewed, both historical and current, has led to conclusions regarding pedagogy. Both positive aspects and critiques of the process approach and the genre approach were identified regarding the pedagogy of each approach. As discussed in relation to reading in Chapter Five, good intentions and knowledge about the teaching of reading can be interrupted by using pedagogies that do not support. The Action Learning Tasks and Reflection Strategies in this chapter have involved examining pedagogy and reflecting upon the ways in which it reflects beliefs and approaches to writing and is appropriate for the school community.

However, there are other factors that can shape how pedagogy around writing evolves, and this has been a major focus of research around writing in recent years. A significant theme has been the influence of high-stakes testing and the prescription of particular teaching practices, together with a changing focus on the aspects of writing being taught. This is because there has been an increasing trend globally to engage in high-stakes testing of literacy. In Australia, the National Assessment Program: Literacy and Numeracy (NAPLAN) was introduced in 2008 with students tested annually in years 3, 5, 7 and 9 and the results for each school (government and non-government) made public on the MySchool website (Turbill et al., 2015). In the U.S., national test-based accountability commenced in 2001 as part of the No Child Left Behind (NCLB) Act. This legislation required states to annually test reading, maths, and later science from grades 3 to 8 and one year of high school (Supovitz, 2009). In the U.K. the trend began in the late 1990s and was continued with the Primary Strategy introduced in 2003 (Alexander, 2004).

Applebee and Langer (2011) sought to update the data on the teaching of writing since the last extensive study conducted in 1979–1980 (Applebee, 1981). The focus of Applebee and Langer (2011) was on the amount of writing currently required of students, the audiences for student work, the impact of high-stakes testing, the approaches to writing instruction and the impact of technology. They focussed on middle and high school classes in English, maths, science and social studies across five U.S. states in schools identified as excellent in teaching writing. They found that students write more in English, but mostly a page or less, and only 19 per cent of students' writing overall was extended writing. Most writing was 'fill in the blank', short answer or copying notes. Students shared their writing with peers, other adults and groups occasionally, but mostly with the teacher. One of the reasons cited for the dominance of short-answer writing was that testing seldom required open-ended responses in any subject area and consequently teachers spent quite some time on test preparation and teaching 'timed writing' for test conditions (Applebee & Langer, 2011, p. 16). Teachers reported that this limited their time on the actual teaching of writing, and they had largely abandoned doing research projects with students because there was not time. The exception to this was in schools that were doing the International Baccalaureate, where more time was spent on writing and reflection as part of learning and testing (Applebee & Langer, 2011, p. 19). Interviews revealed that teachers understood appropriate techniques for teaching writing and observations in some schools indicated innovative and exciting pedagogy around the processes of writing and uses of technology, but competing priorities, teaching curriculum content for testing and teaching writing specific to test conditions and requirements prevented teachers from using the full range of pedagogies they knew were appropriate to fully develop students' writing ability.

The results of this research regarding the influence of technology were interesting, as less than a third of the classrooms made use of any technology (with the exception of maths), and when technology was used, it was by the teacher and largely for presenting information. When students did use technology, it was mainly to aid word processing or to find source materials on the internet and rarely involved the creation of multimodal texts using video, audio or graphics. Applebee and Langer (2011) concluded that the ways in which technology was being used simply reinforced traditional pedagogy with the teacher at the centre of instruction (Applebee & Langer, 2011, p. 23). They also found these results quite surprising given the national Assessment of Educational Progress had begun to assess students' writing progress using computers and computer software.

Applebee and Langer (2011, p. 25) found that as well as writing pedagogy being largely teacher centred, when students were provided with a tool to aid their writing, revision and self-evaluation, there was a tendency for this information to be in the form of a quite prescriptive rubric that was repetitive and resulted in formulaic writing (e.g. requiring discussion of three points or using five paragraphs).

The research of Applebee and Langer (2011, p. 26) identified a dissonance between teachers' understandings about writing pedagogy and the links between writing and learning, and the actual pedagogy and practices of the classroom. Teacher knowledge and understanding about writing pedagogy and its role in learning was simply not present in their practice. As observed and reported by the teachers themselves, their teaching practices were largely constrained by the time devoted to preparing students to write in the ways required for high-stakes testing and knowing content to present in that writing. Applebee and Langer (2011, p. 26) concluded 'Given the constraints imposed by high-stakes tests, writing as a way to study, learn and go beyond – as a way to construct knowledge or generate new networks of understandings (Langer, Envisioning Knowledge, Envisioning Literature) – is rare'.

The research and conclusions of Applebee and Langer (2011) are of some concern given the literature regarding the types of literacy skills, knowledge and processes that have been identified as necessary for students entering the workplace and participating fully in all aspects of everyday life in the 21st century (see Australia's Future Workforce? 2015; Benedikt & Osborne, 2013; Holman, Wall, Clegg, Sparrow, & Howard, 2005; The Foundation for Young Australians, 2017; Chapter One in the companion volume *Foundations of Multiliteracies: Reading, Writing and Talking in the 21st Century*). In addition, the conclusions of Applebee and Langer (2011) indicate that the focus of high-stakes testing and the ways in which it is constraining the teaching of writing are not conducive to developing multiliterate students.

These concerns and findings are not unique to the U.S. Alexander (2003a) suggested that the national curriculum literacy and numeracy programmes and high-stakes testing of their outcomes was influencing classroom talk and consequently the types of learning taking place. In other words it was shaping pedagogy in possibly negative ways. He suggested that because of the amount of content to cover, the **pace** of transmission would increase, and teacher talk would be dominant and privileged. He also suggested that teacher questioning would increase and questions would be largely closed. Alexander (2004) wrote further on the influences of curriculum and testing discussing the ambiguity of intent in, and implementation of, A Primary Strategy 2002-2007 (Department for Education and Skills, 2003a, 2003b). He compared statements about the autonomy of teachers with the guidelines for teaching and the regime of testing implemented by the Department for Education and Skills. He stated,

> Against the ostensible offer of autonomy, we have the continuing pressure of testing, targets and performance tables and the creeping hegemonisation of the curriculum by the Literacy and Numeracy Strategies, with three-part lessons, interactive whole class teaching and plenaries soon to become a template for the teaching of everything.
>
> (Alexander, 2004 p. 15)

Lefstein and Snell (2014) discussed the emphasis on 'best practice' that emerged from The National Literacy Strategy, part of which aimed to provide teachers with specific teaching methods that have been researched and identified as successful. They also had concerns about how the strategy was shaping pedagogy. While intent of this is noble, Lefstein and Snell (2014) pointed out that the assumption that one 'best practice' will transfer successfully to another social and cultural context and different groups of students, teachers and schools is a false one, and can only advance teacher practice to a certain extent. Furthermore, the professional development accompanying this approach emphasised demonstration (often through video) and imitation. Lefstein and Snell (2014, pp. 4–5) asserted that the assumptions about transferability and the methods of professional development ignore the complexities of teaching, presenting it as straightforward and simple. They pointed out that there are multiple factors that shaped the success of teaching, among them:

- The pupils, and the social dynamics among and between teacher and pupils,
- The different levels of ability and learning styles among the students,
- The content being taught and what it demands of students
- The supports in place from the institution (school) or system (e.g. a department of education)
- The physical setting and the teacher's individual skills, manner, values, knowledge and experience.

They suggested that a better approach to professional learning was to enable teachers to investigate successful pedagogies and practices identified in research in the context of their classrooms and discuss their practices with colleagues, sharing successes, challenges and breakthroughs. This recommendation that teachers themselves investigate the implementation of research in their own classroom is concomitant with that of Freebody (2011), which was discussed in Chapter Five and the concept of Action Learning underpinning this book. Such an approach is supported by theory and research, but has the advantage of further investigation and development as it is applied to the unique characteristics of the school, its teachers, students and community. An action learning approach to pedagogy results in the shaping of pedagogies that are robust because they are the result of the application of research and theory further developed for the community in which they are applied.

A further concern of Lefstein and Snell (2014) was that while particular dialogue around literacy learning had been identified as part of 'best practice', dialogue in classrooms needed to be examined in context. They used the example of some of the dialogue presented in their research, indicating that several excerpts occurred in the context of test preparation. They suggested that rather than looking at this dialogue in terms of whether it was 'good' or 'bad' practice, it should be examined in terms of its context: high-stakes test preparation. In this case, they suggested the better question to ask was how teachers and students manage the desire for extended dialogue to aid learning and understanding, with the need to fulfil institutional expectations of high-stakes testing. These are the sorts of issues a school can address as a community of learners conducting action learning in their classrooms and school.

In Australia, Wyatt-Smith and Jackson (2016) examined a possible relationship between the implementation of the NAPLAN in 2008 and a trend in students' results, which in 2015 indicated an increasing number of students falling below the benchmark. The original intent of the use of benchmarks was to inform teachers about the outcomes of their pedagogy and provide data to assist them in targeting areas of need (Wyatt-Smith, 1998). However, there is increasing concern among researchers that there are negative impacts from NAPLAN, in particular large periods of highly focussed instructional time given to teaching to the test and practicing items from previous test (Cumming et al., 2016; Comber & Cormack, 2013). As the tests occur in May, this means that it is possible that students spend a considerable part of the academic year, which commences at the end of January, learning about testing and focussing on a very narrow part of literacy. NAPLAN for literacy includes reading, writing and language conventions (spelling, grammar and punctuation). The parts associated with writing are language conventions, and writing a specific genre (which is identified prior to testing so teachers can prepare students) means that attention to writing is focussed on skills (taught and tested out of context) and writing one particular text type, where skills are also assessed as part of the assessment of the writing. This testing regime and its content does not reflect the conclusions and recommendations from research on the teaching of writing or the research about writing pedagogy that has been reported in this chapter. As Wyatt-Smith and Jackson (2016) concluded, there is a disconnect between the mandated assessment criteria and the English curriculum content and there is no attention to assessing students' progress in learning the process of writing or their ability to produce multimodal texts. High-stakes testing and what is being tested is shaping teachers' pedagogy and the focus of their teaching about writing.

Concerns about assessment and monitoring students' progress have also been raised by Mackenzie (2014), who reported that although NAPLAN testing did not occur until year 3, anecdotal evidence she had collected from large numbers of teachers indicated that teachers felt pressured to focus on the content of the NAPLAN writing test from the moment students entered school. Wohland (2008) had noted a focus on correctness of form in teacher responses to students' early attempts at invented writing, and Mackenzie (2014) had identified that teachers focussed on the linguistic part of the text and tended to ignore the role of images created as part of the text. This is at odds with findings of both historical and current research on the writing process that indicate opportunities for students to attempt writing should be provided and attempts at writing should be encouraged by teachers. These opportunities motivate students to take risks and responsibility and develop understanding that writing a draft for meaning is an important part of the process of crafting a final polished piece of writing for publication.

In addition, research indicates that drawing and writing text together is an important part of rehearsing complex thoughts (Mackenzie & Veresov, 2013). Drawing or creating visual images as part of a text is also part of creating multimodal text and therefore an important part of writing in the 21st century. Mackenzie (2014) followed up her anecdotal evidence by researching teachers' understandings of, and attitudes towards, early literacy development. Part of this included asking teachers to respond to a piece of writing by a student in the fifth week of schooling. The piece included writing, **symbols** (ticks) and a drawing of a female and an animal. The results confirmed Mackenzie's anecdotal findings. All participants responding to the writing focussed on the conventions of print (letters, words, punctuation, directional principles, accurate spelling) as strengths of the writing. Fifty-five per cent of the participants only responded to the conventions of print in the piece of writing. Interestingly, the results of the survey of attitudes and beliefs about literacy development all participants identified a need to understand the conventions of print and 60 per cent identified only conventions of print. The issue here is not whether knowing conventions of print is essential or not (clearly it is), but the balance with other aspects of writing development and the stage of schooling when this should be such a large focus in developing students' understandings about writing. Mackenzie (2014) also reported that in the survey of beliefs most participants agreed that helping children make meaning and express their ideas should be the highest priority of an early years writing program.

The dissonance between teachers' beliefs and practice is of concern. As Mackenzie (2014) pointed out, teachers' responses to, and assessment of, students' writing during the school day is often 'on the run',

and if their responses and talk about the students' writing focusses on conventions rather than meaning, this is sending very clear messages to students about what constitutes good writing. Reporting on
a three-year longitudinal study of the implementation of the writing process conducted by Anstey and
Bull in the 1980s, Anstey (1986) described students in early years of schooling who came from classrooms where conventions were over-emphasised. These students became reluctant to take risks or even
engage in writing beyond copying from 'readers' or known text. They focussed on conventions before
even attempting to write words, for example by first placing full stops at the end of each line. These past
and present results indicate how carefully teachers must monitor the match or mismatch between their
knowledge from research, their beliefs and their actual pedagogy and practice, with particular attention
to teacher and learner talk around text. Teachers need to be aware of the potential for high-stakes testing
and other systemic factors to shape their pedagogy in such a way that they focus on only certain aspects
of the teaching of writing. This is an issue that requires careful reflection regarding if, and how, it might
be addressed. It is both an individual and whole school issue that requires a carefully researched and
measured response.

Applying the Action Learning Cycle to improve the teaching of writing

The major focus of this book has been further exploration of **multiliteracies** through action learning
cycles, and this exploration has been facilitated by the provision of additional information about multiliteracies, the development of multiliteracies through particular pedagogies such as dialogic talk and
detailed information about the Action Learning Cycle together with tools to enable such investigations
to take place. One of the major tools in Chapter One was the Multiliteracies Matrix, which provided an
opportunity for the reader to reflect upon their current understandings of multiliteracies and to what
extent these concepts were being implemented in the classroom. Action Learning Tasks within specific
chapters provided opportunities for more detailed analysis of particular aspects of multiliteracies knowledge and teaching with regard to inquiry, talk, the semiotic systems, reading multimodal texts and in
this chapter, writing multimodal texts. The purpose of these tasks, together with Reflection Strategies,
Theory into Practice Activities and Auditing Instruments, was to provide opportunities for the reader to
examine areas of their beliefs, knowledge, pedagogy and practice with multiliteracies and consider if, and
how, they would like to further investigate, refine, change, improve or develop particular aspects in their
classroom. They also provided strategies and tools the reader could use or adapt to collect data during
their Action Learning Cycle. The Action Plan Proforma was provided to help frame and implement an
Action Learning Cycle that would enable this further investigation of multiliteracies to take place.

In terms of the teaching of writing, historic and current research indicates that there are major areas
around the teaching of writing that need to be addressed in order to teach multimodal authoring, using
a variety of technologies in such a way that students will be able to communicate in all aspects of their
lives using the semiotic systems, technology and text types that are currently used. The research also
indicates that it is necessary that the ways in which writing is taught now equip students with the knowledge, skills, understandings, beliefs and attitudes to respond to the way in which writing, communication
and the production of texts will evolve in the future. For example, issues such as design and redesign,
static and dynamic pedagogies, developing resilience, developing an attitude towards literacy as problem
solving and having the ability to use metacognitive skills and self-monitor were identified as contributing
to being able to respond to change.

A body of research is emerging that identifies a potential global mismatch between and among the expectations of education systems and curricula regarding teaching around multimodal texts, the provision of information and professional learning to support teachers in implementing curriculum expectations regarding the teaching around multiliteracies and multimodal texts and teacher knowledge about multiliteracies and multimodal text (Chandler, 2017). Much of the current research that has been reported in this chapter has identified the vast amount of knowledge, skills and processes important to teaching about multimodal texts – for example understanding technology and software, understanding the actual process of producing multimodal text, having a metalanguage to talk about technology, knowing and being able to analyse and use the codes and conventions of the semiotic systems present in multimodal texts, understanding text structures and how multimodal texts are constructed in different disciplines, and being able to learn through multimodal texts in order to produce a multimodal text to demonstrate learning.

Chandler (2017), concerned about this potential mismatch, investigated fifty-five upper primary school teachers' understanding about some of these and other areas before they implemented a unit of work on multimodal composition that was part of a 3DMAP project implemented in four Australian states. The 3DMAP project was designed to engage students in multimodal authoring. The results indicated that in general respondents were not well prepared to teach about the production of multimodal texts. They did not have the relevant knowledge about technology and software, a metalanguage for talking about the design of multimodal texts or knowledge about, or metalanguage for, the codes and conventions of the semiotic systems in multimodal texts. While they had some knowledge about the genres or text types, this was mostly limited to the text types that had dominated NAPLAN tests (narrative and persuasive), and the level of knowledge about these text types varied greatly. Most teachers were committed to teaching the process of writing but did not have the skills and knowledge specific to the process of producing multimodal texts. Chandler (2017) reported that knowledge was often idiosyncratic to schools where a local school culture or metalanguage had been adopted. He also noted that the source of teachers' knowledge was reported as self-taught or from colleagues, and that while younger teachers had more knowledge (having recently emerged from teacher education) and late career teachers had sought knowledge through professional learning that was available or from colleagues, mid-career teachers had the lowest level of knowledge. These findings are not necessarily a reflection on teachers' desire or ability to teach about multimodal texts. As Chandler pointed out, it identifies a need for systemic action by schools, school systems and teachers themselves to address the gaps in knowledge.

So the question is, what can teachers do while they are waiting for adequate and systemic responses that provide specific curriculum knowledge and professional learning to facilitate the systemic demand that teachers teach about multimodal text and multiliteracies? A growing body of research about the teaching of writing has addressed building teachers' knowledge and expertise in writing through Action Learning Cycles that combine engagement with the writing process themselves, and attempting to implement a more process-oriented approach to the teaching of writing. Several of these pieces of research have specifically focussed on addressing teaching the process of writing with multimodal texts. Cremin and Baker (2010, 2014) postulated that many teachers were not necessarily regularly engaged in writing themselves and therefore did not have an identity as a writer. This in turn made it hard for them to break down the processes of writing and empathise with students about the challenges, decision-making and level of complexity involved in writing. They also suggested that if teachers were not regularly engaged in writing, then it was difficult for them to model the processes involved and identify a consistent vocabulary or metalanguage for articulating the process. Cremin and Baker (2010) investigated these ideas with a small group of teachers in the U.K. who endeavoured to engage in writing themselves and 'become writers' as they taught the writing process to their students. As Cremin and Baker (2010) acknowledged, the study was small but its results revealed that while the teachers found being a writer as well as a teacher of writing was difficult and created some tensions for them when teaching, it did provide better understanding of the students' struggles with the process. Issues arose for the teachers in moving from revealing their struggles as a writer to students and then moving on to the role of teacher of writing, that is moving from the personal to the professional. They concluded that it was necessary to share the personal aspects of the writing process when writing alongside students and return to the professional role of teacher when modelling and demonstrating the craft of writing and teaching aspects such as textual features (Cremin & Baker, 2010, pp. 26–28). One of the other outcomes was that this struggle between the personal and professional helped teachers understand better how their use of language and their actions position and influence young writers. Cremin & Baker (2014) wrote further about teachers as writers and writer identities and suggested that teachers need to reflect upon themselves as writers and the writing they engaged in outside the school context and then use this knowledge to find a range of ways in which they can model being a writer in the classroom. Cremin and Myhill (2012) offered a series of questions that would assist teachers in exploring themselves as writers. These can be summarised as follows:

- What kind of writing do you do?
- What do you enjoy writing most and why?
- What do you dislike most writing and why?
- Do you choose to write outside school?
- Do you use multimedia to write (e.g. Facebook, blogs)?
- What do you see as your strengths and weaknesses as a writer?
- What helps you write?
- What do you remember about learning to write, and what assisted and what did not?

Cremin and Baker (2014) suggested that addressing these questions when actually engaging in writing themselves might assist teachers in modelling how a motivated writer might engage with others. They identified some of the roles a teacher could adopt and model in the classroom as a result:

- engaged and reflective reader
- authentic demonstrator of writing in front of the whole class
- scribe for class compositions
- fellow writer, writing alongside students in small group contexts
- response partner
- editor, co-editor and adviser
- publisher of their own and their students' work
- writer in their everyday lives.

(Cremin & Baker, 2014, p. 5)

In New Zealand, Dix and Cawkwell (2011) responded to concerns that national assessment data indicated students were performing better in reading than writing and research indicating teachers themselves reported that they lacked confidence in teaching of writing, by designing and implemented a two-year research project to address both issues. The teachers engaged in writing workshops that built their understanding of themselves as writers and their writing abilities. Simultaneously the teachers were assisted to shape and implement a related action learning project around their teaching of writing. The goal was to examine how creating a community of writers among the teachers as they met regularly and shared their writing and received input from outside experts might assist them in their teaching of writing. While there were a range of outcomes that Dix and Cawkwell (2011) detailed in three case studies from the project, the overarching outcome was that as teachers engaged in writing as a community of learners these experiences informed their ability to build a community of learners in the classroom.

REFLECTION STRATEGY 6.6

- The purpose of this Reflection Strategy is to think about yourself as a writer, the characteristics of your writer identity and consider the implications for your pedagogy and talk around the teaching of writing. This could be an individual, year level, discipline group or whole school Reflection Strategy. If working as a group, share and discuss the task related to each dot point.
- Use the previously presented summary of questions that Cremin and Myhill (2012) developed to summarise your identity as a writer.
- How might your writer identity be shaping your pedagogy around the writing process? Are there aspects you could use to inform your pedagogy?
- How might your writer identity be shaping your pedagogy around the use of technology for writing and the production of multimodal texts?
- Do you feel you need to expand your writer identity to inform your pedagogy around the teaching of writing? How might you go about this?

As previously reported, Edwards-Groves (2012) used an Action Learning Model that incorporated professional learning for teachers about multimodal texts and contemporary writing practices together with changing classroom pedagogy around technology in the classroom. Her findings indicated that pedagogy does not change simply because teachers know more about technology or multimodal texts. The context of an Action Learning Model created the opportunity for teacher dialogue about the changes they were making, challenges, and successes. It was this dialogue, which encouraged reflection on their pedagogy, together with the expanding knowledge from the professional learning, that changed pedagogy and in particular, the talk in the classrooms. These findings reflect those of Anstey & Bull (2014), who conducted a twelve-month Action Learning Project around multiliteracies and multimodal texts in a Catholic primary school in a suburb of Brisbane, Queensland. The principal reflected upon the process once it was complete and the teachers had presented a report on the process and outcomes of their action learning at a staff meeting. He commented that he had provided professional learning opportunities through attendance at seminars and professional learning courses for staff over seven years but teachers' pedagogy had not changed until engagement in the Action Learning Cycle. He concluded that the combination of a whole school focus, and individual ownership and responsibility for investigating an aspect of their practice, was the reason for this development. The school had become a community of learners and planned to continue engaging in action learning cycles. Individual teachers commented that engagement with the process had challenged them to think about how they engaged with students and talk more with their colleagues.

ACTION LEARNING TASK 6.3

- The purpose of this Action Learning Task is to use the information in this chapter together with knowledge of the students, school and community in which your school is situated, to develop an appropriate set of beliefs and principles to guide the planning, pedagogy and practice around the teaching of writing in your school. If the teaching of writing is a school or personal focus in your action plan, then this task may be useful as a way of reflecting upon, and taking action as a result of professional reading about the teaching of writing.
- Review your work in Action Learning Tasks 6.1 and 6.2, in which you reflected upon what you currently know and believe about the teaching of writing and how it has changed as you read this chapter.
- Conduct final revisions to the sentences you originally wrote about the following items and rewrite them to reflect what you now think:
  o   Why you think it is important to teach writing,
  o   What aspects of writing you think are important to teach,
  o   What approach to teaching writing you currently use and why you have chosen this approach.
- Next, consider the characteristics of your students, the school, the community, the system and curriculum and how they relate to, or inform, the information you have been collating. Consider also your own background, experiences and general beliefs about teaching generally and the teaching of writing in particular that might inform these considerations.
- Extrapolate from these considerations a set of the beliefs you feel would inform the teaching about writing and production of multimodal texts in your school. Then try to develop a set of principles about planning, pedagogy and practice that will help you translate your beliefs when planning for the teaching of writing and inform your pedagogy and practice. It may be useful to think in terms of the following:
  o   'If I believe ... about the teaching of reading, then I need to...'. For example, 'If I believe that understanding the process of writing is important for students, then I must ensure my planning, pedagogy and talk includes modelling the process and opportunities for students to explore and discuss how they engage with the process'.
- Clearly there might be several 'then statements' for each 'belief statement'.
- It will take a considerable time, reflection and discussion with colleagues to begin this process and then revise, reorganise and refine it. However, if it is done carefully and revised regularly as part of a continuous cycle of action learning, then pedagogy and practice will be better aligned with your beliefs and knowledge about the teaching of writing and social and cultural

background and needs of your students and their community. If done as a whole school, it will lead to a consistent approach to planning, pedagogy and practice around the teaching of reading across the school.

- Reference Chapter One on Action Research, Chapter Two on Inquiry, Chapter Three on Dialogic talk, Chapter Four on the semiotic systems and Chapter Five on the teaching of reading may then be useful to inform translation of the beliefs and principles into practice.

ACTION LEARNING TASK 6.4

- The purpose of this Action Learning Task is to audit the commonly used strategies, activities and tasks that you use to teach writing. It is important to review commonly used strategies to ensure awareness of the original learning purpose, relevance to current understandings about the teaching of writing and exactly when and why they might be used. This in turn would inform the talk that is conducted around the activity to ensure its utility is clearly discussed with students.
- Review your planning for a preceding unit of work and list the strategies, activities, and tasks that you have used. Audit the list in terms of how often they are used and reflect upon the variation in use. Why are some used more frequently and some not?
- Retrieve any school-based resources that have been developed, such as lists of strategies and activities that teachers are encouraged to draw upon. Audit the list against your analyses of the strategies you use most frequently and consider the match and mismatch in terms of use.
- Go back to the list of characteristics of a multiliterate person and the understandings about text presented in this chapter, together with Figure 6.2 which shows the design process and examine the strategies being used in terms of how they facilitate these ideas about the teaching of producing multimodal text.
- If you have begun to develop your beliefs and principles, examine the strategies in terms of whether they facilitate pedagogy and practices that would implement these beliefs and principles.
- Generate lists of strategies that would facilitate pedagogy and practices around the teaching of research skills and the production of multimodal texts that would implement these beliefs and principles.
- For each strategy, identify the learning purposes about writing that it would fulfil. Use this list together with the identified learning purposes as a resource for planning the teaching of writing as a way of ensuring your beliefs and principles are matched by your planning, pedagogy and practice.

Conclusion

The focus of this chapter has been on writing and in particular the influence of technology and the production multimodal text. It began with a discussion of what writing is and the challenges involved in producing text, particularly in a multiliterate world, and at various points re-examined designing and redesigning text and the connections between consuming and producing text. The contributions of both historical and current research to the teaching of writing were explored together with the associated pedagogies. Finally, the role of pedagogy was discussed and how action research in classrooms can inform pedagogy about producing multimodal texts in the 21st century.

Two key issues emerged regarding the teaching of writing, the critical role of pedagogy and talk. Regardless of which approach is used, whether producing traditional paper text or multimodal text using a variety of technology or researching online to learn through writing, the ways in which pedagogy and talk facilitated this process were identified as critical. Critiques of both process and genre approaches focussed on pedagogy and much of the investigation of the impact of technology indicated that pedagogy must change to address the complexity of writing multimodal texts. It concluded that it was necessary to teach not only skills to do with technology, but the metacognitive strategies, higher order thinking skills, attitudes and resilience that students will need to problem solve as the focus of writing, ways of producing text and reasons for writing evolve and change with the changes in society. In particular, it is apparent that there must be balance between focussed learning episodes of explicit talk and dialogic talk for exploration, discussion, play, response and modelling. It is imperative to select the appropriate ways of conducting talk between and among students and teacher.

The research also indicated that auditing practice around the teaching of writing regularly is important in order to check that the teaching of writing is responding to the changing practices of writing in society and the impact of technology. Teachers should be auditing their planning and practice in terms of balance among the semiotic systems, technology, software exploration, multimodal texts, traditional paper texts, teaching the process of writing, text types, grammar of all five semiotic systems and developing salience and coherence within, and among, the semiotic systems and meaning making elements of text.

Finally, the increasing politicisation of literacy and the introduction of high-stakes testing regimes, and the foregrounding of particular content and teaching strategies, emerged as a theme in the research around the teaching of writing. Though these issues affect all aspects of literacy and also numeracy, the impact on writing pedagogy and subsequent fall in achievement on testing has been raised by a range of international researchers. How teachers respond to this issue is a difficult problem, but it does indicate the need for constant reflection on teaching practices and being aware of the possible reasons for changes identified in teaching practices.

All the issues identified as critical to the teaching of writing about multimodal texts indicate the need for teachers to continuously engage in Action Learning Cycles, taking current theory and research into their classrooms, collecting data and examining its effectiveness in their specific teaching context, translating and transforming their practice and sharing it with their community of learners, that is their colleagues and their students.

BIBLIOGRAPHY

The Access Center: Improving Outcomes for All Students K-8 2006, 'Science Inquiry: The Link to Accessing the General Educational Curriculum', Research Report, U.S. Department of Education, Washington, DC.

Adelman, C. 1993, 'Kurt Lewin and the origins of action research', *Educational Action Research*, vol. 1, no. 1, pp. 7-24.

Afflerbach, P. & Cho, B. Y. 2008, 'Identifying and describing constructively responsive comprehension strategies in new and traditional forms of reading', in S. Israel & G. Duffy (eds), *Handbook of Reading Comprehension Research*, Erlbaum, Mahwah, NJ, pp. 69-90.

Alexander, R. J. 2001a, 'Border crossings: Towards a comparative pedagogy', *Comparative Education*, vol. 37, no. 4, pp. 507-523.

Alexander, R. J. 2001b, *Culture and Pedagogy: International Comparisons in Primary Education*, Blackwell, Oxford.

Alexander, R. J. 2003a, 'Talk in teaching and learning: International perspectives', New Perspectives on Spoken English in the Classroom, Discussion Papers, Qualification and Curriculum Authority, London, pp. 27-37.

Alexander, R. J. 2003b, *Talk for Learning: The First Year*, North Yorkshire County Council, Northallerton.

Alexander, R. J. 2004a, 'Still no pedagogy? Principle, pragmatism and compliance in primary education', *Cambridge Journal of Education*, vol. 34, no. 1, pp. 7-33.

Alexander, R. J. 2004b, *Talk for Learning: The Second Year*, North Yorkshire County Council, Northallerton.

Alexander, R. J. 2005a, 'Culture, dialogue and learning: Notes on an emerging pedagogy', paper presented at the International Association for Cognitive Education and Psychology Conference, 10-14 July, University of Durham, U.K.

Alexander, R. J. 2005b, *Teaching Through Dialogue: The First Year*, London Borough of Barking and Dagenham, London.

Alexander, R. J. 2008a, *Essays on Pedagogy*, Routledge, Abingdon.

Alexander, R. J. 2008b, *Towards Dialogic Teaching: Rethinking Classroom Talk*, 4th edn, Dialogos, York.

Alexander, R. J. 2010, 'Speaking but not listening? Accountable talk in an unaccountable context', *Literacy*, vol. 44, no. 3, pp. 103-111.

Anderson, L. W. & Krathwohl, D. R. 2001, *A Taxonomy for Learning, Teaching, and Assessing: A Revision of Bloom's Taxonomy of Educational Objectives*, Longman, New York.

Anstey, M. 1986, 'You can't write in a vacuum: Techniques for developing a literature and modelling based process writing classroom', *Reading Around Series*, no. 1, Australian Reading Association, Melbourne.

Anstey, M. 1991, 'Examining classroom talk during literacy instruction: Developing metacognitive strategies', *Australian Journal of Reading*, vol. 14, no. 2, pp. 151-160.

Anstey, M. 1993a, 'Examining classroom talk: Structure talk in literacy lessons examined from a metacognitive perspective', SET, 1, 12, NZCER.

Anstey, M. 1993b, 'Quantitative and interpretative analyses of classroom talk as a cognitive context for learning about literacy', Unpublished doctoral thesis, Griffith University, Brisbane, Queensland.

Anstey, M. 1998, 'Being explicit about literacy instruction', *Australian Journal of Language and Literacy*, vol. 21, no. 3, pp. 206-221.

Anstey, M. 2002a, 'It's not all black and white: Postmodern picture books and teaching new literacies', *Journal of Adolescent and Adult Literacy*, vol. 45, no. 6, pp. 444-456.

Anstey, M. 2002b, *Literate Futures: Reading*, Access Ed, Department of Education, Coorparoo, Queensland.

Anstey, M. 2003, 'Examining classrooms as sites of literate practice and literacy learning', in G. Bull & M. Anstey (eds), *The Literacy Lexicon*, 2nd edn, Pearson Education, Frenchs Forest, pp. 103–121.

Anstey, M. 2009, 'Multiliteracies, the conversation continues: What do we really mean by 'Multiliteracies' and why is it important?' *Reading Forum New Zealand*, vol. 24, no. 1, pp. 5–15.

Anstey, M. & Bull, G. 1987, 'Developing thinking processes in the reading/writing classroom', Proceedings of the 2nd South Pacific Conference on Reading, Hobart.

Anstey, M. & Bull, G. 2004, *The Literacy Labyrinth*, 2nd edn, Pearson, Frenchs Forest, NSW.

Anstey, M. & Bull, G. 2005, 'One school's journey: Using multiliteracies to promote school renewal', *Practically Primary*, vol. 10, no. 3, pp. 10–13.

Anstey, M. & Bull, G. 2006, *Teaching and Learning Multiliteracies: Changing Times, Changing Literacies*, International Reading Association, Newark, Delaware.

Anstey, M. & Bull, G. 2010a, *Evolving Pedagogies: Reading and Writing in a Multimodal World*, Education Services Australia, Carlton South.

Anstey, M. & Bull, G. 2010b, 'Unpublished report to Anon state school on observation of eighteen reading lessons'.

Anstey, M. & Bull, G. 2011a, 'A metalanguage and development sequence for the codes and conventions of the semiotic systems' in M. Anstey & G. Bull (eds), *Viewing Map of Development: Addressing Current Literacy Challenges*, 2nd edn, STEPS Professional Development, Pearson, Frenchs Forest, NSW.

Anstey, M. & Bull, G. 2011b, *Viewing Resource Book: Addressing Current Literacy Challenges*, 2nd edn, STEPS Professional Development, Pearson, Frenchs Forest, NSW.

Anstey, M. & Bull, G. 2012, 'Using multimodal factual texts during the inquiry process', PETAA Paper 184, Primary English Teaching Association, Marrickville, Sydney, NSW.

Anstey, M. & Bull, G. 2013, pers. comm., interview, 30 July.

Anstey, M. & Bull, G. 2014, pers. comm., interview, 17 September.

Anstey, M. & Bull, G. 2016, 'Pedagogies for developing literacies of the visual', *Practical Literacy: The Early and Primary Years*, vol. 21, no. 1, pp. 22–24.

Anstey, M. & Bull, G. 2018, *Foundations of Multiliteracies: Reading, Writing and Talking in the 21st Century*, Routledge, London.

Applebee, A. N. 1981, 'Writing in the Secondary School: English and the Content Areas' Research Monograph No. 21, NCTE, Urbana.

Applebee, A. N. & Langer, J. A. 2011, 'A snapshot of writing instruction in middle schools and high schools', *English Journal*, vol. 100, no. 6, pp. 14–27.

Arizpe, E. & Styles, M. 2003, *Children Reading Pictures: Interpreting Visual Texts*, Routledge Falmer, London.

Australian Curriculum English. 2015, Scope and Sequence PDF, Version 7.5, viewed 6 October 2017, http://v7-5.australiancurriculum.edu.au/english/curriculum/f-10?layout=1.

Australia's Future Workforce? 2015, Report from CEDA (Committee for Economic Development of Australia), viewed 22 February 2017, http://adminpanel.ceda.com.au/FOLDERS/Service/Files/Documents/26792~Futureworkforce_June2015.pdf.

Bain, R. B. 2005, 'They thought the world was flat: Applying the principles of how people learn in teaching high school history', in J. Bransford & S. Donovan (eds), *How Students Learn: History, Mathematics, and Science in the Classroom*, The National Academic Press, Washington.

Baker, C. & Freebody, P. 1989a, *Children's First School Books*, Blackwell, London.

Baker, C. & Freebody, P. 1989b, 'Talk around text: Constructions of textual and teacher authority in classroom discourse', in S. de Castell, A. Luke & C. Luke (eds), *Language, Authority and Criticism: Readings on the School Text Book*, Falmer Press, London.

Baker, E. A. (ed.) 2010, *The New Literacies, Multiple Perspectives on Research and Practice*, The Guilford Press, New York.

Bakhtin, M. N. 1981, *The Dialogic Imagination*, University of Texas, Austin.

Balkwill, L. & Thompson, W. F. 1999, 'A cross-cultural investigation of the perception of emotion in music: Psychophysical and cultural cues', *Music Perception*, vol. 17, no. 1, pp. 43–64.

Banton Smith, N. 1965, *American Reading Instruction*, 2nd edn, International Reading Association, Newark, DE.

Barnes, D. 1976, *From Communication to Curriculum*, Boynton/Cook-Heinemann, London.

Barnes, D. 2008, 'Exploratory talk for learning', in N. Mercer & S. Hodgkinson (eds), *Exploring Talk in School: Inspired by the Work of Douglas Barnes*, Sage, London.

Barnes, D. 2010, 'Why is talk important', *English Teaching Practice and Critique*, vol. 9, no. 2, pp. 7–10.

Barnes, D., Britton, J. N. & Rosen, H. (eds) 1969, *Language, the Learner and the School*, Penguin, Harmondsworth.

Barth, R. S. 1990, 'A personal vision of a good school', *Phi Delta Kappan*, vol. 71, no. 7, pp. 512–516.

Bartlett, B. J. 1978, 'Top-level structure as an organizational strategy for recall of classroom text', Unpublished doctoral dissertation, Arizona State University.

Barton, D., Hamilton, M. & Ivanic, R. 2000, *Situated Literacies: Reading and Writing in Context*, London, Routledge.

Barton, G., Arnold, J. & Trimble-Roles, R. 2015, 'Writing practices today and in the future: Multimodal and creative text composition in the 21st century', in J. Turbill, G. Barton & C. Brock (eds), *Teaching Writing in Today's Classrooms: Looking Back to Look Forward*, Australian Literacy Educators' Association, Adelaide.

Barton, G. & Unsworth, L. 2014, 'Music, multiliteracies and multimodality: Exploring the book and movie versions of Shaun Tan's *The Lost Thing*', *Australian Journal of Language and Literacy*, vol. 37, no. 1, pp. 3–20.

Bearne, E. 2009, 'Multimodality, literacy and texts: Developing a discourse', *Journal of Early Childhood Literacy*, vol. 9, no. 2, pp. 161–193.

Benedikt, C. & Osborne, M. 2013, The Future of Employment: A Working Paper, Oxford Martin Programme of Technology and Employment, Oxford Martin School University of Oxford, Oxford, viewed 22 February 2017, www.oxfordmartin.ox.ac.uk/downloads/academic/The_Future_of_Employment.pdf.

Bennett, S., Maton, K. & Kervin, L. 2008, 'The digital natives debate: A critical review of the evidence', *British Journal of Educational Technology*, vol. 39, no. 5, pp. 775–786.

Bernstein, B. 1960, 'Language and social class', in *Class, Codes and Control, Vol. 1, Theoretical Studies Towards a Sociology of Language*, Routledge and Kegan Paul, London.

Bernstein, B. 1961, 'Social structure, language and learning', *Educational Research*, vol. 3, pp. 163–176.

Bernstein, B. 1962, 'Social class, linguistic codes and grammatical elements', in *Class, Codes and Control, Vol. 1, Theoretical Studies Towards a Sociology of Language*, Routledge and Kegan Paul, London.

Bernstein, B. 1964, 'Elaborated and restricted codes: Their origins and some consequences', in Ethnography and Speech, Monograph Issue of American Anthropologist, March.

Bernstein, B. 1971, *Class, Codes and Control, Vol. 1, Theoretical Studies Towards a Sociology of Language*, Routledge, London.

Bernstein, B. 1973, *Class, Codes and Control, Vol. 2, Applied Studies Towards a Sociology of Language*, Routledge, London.

Bernstein, B. 1975, *Class, Codes and Control, Vol. 3, Towards a Theory of Educational Transmission*, Routledge, London.

Bernstein, B. 1990, *Class, Codes and Control, Vol. 4, The Structuring of Pedagogical Discourse*, Routledge, London.

Bernstein, B. 1996, *Pedagogy, Symbolic Control and Identity: Theory, Research, Critique*, Taylor and Francis, London.

Bezemer, J. & Kress, G. 2014, 'Touch: A resource for making meaning', *Australian Journal of Language and Literacy*, vol. 37, no. 2, pp. 77–85.

Bezemer, J. & Kress, G. 2016, *Multimodality, Learning and Communication: A Social Semiotic Frame*, Routledge, London.

Bloom, B., Englehart, M., Furst, E. J., Hill, E. W. & Krathwohl, D. R. 1956, *Taxonomy of Educational Objectives*, David McKay, New York.

Bloome, D., Carter, S. P., Christian, B. M., Madrid, S., Otto, S., Shuart-Faris, N. & Smith, M. 2008, *Discourse Analysis in Classrooms: Approaches to Language and Literacy Research*, Teachers College Press, New York.

Bolam, R., McMahon, A., Stoll, L., Thomas, S. & Wallace, M. 2005, *Research Report No. 637 Creating and Sustaining Effective Professional Learning Communities*, University of Bristol, Bristol.

Booth, D. & Thornley-Hall, C. (eds) 1991, *The Talk Curriculum*, Australian Reading Association, Carlton, Victoria.

Borg, W. 1981, *Applying Educational Research: A Practical Guide for Teachers*, Longman, New York.

Bransford, J.D. & Franks, J.J. 1977, 'Memory of syntactic form as a function of sematic context', *Journal of Experimental Psychology*, vol. 103, pp. 1037–1039.

Brennan, M. & Williamson, P. 1981, *Investigating Learning in Schools*, Deakin University Press, Victoria.

Brice, A. & Lambert, R. 2009, *Digital Story-Telling*, Curriculum Corporation, Carlton South.

Britton, J. 1970, *Language and Learning*, Allen Lane, London.

Brown, H. & Cambourne, B. 1987, *Read and Retell*, Methuen, Sydney.

Bruner, J.S. 1961, 'The act of discovery', *Harvard Educational Review*, vol. 31, no. 1, pp. 21–32.

Bruner, J.S. 1983, *Child's Talk: Learning to Use the Language*, Oxford University Press, Oxford.

Bruner, J.S. 1996, *The Culture of Education*, Harvard University Press, Cambridge.

Buckingham, D., Banaji, S., Carr, D., Cranmer, S. & Willett, R. 2005, *The Media Literacy of Children and Young People: A Review of the Research Literature*, London Knowledge Lab, London.

Bull, G. 1989, *Reflective Teaching: Using Process and Thinking as Content*, Australian Reading Association, Melbourne.

Bull, G. 2003, 'An investigation of the pedagogy of literature using literature to support learning', in G. Bull & M. Anstey (eds), *The Literacy Lexicon*, 2nd edn, Prentice Hall, Frenchs Forest, NSW, Australia, pp. 145–160.

Bull, G. & Anstey, M. 1993, 'Report on a Three-Year Literacy Study at Surat State School', Language and Literacy Research Unit (LLRU), Faculty of Education, University of Southern Queensland, Queensland, Australia.

Bull, G. & Anstey, M. 1994, 'A Study of the Literacy Attitudes and Practices in the Ravenshoe State School and Community', Language and Literacy Research Unit (LLRU), Faculty of Education, University of Southern Queensland, Queensland, Australia.

Bull, G. & Anstey, M. 1995, 'Adult Literacy Practices in Rural Families and Communities', National Language and Literacy Institute of Australia (NLLIA), Adult Literacy Research Network Node, Queensland, Australia.

Bull, G. & Anstey, M. 1996, 'The Literacy Teaching and Learning Practices of an Urban School and Its Community', National Language and Literacy Institute of Australia (NLLIA), Literacy Research Network Node, Queensland, Australia.

Bull, G. & Anstey, M. 1997, 'Investigating the Literacy Practices of School, Home and Community', Language Australia Child/ESL Literacy Research Network, Queensland Node, Australia.

Bull, G. & Anstey, M. 2000, 'Report on the Harristown State High School Literacy Project', Vol. 1 to 4, Centre for Literacy and Children's Literature in Education (CLEAR), Faculty of Education, University of Southern Queensland, Queensland, Australia.

Bull, G. & Anstey, M. (eds) 2002, *Crossing the Boundaries*, Pearson, Sydney.

Bull, G. & Anstey, M. (eds) 2003, *The Literacy Lexicon*, 2nd edn, Pearson, Frenchs Forest, NSW.

Bull, G. & Anstey, M. 2004, *Inala Multiliteracies Project Report*, submitted to Mark Campling Principal, Forest Lakes State School for Inala Cluster of Schools, Brisbane, Queensland.

Bull, G. & Anstey, M. 2005a, *The Literacy Landscape*, Pearson, Frenchs Forest, NSW.

Bull, G. & Anstey, M. 2005b, *Townsville Multiliteracies Project Report*, submitted to Janelle Pepperdene, Co-ordinator Townsville LDC (Literacy) and Melinda Webb, Education Advisor, Literacy-Productive Pedagogies, Townsville, Queensland.

Bull, G. & Anstey, M. 2007, *Moreton Bay College Multiliteracies Project Report*, submitted to Ngaire Tagney, Head of Primary, Moreton Bay College, Manly West, Brisbane, Queensland.

Bull, G. & Anstey, M. 2010a, *Evolving Pedagogies: Reading and Writing in a Multimodal World*, Education Services Australia, Carlton South.

Bull, G. & Anstey, M. 2010b, 'Using the principles of multiliteracies to inform pedagogical change', in D.R. Cole & D.L. Pullen (eds), *Multiliteracies in Motion*, Routledge, Abingdon, pp. 141–159.

Bull, G. & Anstey, M. 2013, *Uncovering History Using Multimodal Literacies: An Inquiry Process*, Education Services Australia, Carlton South.

Bull, G. & Anstey, M. 2014, *Final Report on the Tasmanian Action Learning Cycle (TALC)*, submitted to Keegan, J. & Rowlands, S., Network Lead Teachers, Literacy/Numeracy (North West), Department of Education, Tasmania.

Buswell, G. T. 1922, 'Fundamental reading habits: A study of their development', *Supplementary Educational Monographs*, no. 21, University of Chicago Press, Chicago.

Cain, S. 2012, *The Power of Introverts in a World That Can't Stop Talking*, Crown, New York.

Calabreze, R. L. 2002, *The Leadership Assignment: Creating Change*, Allyn and Bacon, Boston.

Calkins, L. M. 1983, *Lessons from a Child: On the Teaching and Learning of Writing*, Heinemann, Portsmouth.

Callow, J. 2013, *The Shape of Text to Come: How Image and Text Work*, Primary English Teaching Association of Australia, Sydney.

Cambourne, B. 1988, *The Whole Story*, Ashton Scholastic, Sydney.

Carr, W. & Kemmis, S. 1986, *Becoming Critical: Education Knowledge and Action Research*, Falmer Press, London.

Carrington, V. & Robinson, M. (eds) 2009, *Digital Literacies: Social Learning and Classroom Practices*, Sage, London.

Cazden, C. B. 1967, 'On individual differences in language competence and performance', *Journal of Special Education*, vol. 1, pp. 135-150.

Cazden, C. B. 1970, 'The situation: A neglected source of social class differences in language use', *Journal of Social Issues*, vol. 26, no. 2, pp. 35-60.

Cazden, C. B. 1972, *Child Language and Education*, Holt, Rinehart and Winston, New York.

Cazden, C. B. 1988, *Classroom Discourse: The Language of Teaching and Learning*, Heinemann, Portsmouth, NH.

Cazden, C. B. 2001, Classroom Discourse: The Language of Teaching and Learning, Heinemann, Portsmouth, NH.

Cazden, C. B. 2015, 'Dell Hymes's construct of 'Communicative Competence'', *Anthropology & Education Quarterly*, vol. 42, no. 4, pp. 364-369.

Chambers, A. 1993, *Tell Me: Children, Reading and Talk*, Primary English Teaching Association of Australia (PETAA), Sydney, NSW.

Chandler, P. D. 2017, 'To what extent are teachers well-prepared to teach multimodal authoring?', viewed 17 December 2017, https://doi.org/10.1080/2331186X.2016.1266820.

Churchill, R., Godinho, S., Johnson, N. F., Keddie, A., Letts, W., Lowe., K, Mackay, J., McGill, M., Moss, J., Nagel, M., Shaw, K., Ferguson, P., Nicholson, P. & Vick, M. 2011, *Teaching: Making a Difference*, John Wiley, Milton, Queensland, Australia.

Clay, M. 1978, *What Did I Write? Beginning Writing Behaviour*, Heinemann, Auckland.

Coghlan, D. 2007, 'Insider action research doctorates: Generating actionable knowledge', *Higher Education*, vol. 54, no. 2, pp. 293-306.

Coghlan, D. & Brannick, T. 2010, *Doing Action Research in Your Own Organization*, 4th edn, Sage, London.

Coiro, J. 2003, 'Reading comprehension on the internet: Expanding our understanding of reading comprehension to encompass new literacies', *The Reading Teacher*, vol. 56, no. 5, pp. 458-464.

Coiro, J. 2005, 'Making sense of online text', *Educational Leadership*, vol. 63, no. 2, pp. 30-35.

Coiro, J. 2011, 'Predicting reading comprehension on the internet: Contributions of offline reading skills, online reading skills and prior knowledge', *Journal of Literacy Research*, vol. 34, no. 4, pp. 352-392.

Coiro, J., 2014, 'Online reading comprehension: Challenges and opportunities', *Texto Livre: Linguagem e Tecnologia*, vol. 73, no. 2 pp. 30-43, viewed 19 November 2017, https://doi.org/10.17851/1983-3652.7.2.30-43.

Coiro, J., Castek, J., Sekeres, D. & Guzniczak, L. 2014, 'Comparing third, fourth and fifth graders' collaborative interactions while engaged in online inquiry', *Journal of Education*, vol. 194, no. 2, pp. 1-16.

Coiro, J. & Dobler, E. 2007, 'Exploring the comprehension strategies used by sixth-grade skilled readers as they search for and locate information on the internet', *Reading Research Quarterly*, vol. 42, no. 2, pp. 214-257.

Cole, D. R. & Pullen, D. L. (eds) 2010, *Multiliteracies in Motion*, Routledge, Abingdon.

Comber, B. 2005, 'Making use of theories about literacy and justice: Teachers researching practice', *Educational Action Research*, vol. 13, no. 1, pp. 43-55.

Comber, B. 2012, 'Mandated literacy assessment and the reorganisation of teachers' work: Federal policy, local effects', *Critical Studies in Education*, vol. 53, no. 2, pp. 119-136.

Comber, B. & Cormack, P. 2013, 'High stakes literacy tests and local effects in a rural school', *Australian Journal of Language and Literacy*, vol. 36, no. 2, pp. 78–89.

Comber, B. & Hill, S. 2000, 'Socio-economic disadvantage, literacy and social justice: Learning from longitudinal case study research', *Australian Education Researcher*, vol. 27, no. 3, pp. 151–166.

Comber, B. & Kamler, B. (eds) 2005, *Turn-Around Pedagogies: Literacy Interventions for At-Risk Students*, Primary English Teachers Association (PETA), Newtown.

Cope, B. & Kalantzis, M. (eds) 2000, *Multiliteracies: Literacy Learning and the Design of Social Futures*, Routledge, London.

Cope, B. & Kalantzis, M. (eds) 2015, *A Pedagogy of Multiliteracies: Learning by Design*, Palgrave, London.

Corey, S. M. 1953, *Action Research to Improve School Practices*, Teachers College Press, New York.

Coscarelli, C. V. & Coiro, J. 2014, 'Reading multiple sources online', *Linguagem & Ensino, Pelotas*, vol. 17, no. 3, pp. 751–776, viewed 20 April 2017, www.google.com.au/search?q=Linguagem+%26+Ensino,+Pelotas,+v.17,+n.3,+p.751-776,+set.%2Fdez.+2014&ie=utf-8&oe=utf-8&client=firefox-b&gfe_rd=cr&dcr=0&ei=yOD_WaL1Oc7r8AfZvqWAAw.

Cowey, W. 2005, 'ACTA background paper: A brief description of the national accelerated literacy program', *TESOL in Context*, vol. 15, no. 2, pp. 3–13.

Cremin, T. & Baker S. 2010, 'Exploring teacher-writer identities in the classroom: Conceptualising the struggle', *English Teaching: Practices and Critique*, vol. 9, no. 3, pp. 8–25.

Cremin, T. & Baker, S. 2014, 'Teachers as writers: Implications for identity', PETAA Paper 194, Primary English Teaching Association Australia, Sydney.

Cremin, T. & Myhill, D. 2012, *Writing Voices: Creating Communities of Writers*, Routledge, London.

Crew, G., & Tan, S. 1999, *Memorial*, Lothian, South Melbourne.

Cumming, J. J. & Wyatt-Smith, C. M. 2016, *Literacy and the Curriculum: Success in Senior Secondary Schooling*, Australian Council for Educational Research (ACER), Melbourne.

Darling-Hammond, L. & Richardson, N. 2009, 'Research review/teacher learning: What matters?', *How Teachers Learn*, vol. 66, no. 5, pp. 46–53.

Dawes, L. 2008, 'Encouraging students, contribution to dialogue during science', *School Science Review*, vol. 90, no. 331, pp. 101–107.

Dawes, L. 2010, *Creating a Speaking and Listening Classroom: Integrating Talk for Learning at Key Stage 2*, David Fulton, London.

Dawes, L. 2011, *Talking Points: Discussion Activities in the Primary Classroom*, David Fulton, London.

Dawes, L., Mercer, N. & Wegerif, R. 2000, *Thinking Together: A Programme of Activities for Developing Thinking Skills at KS2*, Questions Publishing Co., Birmingham.

Denscombe, M. 2010, *Good Research Guide: For Small-Scale Social Research Projects*, 4th edn, Open University Press, Berkshire, U.K.

Department for Education and Skills. 2003a, The Core Principles: Teaching and Learning; School Improvement; System Wide Reform, Consultation paper, Department for Education and Skills (DfSE), London.

Department for Education and Skills. 2003b, *Excellence and Enjoyment: A Strategy for Primary Schools*, Department for Education and Skills (DfSE), London.

Derewianka, B. 2011, *A New Grammar Companion for Teachers*, Primary English Teaching Association Australia (PETAA), Sydney.

Derewianka, B. 2015, 'The contribution of genre theory to literacy education in Australia', in J. Turbill, G. Barton & C. Brock (eds), *Teaching Writing in Today's Classrooms: Looking Back to Looking Forward* (pp. 69–86), Australian Literary Educators' Association, Norwood, Australia.

Derewianka, B. & Jones, P. 2016, *Teaching Language in Context*, 2nd edn, Oxford University Press, South Melbourne.

Derewianka, B. M. 1990, *Exploring How Texts Work*, Primary English Teaching Association, Rozelle.

Desimone, L., Porter, A., Garet, M., Yoon, K. & Birman, B. 2002, 'Effects of professional development on teachers' instruction: Results from a three-year longitudinal study', *Education Evaluation and Policy Analysis*, vol. 24, no. 2, pp. 81–112.

Dewey, J. 1910, *How We Think*, Heath, Boston.

Dewey, J. 1916, *Democracy and Education*, Free Press, New York.

Dick, B. 2000, 'A Beginner's Guide to Action Research', viewed 14 August 2017, www.uq.net.au/action_research/arp/guide.html.

Discourse Primer. 2013, 'Tools for Ambitious Science Teaching, National Science Foundation', viewed 5 December 2017, https://people.clas.ufl.edu/rs/files/ScientificDiscourse.pdf.

Ditchburn, G. & Hattensen, S. 2012, 'Connecting with History: Strategies for an Inquiry Classroom', Education Services Australia, Carlton, Victoria.

Dix, S. & Cawkwell, G. 2011, 'The influence of peer group response: Building a teacher and student expertise in the writing classroom', *English Teaching: Practices and Critique*, vol. 10, no. 4, pp. 41–57.

Doecke, B. & Breen, L. 2013, 'Genres and genre theory: A response to Michael Rosen', *Changing English: Studies in Culture and Education*, vol. 20, no. 3, pp. 292–305.

Durkin, D. 1978–1979, 'What classroom observations reveal about reading comprehension instruction', *Reading Research Quarterly*, vol. 14, no. 4, pp. 481–533.

D'warte, J. 2014, 'Exploring linguistic repertoires: Multiple language use and multimodal literacy activity in five classrooms', *Australian Journal of Language and Literacy*, vol. 37, no. 1, pp. 21–30.

Dyson, A.H. 2003, *The Brothers and Sisters Learn to Write: Popular Literacies in Childhood and School Cultures*, Teachers College Press, New York.

Eagleton, M., Guinee, K. & Langlais, Y. 2003, 'Teaching internet literacy strategies: The hero inquiry project', *Voices from the Middle*, vol. 10, no. 3, pp. 28–35.

Edwards, A.D. & Mercer, N. 1987, *Common Knowledge: The Development of Understanding in the Classroom*, Methuen/Routledge, London.

Edwards, A.D. & Westgate, D.P.G. 1987, *Investigating Classroom Talk*, Falmer Press, London.

Edwards, J. & Jones, K. 2001, 'A co-learning agreement to support classroom research on collaborative peer talk', Occasional Papers in Science, Technology, Environment and Mathematics, University of Southampton, Southampton.

Edwards, T. 2003, 'Purposes and characteristics of whole-class dialogue', in *New Perspectives on Spoken English in the Classroom, Discussion Papers,* Qualification and Curriculum Authority, London, pp. 38–40.

Edwards-Groves, C. 1998, 'Reconceptualisation of classroom events as structured lessons: Documenting and changing the teaching of literacy in the primary school', Unpublished doctoral thesis, Griffith University, Queensland, Australia.

Edwards-Groves, C. 2003, *On Task: Focused Literacy Learning*, Primary English Teaching Association of Australia (PETAA), Sydney.

Edwards-Groves, C. 2008, 'The praxis-oriented self', in S. Kemmis & T.J. Smith (eds), *Enabling Praxis: Challenges for Education*, Sense, Rotterdam, pp. 127–148.

Edwards-Groves, C. 2011, 'The multimodal writing process: Changing processes in contemporary classrooms', *Language and Education*, vol. 25, no. 1, pp. 49–64.

Edwards-Groves, C. 2012, 'Interactive creative technologies: Changing learning practices and pedagogies in the writing classroom', *Australian Journal of Language and Literacy*, vol. 35, no. 1, pp. 99–113.

Edwards-Groves, C., Anstey, M. & Bull, G. 2014, *Classroom Talk: Understanding Dialogue, Pedagogy and Practice*, Primary English Teaching Association Australia (PETAA), Sydney.

Edwards-Groves, C. & Ronnerman, K. 2012, 'Generating leading practices through professional learning', *Professional Development in Education*, vol. 39, no. 1, pp. 122–140. https://doi.org/10.1080/19415257.2012.724439

Ellis, R. & Simons, R.F. 2005, 'The impact of music on subjective and psychological indices of emotion while viewing films', *Psychomusicology*, no. 19, pp. 15–40.

Ewing, R. 1994, 'What is a functional model of language?' PEN 95, Primary English Teaching Association, Sydney.

Ferrance, E. 2000, 'Action Research in Action', Northeast and Islands Regional Educational Laboratory at Brown University, viewed 14 August 2017, www.alliance.brown.edu/pubs/themes_ed.act_research.pdf.

The Foundation for Young Australians. 2017, 'The New Work Smarts: Thriving in the New Work Order', The Foundation for Young Australians, Sydney.

Freebody, P. 2011, 'Reading in primary school: Teachers researching comprehension', in M. Kelly & C. Topfer (eds), *Reading Comprehension: Taking the Learning Deeper*, Australian Literacy Educators' Association, Norwood, pp. 8–13.

Freebody, P. & Ludwig, C. 1998, *Talk and Literacy in Schools and Homes*, Commonwealth of Australia, Canberra.

Freebody, P. & Luke, A. 2003, 'Literacy as engaging with new forms of life: The four roles model', in G. Bull & M. Anstey, *The Literacy Lexicon*, 2nd edn, Pearson, Frenchs Forest, NSW.

Freebody, P. O., Luke, A. & Gilbert, P. 1991, 'Reading positions and practices in the classroom', *Curriculum Inquiry*, vol. 21, pp. 435–437.

Freire, P. 1984, *Pedagogy of the Oppressed*, Continuum, New York.

Fullan, M. 2001, *Leading in a Culture of Change*, Jossey-Bas, San Francisco.

Fullan, M. 2002, 'Leadership and sustainability', *Principal Leadership*, vol. 3, no. 4, pp. 1–9.

Fullan, M. 2004, *Leadership and Sustainability*, Corwin Press, Thousand Oaks, CA.

Fullan, M. 2005, 'Resiliency and sustainability', *The School Administrator*, February, pp. 16–18.

Fullan, M. 2007, *The New Meaning of Educational Change*, 4th edn, Teachers College, Columbia University, New York.

Fullan, M. 2008, *The Six Secrets of Change: What the Best Leaders Do to Help Their Organizations Survive and Thrive*, Jossey-Bass, San Francisco.

Game, A. & Metcalfe, A. 2009, 'Dialogue and team teaching', *Higher Education Research and Development*, vol. 28, no. 1, pp. 45–57.

Gardner, P. 2017, 'Worlds apart: A comparative analysis of discourses of English in the curricula of England and Australia', *English in Education*, https://doi.org/10.1111/eie.12138. http://onlinelibrary.wiley.com/journal/10.1111/(ISSN)1754-8845/issues.

Gee, J. P. 1990, *Social Linguistics and Literacies: Ideology in Discourses*, Falmer Press, London.

Gee, J. P. 1992, *The Social Mind: Language, Ideology and Social Practice*, Bergin & Garvey, New York.

Gee, J. P. 2003, *What Video Games Have to Teach Us about Learning and Literacy*, Palgrave, New York.

Gee, J. P. 2004, *Situated Language and Learning: A Critique of Traditional Schooling*, Routledge, New York.

Gee, J. P. 2005, *Why Video Games Are Good for Your Soul: Pleasure and Learning*, Common Ground, Melbourne.

Gilbert, L. C. 1953, 'Functional motor-processing of the eye in relation to reading', *University of California Publications in Education*, no. 2, University of California, pp. 159–232.

Gilbert, L. C. 1959, 'Speed of processing visual stimuli in relation to reading', *Journal of Educational Psychology*, vol. 50, pp. 8–14.

Glasswell, K., Singh, P. & McNaughton, S. 2016, 'Partners in design: Co-inquiry for quality teaching in disadvantaged schools', *Australian Journal of Language and Literacy*, vol. 39, no.1, pp. 20–29.

Glickman, C. D. 1993, *Renewing America's Schools: A Guide for School-Based Education*, Jossey-Bass, San Francisco.

Godinho, S. & Shrimpton, B. 2003, 'Boys and girls use of linguistic space in small group discussions: Whose talk dominates?' *Australian Journal of Language and Literacy*, vol. 26, no. 3, pp. 28–43.

Goodman, K. 1976, Reading: A psycholinguistic guessing game, *Journal of the Reading Specialist*, pp. 126–137.

Goodman, K. S. 1987, *What's Whole in Whole Language?* Scholastic, Ontario.

Goodman, Y. M. 1989, 'Whole language research: Foundations and development', *Elementary School Journal*, no. 90, pp. 113–127.

Gossen, D. & Anderson, J. 1995, *Creating the Conditions: Leadership for Quality Schools*, New View Publications, Chapel Hill.

Graves, D. 1981, 'Donald Graves in Australia', in R. D. Walshe (ed.), *Donald Graves in Australia: 'Children want to write…'*, Primary English Teaching Association, Rozelle.

Graves, D. 1983, *Writing: Teachers and Children at Work*, Heinemann, New Hampshire.

Gravett, E. 2005, *Wolves*, Macmillan, Oxford.

Gravett, E. 2016, *Bear and Hare, Mine!* Macmillan, London.

Greenwood, D.J.& Levin, M. 2007, *Introduction to Action Research*, 2nd edn, Sage, Thousand Oaks, CA.

Habermas, J. 1970, 'A theory of communicative competence', *Inquiry*, vol. 13, pp.360-375.

Hall, W.E.& Robinson, F.P. 1945, 'An analytical approach to the study of reading skills', *Journal of Educational Psychology*, vol. 36, pp.429-442.

Halliday, M. 1973, *Explorations in the Functions of Language*, Edward Arnold, London.

Halliday, M.A.K. 1975, *Learning How to Mean: Explorations in the Development of Language*, Edward Arnold, London.

Halliday, M.A.K. 2004, *An Introduction to Functional Grammar*, Hodder Arnold, London.

Hammond, J. 1996, 'Reading knowledge about language and genre theory', in G. Bull& M. Anstey (eds), *The Literacy Lexicon*, Prentice Hall, Sydney.

Hannon, P. 1995, *Literacy, Home and School: Research and Practice in Teaching Literacy with Parents*, Falmer Press, Brighton.

Hargreaves, A. 1994, *Changing Teachers, Changing Times: Teachers' Work and Culture in the Postmodern Age*, Cassell, London.

Hargreaves, D. 1995, 'School culture, school effectiveness and school improvement', *School Effectiveness and School Improvement*, vol. 6, no. 1, pp.23-46.

Harpaz, Y.& Lefstein, A. 2000, 'Communities of thinking', *Educational Leadership*, vol. 58, no. 3, pp.54-57.

Harris, T.L.& Hodges, R.E. (eds) 1995, *The Literacy Dictionary: The Vocabulary of Reading and Writing*, International Reading Association, Newark, Delaware.

Hartman, D.K., Morsink, P.M.& Zheng, J. 2010, 'From print to pixels: The evolution of cognitive conceptions of reading comprehension', in E. A. Baker (ed.), *The New Literacies: Multiple Perspectives on Research and Practice*, The Guilford Press, London.

Hattie, J.A.C. 2012, *Visible Learning for Teachers: Maximizing Impact on Learning*, Routledge, London.

Hawisher, G.E.& Selfe, C.L. (eds) 2000, *Global Literacies and the World-Wide Web*, Routledge, London.

Heap, J.L. 1982, 'Understanding classroom events: A critique of Durkin with an alternative', *Journal of Reading Behavior*, vol. XIV, no. 4, pp.391-411.

Heath, S.B. 1983, *Ways with Words: Language, Life and Work in Communities and Classrooms*, Cambridge University Press, Cambridge.

Heath, S.B. 1986, 'The functions and uses of literacy', in S.C. deCastell, A. Luke& K. Egan (eds), *Literacy, Society and Schooling*, Cambridge University Press, Cambridge.

Heil, D. 2005, 'The internet and student research: Teaching critical evaluation skills', *Teacher Librarian*, vol. 33, no. 2, pp.26-29.

Hendricks, C.C. 2002, 'A review of the work of Laurence Stenhouse: Questions, ambiguities, and possibilities', *Journal of Research in Education*, vol. 12, no. 1, pp.117-122.

Herbel-Eisenmann, B.& Cirillo, M. (eds) 2009, *Promoting Purposeful Discourse*, National Council of Teachers of Mathematics, Reston, VA.

Herber, H.L. 1978, *Teaching Reading in the Content Areas*, Prentice Hall, Englewood Cliffs, NJ.

Holman, D., Wall, T.D., Clegg, C.W., Sparrow, P.& Howard, A. (eds) 2005, *The Essentials of the New Workplace: A Guide to the Human Impact of Modern Work Practices*, Wiley and Sons, Chichester.

Hoodless, P. 2004, 'Spotting the adult agendas: Investigating children's historical awareness using stories written for children in the past', *The International Journal of Historical Teaching and Research*, vol. 4, no. 2, July (no page numbers).

Hornsby, D. 1988, *Write on*, Pearson Education, Harlow.

Howe, C. 2010, *Peer Groups and Children's Development*, Wiley-Blackwell, Oxford.

Hull, G.& Schultz, K. (eds) 2002, *Schools out! Bridging Out-of-School Literacies with Classroom Practices*, Teachers College Press, New York.

Hymes, D. H. 1972, 'On communicative competence', in J. B. Pride & J. Holmes (eds), *Sociolinguistics: Selected Readings*, Penguin, Harmondsworth.

Ingvarson, L. 2005, 'Getting professional development right', viewed 11 October 2013, http://research.acer.edu.au/professional-dev/4.

Ingvarson, L., Meiers, M. & Beavis, A. 2003, 'Evaluating the quality and impact of professional development programs', viewed 11 October 2013, http://research.acer.edu.au/professional-dev/3.

Ivanic, R. 2004, 'Discourses of writing and learning to write', *Language and Education*, vol. 18, no. 3, pp. 220–245.

Jenkins, H. 2009, *Confronting the Challenges of Participatory Culture: Media Education for the 21st century*, The MIT Press, Cambridge.

Jewitt, C. 2006, *Technology, Literacy and Learning: A Multimodal Approach*, Routledge, Abingdon.

Jewitt, C., Bezemer, J. & O'Halloran, K. 2016, *Introducing Multiliteracy*, Routledge, London.

Jewitt, C. & Kress, G. (eds) 2008, *Multimodal Literacy*, Peter Lang, New York.

Johansen, J. D. & Sendergaard, L. (eds) 2010, *Fact, Fiction and Faction*, University Press of Southern Denmark, Odense.

Julien, H. & Barker, S. 2009, 'How high-school students find and evaluate scientific information: A basis for information literacy skills development', *Library & Information Science Research*, vol. 31, no. 1, pp. 12–17.

Kalantzis, M., Cope, B., Chan, E. & Dalley-Trim, L. 2016, *Literacies*, 2nd edn, Cambridge University Press, Port Melbourne.

Kamler, B. 1992, 'The social construction of free topic choice in the process writing classroom', *Australian Journal of Language and Literacy*, vol. 15, no. 2, pp. 105–122.

Kamler, B. & Comber, B. 2008, 'Making a difference: Early career English teachers research their practice', *Changing English*, vol. 15, no. 1, pp. 65–76.

Kemmis, S. & Grootenboer, P. 2008, 'Situated praxis in practice', in S. Kemmis & T. J. Smith (eds), *Enabling Praxis: Challenges for Education*, Sense, Rotterdam, pp. 37–62.

Kemmis, S. & Heikkinen, H.L.T. 2012, 'Understanding professional development of teachers within the theory of practice architectures', paper presented at the European Conference of Educational Research, September, Berlin.

Kemmis, S. & McTaggert, R. (eds) 1988, *The Action Research Planner*, 3rd edn, Deakin University, Victoria.

Kemmis, S. & McTaggert, R. 2005, 'Participatory action research: Communicative action and the public sphere', in N. K. Denzin & Y. S. Lincoln (eds), *Handbook of Qualitative Research*, 3rd edn, Sage, Beverly Hills, CA.

Kemmis, S., Wilkinson, J., Edwards-Groves, C., Hardy, I., Bristol, L. & Grootenboer, P. 2012, "Changing education, changing practices: Executive summary, A synopsis of findings of the ARC Discovery Project' Leading and Learning': Developing ecologies of educational practices', presented at the projects' Dissemination Seminar, October 17, Canberra.

Kendon, A. 2004, *Gesture: Visible Action as Utterance*, Cambridge University press, Cambridge.

Kenner, C. 2008, 'Embodied knowledges: Young children's engagement with the act of writing', in C. Jewitt & G. Kress (eds), *Multimodal Literacy*, Peter Lang, New York, pp. 88–106.

Kervin, L. 2015, 'Students writing with new technologies: The 2015 Donald Graves address', PETAA Paper 201, Primary English Teaching Association Australia, Marrickville, NSW.

Kervin, L., Verenkina, I., Jones, P. & Beath, P. 2013, 'Investigating synergies between literacy, technology and classroom practice', *Australian Journal of Language and Literacy*, vol. 36, no. 3, pp. 135–147.

Khan, S. & Fine, J. 1991, 'Investigating children's talk', in *The Talk Curriculum*, Australian Reading Association, Carlton, Victoria, pp. 145–151.

Kiili, C., Coiro, J., & Hamalainen, J. 2016, 'An online inquiry tool to support the exploration of controversial issues on the internet', *Journal of Literacy and Technology*, vol. 17, no. 1–2, pp. 31–52.

Kiili, C., Laurinen, L. & Marttunen, M. 2008, 'Students evaluating internet sources: From versatile evaluators to uncritical readers', *Journal of Educational Computing Research*, vol. 39, no. 1, pp. 75–95.

Kim, J. S. 2008, 'Research and the reading wars', *Phi Delta Kappan*, vol. 89, no. 5, pp. 372–375.

Kincheloe, J. 2001, *Getting Beyond the Facts: Teaching Social Studies/Social Sciences in the Twenty-First Century*, Peter Lang, New York.

Knobel, M. & Healy, A. 1998, *Critical Literacies in the Primary Classroom*, Primary English Teaching Association, Newtown, Sydney.

Kress, G. 2000, 'Design and transformation: New theories of meaning', in B. Cope & M. Kalantzis (eds), *Multiliteracies: Literacy Learning and the Design of Social Futures*, Routledge, Abingdon.

Kress, G. 2003, *Literacy in the New Media Age*, Routledge, London.

Kress, G. 2010, *Multimodality: A Social Semiotic Approach to Contemporary Communication*, Routledge, London.

Kress, G., Jewitt, C., Ogborn, J. & Tsatsalis, C. 2001, *Multimodal Teaching and Learning: The Rhetorics of the Science Classroom*, Continuum, London.

Kress, G. & van Leeuwen, T. 1990, *Reading Images*, Deakin University, Burwood.

Kress, G. & van Leeuwen, T. 2001, *Multimodal Discourse: The Modes and Media of Contemporary communication*, Arnold, London.

Kress, G. & van Leeuwen, T. 2006, *Reading Images: The Grammar of Visual Design*, 2nd edn, Routledge, London.

Kruse, D. 2009, *Thinking Strategies for the Inquiry Classroom*, Education Services Australia, Carlton, Victoria.

Kruse, D. 2010, *Thinking Tools for the Inquiry Classroom*, Education Services Australia, Carlton, Victoria.

Kruse, D. 2012, *Assessment Strategies for the Inquiry Classroom*, Education Services Australia, Carlton, Victoria.

Kuhlthau, C.C., Maniotes, L.K. & Caspari, A.K. 2007, *Guided Inquiry; Learning in the 21st Century*, Libraries Unlimited, Santa Barbara.

Labov, W. 1966, *The Social Stratification of English in New York City*, Center for Applied Linguistics, Washington, DC.

Labov, W. 1969a, 'The logic of nonstandard English', in N. Keddie (ed.), *Tinker, Taylor, the Myth of Cultural Deprivation*, Penguin, Melbourne, pp. 21–66.

Labov, W. 1969b, 'A study of non-standard English', *Center for Applied Linguistics*, Washington, DC.

Lai, M.K. & McNaughton, S. 2013, 'Developing effective research-practice partnerships: Lessons from a decade of partnering with schools in poor urban communities', in J. Duncan & L. Connor (eds), *Research Partnerships within Early Years Education: Teachers and Researchers in Collaboration*, Palgrave Macmillan, New York, pp. 49–70.

Langer, J.A. 2011, *Envisioning Knowledge: Building Literacy in the Academic Disciplines*, Teachers College, New York.

Lankshear, C., Gee, J., Knobel, M. & Searle, C. 1997, *Changing Literacies*, Open University Press, Buckingham.

Lankshear, C. & Lawler, M. 1987, *Literacy, Schooling and Revolution*, Falmer Press, London.

Lawton, D. 1968, *Social Class, Language and Education*, Routledge and Kegan Paul, London.

Lefstein, A. 2006, 'Dialogue in schools: Towards a pragmatic approach', *Working Papers in Urban Language and Literacies*, vol. 33, pp. 1–16.

Lefstein, A. & Snell, J. 2014, *Better than Best Practice: Developing Teaching and Learning through Dialogue*, Routledge, London.

Lenhart, A., Arafeh, S., Smith, A. & MacGill, A. 2008, Writing Technology and Teens, PEW Internet and American Life Project and the National Commission on Writing, viewed 8 November 2017, www.pewinternet.org/2008/04/24/writing-technology-and-teens/.

Leu, D.J. 2000, 'Literacy and technology: Deictic consequences for literacy education in an information age', in M.L. Kamil, P.B. Mosenthal, P.D. Pearson & R. Barr (eds), *Handbook of Reading Research* (vol. 3), Lawrence Erlbaum, Mahwah, NJ, pp. 743–770.

Leu, D.J., McVerry, J.G., O'Byrne, W.I., Kiili, C., Zawilinski, L., Everett-Cacopardo, H., Kennedy, C. & Forzani, E. 2011, 'The new literacies of online reading comprehension: Expanding the literacy and learning curriculum', *Journal of Adolescent & Adult Literacy*, vol. 55, no. 1, pp. 5–14.

Levesque, S. 2006, 'Discovering the past: Engaging Canadian students in digital history', *Canadian Social Studies*, vol. 40, no. 1, pp. 1–8.

Levesque, S. 2008, *Thinking Historically: Educating Students for the 21st Century*, University of Toronto Press, Toronto.

Lewin, K. 1946, 'Action research and minority problems', *Journal of Social Issues*, vol. 2, no. 4, pp. 34–46.

Lipscombe, K., Kervin, L. & Mantei, J. 2015, 'Examining the writing process for digital literary text construction', in J. Turbill, G. Barton & C. Brock (eds), *Teaching Writing in Today's Classrooms: Looking Back to Look Forward*, Australian Literacy Educators' Association, Adelaide.

Littleton, K. & Mercer, N. 2010, 'The significance of educational dialogues between primary school children', in K. Littleton & C. Howe (eds), *Educational Dialogues: Understanding and Promoting Productive Interaction*, Routledge, London.

Littleton, K. & Mercer, N. 2013, *Interthinking: Putting Talk to Work*, Routledge, London.

Liu, J. 2013, 'Visual images: Interpretative strategies in multimodal texts', *Journal of Language Teaching and Research*, vol. 4, no. 6, pp. 1259–1263.

Lobato, J., Clarke, D. & Ellis, A.B. 2005, 'Initiating and eliciting in teaching: A reformulation of telling', *Journal for Research in Mathematics Education*, vol. 36, no. 2, pp. 101–136.

Lo Bianco, J. & Freebody, P. 2001, *Australian Literacies: Informing National Policy on Literacy Education*. 2nd edn, Language Australia, Ringwood.

The Lost Thing. 2010, animated short film, Passion Pictures Australia, Richmond. Distributed by IndieFlix, narrated by Tim Minchin.

Luke, A. 1993, Chapter One in L. Unsworth (ed.), *Literacy Teaching and Learning*, Macmillan, Sydney.

Luke, A. 1995, 'When basic skills and information processing just aren't enough: Rethinking reading in new times', *Teachers College Record*, vol. 97, no. 1, Fall, pp. 95–115.

Luke, A., Baty, A. & Stehbens, C. 1989, '"Natural conditions" for language learning: A critique', *English in Australia*, no. 89, pp. 36–49.

Luke, A. & Freebody, P. 1997, 'Shaping the social practices of reading', in S. Muspratt, A. Luke & P. Freebody (eds), *Constructing Critical Literacies: Teaching and Learning Textual Practices*, Allen & Unwin, St Leonards, pp. 185–225.

Luke, A. & Freebody, P. 1999a, 'A map of possible practices: Further notes on the Four Resource Model', *Practically Primary*, vol. 4, no. 2, pp. 5–8.

Luke, A. & Freebody, P. 1999b, Further Notes on the Four Resources Model, viewed 21 March 2017, http://kingstonnet worknumandlitteam.wikispaces.com/file/view/Further+Notes+on+the+Four+Resources+Model-Allan+Luke.pdf.

Lyle, S. 2008, 'Dialogic teaching: Discussing theoretical contexts and reviewing evidence from classroom practice', *Language and Education*, vol. 22, no. 3, pp. 222–240.

Lynch, J. 2017, 'The complexity of teaching internet inquiry with iPads in the early years', *Australian Journal of Language and Literacy*, vol. 40, no. 3, pp. 186–198.

Macken-Horarik, M., Love, K. & Unsworth, L. 2011, 'A grammatics 'good enough' for school English in the 21st century: Four challenges in realising the potential', *Australian Journal of Language and Literacy*, vol. 34, no. 1, pp. 9–23.

Mackenzie, N.M. 2014, 'Teaching early writers: Teachers' responses to a young child's writing sample', *Australian Journal of Language and Literacy*, vol. 37, no. 3, pp. 182–191.

Mackenzie, N.M. & Veresov, N. 2013, 'How drawing can support writing acquisition: Text construction in early writing: What happens when you shift teaching priorities in the first six months of school?', *Australasian Journal of Early Childhood*, vol. 38, no. 4, pp. 22–29.

Mansfield, J. 2014, Unpublished report. *Tasmanian Action Learning Cycle*, North West Coast, Tasmania.

Marsden, J. & Tan, S. 2010, *The Rabbits*, Hachette, Melbourne.

Marsh, J. 2014, 'Online and offline play', in A. Burn & C. Richards (eds), *Children's Games in the New Media Age: Childlore, Media and the Playground*, Ashgate, London, pp. 109–132.

Martin, J.R. 1993, 'Literacy in science: Learning to handle text as technology', in M.A.K. Halliday & J.R. Martin (eds), *Writing Science: Literacy and Discursive Power*, Falmer Press, London.

Martin, J.R. & Rothery, J. 1993, 'Grammar: Making meaning in writing', in B. Cope & M. Kalantzis (eds), *The Powers of Literacy*, Falmer Press, London.

Marwick, A. 1997, 'Primary sources: Handle with care', in M. Drake & R. Finnegan (eds), *Sources and Methods for Family and Community Historians: A Handbook*, Cambridge University Press, Cambridge.

McNiff, J. 2013, *Action Research: Principles and Practice*, Routledge, New York.

McNiff, J. & Whitehead, J. 2006, *All You Need to Know About Action Research*, Sage, London.

McVerry, J.G. 2007, 'Forums and functions of threaded discussions', *New England Reading Association Journal*, vol. 43, no. 1, pp. 785–789.

Meiers, M. 2010, 'Professional Learning Communities', Newsletter of the Australian Literacy Educators' Association, February.

Mercer, N. 1995, *The Guided Construction of Knowledge: Talk Amongst Teachers and Learners*, Multilingual Matters, Clevedon.

Mercer, N. 2000, *Words and Minds: How We Use Language to Think Together*, Routledge, London.

Mercer, N. 2004, 'Sociocultural discourse analysis: Analysing classroom talk as a social mode of thinking', *Journal of Applied Linguistics*, vol. 1, no. 2, pp.137-168.

Mercer, N. 2008, 'The seeds of time: Why classroom dialogue needs a temporal analysis', *Journal of the Learning Sciences*, vol. 17, no. 1, pp.33-59.

Mercer, N. & Hodgkinson, S. (eds) 2008, *Exploring Talk in School*, Sage, London.

Mercer, N. & Littleton, K. 2007, *Dialogue and the Development of Children's Thinking: A Sociocultural Approach*, Routledge, London.

Mertler, C. A. & Charles, C. M. 2008, *Introduction to Educational Research*, 6th edn, Allyn & Bacon, Boston.

Meyer, B.J.F. & Freedle, R. 1979, *The Effects of Different Discourse Topics on Recall*, Educational Testing Service, Princeton, NJ.

Michaels, S. & O'Connor, M. C. 2012, *Talk Science Primer*, TERC, Cambridge.

Michaels, S., O'Connor, M. C., Hall, M. W. & Resnick, L. B. 2002, *Accountable Talk: Classroom Conversation that Works* (3 CD-ROM set), University of Pittsburgh, Pittsburgh.

Michaels, S., O'Connor, M. C. & Resnick, L. B. 2007, 'Deliberative discourse idealized and realized: Accountable talk in the classroom and in civic life', *Studies in Philosophy and Education*, vol. 27, no. 4, pp.283-297.

Mills, G. 2003, *Action Research: A Guide for the Teacher Researcher*, Merrill/Prentice Hall, NJ.

Mills, K. A. 2010, 'A review of the 'digital turn' in new literacies studies', *Review of Educational Research*, vol. 80, no. 2, pp.246-271.

Mills, K. A. 2011, *The Multiliteracies Classroom*, Multilingual Matters, Bristol.

Mills, K. A. & Dreamson, N. 2015, 'Race, the senses, and the materials of writing and literacy practices', in J. Turbill, G. Barton & C. Brock (eds), *Teaching Writing in Today's Classrooms: Looking Back to Look Forward*, Australian Literacy Educators' Association, Adelaide.

Moorman, G. B., Blankton, W. E. & McNaughton, T. 1994, 'Rhetoric and community in whole language: A response to Cambourne, Willinsky and Goodman', *Reading Research Quarterly*, vol. 29, no. 4, pp.348-351.

Morris, A. & Stewart-Dore, N. 1984, *Learning to Learn from Text: Effective Reading in the Content Areas*, Addison Wesley, North Ryde, NSW.

Mortimer, E. F. & Scott, P. H. 2003, *Meaning Making in Science Classrooms*, Open University Press, Maidenhead.

Moyles, J., Hargreaves, L., Merry, R., Paterson, F. & Esarte-Sarries, V. 2003, *Interactive Teaching in the Primary School*, Open University Press, Maidenhead.

Murray, D. M. 1982, *Learning by Teaching: Selected Articles on Writing and Teaching*, Boynton Cook, Montclair.

Murray, D. M. 1985, *A Writer Teaches Writing: A Practical Method of Teaching Composition*, Houghton Mifflin, Boston.

Myhill, D. 2005, *Teaching and Learning in Whole Class Discourse*, University of Exeter School of Education, Exeter.

Myhill, D., Jones, S. & Hopper, R. 2006, *Talking, Listening, Learning: Effective Talk in the Primary Classroom*, Open University Press, Maidenhead.

Nassaji, H. & Wells, G. 2000, 'What's the use of triadic dialogue? An investigation of teacher-student interactions', *Applied Linguistics*, vol. 21, no. 3, pp.333-363.

National Council of Teachers of Mathematics. 2013, *What Are Some Strategies for Facilitating Productive Classrooms Discussions?* National Council of Teachers of Mathematics, Reston, VA.

New London Group. 1996, 'A pedagogy of multiliteracies: Designing social futures', *Harvard Educational Review*, vol. 66, no.1, Spring, pp.60-92.

Newman, J. M. 1991, 'Learning to teach by uncovering our assumptions', in D. Booth & C. Thornley-Hall (eds), *The Talk Curriculum*, Australian Reading Association, Carlton, Victoria, pp.107-121.

Noffke, S. & Somekh, B. (eds) 2009, *The Sage Handbook of Educational Action Research*, Sage, London.

Noffke, S. E. 2008, 'Research relevancy or research for change', *Educational Researcher*, vol. 37, no. 7, pp. 429–431.

Nolen, A. L. & Putten, J. V. 2007, 'Action research in education: Addressing gaps in ethical principles and practices', *Educational Researcher*, vol. 36, no. 7, pp. 401–407.

Nystrand, M., Gamoran, A., Kachur, R. & Prendergast, C. 1997, *Opening Dialogue: Understanding the Dynamics of Language and Learning in the English Classroom*, Teachers College Press, New York.

Nystrand, M., Wu, L. L., Gamoran, A., Zeiser, S. & Long, D. A. 2003, 'Questions in time: Investigating the structure and dynamics of unfolding classroom discourse', *Discourse Processes*, vol. 35, no. 2, pp. 135–198.

Ontario School Library Association. 1999, Information Studies: Inquiry and Research K-12, viewed 1 November 2014, www.accessola.com/action/positions/info_studies/

Oxenham, J. 1980, *Literacy: Writing, Reading and Social Organisation*, Routledge & Kegan Paul, London.

Painter, C., Martin, J. R. & Unsworth, L. 2013, *Reading Visual Narratives: Image Analysis of Children's Picture Books*, Equinox Publishing, Sheffield, U.K.

Palincsar, A. S. & Brown, A. L. 1984, *Reciprocal Teaching of Comprehension Fostering and Mentoring Activities: Cognition and Instruction*, Lawrence Erlbaum, Hillsdale.

Paris, S. G., Cross, D. R. & Lipson, M. Y. 1984, 'Informed strategies for learning: A program to improve children's reading awareness and comprehension', *Journal of Educational Psychology*, vol. 76, no. 6, pp. 1239–1252.

Paris, S. G. & Paris, A. H. 2001, 'Classroom applications of research on self-regulated learning', *Educational Psychologist*, vol. 36, no. 2, pp. 89–101.

Pearson, P. D. & Gallagher, M. C. 1983a, 'The Instruction of Reading', Technical Report 57, Center for the Study of Reading University of Illinois, Champaign, IL.

Pearson, P. D. & Gallagher, M. C. 1983b, 'The instruction of reading comprehension', Technical Report no. 297, Center for the Study of Reading,, University of Illinois at Urbana-Champaign, Champaign, IL.

Pearson, P. D. & Johnson, D. D. 1978, *Teaching Reading Comprehension*, Holt, Rinehart & Winston, New York.

Penuel, W., Fishman, B., Yamaguchi, R. & Gallagher, L. P. 2007, 'What makes professional development effective? Strategies that foster curriculum implementation', *American Educational Research Journal*, vol. 44, no. 4, pp. 921–958.

Perkins, D. N. 2003, *Making Thinking Visible*, viewed 8 November 2017, www.visiblethinkingpz.org/VisibleThinking_html_files/06_AdditionalResources/MakingThinkingVisible_DP.pdf.

Perrott, C. 1988, *Classroom Talk and Pupil Learning: Guidelines for Educators*, Harcourt Brace Jovanovich, Sydney.

Poole, M. E. 1972, 'Social class differences in code elaboration: A study of written communication at the tertiary level', *Australian and New Zealand Journal of Sociology*, vol. 8, pp. 46–55.

Purcell, K., Buchanan, J. & Friedrich, L. 2013, The Impact of Digital Tools on Student Writing and how Writing is Taught in Schools, National Writing Project, PEW Research Centre viewed 8 January, 2018, www.pewinternet.org/2013/07/16/the-impact-of-digital-tools-on-student-writing-and-how-writing-is-taught-in-schools/.

Reason, P. (ed.) 1994, *Participation in Human Inquiry*. Sage, London.

Reason, P. & Bradbury, H. 2007, *Handbook of Action Research*, Sage, London.

Resnick, L. B., Michaels, S. & O'Connor, M. C. 2010, 'How (well-structured) talk builds the mind', in D. D. Preiss & R. J. Sternberg (eds), *Innovations in Educational Psychology*, Springer, New York, pp. 163–194.

Ritchhart, R., Palmer, P., Church, M. & Tishman, S. 2006, 'Thinking routines: Establishing patterns of thinking in the classroom', paper presented at the American Educational Research Association Conference, April, New York.

Ritchhart, R. & Perkins, D. N. 2005, 'Learning to think: The challenges of teaching thinking', in K. Holyoak & R. G. Morrison (eds), *Cambridge Handbook of Thinking and Reasoning*, Cambridge University Press, Cambridge.

Ritchhart, R. & Perkins, D. N. 2008, 'Making thinking visible', *Educational Leadership*, vol. 65, no. 5, pp. 57–61.

Ritchhart, R., Turner, T. & Hadar, L. 2008, 'Uncovering students' thinking about thinking using concept maps', paper presented at the annual meeting of the American Educational Research Association, March 26, New York.

Rivalland, J. 1989, 'Meaning making: A juggling act or helping children become critical thinkers?', *Australian Journal of Reading*, vol. 12, no. 1, pp. 5–21.

Robinson, F. P. & Hall, W. E. 1941, 'Studies of higher level reading abilities', *Journal of Educational Psychology*, vol. 32, pp. 441–451.

Ronnerman, K. & Olin, A. 2012, 'Research circles – enabling changes in site based educational development, paper presented in the symposium Action Research and Site-Based Education Development, Australian Association for Research in Education (AARE), December 2006, Sydney.

Rose, D. & Martin, J. R. 2012, *Learning to Write, Reading to Learn*, Equinox, Sheffield, UK.

Rose, S., Spinks, N. & Canhoto, A. I. 2015, *Management Research: Applying the Principles*, Routledge, London.

Rosen, M. 2011, 'How genre theory saved the world', viewed 3 January 2018, http://michaelrosenblog.blogspot.com.au/2011/12/how-genre-theory-saved-world.html.

Rosen, M. 2013, 'How genre theory saved the world', *Changing English: Studies in Culture and Education*, vol. 20, no. 3, pp. 3–10.

Rowan, L. 2001, *Write Me in: Inclusive Texts in the Primary Classroom*, Primary English Teaching Association, Newtown, Sydney.

Rowe, M. B. 1986, 'Wait time: Slowing down may be a way of speeding up', *Journal of Teacher Education*, vol. 37, pp. 43–50.

Rymes, B. 2009, *Classroom Discourse Analysis: A Tool for Critical Reflection*, Hampton Press, NJ.

Schoenfeld, A. H. & Pearson, P. D. 2009, 'The reading and math wars', in G. Sykes, B. Schneider & D. N. Plank (eds), *Handbook of Educational Policy Research*, Routledge, New York, pp. 560–580.

Schon, D. A. 1983, *The Reflective Practitioner*. Basic Books, New York.

Scott, C. 2009, 'Talking to learn: Dialogue in the classroom', *The Digest*, NSWIT, vol. 2.

Scott, P. H., Mortimer, E. F. & Aguiar, O. 2006, 'The tension between authoritative and dialogic discourse: A fundamental characteristic of meaning making interactions in high school science lessons', *Science Education*, vol. 90, pp. 605–631.

Scott, T. J. & O'Sullivan, M. K. 2005, 'Analyzing student search strategies: Making a case for integrating information literacy skills into the curriculum', *Teacher Librarian*, vol. 33, no. 1, pp. 21–26.

Sekeres, D., Coiro, J., Castek, J. & Guzniczak, L. 2014, 'Wondering + online inquiry = learning', *Phi Delta Kappan*, vol. 96, no. 3, pp. 44–48.

Serafini, F. 2011, 'Expanding perspectives for comprehending visual images in multimodal texts', *Journal of Adolescent & Adult Literacy*, vol. 54, no. 5, pp. 342–350.

Shand, J., & Konza, D. 2016, 'Creating the student writer: A study of writing identities in non-academic senior English classes', *Australian Journal of Language and Literacy*, vol. 39, no. 2, 149–162.

Shapiro, A. M. & Niederhauser, D. 2004, 'Learning from hypertext: Research issues and findings', in D. H. Jonassen (ed.), *Handbook of Research on Educational Communications and Technology*, 2nd edn, Lawrence Erlbaum Associates, Mahwah, NJ, pp. 605–620.

Simpson, A. 2004, *Visual Literacy: A Coded Language for Viewing in the Classroom* (PEN 142), Primary English Teaching Association (PETA), Marrickville, Sydney, NSW.

Simpson, A., Mercer, N. & Majors, Y. 2010, 'Douglas Barnes revisited: If learning floats on a sea of talk, what kind of talk? And what kind of learning?' *English Teaching: Practice and Critique*, vol. 9, no. 2, pp. 1–6.

Sinclair, J. & Coulthard, R. M. 1975, *Towards an Analysis of Discourse: The English Use by Teachers and Pupils*, Oxford University Press, Oxford.

Singh, P., Martsin, M. & Glasswell, K. 2014, 'Dilemmatic space: High-stakes testing and the possibilities of collaborative knowledge work to generate learning innovations', *Teachers and Teaching: Theory and Practice*, vol. 21, no. 4, pp. 379–399.

Smith, F. 1973, *Psycholinguistics and Reading*. Thomson Learning, Toronto.

Smith, F. 1978, *Understanding Reading: A Psycholinguistic Analysis of Reading and Learning to Read*, 2nd edn, Holt, Rinehart and Winston, USA.

Smith, F., Hardman, F., Wall, K. & Mroz, M. 2004, 'Interactive whole class teaching in the national literacy & numeracy strategies', *British Educational Research Journal*, vol. 30, no. 3, pp. 396–411.

Solomon, Y. 2009, *Mathematical Literacy: Developing Identities of Inclusion*, Routledge, London.

Spiro, R. 2004, 'Principled pluralism for adaptive flexibility in teaching and learning to read', in R. B. Ruddell & N. Unrau (eds), *Theoretical Models and Processes of Reading*, 5th edn, International Reading Association, Newark, Delaware, pp. 654–659.

Stenhouse, L. 1981, 'What counts as research?' *British Journal of Educational Studies*, vol. 29, pp. 103–113.

Stenhouse, L. 1983, 'Relevance of practice to theory', *Theory into Practice*, vol. 22, no. 3, pp. 211–215.

Stenhouse, L. 1985, 'Action research and the teacher's responsibility for the educational process', in J. Ruddick & D. Hopkins (eds), *Research as a Basis for Teaching: Readings from the Work of Laurence Stenhouse*, Heinemann, London, pp. 56–59.

Stoll, L. 1998, 'School culture', *School Improvement Network's Bulletin*, Institute of London, no. 9, Autumn, pp. 8–15.

Stoll, L., Bolam, R., McMahon, A., Thomas, S., Wallace, M., Greenwood, A. & Hawkey, K. 2006, 'What Is a Professional Learning Community? A Summary', viewed 14 August 2017, www.decs.sa.gov.au/docs/documents/1/Professional LeaningComm-1.pdf.

Stoll, L. & Fink, D. 1996, *Changing Our Schools: Linking School Effectiveness and School Improvement*, Open University Press, Buckingham.

Street, B. V. 1984, *Literacy in Theory and Practice*, Cambridge University Press, New York.

Street, B. V. 1993, 'The new literacy studies, guest editorial', *Journal of Research in Reading*, vol.16, no. 2, pp. 81–97.

Street, B. V. 1997, 'The implications of the 'New Literacy Studies' for literacy education', *English in Education*, vol. 31, no. 3, pp. 45–59.

Supovitz, J. 2009, 'Can high-stakes testing leverage educational improvement? Prospects from the last decade of texting and accountability', *Journal of Educational Change*, vol. 10, no. 2–3, pp. 211–227. https://doi.org/10.1007/s10833-009-9105-2.

Talking Our Way into Literacy, 1996, Report to Curriculum Corporation of Australia, Carlton, Victoria.

Tan, S. 2000, *The Lost Thing*, Lothian, Port Melbourne.

Taylor, T. 2003, 'Teaching historical literacy: The national history project', viewed 30 November 2017, www.curriculum.edu.au/cc/default.asp?id=9323.

Temple, C. A., Nathan, R. & Temple, C. 1988, *The Beginnings of Writing*, 2nd edn, Allyn and Bacon, Boston.

Thorndike, E. 1917, 'Reading as reasoning a study of mistakes in paragraph reading', *Journal of Educational Psychology*, vol. 8, pp. 323–332.

Trifonas, P. 1998, 'Cross-mediality and narrative textual form: A semiotic analysis of the lexical and visual signs and codes in the picture book', *Semiotica*, vol. 118, no. 1/2, pp. 1–70.

Turbill, J., Barton, G. & Brock, C. 2015, *Teaching Writing in Today's Classroom: Looking Back to Look Forward*, Australian Literacy Educators' Association, Norwood.

Turner, A. 1992, *Patterns of Thinking: Top-Level Structure in the Classroom*, Primary English Teaching Association (PETA), Marrickville, NSW.

Twiner, A., Lyttleton, K., Coffin, C. & Whitelock, D. 2014, 'Meaning making as an interactional accomplishment: A temporal analysis of intentionality and improvisation in classroom dialogue', *International Journal of Educational Research*, vol. 63, pp. 94–106.

UNESCO. 2017, Five Laws of Media and Information Literacy, viewed 23 March 2017, www.unesco.org/new/en/communication-and-information/media-development/media-literacy/five-laws-of-mil/.

United Nations Educational Scientific and Cultural Organisation (UNESCO). 1957, *World Illiteracy at Mid-Century*, UNESCO, Paris.

Unsworth, L. 1988, 'Whole language or procedural display? The social context of popular whole language activities', *Australian Journal of Reading*, vol. 11, no. 2, pp. 127–137.

Unsworth, L. 2001, *Teaching Multiliteracies Across the Curriculum: Changing Contexts of Text and Image and Practice*, Open University Press, Oxenham.

Unsworth, L. 2015, 'Curriculum literacies: Accessing disciplinary discourses', in J. Turbill, G. Barton & C. Brock (eds), *Teaching Writing in Today's Classroom: Looking Back to Look Forward*, Australian Literacy Educators' Association, Norwood.

Vass, P. 2004, 'Thinking skills and the learning of primary history: Thinking historically through stories', *The International Journal of Historical Teaching and Research*, vol. 4, no. 2, July (no page numbers).

Vygotsky, L. S. 1962, *Thought and Language*, The MIT Press, Cambridge.

Vygotsky, L. S. 1978, *Mind in Society: The Development of Higher Psychological Processes*, Harvard University Press, Cambridge.

Walker, T. R. 2006, 'Historical literacy: Reading history through film', *The Social Studies*, January/February, pp. 30–34.

Walsh, M. 2006, 'The "textual shift": Examining the reading process with print, visual and multimodal texts', *Australian Journal of Language and Literacy*, vol. 29, no. 1, pp. 25–37.

Walsh, M. 2007, 'Literacy and learning with multimodal texts: Classroom glimpses', *Synergy*, vol. 4, no. 1, pp. 43–49.

Walsh, M., Asha, J. & Sprainger, N. 2007, 'Reading digital texts', *Australian Journal of Language and Literacy*, vol. 30, no. 1, pp. 40–53.

Walsh, M. & Simpson, A. 2014, 'Exploring literacies through touch pad technologies: The dynamic materiality of modal interactions', *Australian Journal of Language and Literacy*, vol. 37, no. 2, pp. 96–106.

Walsh, S. 2011, *Exploring Classroom Discourse: Language in Action*, Routledge, New York.

Walshe, R. D. 1981, *Every Child Can Write! Learning and Teaching Written Expression in the 1980s*, Primary English Teaching Association, Rozelle, Sydney.

Wells, G. 1987, *The Meaning Makers*, Hodder & Stoughton, London.

Wells, G. 1991, 'Talk about text: Where literacy is learned and taught', in D. Booth & C. Thornley-Hall (eds), *The Talk Curriculum*, Australian Reading Association, Carlton, Victoria.

Wells, G. 1993, 'Reevaluating the IRF sequence: A proposal for the articulation of theories of activity and discourse for the analysis of teaching and learning in the classroom', *Linguistics and Education*, vol. 5, no. 1, pp. 1–36.

Wells, G. 1999, *Dialogic Inquiry: Towards a Sociocultural Practice and Theory of Education*, Cambridge University Press, Cambridge.

Wells, G. (ed.) 2001, *Action, Talk and Text: Learning and Teaching through Inquiry*, Teachers College Press, New York.

Wells, G. 2006, 'Monologic and dialogic discourses as mediators of education', *Research in the Teaching of English*, vol. 41, November, pp. 168–175.

Whitehead, J. & McNiff, J. 2006, *Action Research Living Theory*, Sage, London.

Wiggins, G. & McTighe, J. 2005, *Understanding by Design*, 2nd edn, Association for Supervision and Curriculum Development, Alexandria.

Wilkinson, A. 1991, 'Talking sense: The assessment of talk', in D. Booth & C. Thornley-Hall (eds), *The Talk Curriculum*, Australian Reading Association, Carlton, Victoria.

Williams, F. & Naremore, R. C. 1969, 'Social class differences in children's syntactic performance: A quantitative analysis of field study data', *Journal of Speech and Hearing Research*, vol. 12, pp. 777–793.

Wohland, K. E. 2008, 'From 'What did I write?' to 'Is this right?': Intention, convention, and accountability in early literacy', *The New Educator*, no. 4, pp. 43–63.

Wolf, M. K., Crosson, A. C. & Resnick, L. B. 2006, *Accountable Talk in Reading Comprehension Instruction*, Center for the Study of Education, University of California Technical Report 670, Los Angeles.

Wolfe, S. 2006, 'Teaching and learning through dialogue in primary classrooms in England', Unpublished PhD thesis, University of Cambridge, Cambridge.

Wolfe, S. & Alexander, R. J. 2008, 'Argumentation and dialogic teaching: Alternative pedagogies for a changing world', viewed 29 November 2017, www.robinalexander.org.uk/wp-content/uploads/2012/05/wolfealexander.pdf.

Woolley, G. 2010, 'Developing comprehension: Combining visual and verbal cognitive processes', *Australian Journal of Language and Literacy*, vol. 33, no. 2, pp.108–121.

Wyatt-Smith, C. & Jackson, C. 2016, 'NAPLAN data on writing: A picture of accelerating negative change', *Australian Journal of Language and Literacy*, vol. 29, no. 3, pp.233–242.

Wyatt-Smith, C.M. 1998, 'Interrogating the benchmarks', *English in Australia*, no. 123, pp.20–28.

Yopp-Edwards, R. 2003, 'Comprehension instruction', *Reading Educators' Guild Newsletter*, vol. 32, no. 2, viewed 6 November, http://ed.fullerton.edu/reg/files/2014/07/news3202.pdf.

Zammit, K. & Downes, T. 2002, 'New learning environments and the multiliterate individual: A framework for teachers', *Australian Journal of Language and Literacy*, vol. 25, no. 2, pp.24–36.

Zawilinski, L. 2009, 'HOT blogging: A framework for blogging to promote higher order thinking', *The Reading Teacher*, vol. 62, no. 8, pp.650–661.

Zimmerman, B.J. 2000, 'Attaining self-regulation: A social cognitive perspective', in M. Boekarts, P. Pintrich & M. Zeidner (eds), *Self-Regulation: Theory, Research, and Applications*, Academic, Orlando, FL, pp.13–39.

GLOSSARY

Action Research: Refers to a systematic inquiry undertaken by a teacher with the express purpose of informing and changing classroom pedagogy and practice. The research is conducted in the context of the school and addresses significant educational issues that have been identified by the teacher as important in the teaching and learning processes being realised in a particular classroom.

Appearance: Appearance refers to how the following elements – hairstyle, colouring or costume, clothing, jewellery, make-up and props such as a walking stick – contribute to appearance and indicate personality, social status and culture.

Articulation (voice):   Articulation refers to how clearly the speaker enunciates words.

Bodily contact: Bodily contact refers to the way in which people make contact through touch, where and how they touch, and the parts of their body that make contact. It may indicate emotion, relationships and the nature of those relationships.

Body Language: Sometimes referred to as kinesics, refers to the movement of head, arms, hands, legs and feet. Can indicate emotional arousal or a particular emotional state; for example rough or jerky movements might indicate lack of control. The nature of the gesture can indicate relationships; for example a very emphatic movement of the arm or hand could indicate authority or dominance.

Body Position and Orientation: Body position or orientation refers to how the body is presented to others in the interaction; for example whether participants face one another, are at an angle, turned to the side or away from each other. Body position can indicate power, intimacy, aggression, compliance or respect in relationships.

Codes: A terminology that can be used to create meaning in a particular semiotic system.

Cohesion and Coherence: Using codes and conventions to indicate the relationships among meaning making elements. For example the repetition of a descending pitch in the soundtrack of music accompanying a film whenever something confronting is about to happen helps the consumer anticipate meaning and look for other clues among the codes that indicate what 'confronting activity' is about to take place. Coherence or cohesion may also be space based, for example using codes and conventions to indicate relationships among meaning making elements in a single scene, screen page or image. They may also be time based, for example using codes and conventions to indicate chronology of events in a report, narrative or film.

Communicative competence: Refers to the ability of middle class students to understand when it is appropriate to use standard or non-standard dialects (or elaborate and restricted codes) in formal or less formal contexts. While working class students know both the codes or dialects, they are unable to judge when it is appropriate to use them. They are therefore not communicatively competent.

Complementary meaning making elements: The two elements confirm and elaborate the same meaning. For example a diagrammatic image shows the sequence of a process, and the size of the font in the labels indicates the relative importance of each process.

Constructivism: An approach to teaching and learning that is based on the idea that students should be actively involved in their own learning by accepting responsibility for their own learning. In this way students engage in identifying problems and becoming problem solvers through collaborative learning. Students are said to become more successful learners by making sense of what happens to them in the course of actively constructing a world for themselves.

Consuming/Consumption: Making meaning with multimodal text in order to fulfil a particular purpose in a particular context. It may involve interaction with others to achieve the purpose. The text may be disseminated via a range of technologies.

Conventions: Conventions are the agreed-upon or accepted ways of using the codes. Together the codes and conventions are the tools that come together to enable a reader/viewer to make meaning. There are codes and conventions that are associated with each semiotic system.

Deficiency Hypothesis: A belief that poor performance by students from working class backgrounds can be attributed to factors operating within the home. This 'blame the victim' approach shifts responsibility for educational failure away from the school to families because of deficiencies that are believed to be present within the context of the home.

Design (noun): Refers to the components of meaning, for example the form or structure of a text.

Design (verb): The process of making meaning as the selected repertoire of resources are combined and recombined to interpret, communicate and represent meaning through a text.

Dialogic talk: Dialogic talk takes place when the climate of the classroom encourages student-to-student talk, student-to-teacher talk and teacher-to-student talk. In dialogic talk, students feel confident and competent to initiate talk and freely exchange ideas with others. Dialogic talk will only be successful if students listen respectfully to others, especially to fellow students, building on each other's ideas through talk and allowing everyone to participate in discussions.

Difference Hypothesis: Language and literacy practices present in the families of minority groups can be seen as alternative forms of standard English. The differences, termed linguistic relativity, can be interpreted as differences of dialect rather than as some form of penalty or explanation of poor performance at school. It then becomes the responsibility of the school to accommodate these differences rather than blaming the home.

Distance: The spatial distance between objects can indicate relationships between people, places and things.

Distance, Angle: The angles at which people, places and things are positioned in space, as well as the distance can provide information about the relationship. A direct frontal angle can indicate stronger engagement between the people, places or things while an oblique angle can mean someone or something is detached or sidelined.

Distance, Degree: Different degrees of space between people, places and things signify different degrees of formality or intimacy.

Editing: Editing refers to how the director puts together (edits) the scenes that have been shot in order to achieve his or her communicative objective.

Elaborate code: Proposed by Bernstein (1961) as almost the direct opposite of the restricted code and having the following characteristics: accurate and complex sentences; a discriminating selection of a range of conjunctions, adjectives, adverbs and prepositions; frequent use of the personal pronoun; use of subordinate clauses; use of generalised statements; complex and explicit meanings; and language of possibilities. These characteristics result in a wide range of syntactical alternatives and a flexible approach to syntactic organisation.

Exploratory talk: This type of talk involves exploring new ideas within a group of students in order to achieve a collective conclusion to a shared problem. Because it involves new ideas, this type of talk is likely to be hesitant and incomplete and require an element of risk taking. Both teachers and students need to be comfortable, at ease and confident with a degree of uncertainty because ideas are being developed and sometimes unexpected conclusions are reached.

Facial expression: Facial expression includes eyebrow position, shape of eye (e.g. narrowing or wide-eyed) position and shape of mouth and size of nostrils. These aspects of facial expression can all be used singly and in combination to indicate relationships and the nature of them and also emotion, mood, agreement, disagreement or disinterest. They are all are socially or culturally constrained.

Faction: Refers to those texts that contain a significant amount of factual information but still include a narrative.

Field, Tenor, Mode: Halliday (1974) suggested that while language may vary, the ways humans use language is shaped by three functions and their related metafunctions. He identified three features of a situation (that is the context) which may influence the way language is used in a text: field (what the text is about), tenor (the relationship between the producer of the text and the consumer of the text) and mode (how the text is constructed).

Focussed Learning Episode: Focussed learning episodes are lessons in which specific knowledge, strategies, processes or skills are introduced. They are usually used to provide foundational knowledge that students will need in order to develop further and deeper understandings.

Framing (Spatial Semiotic System):   Frames, real or implied, separate or bring together people, places or things in a text. Similarly, they can separate or bring together items in a composite text (e.g., bringing together or separating linguistic and visual text, or two parts of a visual or a linguistic text). This influences how the consumer will attend to a text, how they will direct their meaning making path through the text and how they might combine or relate parts of the text.

Framing (Visual Semiotic System), Camera shots: Framing can also be achieved by the use of particular camera shots: close-up, medium or long shot. For example, a close-up shot may provide detail of one particular aspect of a scene, while a long shot may provide contextualising information rather than detail.

Framing, Cropping: Cropping (removing part of the image, making it invisible to the consumer) an image is a way of achieving what is available or not available to the consumer.

Functions of teacher talk: Refers to the ways in which teacher talk can shape students' understandings about literacy, literate behaviour and what constitutes literate practice. Teacher talk can be examined in order to understand where the focus of teacher talk lies in lessons, and appreciate its function in focussing the way in which literacy is practised in the classroom and how it affects students' perceptions of, and learning about, literacy.

Gaze and Eye Movement: Gaze and eye movement refers to the way in which a person's gaze is realised and where it is directed. it can indicate relationships or the relative importance of something. Gaze can be directed (specifically and intentionally focussed on someone or something) or non-directed (general scanning that is not focussed).

Gaze and Eye Movement, Angle: The angle of the gaze can indicate attitude, relationships and power; for example an eye-level gaze could indicate equality between the participants, top down dominating someone or something, and bottom up would indicate that someone or something has power over what is being portrayed.

Gaze and Eye Movement, Demand: The gaze of a participant represented in a text can be directed at the consumer of the text. The effect of this direct gaze is to demand the attention of the consumer and a relationship with the participant (the person gazing at the consumer). This will influence the meaning making of the consumer.

Gaze and Eye Movement, Length: The length of gaze (time spent) can indicate power, intimacy or dismissal. The length of the gaze (how the eyes are used and how long the gaze lasts) can modify the intention. For example, an eye-level gaze that is prolonged with narrowed eyes could be confrontational rather than equitable.

Gaze and Eye Movement, Stability: The stability of gaze can also modify intent; it might be steady, fluctuating or hesitant, each of which implies different emotions, moods or relationships. For example, a hesitant gaze may indicate a relationship that is new or just beginning, while a fluctuating gaze may indicate suspicion.

Head Nods: Head nods can indicate agreement or disagreement, but angle and tilt of head towards others when nodding can also effect interaction and indicate power, intimacy, aggression, compliance or respect.

Hierarchical meaning making elements: The role of elements varies terms of relative importance over time. For example in a film dialogue may provide most information to begin with, but then the actions of the people may become dominant in terms of meaning.

Hypertext: Hypertext is text that links to other information. By clicking on a link in a hypertext document, a user can quickly jump to different content. Hypertext is usually associated with online reading and is carried out by clicking text-based links that open new pages. These links are often blue and underlined and allow the user to jump from page to page.

Ideational, Interpersonal and Textual Metafunctions: The term metafunction was first coined by Halliday (1974) who, having identified field, tenor and mode as the features of a situation which may influence the way language is used in a text, then identified three related metafunctions that he postulated guided the actual selection of language and textual features to be used in the text: *ideational, interpersonal* and *textual* (see Ewing, 1994).

Inquiry: A form of active learning that begins by posing questions or scenarios. Individuals identify and investigate issues or questions to develop their knowledge or find solutions to particular issues. Inquiry is based on problem solution and involves individuals in learning the skills of critical thinking and research. Inquiry occurs across all disciplines and is not limited to English, although many of the necessary skills and strategies rely on the development of particular literacies.

Inquiry-based teaching: An approach to the teaching of the inquiry process that involves explicit instruction about the skills and strategies of inquiry. It provides students with knowledge about the inquiry process so that they can become self-regulated learners. It is based on the idea of learners taking control of their own learning and teachers implementing a student-focussed rather than a teacher-focussed pedagogy.

Inserts: Inserts occur when a scene is added, which appears out of place or does not advance the plot, but later its relevance is revealed.

Intonation and Stress (voice):   Particular pitch and stress patterns may be used within an oration to emphasise particular words and can therefore change meaning. (See also Rhythm and Rhythm Patterns.)

IRE: A question and answer sequence or exchange that consists of a three-part structure. This structure is typically made up of an initiation by the teacher (I), most often a question, followed by a response (R) from a student and ending in some form of evaluation (E) by the teacher.

Juxtaposition: Juxtaposition is to do with the boundaries of an object and its relation to others, that is how objects are arranged in relation to one another.

Kinesics: Kinesics, sometimes referred to as body language, refers to the movement of head, arms, hands, legs and feet can indicate emotional arousal or a particular emotional state. For example rough or jerky movements might indicate lack of control. The nature of the gesture can indicate relationships; for example a very emphatic movement of the arm or hand could indicate authority or dominance. (See also Body Language.)

KWL: A retrieval chart is constructed by the teacher, or by each individual student which has three vertical columns. The columns are titled What do I Know? What do I Want to know? and What have I Learnt? In the three columns students generate questions that they wish to investigate, reflect on their prior knowledge, and set themselves an inquiry. Sometimes an extra column is added to ask How will I use this information? (KWLH)

Lighting: The absence, presence or degree of light can be used to denote mood, emotion, time of day or draw attention to items or characters in a scene or image. This can be achieved through the way in which lighting is used (e.g. soft, bright, spotlighting) or the direction from which light comes (e.g. side, top, bottom).

Line – actual or implied: Lines can be actual but they can also be implied through repetition of colour or objects across a page or screen.

Line – quality: The quality of a line refers to how it is depicted and can be achieved through the media or software employed and how the line is applied (e.g. thin, thick, heavy, hesitant).

Line – type: Lines may be vertical, horizontal, diagonal, jagged, curved, right-angled or forming a doorway. Each of these has significance; for example in Western society, repeated vertical lines infer loneliness or isolation.

Literacy identity: Life experiences provide a repertoire of resources about literacy and literate practices that contribute to an individual's literacy identity. Students bring to school a range of experiences from their social and cultural life, their lifeworlds – that is everything that happens to them outside of school. Those experiences that take place in classrooms, after careful guidance by a teacher, form the student's school-based world.

Meaning making element: The specific parts of a text that represent and convey meaning; for example in an image, the items/people depicted, a caption or label, a logo, a voice-over. Each of these elements will be conveyed by a semiotic system and particular codes and conventions will be employed to convey particular meanings about the element. For example in an image the items may be arranged to convey what is important or to lead the eye through the image (spatial semiotic system) but may also be coloured to convey mood or draw attention (visual semiotic system). If delivered digitally, the voice-over may use pitch, pause and volume (audio semiotic system).

Media/Opacity/Transparency: The use of different media; for example watercolour, gouache or colour software can produce transparent colours (see-through) or opaque (dense).

Metacognition: Knowledge, monitoring and control of one's thinking processes in order to employ the most appropriate strategies to achieve a goal.

Metalanguage: In the context of a multiliterate classroom, metalanguage refers to terminology that enables producers and consumers of multimodal text to clearly articulate and describe all features of a multimodal text, including the codes and conventions of the semiotic systems and technologies used in its construction, together with the processes of consuming and producing the multimodal text.

Modulation (voice):   Modulation refers to the way in which volume and tone varies during dialogue, voice-over, narration and song lyrics.

Monologic Talk: Monologic talk resembles a monologue by the teacher. Talk is dominated by the teacher who acts as the source of all knowledge and provides little, or no, opportunity for student-initiated talk.

Motifs or Musical Phrases: A group of sounds that are composed and come together in a short phrase, may be repeated when a particular character appears, or when a character exhibits particular emotions. This groups of sounds or musical phrase can then referred to as a motif.

Multiliteracies: A concept of literacy as being multimodal rather than language dominant, being made up of multiple literacies and multiple literate practices that continuously evolve as local and global society, culture and technology change the contexts in which literacy is practiced. Multiliteracies enable capacities to cope with change and effectively participate and contribute to all aspects of society: workplace, leisure, social, cultural and civic environments.

Multimodal texts: Texts that are formed by the combination of two or more semiotic systems (linguistic, visual, audio, spatial or gestural). Multimodality refers to the making of meaning through the interrelating of two or more semiotic systems.

Oppositional meaning making elements: The elements have different meanings that are in opposition to or contradict one another, for example in film where violence is depicted through the actions of the character but the music is serene.

Pace (Audio Semiotic System):   Pace refers to the speed at which sound is delivered. It can denote mood or action. For example fast-paced sounds tend to indicate action or excitement, while slow-paced sounds tend to have a more calming effect.

Pacing (Visual Semiotic System):   Pacing refers to the overall way in which the plot or information in a film can be presented over time. The film or play may be fast paced or slow paced. For example, fast pace may focus on action, whereas slow pace may focus on character development or detail.

Parallel cutting: Parallel cutting refers to cutting backwards and forward from one scene or character to another to depict simultaneous events and/or create increasing tension. It can also be achieved through the use of a split screen.

Pedagogy: The concept of pedagogy explains the relationship between teaching and learning. It defines the conditions necessary for students to fully participate in learning while also describing the teaching practices necessary to support such learning. Literacy pedagogy needs to take account of developments in contemporary society such as cultural and linguistic diversity and also the range of new texts produced by the semiotic systems and the new technologies, the advent of new literacies and consideration of literacy identity.

Person oriented family: A family where power and status is gained by an individual by virtue of personal competence (a particular talent). Child-rearing is accompanied and associated with reasoning language and practices (let's negotiate this).

Personal Space: Personal space is a critical aspect of proximity. It refers to the level of proximity a person can tolerate with comfort (the size of their personal space), that is how tolerant they are of how close someone is to them. The comfort of those involved and the nature of their relationship influences personal space. Personal space is also influenced by social and cultural conventions and context. (See also Proximity.)

Phase structure of lessons: Phases refer to changes in focus or task during a lesson. Phase divisions or changes can be signalled both orally and physically. Two oral signals can be given, either an explicit statement or instruction to move on to another task or change focus (for example 'Our next task is…') or a tag utterance which is known and recognised by all members of the class as a signal of change (for example, 'OK…', 'Alright…'). Physical signals can be of three kinds: a change in activity by students, physical reorganisation of the room or students moving (for example from sitting on the floor to their desks) or use of equipment (for example starting a film to be watched.)

Phrasing: Phrasing refers to the way the overall audio message is broken up into smaller sections. For example, a speaker may use phrasing to break up information into smaller, more easily processed pieces.

Pitch: Pitch refers to how high or low the sound is.

PMI: A strategy originally developed by Edward de Bono intended to assist in evaluating information about an issue. It is a retrieval chart with three vertical columns where students enter positive elements about the issue in the **P**lus column, negative elements in the **M**inus column, and elements that are neither positive or negative but nevertheless **I**nteresting in the final column. It encourages students to see both sides of an argument and understand different points of view. It can support students in their inquiry particularly if they are engaged in guided or open/independent inquiry. The strategies are termed routines by Ritchhart et al. because they form part of the everyday fabric of many classrooms and part of the core practices of many teachers. Ritchhart and his colleagues concluded that the routines are attractive to teachers and students because they are established by repeated practice, they are concrete examples of visible critical thinking, and as such can be explicitly taught.

Point of View: Point of view refers to where the consumer is positioned to view the scene or image.

Point of View - Bird's Eye or Top Down: Bird's eye or top down positions the consumer above the scene or image looking down on it.

Point of View - Eye Level: Eye level positions the consumer at the same level as the participants in the scene.

Point of View - Worm's Eye or Bottom Up: Worm's eye or bottom up positions the consumer below the scene or image, looking up at it.

Position, Centre-Margin: In Asian culture, importance is indicated by placement at the centre of the layout, while objects or information placed at the margins are either less important or ancillary. However, these spatial relationships can be found in Western culture as well with similar meaning. Centre and margin layouts are used more frequently in non-fiction than narrative genres.

Position, Foreground - Background: The placement of objects in the foreground indicates importance and placement in the background lesser importance. Degrees of importance can be indicated by placement closer to foreground or background.

Position, Left-Right: In Western society, the position or placement of information or objects on the left and right indicates different values. On the left is what is known, while on the right is the new. This can apply within an image or on a page or screen layout.

Position, Top-Bottom: In Western society, the position or placement of information or objects placed at the top or bottom of the page indicates different value. Information at the top will be that which is more salient or palatable. Sometimes this referred to as ideal (top) and real (bottom).

Position oriented family: A family where power and status is gained by an individual by virtue of their position in the family (father, mother, child). Child rearing is accompanied and associated with threatening language and practices (do as I tell you).

Posture: Posture refers to the way in which a person stands, sits or lies and can indicate interpersonal attitudes, their emotional state or the nature of their character. For example a rigid upright posture leaning towards and over another person could indicate superiority or a person who likes to dominate.

Producing/Production: Engagement in the design and creation of a multimodal text, together with the selection of an appropriate means of dissemination, that will fulfil a particular communicative purpose, for a specific audience and context. May involve collaboration with others to access specific, needed expertise.

Projection (voice):   Projection refers to how well the speaker or singer projects (throws) their voice out to the audience so it is easy to hear.

Proximity: Proximity refers to the space (or distance) between people and can indicate a relationship and the nature of that relationship. Its meaning and interpretation are modified by cultural and social conventions. (See also Personal Space.)

Redesign/Redesigning: The combining, recombining and reworking of the selected resources to consume or produce a unique multimodal text.

Reinforcing meaning making elements: The two elements represent the same information. For example the position of the character in the space (three-dimensional or two-dimensional) indicates they are the most important and light is only focussed on the character, reinforcing their importance.

Repertoire of Resources: The available designs that may be drawn upon when consuming or producing a text.

Restricted code: Originally described by Bernstein (1960, 1962, 1962, 1964) as having the following characteristics: short, simple and often unfinished sentences; limited use of adjectives, adverbs and subordinate clauses; infrequent use of personal pronouns; use of categorical statements; use of repetitive expressions; and implicit meanings. These characteristics result in a narrow range of syntactical alternatives and a rigid approach to syntactic organisation.

Rhythm and Rhythm Patterns: In music, sound effects or oration, stress patterns can be realised through rhythm, for example short sharp rhythms might accompany fast or rough actions and a regular flowing rhythm might accompany gentle actions. A particular rhythm pattern might be used repeatedly to develop an association with a particular character, action or emotion. (See also Intonation and Stress (voice).)

Safe classrooms: Refers to those classrooms where students feel safe to talk because they are encouraged to talk by their teachers by virtue of the fact that there is a balance between teacher talk and student talk. The teacher creates opportunities for student talk by reducing the amount of teacher talk and also by allowing silences to develop by reducing the number of questions asked and by pausing more often and for longer periods of time. The teacher, by engaging in fewer IRE sequences, encourages students to provide responses to questions when they are not sure of the answer and maybe hesitant. Students then begin to develop confidence in their thinking and competent in their learning. The climate in the classroom then begins to feel safe for students to negotiate their learning.

Salience: Using specific codes and conventions to indicate to a consumer the relative importance among the meaning making elements on a page, and therefore where the consumer's attention should be first directed. For example using a spotlight to draw attention to a particular character or activity in the scene of a film or a live play, or placing an object in the foreground of an image to indicate it is more important than other items which are behind it and that the consumer should attend to it first.

Saturation: Saturation refers to the purity or intensity of the colour. When other colours are added, it dilutes its intensity.

Semiotic system: A system of signs and symbols that have agreed-upon meanings within a particular group.

Shape: Shape refers to the actual visual outline of an object and provides a way of identifying objects by using visual memory.

Social Practice: The recognised, agreed and accepted behaviour (acting and interacting), talking and valuing among a social or cultural group. The social or cultural group will use these ways of behaving and talking in particular contexts. They may have a shared language (e.g. slang) and ways of dressing or ways of wearing clothes. They may also share ways of viewing or acting towards particular social or cultural groups.

Speed: Action in film can be presented at normal or real speed, sped up or in slow motion to create particular moods or draw attention to an aspect of a scene. For example car chases are often sped up to increase the excitement.

Symbols: Symbols, are simplified shapes used to represent items in diagrams and figures or convey information in everyday settings.

Synthesising: The ability to engage in the processes necessary to move back and forth among a repertoire of resources, including semiotic systems, to make or represent meaning.

Texture: Texture refers to the tactile feel of an object. In an image, texture provides a link between tactile memory and the object depicted.

Think-Pair-Share: A question and answer strategy involving all, or most, of the class engaging in addressing a particular question. The teacher asks a question that requires each student to think about a possible answer (think), the students then discuss their answer with a partner (pair), and then share the answer with the whole class (share).

Timbre: Timbre is the particular quality of a voice that is characteristic or unique to an individual, for example a reedy, thin quality or a dark, throaty quality. Musical instruments also have unique timbrel qualities.

Tone (Audio Semiotic System):   In music, the term tone refers to pitch and translates to a specific level of sound on the musical score (e.g. middle C).

Tone (Visual Semiotic System):   Tone refers to the amount of light (white) or dark (black) in a colour.

Top-Level Structures: Strategies that are based on organisational patterns in texts and reflect common text structures such as comparison-contrast, cause-effect and problem–solution. These structures can be found at the macro-level such as whole chapters or at the micro-level at the sentence or paragraph level. Top-level structures are strategies that students can use when extracting or organising information particularly when engaging in note-taking or constructing an outline.

Transformation: The result of the process of design. The consumer will have been transformed by engaging with the available resources and multimodal texts in new ways in order to make meaning. Conversely, the production and dissemination of a multimodal text will transform those who engage with it.

Transitions: This is the method of moving from one scene to another in film. This can be achieved by fading to black or white or one scene slowly dissolving into another.

Utterance: In a lesson transcript the turns of talk or 'utterances' by each participant are numbered in the order they occur, to enable analysis and discussion of the transcript.

Vector/vectorality: refers to the way the eye is led through a text by actual or implied lines (see Line – actual or implied).

Volume/Audibility: Volume and audibility refer to the loudness or softness of the sound.

INDEX

Note: Page numbers in italic indicate a figure and page numbers in bold indicate a table on the corresponding page.